ITALY DISH BY DISH

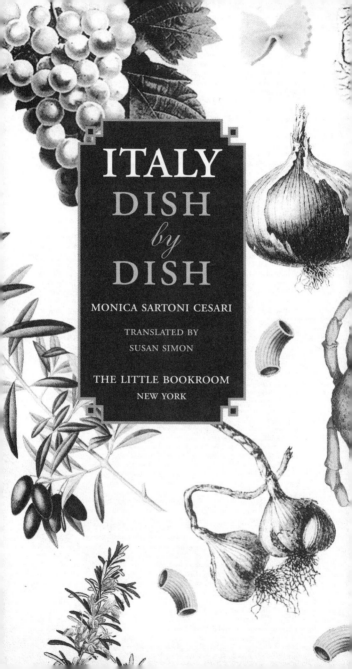

ITALY
DISH
by
DISH

MONICA SARTONI CESARI

TRANSLATED BY
SUSAN SIMON

THE LITTLE BOOKROOM
NEW YORK

Italy Dish by Dish © 2011 The Little Bookroom
Originally published as *Mangia Italiano* by Monica Cesari Sartoni
© 2005 Morellini Editore, Milan, Italy
English translation © 2011 Susan Simon

Design: Katy Homans, New York
Cover pattern: Lauren Ruggeri

Library of Congress Cataloging-in-Publication Data
Cesari Sartoni, Monica.
[Mangia Italiano. English]
Italy dish by dish / by Monica Sartoni Cesari ;
translated by Susan Simon.
p. cm.
Includes index.
ISBN 978-1-892145-90-1 (alk. paper)
1. Cookery, Italian. 2. Cookery--Italy. I. Title.
TX723.C458 2010
641.5945--dc22

2010013290

Published by The Little Bookroom
435 Hudson St., 3rd floor
New York, NY 10014
www.littlebookroom.com
editorial@littlebookroom.com

ISBN 978-1-892145-90-1

10 9 8 7 6 5 4 3 2 1

Printed in the United States of America

CONTENTS

PIEMONTE (PIEDMONT) AND VAL D'AOSTA

From its valleys to its rolling hills to the clear, luminous foothills of the Alps, Piedmont dispenses an extraordinary range of food, rich in flavors and exquisitely refined.

Almost half of the rice consumed in Italy is grown on the plains in the provinces of Novara and Vercelli on the border with Lombardy. The prestigious *superfino* Carnaroli and the *semifino* Vialone Nano and Maratelli are among the types of rice grown in the region. This indigenous production gives birth to exceptional rice dishes: paniscia Novarese or panissa Vercellese, as well as riso con porri (rice with leeks) from Asti and the delicious risotto alla canavesana.

Moving up towards the hills of the Langhe and Monferrato area, with its clay-like soil, you will find distinctly flavored produce of outstanding quality: the "meaty" sweet peppers of Carmagnola, excellent cardoons, Jerusalem artichokes, the splendid asparagus from Sàntena, tasty leeks, perhaps the tastiest hazelnuts in the world and, above all, the mythical white truffles from Alba. The alpine area of Piedmont also produces some of the most important and highly esteemed cheese and dairy products in all of Italy. The streams that course through the mountains are filled with trout and other freshwater fish like salmerini and temoli.

If it's true that the cuisine of a region is born from the relationship between the products of its terrain and the way that people use them, Piedmont offers an abundant gastronomic tradition divided into three very distinctive classes of food — common, noble and above all, *borghese*, or middle class.

Common or working class dishes are defined by the occupations of their creators.

For example, vegetable vendors are known for dishes made with leeks; olive oil–preserved tuna, mackerel or other fish; and little rabbits that have been fed with wild willow leaves. The food of cattlemen, carriage drivers, and attendants is just like what you find at roadside inns: tripe soup, bread and oxtails, chick peas and pig's heads, bean salad, onions and boiled meat or olive oil–preserved fish, pickled vegetables and fish, and hearty, cooked salami. Masons favor stews, agnolotti (pasta filled with meat) and polenta with gorgonzola or brôs, a local cheese.

Fisherman like eel cooked in red wine and pickled freshwater fish.

Peasant or modest food, for instance soma d'ai (thick slices of bread rubbed with garlic, soaked with olive oil, then sprinkled with salt), makes up in flavor what it lacks in rich ingredients. The food that comes out of the courts and palaces of the nobility was inspired by the food of Piemonte's neighbor, France. There is evidence of this influence in the complex meals made with game or the great and rich risottos.

However, the biggest influence on the food of the region is *la cucina borghese* or the food of the middle class. Characterized by a great variety of tasty, well-balanced ingredients, it is exemplified in dishes such as finanziera, bollito misto accompanied by its incomparable sauce, bagnet and other excellent meat, the region's version of fritto misto and an infinite range of antipasti.

Val d'Aosta has managed to preserve ancient food traditions. There's testimony to this fact depicted on a series of frescoes in the Challant family castle at Issogne. They show various market scenes including butcher shops, bakeries and pharmacies—and the foods that are still popular in the region: large pieces of cheese, prosciutto, lambs, salami, butter, lardo and spit-roasted game. And so, the food of the Val d'Aosta is to this day rich with butter, cheese and strong, salted meats preserved in barrels with garlic, sage and rosemary.

While traveling around the region one might easily discover an isolated valley, with an inn that serves the most extraordinary sliced lardo, milk and chestnut soup, polenta slices with buttery cheese or tasty, preserved meat stew or game. You may find yourself in the Valle di Gressoney with its ancient German population still maintaining the traditions of their homeland—especially the culinary ones. From there travel through the valleys from the Dora massif on to Monte Rosa where you'll find dishes very similar to those found in the Teutonic-influenced Alto Adige region.

However, French influence takes center stage in this region's kitchen in its profuse use of butter and marvelous fatty cheeses. The pairings of these cheeses with Martin Sec pears, apples or the highly fragrant quince of the area are legendary. Rich soups and big plates of polenta keep away the chill of the glacial mountain air and warm the body. Pasta dishes are almost nonexistent.

It's almost obligatory to end a meal in Val d'Aosta with a little glass of Génépy, an alpine liqueur made from the eponymous plant.

Agliata verde monferrina A type of pesto made with parsley, basil, celery leaves, lots of garlic, salt, pepper and fresh lemon juice that is mixed with robioletta or toma delle Langhe fresca to make a very tasty cream cheese often served with *cipollata rossa monferrina* (page 4).

Antipasto Chaumière A dish made with boiled potatoes cooked with blood sausages and Valdostane sausages for a few minutes and served hot.

Bagna cauda or **bagna caôda** A traditional Piemontese sauce made with olive oil, butter, garlic and anchovies. It is kept warm in its own specially designed terra cotta pot that sits on top of a little heater to insure consistent temperature. Diners then dip into this warm bath a selection of raw vegetables (such as cardoons, artichokes, peppers, celery, Jerusalem artichokes, cauliflower, radishes and cabbage leaves) or cooked vegetables (such as potatoes, carrots, onions and turnips). In some areas of the Monferrato, you may find a cup of Barbera wine, milk-soaked garlic or more minced garlic added to bagna cauda. Nothing of the bagna cauda is wasted because any leftover vegetables are typically scrambled with eggs to make another delicious dish.

Ballotte di ricotta, tonno e basilico "Little balls" made with Piemontese ricotta (sciràss) combined with robiola cheese, hard-cooked egg yolks, olive oil, lemon zest and juice, grated Parmesan cheese, flaked tuna fish, basil, parsley, capers and black pepper. Each ball is wrapped in a fresh basil leaf and served at room temperature with a drizzle of extra virgin olive oil. You will find this typical dish on the finest tables in Turin and Cuneo.

Bergne Cured, prosciutto-style lamb or mutton typical of the high Val Sesia.

Biova or **pane biove** A large, round bread, typical of the Piedmont region, made with hard wheat.

Boudin Large salami made with pork blood, potatoes and lardo, served boiled and sliced.

Brusch delle Langhe A type of headcheese with an aspic-like texture; a mixture of pork head, tongue and hocks held together in a gelatin base.

Carne all'albese Very thinly sliced pieces of beef dressed with olive oil, lemon juice, salt and pepper. Shards of

Parmesan cheese and shaved white truffles are scattered over the top.

Castagne al caramel From the Val d'Aosta, a sweet antipasto of chestnuts cooked in whey and then caramelized in melted butter and sugar.

Castellana di peperoni A classic antipasto from the village of Costigliole d'Asti made with peppers that have been baked, peeled, cut lengthwise and then rolled around pieces of prosciutto and fontina cheese.

Cipollata rossa monferrina A very tasty cream cheese made with robiola or very fresh toma delle Langhe in combination with peeled red peppers, scallions, paprika, fresh lemon juice, olive oil and salt. It's served with slices of toasted rustic bread.

D'la duja See *salamin d'la duja* (page 5).

Erbj con el salam A springtime specialty from the province of Vercelli; a sauce, made with wild asparagus cooked with salami and pancetta, served with room-temperature polenta.

Fonduta A specialty of Piedmont and of the Val d'Aosta (with some variations), made by macerating the best quality fontina with milk and then cooking it in a double boiler with egg yolks. The result is a very delicate cream that is served hot with little toasts and white truffles from Alba (no truffles are used in the Val d'Aosta version). It would seem to be a simple preparation, but in fact it's quite risky because the mixture can easily seize up. It should be served as soon as the cream is achieved — it can't wait!

Insalata capricciosa A salad made with a julienne of celery root, pickled tongue, boiled ham, cheese, olive-oil–marinated mushrooms, etc., dressed with fresh mayonnaise.

Insalata di riso alla novarese A rice dish typical of the province of Novara made by layering cooked rice with thinly sliced white truffles. The whole thing is dressed with a sauce made with olive oil, anchovies, garlic and parsley. The dish is briefly heated before serving.

Marzapane A blood sausage made with pork blood, tiny pieces of lardo, breadcrumbs, garlic and spices. It is meant to be boiled; then it is sliced, dipped in beaten eggs and fried.

Mocetta Salami from the Val d'Aosta that is cured similarly to prosciutto. It was originally made with the leg of a steinbock, a wild goat native to the Alps. Nowadays it's usually made with deer or leg of domestic goat. To thoroughly enjoy its flavor, it is best eaten on thinly sliced, buttered dark bread, possibly with a drizzle of honey.

Pane all'ospite Sliced whole-wheat bread covered with fresh butter and *salagnun* (page 24).

Pecc ed vaca Pressed, boiled udder, sliced, then covered with salsa verde.

Pomodori farciti alla novarese Tomatoes, stuffed with rice, which are then topped with cheese and pepper, dipped in a batter, and either deep-fried or baked.

Prosciutto di Bosses con crostini Nothing more than whole-wheat toasts that have been prepared with butter, then spread with a pâté made from calves' liver and prosciutto.

Quagliette Cabbage leaves stuffed with a rich meat mixture (see *caponet*, page 14).

Salamin d'la duja A typical Piemontese salami. The *duja* in the name refers to the earthenware crock in which the salami is cured. Because of the humid conditions in many areas of the region the salami is sealed with fat and then left to age undisturbed.

Sandwiches piemontesi Sandwiches made with thinly sliced white bread filled with a combination of ricotta, cooked ham, chopped capers, hard-cooked egg yolks, horse-radish and rum. The finished sandwiches are dusted with sieved hard-cooked yolks.

Sobrìch In Piemontese dialect, "fritters." You can find many varieties but they are mostly vegetable-based (spinach, cauliflower, leek, cardoon, potato, zucchini or eggplant).

Tartrà A modest savory pudding with Spanish or "Barbarian" origins made with eggs, milk, cream, onions, grated Parmesan cheese, sage, bay leaf, rosemary, freshly ground black pepper and nutmeg. It is a real "grandma dish" — *un piatto delle nonna*.

Tettarina dell'alpeggio A dish in which an udder is covered with salt and left to macerate for a few days. It is then boiled and weighted down to compress before being thinly sliced to serve, sometimes accompanied by a sauce.

Tomini alle erbe di Peranche Little cheeses from the valleys that are marinated in olive oil, vinegar, black pepper, nutmeg, parsley, garlic, sage, celery, piripilli (a small French hot pepper) and ejseppo (a variety of wild thyme).

Torta di San Pietro A delicious savory pie filled with puréed chestnuts, potatoes and fava beans. It's served with melted butter and rosemary.

Torta verde A savory pie filled with rice, spinach, eggs and Parmesan cheese.

Vitel tonné Veal that is poached in a broth with carrots, onions and celery. The cooled veal is then thinly sliced and covered with a mayonnaise made with tuna, anchovies and capers.

PASTA, GNOCCHI, RICE, POLENTA AND GRAINS

Agliata A pasta dish, usually made with tagliatelle, dressed with walnut pesto, garlic, butter and breadcrumbs.

Agnolotti The typical square Piemontese ravioli. The fillings can vary greatly, but the classic one consists of a mixture of beef pot roast, roast pork, rabbit, sausage, brains, escarole, eggs and Parmesan cheese. Agnolotti are cooked in broth but are drained, then dressed with a sauce made with some of the meats used in the filling. The fillings may vary by being made with leftover boiled, stewed or roast beef, or with rabbit, chicken, veal, beef, sausage, beef tendons, sweetbreads, brains and marrow. Escarole mixed with endive, chard, cabbage or spinach may be added to the mixture as well. At one time a simple Parmesan cheese risotto was added to soften the filling mixture. You may find a lighter variation of agnolotti that are referred to as *di magro* (lean) with truffles added to the filling.

Agnolotti alla Marengo Ravioli made with a filling of beef or pork that has been marinated in red wine and various spices, and then braised with onions, carrots, celery, chopped garlic, bay leaf, rosemary, sage, cinnamon, cloves, pepper and nutmeg. The finely chopped cooked meat is then mixed with sausage, cabbage, eggs, Parmesan cheese and breadcrumbs. Agnolotti are dressed with the sauce in which the meat has cooked. They are about 3 cm long.

Agnolotti canavesani (agnulót) Agnolotti with a filling made with wine, rice cooked in red wine, rice cooked in milk, sausage, Grana cheese, eggs, pepper, nutmeg, garlic, truffles and chopped cabbage sautéed with pancetta and prosciutto. They're dressed with a meat sauce and then garnished with melted butter and shaved white truffles.

Agnolotti di spinaci Agnolotti with a filling made with braised beef, rice boiled in milk, lots of spinach, eggs, Grana cheese, pepper and nutmeg. They're best when dressed with a ragù made with chicken livers and mushrooms.

Brudera A dish typically served on the day when a pig is slaughtered. It is actually a risotto dressed with sausages and pork ribs, and slightly whipped pig's blood that is still warm. This is a specialty of the province of Vercelli, in particular the villages of Costanzana, Desana and Pezzana.

Cabiette piemontesi Gnocchi made with potatoes, nettles, whole-wheat flour and Piemontese toma cheese. They're dressed with a layer of sautéed onions, then sprinkled with breadcrumbs and baked. The dish is typical of the village of Rochemolles, just outside of Bardonecchia near Turin.

Cannelloni A sumptuous dish with origins in the village of Limone Piemonte near Cuneo. Cannelloni are made with precooked egg pasta squares and stuffed with a filling made with veal, cooked prosciutto, spinach, Parmesan cheese and beef ragù. They are rolled up into cylinders, placed in a baking dish, covered with béchamel and gratinéed in the oven.

Cannelloni alla Barbaroux Very rich cannelloni made with crêpes that are filled with veal, prosciutto, cheese and eggs. They are covered with béchamel and gratinéed in the oven. The name of the dish refers to its inventor, Count Giuseppe Barbaroux, a legal aide to the nineteenth-century king, Carlo Alberto.

Ceresolini A type of *tajarin* (page 10), tagliatelle typical of the village of Ceresole d'Alba.

Dunderet di patate A type of Piemontese gnocchi made with flour, eggs, potatoes and nutmeg. The dough must be almost batter-like because it is tossed by the spoonful into boiling water, then cooked until the dumplings are solid. They are served dressed with meat sauce or butter, sage and cheese.

Gnocchi all'ossolana Little gnocchi found all around the area near the Swiss border town of Domodossola made with flour, eggs, pepper, nutmeg and cheese and served with butter and sage.

Gnocchi alla bava Potato gnocchi, typical of the Piedmont region, usually made with part buckwheat flour and part whole-wheat flour. They're smaller than potato gnocchi made with white flour. They are dressed with toma and fontina cheeses. Some people add cream and egg yolks to the sauce. There's also a version called gnocchi della festa ("special occasion gnocchi"). For that version, boiled chicken is ground and barely sautéed in butter, then added to the dough and then barely sautéed in butter again. The gnocchi are then tossed with the same cheeses.

Gnocchi di patate alla piemontese Piedmont, just like the Veneto, Emilia-Romagna, Lazio and Friuli regions, would like to take ownership of this simple and refined dish of potato gnocchi. In Piedmont they are usually made with flour and potatoes, then dressed with a sauce made with beef pot roast cooked in tomato sauce and topped with grated Grana cheese.

Knolle A type of gnocchi made with yellow (corn) flour typical of the village of Gressoney La Trinite near Aosta. They're often served with boiled speck, accompanied by sauerkraut, boiled potatoes and carrots.

Lasagne albesi A historic recipe created, like so many others, in order to use various parts of the pig on the day it was slaughtered. For this dish, fresh pig's blood is slowly thickened in milk and then spread on cooked, fresh pasta rectangles (1 cm x 8 cm). The pasta is dressed with a sauce made with onions, butter, olive oil, glandular fat from the pig, sausages, veins, sweetbreads and ground shoulder meat.

Paniscia novarese A preparation in which rice is added to a sauté of lardo, onions and *salamin d'la duja* (page 5), then to minestrone made with borlotti beans, celery, carrots, cabbage, tomatoes and pork cracklings.

Panissa vercellese A preparation in which the rice is added to the same sauté as in *paniscia novarese* (above), then spritzed with Barbera or Nebbiolo wine. The rice then finishes cooking in a broth in which borlotti beans and pork cracklings have been cooked.

Polenta alla piemontese A preparation in which cooked polenta is sliced into thin pieces and layered in a baking dish with chopped, leftover roast meat that has been sautéed in butter. The whole thing is covered with a few teaspoons of milk and grated Parmesan cheese, and baked for about an hour before serving.

Polenta alla rascard Polenta typical of the valleys of the region. Cooked polenta is cut into slices that are layered in a baking dish with a chopped meat ragù, sausage and fontina cheese. A *rascard* is the typical traditional wood farmhouse of the region.

Polenta concia (cùnsa) or **polenta d'Oropa** A very substantial dish found throughout the Val d'Aosta. It's made with either soft or hard polenta, then served layered with fontina cheese from the Valdostana or fresh toma, butter and Parmesan cheese. The dish is gratinéed before serving.

Polenta dei siouri A polenta dish from the city of Tortona. The cooked polenta is sliced and placed in a baking dish with a copious amount of meat sauce, cheese and shaved white truffles, and gratinéed before serving.

Polentobocce Balls of polenta about the size of oranges, which are stuffed with cheese, breaded and fried in butter; typical of the Valdostana.

Polpettine di polenta alla piemontese Little polenta balls prepared by mixing cooked polenta with a thick sauce made with Gruyère, Parmesan cheese, flour, salt, pepper, nutmeg, milk, egg yolks, diced filet of beef and white truffles. Once the mixture has solidified, a cutter is used to make rounds that are dipped in egg and breadcrumbs, and then fried.

Puccia Polenta from the city of Alba, made with white and yellow corn flour and served with pork and cabbage stew, butter and grated Grana cheese.

Rabatòn A creation from the city of Alessandrina. These "little sticks" are formed with dough made with chard, ricotta, breadcrumbs, eggs and garlic. They are cooked in broth, drained and transferred to a baking dish. They are then covered with butter and fresh sage leaves and gratinéed before serving.

Ris e riondele A dish of rice cooked with mallow leaves and milk; a specialty of the city of Biella.

Riso alla canavesana A dish of rice boiled in a broth made with beef and chicken. The cooked rice is finished off with fontina, emmenthal and Grana cheeses. These three melting cheeses not only give the dish its flavor but also its pleasantly creamy texture.

Riso e porri degli ortolani d'Asti A delicious risotto made with a base of leeks, garlic, bay leaves fried in butter and diced lardo. Just before serving, the risotto is enriched with Parmesan, Gruyère and fontina cheeses. A *nonnulla* (an Italian word worth knowing, which means "a little nothing" or "a trifle") of nutmeg is grated over the top.

Riso in cagnon There are three versions of this rice dish with a mysterious name: Lombardian, Ligurian and Piemontese. Basically, it is nothing more than boiled rice dressed with browned butter and fontina cheese.

Risotto alla novarese A traditional risotto made with Barbera wine, then enriched with butter and Parmesan cheese.

Risotto alla piemontese A classic risotto made in the traditional way by sautéing onions in butter before adding the rice and some white wine. The risotto is cooked with broth and additional butter and grated Parmesan cheese is added at the end. There are variations, however; for example, some add the sauce from roast meat, Barbera or Barolo wine, pancetta, lardo and a sprinkling of nutmeg. In the province of Alba fragrant white truffles are often added. There's also a *rossa* or red version (the above is considered a risotto bianca, a white risotto) that is identical to the classic risotto but with the addition of tomato purée.

Risotto Gran Paradiso A risotto, typical of the Valdostana area, made with pancetta, toma cheese, onions, asparagus, peas, porcini mushrooms and parsley.

Tajarin Fresh egg pasta tagliatelle from the Langhe area. They're the true, native pasta of Piedmont, no larger than 3 mm. In some recipes olive oil and a handful of grated Parmesan cheese are added to the pasta dough. A traditional sauce, called al brucio, made from roast meat, is used with tajarin. However, the tajarin pair very well with white truffles or a chicken liver ragù. They can also be served in broth or in bean minestrone (made with fava beans in the summertime). The so-called combinata monferrina is tajarin and fava bean soup with an added cup of Barbera.

SOUPS

Al macc A soup typical of the area around Biella made with rice, milk and chestnut cream.

Asulette A soup made with whole-wheat flour and served garnished with slices of bread and fontina cheese.

Brodera The same as *brudera* (page 6).

Cisrà A traditional soup made with chickpeas. The word *cisrà* in Piemontese dialect is not only the name of this soup but also the name of one made with dried and skinned black chickpeas imported from Asia. Until 1920 it was easy to find these black chickpeas in most grocery stores in the Monferrato area and around the province of Vercelli. By 1932 the importation of the black chickpeas ceased, so the "original" cisrà never returned to the Piemontese kitchen.

Machet A soft polenta thinned with milk, then enriched with chestnuts. You'll find this soup in the province of Vercelli.

Minestra di riso alla valdostana A very simple soup made with rice, turnips and butter.

Minestra di trippa alla piemontese A delicious soup made with veal tripe, cabbage, potatoes and leeks.

Minestra marià A soup that is usually found in the southern part of Italy. However, in Piedmont you'll find a springtime version of it made with rice, spinach and eggs.

Seupa de gri A highly flavored soup made with barley, pork ribs, pancetta, onions, celery, potatoes, carrots, leeks and other seasonal vegetables.

Skilà A long-cooked soup made by the Valsesiani shepherds of onions, garlic, leeks and celery. Pieces of whole-wheat bread and cheese are added to the soup at the end.

Soupe Cogneintze A soup made with whole-wheat breadcrumbs, fontina cheese, beef broth and rice. It's typical of the village of Cogne in the province of Aosta.

Soupe grasse A tasty soup made by pounding stale whole-wheat bread in a mortar with a pestle until it is reduced to a finely ground powder. The powder is then cooked with butter, broth and toma cheese. The cooked soup is garnished with onions, juniper berries, freshly ground black pepper and nutmeg sautéed in butter. This is a specialty of the Valle di Susa.

Soupe paysanne A soup from the Valdostana made with crumbled whole-wheat bread, beef broth, pieces of toma cheese, butter, onions and various herbs.

Soupe Valpellinentze The Valpelline valley is found on the way to Gran San Bernardo. This substantial soup—made with bread, cabbage, fontina cheese and beef broth, then gratinéed—is often prescribed to those who are ill or convalescing.

Tofeja The word refers to the cylindrical-shaped terra cotta pot in which a soup of the same name is cooked. The pot narrows toward the bottom and has four handles. This historic preparation, also called fasoi grass ("fatty beans"), is usually served during the Carnival celebrations just before Lent. The soup is made with beans and various pork parts including hocks, cheeks, tail, ears, ribs and cracklings. It's a specialty of the Canavesana area.

Zuppa alla canavesana A very dense and substantial soup made with boiled cabbage or Savoy cabbage or turnips layered with toasted bread in a casserole. It's topped with meat sauce, lardo, onions, garlic, sausage and cheese. Broth is poured over everything; it is then gratinéed before serving.

Zuppa alla ueca A soup made with barley, pork ribs and greens. It is topped with toasted black bread, fontina cheese and a mixture of chopped parsley, basil and garlic, then gratinéed to serve.

Zuppa biancomangiare A very refined soup that dates back to the sixteenth century, made with chicken broth, breast of chicken, almonds, white bread and milk.

Zuppa di Arey A specialty of the mountain town of Courmayeur. The soup is prepared with milk, red wine, eggs, sugar, walnuts, cinnamon, nutmeg and broken breadsticks.

Zuppa mitunà A soup made by toasting pieces of bread in butter in a casserole. The toast is covered with a sprinkling of grated Grana cheese, then with broth, and then gratinéed. Some cooks beat egg yolks into the broth in order to achieve a more substantial soup.

CONDIMENTS, SAUCES, SALSAS AND EGGS

Bagnet piemontese *Bagnet* is a Piemontese term that's used to describe two sauces, il bagnet verd and il bagnet ross, that accompany boiled meats. The first one is a type of raw green sauce made with parsley, garlic, anchovies, the white part of bread soaked in vinegar, hard-cooked egg yolks and olive oil. The second one is a cooked sauce made with tomatoes, garlic, carrots, onions, vinegar and hot peppers.

Frittata rognosa A mouth-watering frittata made with Parmesan cheese and *salamin d'la duja* (page 5) cut into little pieces. Very often wild herbs such as nettles, rosolacci, San Pietro grass and leftover roast meats are added as well.

Salsa del povr'om A delicious sauce with two versions. The first one, the historic version, is made with pan drippings, broth, vinegar, scallions, chopped onions, parsley, breadcrumbs and freshly grated black pepper. The second much simpler variation is made with butter, eggs, flour, garlic and vinegar. Both sauces are good with cooked vegetables such as asparagus, chard ribs and cauliflower, or slices of boiled meat.

Uova a la bela Rosin A preparation, typical of the Piedmont region, made by cutting hard-cooked eggs in half, placing them yolk-side down, covering them with mayonnaise, and then dusting them with sieved hard-cooked yolks. The name refers to the beautiful commoner, Rosa Vercellana, who later became the mistress of King Vittorio Emanuele II. She gave him two children and he gave her the title Contessa di Mirafiore.

Uova alla piemontese A very tasty frittata made with Parmesan cheese and white truffles.

FISH, CRUSTACEANS AND SHELLFISH

Acciughe tartufate Fresh, raw anchovies marinated in layers with olive oil and white truffles.

Pesce ragno all'astigiana Actually, sea bass (branzino or spigola), although *pesce ragno* means "spider fish." It's cooked in copious amounts of aged white wine and butter and served sauced in a reduction of its cooking liquid surrounded by steamed potatoes and parsley. The same preparation is often used with pike.

Tinche all'agro A preparation in which a freshwater fish, tench, is floured, fried in butter and garlic and served with a sauce made by deglazing the pan with vinegar, white grape juice, parsley, sage and lemon peel.

Tinche in carpione A dish in which tench is floured and fried, then put into a warm marinade made with onions, sage, garlic, oregano and vinegar. The same preparation is used with other freshwater fish such as carp and whitefish.

Trote all'astigiana Little trout that are deboned, but left whole, their cavities stuffed with bay leaves, sage, parsley, butter, salt and pepper, then covered with white wine (Cortese or Arneis), sliced onions and freshly ground black pepper.

Trote alla piemontese Trout sautéed in olive oil, celery, onions, garlic, sage and rosemary, then topped with vinegar, lemon peel and raisins. A sauce for the fish is made by deglazing the pan then adding flour to the sauce to slightly thicken it.

Trote del Sesia in carpione A dish that may be made with Marmorata, Fario or Iridea trout that are fried in wild thyme- or sage-flavored butter and then immersed in a warm marinade of vinegar, wine, parsley, celery, bay leaf and juniper berries.

MEAT

Anatra alla novarese A mute duck (considered the tastiest) stuffed with its chopped innards, cabbage, rice, sausage, pancetta, lardo and mixed herbs. It may be roasted, baked in a casserole or boiled to serve.

Bale d'asu Large, round, cooked salami; a specialty of Mondovi near Cuneo.

Batsoà Made by boiling pork hocks in good-quality vinegar, then letting them rest in their cooking liquid. They are then de-boned, sliced, breaded and fried. The name comes from the French, *bas de soie* (silk stockings).

Bollito misto alla piemontese A mix of boiled meats composed of various cuts of beef and veal (breast, ribs, shoulder, tip, head, hocks, tail, tongue) and, in addition, hen or capon, cotechino, zampone and sausages. The cooking water is usually flavored with a clove-studded onion, celery, carrots, parsley sprigs and peppercorns. Among the sauces that are served with this assortment are *bagnet verd* and *bagnet rosso* (see *bagnet piemontese*, page 12); cognà, which is prepared with a purée of raisins reduced with apples, pears and figs; and sausa d'aviè, which is made with honey, walnuts and mustard powder. There's something similar to the sausa d'aviè in Valsesia called *uberlekke* (page 21).

Brasato al barolo An excellent dish made with a good cut of beef such as top round or rump roast that is cooked very slowly with celery, carrots, onions, garlic, herbs (such as parsley, sage, rosemary, bay leaf), a grating of nutmeg, a bit of lardo and Barolo wine. The cooking sauce is strained, then served on top of the sliced beef, which should be accompanied by polenta or mashed potatoes. In the classic version of this dish the meat is marinated in the wine and herbs before cooking (see recipe, page 32).

Camoscio alla piemontese A stew made with large pieces of venison marinated in white wine vinegar, carrots, celery, sage and rosemary. The pieces of marinated meat are then dredged in flour and added to a casserole where onions have been sautéed in butter and olive oil. The venison is slowly stewed until tender.

Caponet A dish consisting of bundles of cabbage leaves filled with leftover boiled meats and cooked salami (d'la duja). In the area around Vercelli, rice is added to the filling and the dish is called caponot. In the province of Novara this dish is called quagliette (little quails).

Capriolo (or **camoscio) alla valdostana** A stew made with leg of venison marinated in red wine and herbs. It is sautéed and bathed in grappa, then cooked in its marinade. It's best served with polenta.

Carbonade or **carbonata** A dish typical of the Valdostana made with sliced beef (at one time salted beef was used) cooked in an abundant amount of onions, red wine and herbs. Although the dish is Belgian in origin, there are variations found in the mountain towns of Saint Vincent, where the beef is cut into baton-shaped pieces, and in Cervinia, where the beef is sliced but cooked in beer instead of red wine. The dish is served very hot, almost always with polenta.

Cima alla piemontese This dish is very similar to one that's made in Liguria (page 41). It's prepared by making a pocket in a piece of veal belly and filling it with a stuffing made with sweetbreads, brains, chicken, Grana cheese, eggs, carrots, parsley, basil and garlic. It's weighted down and then baked, and served sliced with a side dish of seasonal vegetables.

Civet or **civè** or **sivè** A French term used in Piedmont to designate a type of wild game stew (hare or venison) that is marinated in red wine and herbs. Onions, carrots, celery, garlic, sage, rosemary, parsley, juniper berries, bay leaf, cloves and cinnamon play a big part in the marinade. The finished dish is bound together with the animal's blood and liver. This preparation is somewhat like salmì except blood is not used to bind that dish; instead, the pan drippings are strained and added back to the pot.

Coniglio Rabbit.

Coniglio all'astigiana Pieces of rabbit that are braised with butter, onions, sage, rosemary, bay leaf, thyme, pancetta and Grignolino wine. A finely chopped mixture of garlic, parsley and rabbit liver is added at the end.

Coniglio alla canavesana A dish in which pieces of rabbit are marinated in vinegar, onions, sage, a bit of cinnamon and cloves, then very slowly cooked.

Coniglio in peperonata A very tasty preparation in which rabbit is sautéed in a mixture of veal kidney fat, butter, rosemary and bay leaf. About halfway through the cooking process, pepper stew (peperonata), seasoned with anchovies, garlic and vinegar, is added to the rabbit.

Costata alla losa A rib eye steak that is marinated in olive oil and fragrant herbs and then cooked on a *losa*—a split shale stone like the ones that cover the roofs of rustic mountain homes.

Costoletta alla castellana See *quaietta* (page 19).

Costoletta or **cotoletta alla valdostana** A veal chop that has had a pocket cut into it, which is filled with pieces of fontina cheese, then breaded and fried. During the season, shards of white truffle are added to the filling.

Cotletta 'd crin a l'astesana A dish in which a pork chop is marinated in olive oil, breaded, and then cooked in olive oil, butter and anchovies. The chop is topped with shaved white truffles and it's finished in the oven; a specialty of the province of Asti.

Cotolette di crema tartufata A type of pudding made with semolina, white flour, Parmesan cheese, nutmeg, eggs, milk, cream, Gruyère cheese and white truffles. The cream is chilled in a flat pan and cut into shapes, dipped into egg and breadcrumbs, and fried—delicious, if not exactly light.

Fagiolata Beans from Saluggia that are stewed with tomatoes and pork cracklings. Sometimes cotechino or a calf's head is added to the stew. Its ideal companion is polenta.

Fassone A type of cattle that has a genetic anomaly which makes its hind quarters grow to almost double the normal size.

Fegato alla paesana Liver cooked in a skillet with onions, chopped garlic, parsley, lardo, red wine and a little flour to thicken.

Filetti di manzo con salsa brusca Little slices of beef fillet sautéed in a skillet then dressed with sauce made with chopped hard-cooked eggs, mustard, olive oil and freshly ground black pepper.

Finanziera alla piemontese A sumptuous and elaborate sauce typical of the Piedmont region. It's made with cock's combs, wattles and testicles; unborn eggs and chicken livers; beef fillet; veal rump and saddle, tendons, sweetbreads and brains; olive oil–marinated porcini mushrooms and assorted herbs. It's all made into a velouté, a cream to which dry Marsala wine is added. The finanziera sauce can then be used to fill vol-au-vent, as an accompaniment to a plain white risotto, made into a mold or served as a very refined, hot antipasto. There are variations for this recipe; the most notable includes pickles. The name of the dish dates to the nineteenth century when this was one of the favorite dishes of the bankers of Turin — especially during their working lunches. The term *finanziera* comes from classic French cuisine — it may refer to a garnish or a sauce that is somehow linked to the concept of great wealth.

Flisse or **frisse** Very similar to *grive* (page 17) but made with different ingredients. Frisse are in fact meatballs made with pork leg, lungs, hearts, liver and sausages, then flavored with juniper berries just like grive. The meatballs are covered in caul fat and cooked in a skillet.

Fricandeau astigiano Pieces of beef and pork that have been dredged in flour, flavored with finely chopped garlic, rosemary and sage, then cooked with onions, celery, carrots, white wine, red wine, broth and a little bit of tomato purée. This preparation is cooked for a long time. About halfway through, small white onions (cipolline d'Ivrea) and diced potatoes are added. The finished dish may also be used to dress fresh egg tagliatelle.

Fricia or **fritto misto alla piemontese** An extraordinary and very rich mixture of fried sweet and savory ingredients including sweetbreads, both veal and pork livers, brains and little pieces of veal rump, chicken combs and croquettes, beef fillet, lamb chops, sliced eggplant and zucchini, squash blossoms, artichoke bottoms, mushrooms, amaretti cookies, sweet semolina pudding, apple slices and more. Naturally, the ingredients depend upon the season. Most of the ingredients are dredged in flour and dipped in a batter before they're fried. Some serve this mixture with *flisse* (page 16) or *grive* (below). In the area near Asti, the fried mixture is served with sliced buttered carrots.

Grive Lean pork meatballs typical of the Langhe area. Ingredients, in addition to pork, include brains, liver, bread, cheese, eggs, juniper berries and assorted herbs. The meatballs are covered with caul fat, then cooked in a skillet with butter and olive oil.

Involtini alla canavesana Meatballs made with chopped veal liver, sausage, raisins, juniper berries and Parmesan cheese. They're covered with caul fat then stewed with tomatoes. They go splendidly well with puréed potatoes.

Lepre Hare.

Lepre alla vignarola For this preparation, hare is marinated in white wine with grapes for a few days; spices and herbs are then added and it's very slowly cooked. The pan juices are strained to make the sauce, and then enriched with cream and a drop or two of Marsala wine. The hare is served covered with the sauce and garnished with grapes. This is definitely an autumn dish and is rather rare.

Lepre in civet See *civet*, page 15.

Lepre in salmì See *salmì*, page 20.

Lingua al giardino Boiled pork tongue cut into very fine slices and dressed with a sauce made with onions, carrots and celery sautéed in olive oil with parsley, capers, tomato sauce, hot pepper flakes, broth, vinegar and a bit of flour to thicken. This nineteenth-century dish is typical of the Langhe area.

Lumache al Barbera Snails that are thoroughly purged, then removed from their shells and fried in olive oil, celery and onions. Barbera wine is added at the end. Just before serving, the snails are garnished with chopped walnuts and a splash of brandy.

Lumache all'ossolana In this dish, snails are baked in their shells along with a filling made with crumbled amaretti cookies, chopped walnuts, eggs, garlic and parsley. In another version, the snails are braised with leeks.

Lumache alla piemontese A dish made with snails that are first purged by boiling in water and white wine, and then sautéed with onions, tomato sauce, broth, bay leaf and thyme. They're put back into their shells after they've been cooked. Walnuts, pine nuts and anchovies are then mashed in a mortar with a pestle and added to the sauce along with chopped parsley. The snails are covered with the sauce, then reheated in the oven and served with buttered toasts.

Lumache e salsiccia alla cunese An unusual sauce made with snails and sausage cooked in wine and served with polenta.

Marzapane novarese A type of salami similar to blood sausage made with pork blood, bits of bread and fatback chopped with garlic, salt, pepper and spices. It's stuffed into casings, hung and left to dry for two days. It's boiled for twenty minutes to serve.

Masarà An extremely tasty stew made with little sausages (*d'la duja*, page 5) that are sautéed in butter, olive oil, lardo and onions. Tomatoes, zucchini and potatoes are added a little more than halfway through the cooking process. Historically, this dish is served with corn bread.

Meiroun 'd crava Goat that has been smoked or corned, then boiled before serving. It's a specialty of Mondovi near Cuneo.

Milza ripiena This dish is sometimes called the poor man's cima. It's made by cutting a pocket into the spleen, then stuffing it with boiled meats, leftover roast meats, parsley, garlic, Grana cheese and eggs. The stuffed spleen is then boiled in water flavored with celery, carrots and onions and served at room temperature with a side dish of buttered, cooked vegetables.

Montone in salsa This dish, typical of Domodossola near the Swiss border, is a whole mutton grilled over a wood-burning fire. It's continuously basted with a mixture of olive oil, vinegar, mixed herbs and hot peppers.

Oca alla piemontese A goose cooked in water, garlic and rosemary. The cooked goose is then covered with its rendered fat in order to preserve it for a while. It may be served hot or cold and it goes very well with polenta.

Pitò al fieno maggengo A preparation in which a turkey (*pito*) is boiled in an abundant amount of salted water and hay from the May harvest. This historic, rather rare recipe can be found in the village of Roccaverano near the province of Asti.

Pollo alla babi A young chicken, split open, covered in assorted herbs and grilled over a wood-burning fire.

Pollo alla Marengo According to legend, this recipe was created at the last minute by Napoleon's chef, Dunand, on the evening of the battle at Marengo. The ingredients include what was available: pieces of chicken sautéed in a skillet with onions, garlic, tomatoes, bay leaf, mushrooms, freshwater shrimp, Madeira wine, celery and carrots. The dish was served with toasted bread and fried eggs.

Polpettone alla moncalvese A type of "meat loaf" from Moncalvo in the province of Asti that is is actually a veal top round wrapped in prosciutto or pancetta, then roasted in white wine.

Puloti alla vercellese Little water birds (moorhens) that live in the marshes at the edge of rice fields become very fat and tasty from eating grains of ripe rice. In the area near Vercelli, Novara and Lomellina, they're wrapped in pancetta, then cooked in a casserole with celery, carrots, onion and bay leaf. This is a typical September dish and is usually served with a plain risotto alla piemontese.

Quaietta This dish, from the area around Saluzzo in the province of Cuneo, is referred to as a "restorative" dish. It's made by making a pocket in a veal fillet and stuffing it with chopped roasted meat, cheese and truffles.

Quartiretto A dish typical of the village of Limone Piemonte near Cuneo, but found throughout Piedmont. In it, the hindquarters of a kid are deboned and stuffed with a filling made of eggs, cheese and spinach, and then baked.

Rane Frogs.

Rane alla vercellese Frogs that are floured and fried then stewed in tomatoes, garlic, parsley, beet tops and white wine.

Rane fritte alla novarese Frogs that are floured and fried, then left to marinate in vinegar, onions, celery, parsley and cloves for at least two hours.

Rane ripiene A recipe typical of the village of Cassalvolone near Novara, in which frogs are marinated for at least two hours in water, vinegar, garlic, onions and celery. They are then stuffed with a filling made with *salamin d'la duja* (page 5), breadcrumbs, eggs and spinach before being dredged in flour and fried.

Rolata di vitello A dish made with a good-sized piece of veal breast filled with chopped garlic and rosemary, prosciutto, mushrooms, eggs, greens and sausage. It's rolled, tied, then cooked in a casserole and basted with broth.

Rostòn A stew typical of Alba and the Langhe area made with fillet of *sanato* (page 20) that has been studded with pieces of white truffle and cooked with herbs, greens and porcini mushrooms.

Rustida or **rostida** A dish typical of the Piedmont countryside in which the heart, lungs and chunks of lean pork, onions and sausages are stewed with tomatoes. It's served with polenta.

Saccoccia See *tasca ripiena* (below).

Salame di patate A "salami" made with a purée of potatoes in combination with mixed pork meat (like a sausage mixture), salami spices and garlic stuffed into a casing. This strange salami is left to rest for twenty-four hours; then baked. It's served with small white onions (cipolline d'Ivrea).

Salmì A term that is a derivative of the French word *salmis*, which is a method of cooking game. In Piedmont, salmì is most often associated with hare and is similar to *civet* (page 15). However, in the Piedmont preparation the garlic, herbs and spices are eliminated. The sauce isn't thickened with blood or liver but instead is made by straining the pan drippings.

Sanato A term that refers to a breed of veal, usually Piemontese, that hasn't been weaned, but is fed a mixture of its mother's milk and egg yolks. The authentic sanato is quite large, has very white meat, a delicate flavor and is easily digested. A particularly tasty version is *al latte*—cooked slowly in milk, prosciutto, onions, celery and carrots.

Subrics Croquettes typical of the city of Cuneo made with apples, ground veal and eggs. The croquettes are floured and fried, then basted with red wine and sugar.

Tacchinella ripiena alla piemontese A young female turkey stuffed with rice, peppers and chicken livers. The roasted bird is served with a sauce made from its pan drippings.

Tapulone This very strange dish, from the area around Novara, is made with donkey and mule meat, ground, then cooked with cabbage, herbs and wine. It's often made with a combination of donkey, horse and beef. According to local legend, about a thousand years ago a group of pious villagers from the Ossolano area made a pilgrimage to the San Giulio church on a little island of the same name in Lago d'Orta. On their way home they were overcome with hunger and decided to kill and cook one of their donkeys. It was so tough that it was inedible. They used a knife called a *tapule* to cut it into bite-sized pieces.

Tasca ripiena A dish made by cutting a pocket into a piece of the top round of veal and stuffing it with a filling made of veal ground with salami, scallions, parsley, garlic, eggs, black pepper and grated Grana cheese. The stuffed meat is then covered with cloth and boiled. This specialty of the area around Asti and the Monferrato is served cold.

Tonno di coniglio A dish made by cooking a rabbit in vegetable broth with various herbs. The rabbit is then cut into pieces, layered in a ceramic dish that has been rubbed with olive oil, garlic and fresh sage, and left to rest in a cool spot for about forty-eight hours. This peasant preparation is typical of the Monferrato area.

Trippa alla savoiarda Tripe stewed with onions, celery, carrots, tomatoes and basil.

Uberlekke A very rich mixture of boiled meats typical of the Valsesia area. The mixture — beef rump, veal top round, head and tongue, pork ribs and leg of lamb — is preserved in salt for a few days before it's boiled. Once cooked, it is combined with liverwurst, ham shank, cotechini and pork skins stuffed with hot peppers (all individually cooked) to serve, accompanied by potatoes, turnips, carrots and horseradish sauce.

VEGETABLES

Asparagi alla Monferrina For this dish, steamed asparagus is placed in a baking dish with tips pointing toward the center, covered with butter and grated Parmesan cheese, cooked in a moderate oven and often served with butter-fried eggs.

Baggianata A ratatouille made with beans and tomatoes; a specialty of Domodossola.

Carciofi ripieni alla torinese A dish in which artichokes are cut in half and the fuzzy choke removed before stuffing the cavity with a filling made of ground veal or chicken, prosciutto and parsley. The artichokes are then covered, first with thin slices of roast pork loin, then with a sauce made with the roast meat and white wine, and then slowly stewed in a skillet.

Cavolo farcito A substantial vegetable (but not vegetarian) dish made by stuffing a whole cabbage with a filling consisting of half-boiled rice, sausage, parsley and lemon juice. The cabbage is covered with cheesecloth then boiled. It's served hot garnished with sage fried in butter, grated Grana cheese, parsley, breadcrumbs and finely chopped, hard-cooked egg yolks.

Cime di luppolo alla biellese Hops greens that have been boiled, drained, covered with grated Parmesan cheese and then topped with butter-fried eggs.

Cipolle Onions.

Cipolle di magro Onions that are stuffed with a filling made with a purée of squash, fruit mostarda, eggs, crumbled amaretti cookies and nutmeg. The dish is considered a specialty of the extreme eastern part of the Piedmont region in the area between the Po River and the old customs station near the border with the Lombardy region.

Cipolle ripiene A simple, fragrant dish prepared with the best-quality Piemontese onions. The large onions are half-cooked, and then the centers are scooped out. The cavities are stuffed with a filling made of chopped beef sautéed in butter, eggs, cheese and freshly ground black pepper. They are topped with a splash of grappa and then baked.

Giardinetto alla piemontese A combination of vegetables that have been cooked — or prepared — then dressed separately but served on the same plate. The composition consists of boiled new potatoes, carrots, radishes, little artichokes and lettuce.

Salada 'd coconj A splendid salad made with ovoli mushrooms and usually dressed with a sauce made with anchovies, parsley, eggs, lemon, garlic and olive oil.

Sedani crogiolati A dish of sliced celery root that is parboiled then finished in a sauce made with butter, flour, onions and broth. It's served on toast.

Soria A stew made with green beans, potatoes, onions, lardo and fragrant herbs. It's typical of Valdostano.

Tartufi all'acciuga A very tasty dish made by mixing cubes of bread with an abundant amount of shaved white truffles, then covering it with a sauce made with anchovies, garlic, rosemary, sage, game pan drippings, cream and a bit of Marsala wine.

Turinèisa A dish made by parboiling zucchini, cutting them in half lengthwise, scooping out the middle and stuffing them with a filling made with sausage, pieces of veal that have been cooked in butter, garlic, parsley, San Pietro herb, Parmesan cheese, nutmeg and eggs. The stuffed zucchini are sprinkled with white wine and then baked. This same filling is also used for onions and squash blossoms.

CHEESE AND DAIRY PRODUCTS

Acceglio A traditional fresh cheese produced in Valle del Maira in the province of Cuneo. It's made in the summertime with skimmed cow's milk and is a very light cheese with a slightly acidic but clean flavor.

Bettlmat A real fontina — even though it has not been given an official designation — typical of the Val d'Ossola.

Bra The origins of this cheese are remote, but it's the namesake of the citizens of an eponymous town in the province of Cuneo. You can find tender and hard versions of this semi-fat cheese (32% fat) made with uncooked cow's milk. Sometimes sheep or goat's milk is added to the paste. You'll find it made into square or round forms. Tender Bra has a light gray, smooth, elastic rind and the body's color can range from milky white to ivory with small fissures. It has a mildly sharp flavor and makes a good table cheese. Hard Bra has a light brown rind and the body is straw- or ochre colored. The sharply flavored cheese is good for grating.

Brôs or **bruss** or **brüs** or **brussu** A cheese typical of the area that saddles the Appenine mountain range between Liguria, Piedmont and the Langhe region. However, you'll find this cheese in almost all of the Italian regions that border the Alps. It's made with leftovers of soft cheeses. The best version is made with *robiola del bec* (page 24), a mixture made with crumbled, leftover robiola, olive oil, vinegar, salt, pepper, grappa or cognac, garlic, chives and spices. The mix is placed in a terra cotta or glass vessel and left to age for about a month. The result is an extraordinarily robust and flavorful cream cheese.

Castelmagno A cheese that takes its name from the most famous center of its production, Castelmagno near Cuneo. It's a semi-fatty cheese with a hard body with striations of mold. It's usually made with cow's milk, but sheep or goat's milk may be used as well. The thin, elastic rind is reddish-yellow which, as it ages and thickens, becomes wrinkled and brown. The body changes in color from pearly white to golden yellow veined with striations of mold. The young cheese is crumbly but becomes compact. It's a fragrant cheese with a refined and delicate flavor. However, the older it gets, the stronger and more pungent the flavor. It's a perfect table cheese.

Fontina The most famous cheese of the Val d'Aosta, fontina is a fatty cheese made with whole cow's milk and is slightly cooked. The reddish brown rind is thin and compact. The soft and elastic body is straw colored. The rounds of cheese are short — especially the best quality ones. It's highly aromatic, especially that produced in the summertime in the hilly areas of the region. This is both a table and a cooking cheese used to make fonduta, etc.

Montemagno A fatty cheese whose rather harsh, almost

repellent odor comes from the fact that it's aged under a heap of chestnut leaves that go bad and, finally, completely rot.

Murazzano Named for the town near Cuneo where it's produced, this is a fresh, fatty cheese made with sheep's milk or a mixture of sheep and cow's milk. It's made into little forms measuring about four inches wide by an inch and a quarter high. Its soft white body doesn't have a rind but there are small undulations on the surface. This typical table cheese is usually dressed with extra virgin olive oil and freshly ground black pepper to serve.

Murianengo A cheese from the town of the same name, very similar to *castelmagno* (page 23), but slightly more flavorful, produced in the pastures of the Moncenisio area.

Raschera This cheese is made all over the province of Cuneo, but the classic version is made in the Raschera Alps in the Maritime Alps. Raschera is a semi-fat cheese, made with cow's milk that is cooked then pressed. Sometimes a bit of sheep or cow's milk is added to correct the flavor. Its thin, reddish-gray rind becomes wrinkled and darker as it ages. The body is ivory colored with small, sparsely spaced fissures. Raschera is sweetly aromatic, especially the cheese produced in the Alps. As it ages, it becomes more savory and develops a pungent overtone. It's a traditional table cheese.

Reblèque This fresh cheese from the Valdostana is made with heavy cream and is eaten, just after it curdles and has been drained, with sugar and cinnamon.

Robiola del bec *Bec* is dialect for billy goat. The most refined consumers of this cheese prefer to eat that which is produced in October and November — the months when female goats are in heat. This robiola has similar characteristics to *robiola di Roccaverano* (below). Although they are produced in the same area, the main differences are found as the cheese ages. Because goat's milk is used, this one has a more savory flavor and is usually aged for a longer period of time.

Robiola di Roccaverano Robiola cheese is produced in several villages in the provinces of Alessandria and Asti. This fatty, fresh one from the village of Roccaverano is made with cow's, sheep's and goat's milk. It is soft, tender and spreadable, formed into tiny cylindrical shapes, and may be milky white or straw colored. It's delicately fragrant, with a full but slightly acid flavor and is served as a table cheese.

Salagnun This cheese, typical of the lower Val d'Aosta, is actually a ricotta made from the whey of fontina or toma. It's usually flavored with fennel seeds, hot peppers and olive oil.

Seirass del Lausùn A type of curdled milk enclosed in a cloth sack, typical of the village of Pinerolo in the province of Turin.

Toma A hard cheese made with unfermented cow's milk. There are varieties that are more or less fatty. The young cheese is sweetly flavored, becoming more pungent and aromatic as it ages. The best toma comes from Valle del Cervo, Valle dell'Elvo, Valle dell'Orco or from Locano, Val Casotto, Valsesia, Val Stura, the Langhe (at one time made with only sheep's milk), Maccagno, Pesio or Lanzo.

Tomini These little fresh cheese forms—they never weigh more than a quarter of a pound—are made with cow's milk or a mixture of milks. They are formed into cylinders, rectangles or squares and eaten either plain or dressed with olive oil, black pepper and hot pepper, or with salsa verde. In recent years it's become fashionable to stuff the cheese forms with mushrooms, prosciutto, walnuts, arugula and other ingredients before baking or grilling them.

SWEETS AND LIQUEURS

Baci da dama These typical Piemontese cookies are a specialty of the city of Tortona in the province of Alessandria. They are essentially two round almond, shortbread-like cookies that are sandwiched together with a chocolate or apricot jam filling.

Bicciolani These ribbon-shaped ridged cookies are a specialty of the province of Vercelli. They are made with flour, sugar, eggs, butter, cloves, mace, coriander seeds, vanilla, nutmeg and white pepper.

Blanc manger A pure white pudding, a specialty of the Val d'Aosta, which made its way there from the Savoy region of France. It is made with milk, sugar and vanilla.

Bonet A traditional Piemontese pudding made with milk, eggs, cocoa, coffee, rum, Marsala wine and amaretti cookies. There are variations on the theme: *bonet giallo* or "yellow beret" is made by eliminating the cocoa and coffee. It refers to the mold in which the pudding is cooked, which looks like an eighteenth-century cap.

Brochat A very dense cream made by boiling milk, wine and sugar for a long time. It's eaten with sliced bread.

Brutti ma buoni Delicious cookies, from the village of Borgomanero in province of Novara, made with egg whites, almonds and sugar.

Bugie Crumbly ribbons of deep-fried dough that are covered with powdered sugar and typically served during the Carnival period. The name changes according to the area where they're made.

Canditi di Carignano Candied orange peel.

Canestrelli Piemontese sweets made with yellow flour, white flour, eggs, butter, cocoa and vanilla, and cooked in a waffle iron. A Ligurian version is made with almonds.

Ciambelline d'Aosta Ring-shaped wedding cookies made with very finely milled yellow flour, a bit of white flour, sugar, eggs, butter and lemon zest.

Confortini The Piemontese version of cat's tongue cookies (lingue di gatto). They are very thin and crunchy and can be stored for a long period.

Coppa Torino For this preparation, a goblet is lined with sponge cake that is moistened with rum. The goblet is then layered with pastry cream and crumbled candied chestnuts (marrons glacées). The top layer is whipped cream. It's garnished with cherries.

Crumiri di Casale Crumbly dry cookies made with white and yellow flour, eggs, sugar and vanilla.

Cuneesi al rum Delicate little meringues dipped in rum and then covered with chocolate.

Dolce savoiardo Very finely textured sponge cake.

Eporediesi al cacao A type of amaretto cookie made with almonds, hazelnuts, sugar and cocoa, typical of the Canavese area.

Fiandolein A type of zabaione made with egg yolks, sugar, milk, rum and lemon peel.

Finocchini Little cookies typical of the village of Refrancore in the province of Asti.

Genepy A juniper berry liqueur from Valdostana.

Giandujotti Traditional Piemontese chocolates made with a soft chocolate fondant, a cream of toasted hazelnuts from the Langhe, vanilla and sugar. Gianduja chocolate was created in Turin in 1865 during Carnival by the confectioners Caffarel e Prochet, who wanted to make a chocolate molded into the shape of the hat worn with the most popular Turinese carnival mask, that of the merry gentleman of the region's countryside, the Gianduia.

Melicotti Typical crunchy Piemontese cookies made with white and yellow flours, sugar, butter and eggs.

Monte bianco A classic dessert found throughout Piedmont and Lomdardy regions. French in origin, it's made with a purée of chestnuts, milk and sugar. The mixture is made into a little mountain, and then covered with whipped cream. It may have various garnishes, very often shaved chocolate.

Nocciolini Tiny sweet amaretti cookies typical of the village of Chivasso in the province of Turin.

Panna cotta A very fashionable "spoon sweet," typical of the Piedmont region, made with cream and various flavorings, then set with gelatin.

Pazientini Little baton-shaped cookies made with the same ingredients as meringues but with flour added.

Pesche ripiene Fresh peaches cut in half, stuffed with a filling made of almonds, amaretti cookies and cocoa, topped with a splash of Marsala wine, and baked.

Pilot Fritters made with ground grissini (breadsticks), eggs, milk, flour and sugar.

Polenta d'Ivrea A rustic cake made with yellow flour, eggs, butter, sugar and vanilla.

Ratafià A liqueur typical of the Piedmont region made with an infusion of fruits (sour cherries, apricots, oranges, currants, plums, walnuts, lemons, broom and, most important, maraschino cherries) to which sugar is added. It is distilled several times. It has a sweet, fruity flavor and is dark in color.

Salame del papa This Easter sweet, typical of the province of Alessandria, is made by folding crumbled crackers or cookies into a mixture of butter, sugar, eggs, cocoa and rum. The mixture is then formed into a cylindrical shape, wrapped in waxed paper, chilled and then sliced to serve.

Savoiardi Long, very, very light and almost foam-like cookies used mostly as liners or the base for other more complex desserts.

Seiras A dessert made with ricotta cheese softened with cream and flavored with liqueur.

Spumone alla piemontese A light spongy pudding made with mascarpone, eggs, sugar, rum and candied citrus fruits.

Tegole d'Aosta Crunchy cookies made with almonds, recognized by their tile-like (*tegole*) shape. They are sometimes dipped in chocolate.

Torcetti Ring-shaped, dry yeast cookies typical of the village of Saint Vincent in the province of Aosta. Another version from the village of Rivoli in the province of Turin is made with puff pastry.

Torta Gianduja This fancy cake is a Piemontese pastry shop specialty. It's a chocolate-hazelnut cake doused with a liqueur, filled with apricot preserves and then topped with a chocolate glaze.

Zabaione This very famous dessert, found throughout Italy, is thought to be Piemontese in origin. Made by whipping egg yolks, in a double boiler, with Marsala wine and sugar, it's served in a goblet accompanied by dry cookies. Zabaione is also used as an ingredient in more complex desserts. It's said that the name comes from San Giovanni Baylon, the patron saint of pastry makers, who's venerated in the church of San Tommaso in Turin.

Zesti Candied orange and lemon peel typical of the village of Carignano in the province of Turin.

WINES

The best red wines in all of Italy are said to come from this region. Piedmont also produces excellent white wines, however, from the celebrated Moscato from the hills of the province of Asti, to the elegant Gavi from Alessandria and the fragrant Blanc de Morgex from the highest vineyards in Europe, just under Mont Blanc. Turning to fragrance: all the wines from Piedmont and Val d'Aosta have, when aged, a characteristic fruity aroma. The grapes of these regions benefit from the severe northern climate and cold winds that allow them to ripen slowly while preserving their delicate fragrance.

Arneis A light-bodied, dry white wine. It makes a wonderful aperitif but is also a good wine to serve with simple fish dishes.

Barbaresco Made from the same varietal as Barolo (Nebbiolo) and by the same vinification process, the difference between the two is the result of the few kilometers that separate the individual productions. Barbaresco is produced in a slightly warmer climate than Barolo. The wine that comes from the cellars in the town of Barbaresco in the province of Cuneo is a bit less austere, gentler, more beguiling than Barolo, but always of the same high caliber. Just like Barolo, Barbaresco is a good match for rich red meat roasts and aged cheeses. It must be labeled D.O.C.G. (Denominazione di Origine Controllata Garantita), an official designation guaranteeing the quality of the wine.

Barbera This is a generous wine: ruby colored, with shades of violet, an intensely winey nose and decisive flavor. It's a good friend — perfect for those evenings of happy celebrations. When it's young and slightly sour it's a good companion to bagna cauda, as it's able to quash the heat of the sauce. As it barrel-ages it softens and grows more elegant. It's the perfect wine for substantial meat dishes.

Barolo We are indebted to the Marchese Falletti for this wine — the marchese and the vineyard workers he brought to Piedmont from France in the nineteenth century. It was then that the Nebbiolo grape began to be cultivated as if it were Bordeaux. Instead of the old, soft-to-the-mouth wine, "His Majesty's" Barolo — dry and austere — was born. The wine was adored by Cavour, a leading figure in the unification of Italy, and so appreciated by King Carlo Alberto that it was served at the royal table with all game dishes and roasted red meats. Barolo is a versatile wine and may easily be used as an ingredient in various dishes of the area where it's made. When it's young, Barolo is ruby colored and fragrant with violets; as it ages, shades of orange appear and its aroma deepens to tar and resin. Nowadays you find Barolo used to flavor risotto, zabaione and braised meats. Barolo is one of two Piemontese wines to garner the all-important D.O.C.G.

Blanc de Morgex This platinum-colored wine is produced in the Alps at elevations up to 4,000 feet where no one would think grapes could grow. Very fragrant, very dry, light and elegant, this wine really has nothing of the Mediterranean about it and yet, thanks to its mysterious alchemy, perfectly marries with fish dishes cooked on the Italian coasts.

Brachetto This lightly sparkling red dessert wine is typical of the area around Asti and the province of Alessandria. It's sweetly flavored, without being tedious, and has a delicate nose. It's the ideal wine to serve with pears cooked with cinnamon accompanied by panna cotta, a dessert that highlights the fragrance and softness of the wine.

Caluso passito This varietal is the same as *Erbaluce* (page 30). Caluso grapes, however, are left to wither on the vine or are harvested when they have fully ripened and then put in greenhouses to ferment. To augment the alcohol content, brandy is sometimes added to the wine, resulting in a very sweet, golden, intensely fragrant nectar. It goes well with dry pastries and sweets made with almonds.

Chiaretto di Cavaglià This wine, with its beguiling rose pink color, winey nose and sweet flavor, goes well with dry pastries. This long-lasting wine can be drunk for up to one hundred years.

Dolcetto You'll find this varietal growing at elevations of almost a mile in the Langhe area. Its growing area extends into the province of Alessandria. Actually, there are at least seven Dolcetto D.O.C.'s (Denominazione di Origine Controllata), all produced in the Piedmont region and each with its own unique characteristics. The common thread is their drinkability with all meals. Dolcetto is a deep ruby color, with a winey nose and a dry flavor reminiscent of almonds.

Donnaz Produced in the glacial terrain in the area around Pont St. Martin in the province of Aosta from a grape closely related to the Nebbiolo, Donnaz has a garnet red color and a complex, sometimes rough bouquet that softens as it ages, similar to the Nebbiolo varietal. When young, it goes well with dishes made with fontina cheese. The mature Donnaz is perfect with game.

Enfer d'Arvier A wine made from the Valdostana varietal, Petit Rouge. It's bright red, fragrant and medium-bodied, making it the perfect wine for most of the typical dishes of the Valdostana, especially meat-based ones.

Erbaluce This very dry, straw-colored, delicately fragrant wine goes well with not only fish — especially freshwater fish — dishes, but is also wonderful served as an aperitif.

Favorita A varietal typically found on the table in the days before the unification of Italy. Today it's made into a simply structured, delicately colored and interestingly flavored white wine. It goes well with a full meal or as an aperitif.

Freisa This not-too-intensely-colored red wine has an air of raspberries. When it's dry and slightly sparkling, it goes well with the cured meats that are typical of the Piemontese valleys because it balances their fatty texture. When it's sweeter and sparkling, it's a good wine to serve with desserts, especially with those made with walnuts.

Gavi or **Cortese di Gavi** The most elegant white wine of the region. It goes well with simple, almost delicate first courses and fish dishes. It's also an excellent aperitif. The principal gift of this lightly fragrant wine is its freshness — evidenced by its almost absence of color, which makes it appear pale green — and its slightly acidic flavor.

Grignolino This lightly colored and flavored red wine is best when young and still full of tannins. With its bitter herb flavor it contrasts very well with regional dishes like fritto misto made with amaretti cookies or sweet semolina. It's good served throughout an entire meal, too.

Malvasia This slightly sparkling, sweet red wine with a delicate nose is good with desserts, particularly with dry Piemontese pastries and cookies.

Malvasia di Nus Made from the Malvoisie de Nus varietal, this soft, sweet and highly fragrant dessert wine is surprisingly good with veined cheeses. Try it with bruss, toma or fermented ricotta.

Moscato d'Asti spumante This sweet, intensely fragrant, straw-colored wine, with light, ever-present foam is a visual treat. Its bouquet is true to the grape, moscato, from which it's made. It's a perfect dessert wine, an elegant companion to the Christmastime panettone, and wedding or birthday cakes. You can find this wine in a non-sparkling version as well.

Muscat passito de Chambave This precious and original golden yellow dessert wine is made by harvesting bunches of Moscato grapes when they're ripe, then hanging them in an open-air shed. When the temperature drops, the grapes freeze and preserve all their sugar. With its intensely sweet flavor, it goes well with a variety of desserts, and is a wine to savor and meditate upon with respect.

Nebbiolo This varietal forms the base of several different wines that are created according to their individual locations. Some examples: Nebbiolo, in glacial terrain, becomes the elegant Gattinara (perfect with aged toma cheese); the velvety-smooth Carema, redolent of antique roses; the rare Lessona, Ghemme, Fara and Bramaterra; all are great wines to serve with roast meats. On the left bank of the Tanaro River you'll find the lighter and very drinkable Roero, a good wine to serve throughout a meal. Nebbiolo itself is a red wine that marries marvelously well with dishes made with white truffles, and with meat.

Rubino di Cantavenna Created from a mixture of Barbera, Grignolino and Freisa grapes, this is a medium-bodied, light red wine with a winey nose. It marries well with first courses and chicken dishes.

Torrette This light ruby-colored wine is made with the Petit Rouge varietal that grows in the town of St. Pierre in the province of Aosta. With its slightly bitter but pleasing flavor it goes well with carbonade, and when aged, it can hold its own with game.

Brasato al Barolo
Serves 6

¼ pound lardo or prosciutto fat
2 pounds lean beef, such as top round
2 tablespoons unsalted butter
2 tablespoons olive oil
2 tablespoons parsley leaves
2 large sage leaves
1 sprig rosemary
2 cloves garlic
1 bay leaf
2 teaspoons freshly ground black pepper
A pinch of ground cinnamon
A pinch of nutmeg
1 whole clove
2 onions, chopped
2 carrots, chopped
1 rib celery, chopped
1 teaspoon salt and some more for rubbing
   the meat
1 bottle Barolo wine
Broth as needed

Cut the lardo into strips and use a larding needle to lace it into the beef. Tie it up with kitchen twine in a way so it keeps its shape. In a large casserole over medium heat melt the butter in the olive oil. Brown the meat on all sides. Chop together the parsley, sage, rosemary leaves and garlic. Add the mix to the casserole with the bay leaf, pepper, cinnamon, nutmeg and clove. Remove the meat from the pot and sauté the onions, carrots and celery. Add the salt. Lightly rub the meat with salt and put it back into the casserole. Pour in the entire bottle of Barolo. Cover and turn down the heat to low. Cook for at least 3 hours, adding broth as needed. It must be very tender. Continue to cook until it is. Remove the meat from the pot and let it rest for a few minutes. Remove the wine, slice the meat, and serve covered with the pan sauce as is, or strained. This braised meat is excellent served with sliced, roasted polenta or boiled potatoes.

Note: If you would like a more strongly flavored dish, you can marinate the meat in the herbs, spices and wine overnight before cooking.

Suggested wine: Barolo

LIGURIA

Ligurians are not gluttons, they are connoisseurs. The food of this charming region is basic and well defined, and at the same time inventive and creative. The dishes of Liguria, a narrow ribbon of land between the Mediterranean Sea and the Appenine mountain range, emphasize products from the sea and land. It is blessed with a mild, sunny Mediterranean climate, allowing the cultivation of many fruits, vegetables — including some rare varieties — and aromatic herbs. The olives that grow in the region, particularly the taggiasca, produce exceptionally good, subtle and refined oil, with an aftertaste of pine nuts, that pairs brilliantly with the region's great natural products. The incomparable vegetables growing along the Riviera include stringless green beans, tender salad leaves, tasty Albenga artichokes and delicious white beans from Conio. Mushrooms grow next to assorted wild greens and herbs.

The food of Liguria is considered *di magro* — lean, almost vegetarian — created, like most cuisines, in order to use what was readily available. Traditionally, seafaring Ligurians spent long periods of time at sea eating only preserved foods; back on land their overwhelming desire was to eat only fresh products, that is, vegetables. This nautical culture provided the opportunity to transport goods all over the world (dry pasta, with its long shelf life, was popular cargo — today, Liguria is considered the home of pasta) and exposure to the gastronomy of Arab, Spanish and Sicilian ports of call, which has helped define and distinguish the food of the region.

Nonetheless, Liguria's cuisine remains profoundly basic, free of spices or aggressive flavors. The region's simple approach to food makes it one of the most modern of the entire peninsula.

ANTIPASTI, CURED MEATS, BREAD, FLATBREADS AND SAVORY TARTS

Bianchetti Newborn anchovies or sardines that may be blanched and dressed with oil and fresh lemon juice, deep-fried, made into fritters or mixed into a frittata.

Boghe in scabecio Boghe are fish from the same family as the snapper-like group of fish called sparidi. Scabecio is the Ligurian version of the Lombardian *carpione* (page 47) or the Venetian *saor* (see *sarde* or *sardeli in saor*, page 73) — dishes in which the fish are dredged in flour and fried, then immersed in a marinade of vinegar mixed with fried garlic, onions, rosemary, sage and bay leaf.

Cappon magro A traditional Ligurian salad that uses fish and vegetables as its base. The ingredients include thick sailor's crackers soaked in water and crumbled; *mosciame* (page 35) or *bottarga* (page 275); cauliflower, green beans, celery, carrots, beets, potatoes, black salsify; fish such as sea bass or hake; crustaceans and shellfish such as shrimp, lobster and oysters. This complex and regal dish is then dressed with a salsa verde made with anchovies, garlic, pine nuts, capers, hard-cooked eggs, parsley, olive oil and vinegar.

Capponalda or **capponada** A Ligurian antipasto made with sailor's crackers that are tossed with olive oil, salt, capers, chopped olives, anchovies and slices of mosciame or bottarga.

Cuculli Yeasted fritters made with chickpea flour and usually flavored with a pinch of marjoram. Cuculli also may be made with potatoes, pine nuts and marjoram.

Farinata di ceci or **faina** A thin Ligurian focaccia more or less made with only chickpea flour and olive oil. There are variations: in the town of Oneglia in the province of Imperia, the farinata is topped with sliced onions before it's baked, and in the city of Savona, fresh rosemary leaves are sprinkled over the top. In some places it's garnished with freshly ground black pepper. In the town of Sanremo, the farinata is very thin and is served with radicchio as a *piatto di mezzo* — an intermediary course.

Favetta A mush made with fava bean flour that has been left to thicken. It is then cut into pieces and sautéed with green onions. The same dish may be transformed into a soup — the mush has to be softer and looser.

Focaccia con le polpe A yeasted focaccia in which olive pulp (the dregs that remain after the oil has been pressed) is added to the dough. It's typical of the town of Rapallo.

Frisceu A Ligurian word that means "fritter." The fritters can be made with *gianchetti* (below), baccalà, liver, brains, sweetbreads, lettuce, squash blossoms, borage, zucchini, squash or any other in-season ingredient.

Galletta A flat round cracker made with flour, water and a bit of yeast. Typical of Liguria, it's also called galletta da marinaio ("sailor's cracker"), and at one time was widely used on ships because it has such a long shelf life.

Galletti See *cuculli* (above).

Gianchetti Small anchovies, more or less like *bianchetti* (page 33).

Granatine di riso Rice croquettes. The rice is mixed with sautéed chopped veal, made into balls, breaded and fried.

Manene Little fried focaccine made with yeasted dough mixed with puréed potatoes or polenta and olive oil.

Manuelina Focaccia from the town of Recco in the province of Genoa made by placing a thin layer of dough in a baking pan, topping it with fresh cheese, then covering it with another layer of thin dough. The preparation is named for Emanuela Capurro, the owner of an eponymous nineteenth-century trattoria in Recco.

Moscardini all'inferno Tiny octopus stewed with tomatoes, olive oil, garlic and rosemary.

Mosciame or **Musciame** At one time made with dried dolphin meat, today, because dolphin fishing is prohibited, this preparation is made with tuna or other large fish. The meat is pressed into a cylinder shape to dry, then sliced and soaked in olive oil for a few hours in order to soften before eating. Mosciame is usually a deep red or brownish color. It often accompanies a tomato and onion salad and is an ingredient in cappon magro. Although this is a Ligurian specialty, it may be found in Sicily as well.

Paniccia or **panissa** or **panizza** A focaccia made with chickpea flour (sometimes mixed with corn flour) found throughout Liguria, but particularly in the province of La Spezia. Often, after the paniccia cools, it's cut into diamond shapes and fried or cut into squares and sautéed with onions and chives.

Pissadella or **pissaladeira** or **piscialandrea** or **pizza all'Andrea** The Ligurian version of the famous pissaladiere recipe from Provence in the south of France, made using a type of pizza or focaccia that is garnished with anchovies, onions, olives, capers, garlic and tomatoes.

Pontine Little sardines similar to *bianchetti* (page 33).

Sardenaira See *pissadella* (above).

Stecchi fritti alla ligure A typical dish from the town of Chiavari in the province of Genoa prepared by moistening wafers then wrapping them around a filling—made with the chopped head, sweetbreads, testicles and saddle of veal with chicken crests, marjoram, eggs, Parmesan cheese, mushrooms, artichokes and herbs—to form a twig shape. They're then fried to serve.

Torta cappuccina Made somewhat like the *torta pasqualina* (page 36), except that all the ingredients are mixed together.

Torta pasqualina A savory pie typical throughout Liguria. It's so named because it's prepared and served on Easter (Pasqua). There's a bit of an ongoing argument between the cities of Genoa and Savona as to how many layers are needed to make the pie — the citizens of Genoa say twenty while those of Savona say thirty-three (the years that Christ lived). The filling includes cooked chard, *prescinsoea* (page 42), Parmesan cheese and herbs. Before this pie is assembled, the layers are moistened with good olive oil. Once the layering is complete, several holes are poked into it and eggs are cracked into them before baking.

PASTA, GNOCCHI, RICE, POLENTA AND GRAINS

Corzetti alla polceverasca A traditional pasta dish from the Val Polcevera but served throughout Liguria. Corzetti are made from simple flour-and-egg pasta dough that is cut into pieces. Each piece is worked into a figure-eight shape. There are molds made specifically for making this pasta. The cooked pasta is classically dressed with melted butter, fresh marjoram, pine nuts and Parmesan cheese. Frequently, however, a *tocco* (a "touch") — Ligurian dialect for sauce — of meat or mushrooms is added.

Fregamai Dumplings made with farina, grated Parmesan cheese and freshly ground black pepper.

Gasse Butterfly-shaped pasta made with a simple dough of flour, egg and water. They're really good when dressed with an artichoke sauce made with the renowned carciofi d'Albenga (artichokes), onions, dried mushrooms, garlic, parsley, tomatoes and white wine.

Mandilli de saea This unusual Ligurian name for square lasagna noodles with pesto means "silk handkerchiefs." The name refers to the large (15 cm), square shape of the pasta, which also must be extremely thin.

Pansoti or **pansotti** or **pansooti au preboggion** Triangle-shaped, filled ravioli typical of Liguria. The pasta dough is made with flour, water, salt and white wine. The filling is made with *preboggion* (an herb mixture that can include borage, wild chard, parsley, anise, alpine thistle, etc., page 42), *prescinsoea* (a curdled cheese, page 42), ricotta, ground veal, tendons, sweetbreads, brains, eggs, grated cheese and a pinch of fresh marjoram. Classically the pasta is dressed with a sauce made of ground walnuts, more prescinsoea and garlic.

The name pansotti derives from *panciuti* ("pot bellied"), which refers to the shape of the pasta.

Picagge or **piccagge** A pasta dish typical of Liguria that originated in the area near the city of Savona made with wide fettuccine or narrow lasagna noodles dressed with pesto or a sauce made with mushrooms or artichokes. Picagge verdi, a variation of the pasta made with borage leaves added to the dough, are usually dressed with a sauce made with roast meat and Parmesan cheese or beef sauce. The name of the pasta refers to the frill-edged fettuccine that look like dressmakers' trimmings.

Ravioli liguri Ravioli made with egg pasta stuffed with a filling of escarole, borage, ground breast and saddle of veal, ground pork, sweetbreads, sausage, eggs, bread soaked in broth, Parmesan cheese and marjoram. The filling is placed by the teaspoon on a pasta sheet then folded in half. The filled pasta is then cut into rectangles or squares with the appropriate pasta wheel. The ravioli are dressed with sauce made with roast meat and Parmesan cheese. There are several variations on the fillings including one where the meat is replaced with monkfish, mullet, potatoes or artichokes.

Riso arrosto or **risotto del campagnolo di ponente** A type of flan made with rice, onions, mushrooms, artichokes, sausage, *regaglie di pollo* ("gifts" from the chicken including the heart, gizzards and liver) and grated Grana cheese.

Testaroli A dish typical of the town of Pontremoli in the province of Massa Carrara but found throughout the Lunigiana area and in parts of Liguria. It's an important historic find because it demonstrates yet another way, among thousands of others, to make pasta. The dough is made with whole-wheat or chestnut flour, water and salt and cooked on cast iron or terra cotta disks that have been heated over a wood-burning fire. The cooked "pancakes" are cut into diamond shapes, boiled for a few seconds and dressed with pesto. It's not easy to find—or use—the disks used to make the testaroli. Testaroli are similar to testetti found in the Ligurian town of Chiavari or the crosetti found in the town of Bedonia in the province of Parma.

Trenette al pesto This is one of the most typical pasta dishes of Liguria. Trenette are long, narrow (2–4 mm) pieces of flattened pasta. "Real" trenette are boiled with diced potatoes and cut-up green beans, drained together, then dressed with pesto. Avvantaggiate trenette are made with whole-wheat flour.

Trofie Little dumplings made with a mixture of flours, including whole wheat, and water. Each piece is twisted until it becomes thin and narrow at each end. Sometimes chestnut flour is added to the dough mixture because it goes so well with pesto. Sometimes the trofie are tossed with boiled white beans. The birthplace of trofie is the area between the seaside town of Camogli and the town of Bogliasco — even more specifically, Recco — all in the province of Genoa.

Zembi d'arzillo A typical Ligurian dish, and the only traditional Italian dish in which the pasta encloses a fish filling. The classic filling requires a mixture of various kinds of fish fillets (snapper, sea bream, bass, etc.) ground up and mixed with borage, chard, ricotta and Parmesan cheese. Zembi can be dressed with a clam or mussel sauce, or one made with chopped squid, etc. They may also be served in a fish broth — but when served that way, the vegetables are eliminated from the filling.

SOUPS

Lattughe ripiene in brodo This difficult-to-find Ligurian soup is made with lettuce leaves that have been filled with a stuffing made with beef, brains, veal breast and sweetbreads mixed together with chopped mushrooms, garlic, parsley and other vegetables and herbs. The lettuce leaves, which are tied together to resemble little trunks, are cooked then served in beef broth.

Mesciùa or **Mesc-ciua** A soup typical of the city of La Spezia and its surroundings, made with dried cannellini beans, chickpeas, farro (or spelt, a wheat-like grain) or wheat berries and good Ligurian extra virgin olive oil. In bygone times, when the cook could afford it, pieces of meat were added to the soup.

Minestra di bianchetti This splendid soup is made by cooking very thin angel hair pasta, diced zucchini, tiny peas and *bianchetti* (page 33) in a fish broth. Just before serving it's thickened with a beaten egg and garnished with a few leaves of fresh marjoram.

Minestrone alla genovese This "big" soup is made with a variety of seasonal vegetables and finished with a dollop of good quality pesto alla genovese. Different kinds of pasta, from penne to fresh tagliatelle to rice, are added to the soup.

Sbira This soup, typical of Genoa, is probably named for the *sbirri*, the men who, in the cold and humid climate of the city, stood guard at its gates. It's a robust tripe stew served in a boiling hot broth with toasted bread, Parmesan cheese and a beef sauce.

Zimino di ceci *Zimino* is a Ligurian term that refers to a method of preparing fish stews (squid, baccalà, etc.) that typically include chard or spinach. However, in this particular recipe, fish is not one of the ingredients. The zimino here refers to a chickpea sauce enriched with tomatoes, dried mushrooms and chard that is turned into a soup by adding the water in which the chickpeas have cooked.

CONDIMENTS, SAUCES, SALSAS AND EGGS

Agliata or **aggiadda** A Ligurian salsa good not only with boiled meats but also with baccalà (salt cod) fritters. It is prepared by pounding garlic in a mortar with a pestle then adding the white part of bread soaked in vinegar, salt and olive oil. It's very similar to the French aillade (not to be confused with aioli).

Machetto A typical fisherman's preparation made with tiny anchovies and sardines covered with salt, and mixed daily until a smooth and tasty paste is achieved.

Marò or **pestun di fave** A salsa, made in the area between the cities of Sanremo and Imperia, of fresh skinned fava beans mashed with garlic, olive oil, Pecorino cheese and mint leaves. It's a particularly good companion to boiled meats, but goes well with other dishes as well.

Pesto alla genovese This is the vaunted Ligurian sauce — and one of interminable discussions as to its origins. It's well known that there are many versions of pesto, whether in Liguria or in France, where it's called pistou. The two fundamental versions of pesto are the di Ponente (from the western part of Liguria that includes Genoa), a simple and bright recipe, and the di Levante (from the eastern part of the region), which uses a bit less garlic and more "refined" ingredients. A cardinal rule of pesto making is that it must be made in a mortar with a pestle using the tiny, flowering Ligurian basil leaves together with top quality Ligurian extra virgin olive oil, Pecorino and Parmesan cheeses and pine nuts or walnuts. Pesto shouldn't be stored for long periods of time because the basil will loose its characteristic aroma. Pesto is used to dress trenette, trofie, lasagne and gnocchi and to flavor minestrone and many other dishes.

Pestun di fave See *marò* (above).

Salsa di noci or **tucco de nuxe** This Ligurian sauce, made with walnuts, garlic, olive oil, the white part of bread and *prescinsoea* cheese (page 42), is mostly used to dress *pansoti* (page 36).

Tocco "Sauce" in Ligurian dialect. There are many varieties, the most common being tocco di funghi (mushroom sauce), tocco di carne (meat sauce) and tocco di stufato (a sauce made with pot roast).

Tucco de nuxe See *salsa di noci* (above).

FISH, CRUSTACEANS AND SHELLFISH

Bagnun de anciue An anchovy soup typical of the eastern Riviera or Levante made with olive oil, tomatoes and herbs and served with sailor's crackers or croutons.

Boldrò Monkfish.

Buiabesa A substantial fish soup similar to bouillabaisse and a specialty of the province of Imperia. Its name comes from the French preparation.

Buridda A delicious Ligurian fish soup very much like the French Provencal preparation, bourride. Among the fish that may go into this soup are scorpion fish, catfish, sea bream, dog fish, sea bass, wolf fish, monkfish, squid, octopus, shrimp, etc. Among other ingredients are celery, carrots, onions, garlic, anchovies, walnuts and dried mushrooms. An ancient version of this recipe uses stoccafisso (dried fish), wine, bay leaf and walnuts and is thickened with diced potatoes.

Cappon magro See page 34.

Ciuppin A traditional Ligurian fish soup made with a variety of fish that may include sea bream, white bream, skate and mullet; sometimes shellfish or crabs are added. Other ingredients include carrots, onions, celery, garlic, parsley, a modest amount of tomatoes and white wine; there are those who include anchovies and hot peppers as well. Ciuppin is served with toasted bread.

Pesce in ciappa This is a technique of cooking fish on a slate slab, typical of the town of Lavagna in the province of Genoa.

Seppie in zimino A squid stew to which chard or other greens are added.

Stoccafisso accomodato This dried fish or baccalà stew is made by cutting the soaked fish into pieces then sautéing them in a casserole with olive oil and anchovies to which potatoes, pine nuts, olives and herbs are added.

Cima alla genovese This labor-intensive dish is made by cutting a pocket into a piece of veal and filling it with ground veal that has been cooked with sweetbreads, eggs, cheese, peas and fresh marjoram. The pocket is stitched closed and the veal is then boiled, chilled and sliced to serve. There are other versions of the recipe in which more varieties of meat, giblets, more herbs and vegetables are added to the filling.

Lacetti Sweetbreads that are cleaned, then boiled, then dredged in flour, dipped in beaten eggs and fried.

Tomaxelle Stuffed veal roll-ups. The filling is made with a mixture of meat: veal breast, saddle and sweetbreads cooked in a casserole with chopped onions and dried mushrooms to which eggs, the white part of bread soaked in milk, Parmesan cheese, parsley, marjoram, garlic, black pepper, cloves and a grating of nutmeg are added. The tomaxelle are then dredged in flour and cooked in a skillet with bay leaf and white wine. They go very well with puréed potatoes.

Vitello all'uccelletto Pieces of veal stewed in a saucepan with butter, olive oil, bay leaf and white wine. When artichokes are in season, they are added to the dish as well. In the western part of the region, the Ponente, a sauce made with black olives is used.

VEGETABLES

Bacilli The Genovese word for dried fava beans.

Barba di Becco The wild version of salsify, a long root vegetable with a yellowish skin, white and tender flesh and a slightly bitter flavor.

Condiggion A big, composed salad typical of Liguria. Sailor's crackers (gallette da marinaio) that have been rubbed with garlic, then soaked in water and vinegar, are layered with cucumbers, tomatoes, yellow peppers, red onions, new potatoes, salad greens, hard-cooked eggs, all dressed with olive oil, vinegar, garlic and fresh basil leaves. The whole thing is garnished with slices of *mosciame* (page 35) or *bottarga* (page 275) and Taggia olives.

Fratti Lettuce leaves wrapped around a filling made with breadcrumbs, garlic, parsley, marjoram, eggs, milk, cheese and pine nuts. They're cooked in a casserole with peeled tomatoes and broth.

Funghi a funghetto This dish, with the odd name that

means "mushrooms cooked mushroom-style," is made by cooking mushrooms in a skillet with olive oil, garlic, oregano or parsley and an optional, simple tomato sauce.

Funghi alla genovese Porcini mushrooms cooked in a casserole on top of sliced potatoes with olive oil, garlic and basil.

Geè A special type of Ligurian chard.

Imbrogliata di carciofi Scrambled eggs with artichokes.

Preboggion A typical Ligurian mixture of various greens and herbs — mostly wild — that changes according to the season and location. Generally, it consists of the first cabbage of the season or wild chard, borage, cicerbita, anise, dente di leone, etc. The mix is used in frittatas, soups and fillings.

Rattatuia This dish, similar to the French ratatouille, is a combination of fresh vegetables such as green beans, carrots, celery, onions, zucchini, eggplant, peppers and tomatoes cut into cubes and cooked with olive oil and basil.

Scorzonera fritta Fried black salsify. Oddly enough, the origin of this root vegetable's name is not derived from the color of its skin (*scorza*), which is black (*nera*), but instead from a Catalan word for a snake — *escorso*. In the Medieval period it was thought that the root was an antidote to snake bites. It's usually boiled to serve, but almost any carrot recipe works well with scorzonera. In Liguria, it's often cut into pieces, parboiled, then dipped in beaten eggs, then breadcrumbs, and fried.

CHEESE AND DAIRY PRODUCTS

Pecorino delle Navette This fresh cheese, made only with sheep's milk, is produced in the province of Imperia and around the Col di Nava, above the Pornassio area. It's prized for its agreeable flavor that comes from an outstanding and diverse selection of alpine herbs from the floral pastures in which the sheep graze.

Prescinsoea or **prescinseua** This slightly sour curdled cow's milk cheese is unfortunately now difficult to find. It is made by adding curds to a cloth and then letting them drain. The finished product is used in various Ligurian recipes.

SWEETS AND LIQUEURS

Biscotti del lagaccio These long-lasting cookies are what we call *biscotti* — "twice cooked." They're made with flour, butter, sugar, yeast and fennel seeds. The dough is made into log shapes, then baked and cut into slices that are then toasted in the oven.

Bugie These crumbly ribbons of fried dough are covered with powdered sugar and are typically served during the Carnival celebration. The names of these confections vary according to the areas where they're made.

Canestrelli di pasta di mandorle Pounded almonds are the base of this cookie dough. A special cutter is used to form the cookies. The edge resembles a scallop (*canestrello*).

Cavagnetti These little baskets made with sweet dough are filled with a whole egg in its shell. They're often covered with multi-colored sprinkles.

Cavolini These puffs are very similar to beignets. They are often filled with zabaione or whipped cream, then covered with powdered sugar.

Ciavai This is a white layer cake. It is first cut in half horizontally and each half doused with orange liqueur. One half is then coated with whipped cream and Marsala zabaione and then covered with the other half. The whole thing is then covered with a thin layer of whipped cream. The scraps that come from cutting the cake out of its pan are crumbled and sprinkled over the cake. The sides of the cake are bordered with lingue di gatto cookies, and finally, the cake is dusted with powdered sugar.

Cobelletti Little pastries made with shortbread dough and filled with jam or peaches.

Giardiniera dolce A pie filled with mixed cooked fruit, candied fruit and a bit of rum.

Latte alla grotta See *sciumetta*, page 44.

Marzapane quaresimale A traditional Ligurian Lenten recipe for little cakes made with almond paste. The cakes are covered with chocolate- or mint-flavored icing before they are baked. This very old recipe shows up in history books as a torta Genovese; it was made by Genoa's pastry chefs and sent to the courts of Mantua and Ferrara.

Pandolce A Christmas cake similar to panettone. The compact cake is filled with candied and dried fruits, aniseed, orange blossom water and Marsala wine.

Risiny A pudding made with flour, butter, sugar, eggs and lemon peel.

Sacripantina A sponge cake doused with Marsala wine and then filled with coffee and chocolate buttercream. It is iced with a coffee-flavored cream, then covered with crumbled amaretti and other dried cookies.

Sciumetta A Ligurian version of the French dessert, île flottante, made by whipping egg whites with sugar and then poaching scoops of them in milk. They are served with a crème anglaise (pouring cream), pistachio nuts and a dusting of cinnamon.

WINES

In the mild, low latitude of Liguria, grapes ripen quickly causing the fragrance of the region's wines to diminish. However, what they lose in aroma they make up for in palate. The salty Mediterranean breezes and rich coastline terrain endow the grapes of the region with traces of their salt and the flavor of aromatic herbs. The light-bodied wines are fresh, drinkable and perfectly adapted to the local cuisine — simple and tasty.

Cinque Terre The Bosco grape makes up about 60% of this sapid, floral and herbaceous white wine. It's a perfect companion to fish or vegetable soups, minestrone with pesto and ravioli filled with borage, and incomparable with frutti di mare.

Pigato Made in the area around Albenga in the province of Savona, this wine is yellowish-green with a faint nose and a slightly salty flavor. It's perfect with *ciuppin* (page 40), baked anchovies and all Ligurian seafood dishes.

Rossesse di Dolceacqua A full-bodied red wine that is slightly sour when young but after aging for a few years becomes more harmonious, as a hint of aromatic herbs is emitted. This highly tannic wine is perfect with rabbit dishes and all things made with barnyard animals. It is rarely aged for long periods.

Sciacchetrà This wine is made with the best grapes — ones with the best exposure to the sun — from the *grand cru* vineyards of the Cinque Terre. The grapes are left to slowly dry until their flesh becomes concentrated sugar and then after vinification become the mythical Sciacchetrà. The limited production results in very high prices. This wine is sweet but not sickeningly so; it's fragrant with yellow fruits and as it ages its aroma is transformed into a hint of honey and jam. It is typically served as a dessert wine.

Vermentino The grapes used for this wine are like the mix that goes into the Cinque Terre wine; however, in some areas the grapes are vinified alone. Until recently, Vermentino was considered an unpretentious white wine. Now, in the villages of the Valle del Magra, there are small but dedicated vineyards that produce quality Vermentino with good body and structure and a weak but persistent aroma that holds its own with demanding fish and crustacean dishes.

Trenette al pesto
Serves 6

45 leaves Genoese basil (little leaves)
2 cloves garlic
A handful of pine nuts
A pinch of sea salt
Extra virgin olive oil
1 tablespoon grated Pecorino cheese
1 medium potato, cut into medium cubes
¼ pound green beans cut into medium
   pieces
A little more than a pound of trenette or
   tagliatelle, preferably whole wheat

Add the basil, garlic, pine nuts and salt to a marble mortar and pound it with a pestle while slowly adding the olive oil, then the grated cheese, until a smooth paste is achieved. Add the potatoes, then the green beans, then the pasta to a large pot of salted, boiling water. When the pasta is *al dente* use a wire mesh strainer to remove ingredients from the pot and add them to a large serving bowl. Dress with the pesto and a bit of the pasta water.

Suggested wine: Cinque Terre

LOMBARDIA (LOMBARDY)

Is there a real Lombardian cuisine? No, not if you're looking for a homogeneous gastronomic tradition. The region's political and cultural history and its terrain make it difficult to assign one distinct food style to the area. Lombardy is naturally divided into distinct zones: the plains, the lakes, the foothills of the Alps and the mountains. In effect, you could say that the region has nine — the number of its provinces — separate cuisines.

The cuisine of the capital of the region, Milan, is essentially middle class. Most of the dishes are slowly cooked things like risotto, or a veal chop that is cooked in ten minutes elsewhere but takes at least an hour in Milan.

However, the most emblematic cuisine of Lombardy comes out of the province of Mantua. Born in the Renaissance kitchens of the court of the Gonzaga family, its influence is evident in recipes that use spices, and in sweet-and-sour preparations. The general populace has also had a major role in the creation of the province's food because of the way they've consolidated the cooking of the surrounding regions, Emilia-Romagna and the Veneto, to form their own.

Cremona is known for its extraordinary torrone (nougat), for its sharp mostarda and most of all for the generosity of its cuisine. Pavia can boast about its *di magro* or lean dish, risotto alla Certosina, garnished with freshwater shrimp and frogs. Sondrio and the Valtellina in general represent mountain food at its best with polenta dishes, fatty cheeses, pizzoccheri (a buckwheat pasta dish) and bresaola (cured beef). Bergamo has felt the influence of the neighboring region, the Veneto, but because Bergamo's countryside is relatively poor, the food is made with very simple ingredients: a filled pasta called casonsei and polenta with little birds. Brescia has a great affinity with Bergamo, but is just a bit richer. While citizens of Bergamo might spit-roast meats basted with lardo, in Brescia they'll cook meat in a terra cotta pot with butter. Como and Varese have cuisines rich with preparations for their lake fish.

The long Lombardian winters, wrapped in fog, conjure up memories of aroma-filled, steamy kitchens with bubbling soups, large fireplaces and comfort foods.

Bevr'in vin A cup of hot beef broth diluted with a bit of good red wine. The habit of drinking this before a meal was born in Mantua where tradition dictates that the diners should be standing, facing a fireplace, while doing so.

Bissetta A type of eel *carpione* (below). The fish is cut into chunks, dredged in flour, fried and then immersed in a cooked marinade made with vinegar, a bay leaf or sage, celery, carrots, onions and garlic.

Bresaola Cured meat, typical of the Valtellina, prepared with very lean beef fillet or top round that is lightly marinated in red wine and herbs, then aged. It's eaten raw, thinly sliced and dressed with olive oil, lemon, salt and freshly ground black pepper.

Carpione A dish found in the lake districts. Freshwater fish is floured, fried and marinated in a mixture of vinegar, white wine, olive oil, sage, fennel seeds and marjoram. The ingredients may vary — sugar, bay leaf, cloves and wild thyme may be added to the marinade.

Carpione all'uova The same dish as above, but with the addition of eggs and chopped parsley.

Chisola See *schissoeula* (page 49).

Chisolini or **Chisülein** A fried dough preparation similar to *crescente* (page 121) made by cutting a thin sheet of pasta into triangular shapes. They're eaten with cured meats.

Cicc A very thin flatbread from the Valtellina area made with buckwheat polenta and cheese, then fried in lardo. There's also a sweet version in which the polenta is cooked in milk with sugar and vanilla.

Ciccioli d'oca These crunchy chips are made by cooking pieces of goose skin in water until they lose all their fat and become crisp. They're a specialty of the lower Lodigiano area.

Croste con midollo di bue al vino rosso A dish made with slices of a loaf of white bread. The insides are removed so all that remains are the crust-frames, which are fried. The little frames are then filled with diced, parboiled beef marrow and dressed with a red wine sauce and freshly chopped parsley.

Fitascetta or **filascetta** Ring-shaped white bread that is covered with sliced red onions that have been softened in butter. The whole thing is sprinkled with sugar — and sometime slices of fresh cheese — just before baking. Fitascetta is a specialty of the province of Como.

Frittelle di polenta alla lodigiana These thin, little rounds of polenta are layered with prosciutto, fontina cheese and shards of truffles, then covered with another polenta round. Lastly, they are dipped in eggs, then breadcrumbs, and fried. They are often served with tomato sauce.

Frittura di sangue di pollo This hard-to-find dish is made by dripping the blood of a freshly killed chicken on slices of bread, then frying the slices in butter and, to serve, sprinkling salt or sugar on top.

Mantovana A long loaf of bread with a slash across the length of its top, and with a soft interior and shiny crust. It's typical of the bassa Padana, the lower part of the Lombardy region.

Margottini Little flans made by layering semolina polenta — enriched with butter, Parmesan cheese and pepper — with slices of Gruyère-like cheese and another layer of polenta. They are baked and served hot. During their season, truffles are added to this specialty of the province of Bergamo.

Micca A large, round loaf of bread with a cross slashed across its top, which is done to help the bread rise. Micca is a specialty of Milan, the capital city of the region.

Miccone A plain everyday bread from the province of Pavia.

Michetta A round, crunchy, typically Lombardian roll shaped like a rose with five petals. It has a golden crust; what little insides it has are full of holes.

Missoltitt or **missolte** These little fish that come out of Lake Como in the spring and fall are salted and hung to dry in the sun and wind. They're preserved in jars with bay leaves. To serve, they're grilled or heated in a dry skillet until the skin detaches from the flesh. The skinned fish are flavored with salt and vinegar and served with polenta as an antipasto.

Mondeghili An historic specialty of Milan, mondeghili are meatballs made with leftover chopped, boiled meat mixed with eggs, sausage, liverwurst, Grana cheese and the white part of bread that has been soaked in milk, garlic, nutmeg and lemon peel. The meatballs are dipped in beaten eggs, dredged in flour and fried in butter. Of course, they can also be made with fresh, chopped beef. The word *mondeghili* dates back to the time when Milan was under Spanish rule. It's derivative of the Spanish-Arabic word for meatball, albondiga.

Nervetti or **nervitt** A Lombardian term used to describe the knee and shin cartilage from boiled veal. Nervetti are very thinly sliced and dressed with olive oil, onions, parsley, garlic and vinegar, with the optional addition of capers.

Oca conservata nel grasso In the area around Lodi, it is customary to cook geese in this way to preserve them for the winter. The flesh of the goose is covered with salt, spices and garlic for an hour or so, then put into glass jars and covered with fat that is rendered when *ciccioli* (page 47) are made. It's possible to eat the meat—raw or fried—after a week. The preserved goose can last up to five months.

Schissoeula An old-fashioned focaccia or schiacciata ("very flat bread") made with corn flour, eggs, raisins and ciccioli.

Sciatt Fritters made with buckwheat flour, grappa and *scimud* (page 63) that are a specialty of the Valtellina. The name, in dialect, means "frog."

Strinù A very tasty sausage from the Val Camonica made with pork and beef. It's grilled to serve.

Valigini mantovani These little "suitcases" are cabbage leaves filled with chicken, potatoes, parsley, garlic, Parmesan cheese, eggs and breadcrumbs. They are stewed with tomatoes and onions.

Violini Cured leg of venison from the town of Chiavenna in the province of Sondrio. The venison is treated just like prosciutto—salted and aged. Its interesting name comes from the movement made when it's sliced by hand—like a bow playing a violin.

PASTA, GNOCCHI, RICE, POLENTA AND GRAIN

Agnoli These ravioli, a specialty of Mantua, are historically filled with a mixture of boiled capon, marrow, cinnamon, cloves, cheese, eggs and herbs. The recipe refers to one from Bartolomeo Stefani, who was the chef of the Gonzaga court. Usually, these agnoli, very similar in shape to capelletti, are served in a capon broth.

Agnolini These little ravioli are similar in shape to tortellini except that the two ends don't cross over each other. They are filled with a mixture made with beef stew (cooked until it practically resembles a cream of beef), eggs, cheese, sausages and nutmeg, etc. They can be served in broth or dry with a meat sauce, or with butter and Parmesan cheese.

Bardele coi marai Very wide fettuccine made with flour, eggs and a strained purée of borage leaves (marai). They're dressed with melted butter and grated cheese.

Caicc Very large ravioli, typical of the village of Breno in the province of Brescia in the Val Camonica, filled with braised beef and Parmesan cheese. They're dressed with butter and more Parmesan cheese to serve.

Cappelloni Enormous capelletti typical of the Lomellina area filled with beef stew, little sausages that have been preserved in pork fat and other ingredients.

Casônsei Fresh, filled pasta.

Casônsei bresciani These casônsei resemble tubes that are folded and sealed at both ends. They're filled with sausage, breadcrumbs, Parmesan cheese, San Pietro herb or spinach and other fresh herbs. You'll find the addition of crumbled amaretti cookies and raisins in some recipes.

Casônsei della Val Camonica These casônsei are made by placing a filling of potatoes, chard, sausage and mortadella on a disk of pasta, then covering it with another disk. In a somewhat complicated closure, the sides are gathered and pleated together to make a little bundle.

Gnocchi A boiled or baked potato, flour or semolina dumpling usually served with a sauce or grated cheese.

Gnocchi alla lariana In this preparation the batter is made with flour, eggs, milk and other flavorings then added by the spoonful to boiling water. The cooked dumplings are dressed with cubes of fresh cheese and meat or tomato sauce.

Gnocchi di zucca These dumplings are made with a purée of winter squash mixed with flour and whipped egg whites and dressed with garlic and rosemary-scented butter. The inclusion of squash indicates that this is a specialty of the province of Brescia by way of Mantua.

Malfatti Little balls or dumplings made with spinach, flour, mascarpone or ricotta, bread, grated cheese, herbs and egg yolks. After cooking in boiling water they may be simply dressed with melted butter, sage and Parmesan cheese or placed in a baking dish, topped with butter and Parmesan cheese, then gratinéed.

Marubini Small, round ravioli with a crimped edge that are filled with breadcrumbs, grated Grana cheese, beef marrow, eggs, nutmeg and other spices. Another version is filled with braised beef, roast veal or pork and boiled brains. Without fail marubini are served in a rich broth called tre brodi because it's made with beef, chicken and a sausage produced in the area around the province of Cremona, where this pasta is found.

Pasta cunscia Pasta cooked with pieces of potato then drained and served with a tomato sauce made with butter, garlic and sage. The dish is found in the area around the province of Como.

Pizzoccheri Long and wide tagliatelle made with buckwheat flour; a specialty of the Valtellina. Pizzoccheri are cooked with cabbage or chard and sliced potatoes. After draining, they're dressed with butter-fried garlic and *bitto* (page 62), a sharp mountain cheese. Sometimes the dressed dish is baked for a few minutes before serving. Sometimes, the citizens of the Valtellina eat pizzoccheri with raw ramolacci, a root vegetable similar to turnips, dipped in salt.

Polenta alla lodigiana Basically, a polenta sandwich. Two slices of polenta are filled with cheese, then breaded and fried.

Polenta concia This preparation, typical of the Brianza area but found throughout Lombardy, owes a debt to similar recipes from the regions of Val d'Aosta, Piedmont and Friuli. It's made by layering polenta with Parmesan or other cheeses, garlic or onions and sage fried in butter.

Polenta e osei A dish typical of the province of Bergamo, but also found in the province of Brescia and in the Veneto region, in which small birds (sparrows, thrushes, larks, etc.) are split open and filled with lardo, juniper berries and peppercorns. They are then skewered with chunks of lardo or pancetta and sage leaves, and cooked in a skillet or roasted in a pan. The birds are served with polenta that has been dressed with the pan drippings.

Polenta Taragna The emblematic dish of the Valtellina made with buckwheat and corn flours, and dressed with bitto and scimud cheeses and melted butter.

Riso e trigoli A fall dish from the province of Mantua, this is a simple risotto made with trigoli, the water chestnuts that grow in the province's rice paddies.

Riso e zucca Rice boiled with chunks of squash, which is then drained and dressed with butter and Parmesan cheese.

Riso in cagnon There are three versions of this curiously named rice recipe: one from Liguria, one from Piedmont, and the most typical from Lombardy. It's simply boiled rice dressed with melted butter, garlic and sage.

Risotto al pesce persico A plain white risotto topped with golden-fried fillets of perch. It's a typical dish of the little villages along the banks of the lakes, in particular, Lake Como.

Risotto al salto At one time this exquisite specialty of Milan was part of the traditional after-theatre (La Scala) dinners. It was created in order to use leftover risotto alla milanese. After the rice has cooled, it's pressed into little, flat cake shapes then browned on both sides, in butter, in a cast iron skillet. The idea is to achieve a crunchy crust and soft interior.

Risotto alla campagnola Typical of the province of Lodi, a risotto made with rice, beans, tomatoes, pork rind and sausages.

Risotto alla certosina According to popular legend this dish was created in the kitchens of the *certosa* (charterhouse) of Pavia. It came from the monks who, twice a year, were obliged to eat a "lean" diet. The authentic recipe, which is rarely found these days, is a risotto made with a freshwater shrimp and frog broth. It's garnished with frogs, freshwater shrimp, perch fillets, mushrooms, peas and various herbs.

Risotto alla milanese In the classic version of this recipe, the rice should be tossed with onions sautéed in butter and beef marrow. It's cooked with beef broth and colored with saffron dissolved in a bit of broth, then removed from the heat and finished with butter and Parmesan cheese. The risotto should be *all'onda* (wave-like) — loose, almost soupy. There are other ways to make this risotto. One of the oldest recipes calls for the addition of cervellato, salami made with lardo and beef marrow; another recipe uses the pan drippings from roast meats.

Risotto alla pilota This classic dish, a specialty of the province of Mantua and the surrounding rice-growing area that extends all the way to Verona, was created by the paddy workers (*piloti*) who cleaned the rice. The rice is cooked in plain water then dressed with fried sausages and an abundant amount of Parmesan cheese.

Risotto alla pitocca A specialty of the province of Brescia, this risotto is made with rice, chicken broth, chicken and chicken livers.

Risotto col puntel Just like risotto alla pilota, this dish originated in the province of Mantua. However, instead of being served with sausages, it is served with grilled pork cutlets with their bone (*puntel*).

Risotto con le rane A risotto made with sautéed garlic instead of onions. The rice is cooked with frog broth and garnished with frog's legs and lots of freshly chopped parsley. It is a specialty of the province of Pavia and the rice-growing area of the Lomellina.

Risotto con le tinche This risotto is made with garlic as well. The rice is cooked in a broth made from the bones and head of tench (a freshwater fish) and other ingredients. It's garnished with sautéed tench fillets and freshly chopped parsley. In order to remove the muddy flavor from the tench, the fish are forced to swallow a spoonful of vinegar while they're still alive.

Sorbir d'agnoli In order to make this delicious dish, eight or ten agnolini are added to hot broth that's then diluted with some red wine.

Timballo di piccione This sumptuous dish comes straight out of the Renaissance. Its origins are easily traced to the province of Cremona. It's made with rigatoni or a similar pasta shape, mixed with boned, stewed pigeon, then wrapped and baked in short crust.

Tortelli alla cremasca A filled pasta, made in the shape of a butterfly, tortelli actually look more like candies wrapped in paper with both ends closed with a twist or simply folded into a triangle. They are filled with a mixture of amaretti cookies, raisins, candied citron, Grana cheese, the white part of bread, dry Marsala wine and nutmeg. They're dressed with melted butter and Parmesan cheese. The filling might also include special spice cookies from Crema called mostaccini and pears or peaches.

Tortelli di zucca The most widely used preparation of this typical dish is the one from the province of Mantua. These tortelli are served on Christmas Eve because this is considered a "lean" dish. The classic filling for the pasta is puréed winter squash (zucca), crumbled amaretti cookies, apple mostarda and Parmesan cheese. They are dressed with melted butter and Parmesan cheese. There are many variations found in the provinces of Ferrara, Reggio Emilia, and Parma. The shape and the sauces may change but the filling always has squash as its base.

SOUPS

Brofadei See *sbrofadej* (page 55).

Buseca, busecca or **zuppa di trippa** This tripe soup, so entrenched in the cuisine of Lombardy, is called busecconi ("big tripe soup") by the Milanesi. It's made with three different parts of the tripe: *foiolo* (the part that looks like pages of a book); *reticolo* (the part that looks like a net); and *duodeno* (the first part of the stomach). The soup is cooked with various vegetables and herbs and served with grated Parmesan cheese. In some recipes large white beans are added.

Busecca matta in brodo This is a poor man's busecca that uses sliced cabbage as a substitute for the tripe. All the other ingredients are the same. It's served with sliced corn bread.

Ceci con la tempia A soup made with chickpeas and chopped parts of a pig's head. In Milan it is traditionally eaten on November 2, the Day of the Dead.

Crema di asparagi alla milanese This very delicate cream of asparagus soup is thickened with egg yolks and served with tiny croutons.

Gnocarei A soup, typical of the city of Brescia, made with chicken broth, pieces of chicken and cubes of leftover polenta dipped into beaten eggs.

Mach An historic soup, made with rice, chestnuts and butter, found in the Val Travaglia.

Mariconde Tiny little balls made with cheese, milk, butter, nutmeg and the white part of bread. They are served in a meat broth. Sometimes chopped chicken livers sautéed in butter are added to the soup.

Minestra di riso con luppoli A soup is made with onions and hops sprouts fried in lardo, then cooked in beef broth with rice and Parmesan cheese.

Minestra di riso e fegatini A soup made with rice, chopped chicken livers sautéed in butter, freshly chopped parsley and Parmesan cheese (or even better, aged Lodigiano cheese) cooked in a rich beef broth. Sometimes semini, a pasta shaped like seeds, or angel hair pasta is used instead of rice.

Minestra mariconda Same as *mariconde* (above).

Minestrone alla milanese This very rich "big" soup includes every kind of vegetable — tomatoes, borlotti beans, peas, zucchini, potatoes, celery, carrots, cabbage, onions, etc. — and the all-important rice and pancetta cubes. Sometimes pork rind is added. The soup is finished with basil, parsley, sage and garlic; sometimes bay leaf and rosemary also.

Minestrone con la zucca Broken spaghetti are cooked in a purée of pumpkin diluted with milk to make this soup. It's served with butter and Parmesan cheese.

Pàntrid màridaa or **panada** This historic Lombardian recipe is served with the Easter meal. It's made by moistening bread crumbs with a bit of broth, frying them in butter and then adding beaten eggs and Parmesan cheese to the mixture. It's covered in piping hot broth to serve.

Pasta rasa To make this soup, fresh egg pasta is grated and left to dry. It is then cooked in a soup made with tomatoes, beans, lardo, potatoes, onions and garlic and served with Parmesan cheese.

Rapata This soup is made by first sautéing onions in lardo and prosciutto fat; rice and water are then added. The soup is finished with sliced turnips sautéed in butter and chopped parsley. This delicious soup loves Parmesan cheese.

Rasida Same as *pasta rasa* (page 54).

Ris e coràda This typically Milanese soup is made with rice, leeks, pancetta, sage and boiled veal lungs (coràda) cut into pieces.

Sbrofadej in brodo For this soup, dough made with flour, Parmesan cheese, eggs and nutmeg is pressed through a potato masher in order to achieve little worm-like shapes similar to *passatelli* (page 129). The pasta is immediately cooked in broth. The soup is a specialty of Milan and the province of Brescia. However, in Brescia the dough is made with butter and milk instead of the Parmesan cheese, and it's not passed through a potato masher but instead cut into little squares. In the area around Lake Garda a bit of corn flour is added to the dough.

Zuppa alla pavese Although this soup has its origins in the city of Pavia, nowadays it's considered one of the most emblematic Italian dishes. It's made by placing an egg on top of a piece of sliced bread, then pouring hot broth over it until the white solidifies but the yolk remains liquid. It's served with freshly grated Parmesan cheese.

CONDIMENTS, SAUCES, SALSAS AND EGGS

Frittatine alla lodigiana Very thin, almost crêpe-like, frittatas that are filled with *raspadura*—curls of fresh Grana cheese.

Mostarda di Cremona A spicy condiment made with candied fruit preserved in sharp mustard syrup. This mostarda is a typical accompaniment for bollito misto.

Salsa di corniole Salsa made with sugar, lemon and the strained flesh of the corniole fruit. Corniole is the fruit of a tree, similar to dogwood, found in the central part of Italy. The fruit itself is red, olive-shaped and has a lightly acid flavor. The salsa is good with boiled meats.

Saorina This sweet salsa, a specialty of Mantua, is made with cooked wine. It goes well with desserts as well as with boiled meats.

Uova in cereghin Simply, fried eggs.

Uova in trippa, trippate, or **busecca matta** Frittatine—thin frittatas—that are cut into strips and then added, just before serving, to a stew made with the same ingredients as tripe soup. You'll find this dish throughout Lombardy.

Agoni alla comasca Agoni are little freshwater fish that live exclusively in the pre-alpine lakes. On Lake Como they are dried and made into *missoltitt* (page 48) — a dish in which the dried fish are marinated in olive oil and lemon, fried and then served with a sauce made with a bit of the marinade, vinegar and anchovy fillets.

Alborelle fritte Alborelle are little fish found in Lake Como. They're floured and fried to serve.

Anguilla Eel.

Anguilla alla borghigiana Pieces of cut-up eel sautéed in butter with onions, red wine, parsley, bay leaf and other herbs. The name references the area around Borgo Ticino where it's thought that the dish originated.

Anguilla alla lariana To make this dish, cut-up pieces of eel are floured, then sautéed with celery, carrots and onions. The dish is finished with dried mushrooms, aromatic herbs, tomato pulp and red wine. This dish likes to be served with boiled potatoes.

Anguilla ripiena A preparation in which whole eel is stuffed with a filling made with bread crumbs, cheese, garlic and spices, and then baked. It's typical of the village of Clusone on Lake Iseo.

Aole alla cipolla Aole are fish found in Lake Garda. For this dish they are sautéed with an abundant amount of onions.

Curadura The innards of the agoni fish slowly cooked with a bit of olive oil, breadcrumbs, lemon peel and other herbs. The cooking process results in a kind of bitter-tasting cake. It's served with toasted polenta. This rare dish is found in the Lake Como area.

Lavarelli A type of lake fish.

Lavarelli al vino bianco Lavarelli that are filleted, then sautéed in butter with scallions, parsley and white wine.

Lavarelli alla Salvia A preparation in which lavarelli are dredged in flour then baked with butter and fresh sage leaves and served with lemon wedges.

Luccio in salsa A whole pike poached in a court bouillon. The poached fish is then boned, marinated in a sauce made with olive oil, anchovies, capers, peppers, vinegar, garlic, a bit of onion and parsley, and then briefly heated. Traditionally, it's served cold with hot, toasted polenta. The dish is a specialty of Mantua.

Missoltitt See page 48.

Pesce persico alla laghista Breaded perch fillets fried in foamy butter.

Sformato di baccalà alla certosina This molded dish is made with a layer of potato purée mixed with other vegetables, Parmesan cheese and egg yolks, a layer of boiled baccalà (salt cod) flavored with a mushroom sauce, and finished with a layer of the potato mixture. It's baked to serve.

Stoccafisso alla certosina This dish is made with dried cod that has been hydrated, cleaned, and then slowly cooked with butter, olive oil, salt, black pepper, lemon juice and a pinch of baking powder.

Tinca a cappone For this dish, tench, a fish from Lake Iseo, are filled with a stuffing made with breadcrumbs, Parmesan cheese, cloves, cinnamon, parsley, garlic, olive oil and black pepper. They're baked with bay leaves and served with fried polenta.

Tinca alla lariana A dish in which large fillets of tench are stewed with onions and potatoes, or, according to some recipes, with peas, mushrooms and sage.

Tinca con piselli alla lariana Again, large fillets of tench are stewed — this time, with tomatoes, peas and fresh mushrooms.

Tinca ripiena Another version of the tinca a cappone — this one made by filling a whole tench with a stuffing of Grana cheese, breadcrumbs and herbs, then baking it with olive oil, butter and bay leaves.

Torta di bosine Bosine are tiny little fish that come from Lake Iseo. They're cooked in a pie dish with cheese, breadcrumbs, spices, butter and olive oil. This fish pie is served with slices of toasted polenta.

Zuppa di pesce alla tremezzina For this soup, a variety of boned fish fillets are floured and fried, then added to a broth made with the fish bones, fish heads, tomatoes and other vegetables. The soup is finished with saffron and hot pepper flakes

MEAT

Animelle in agrodolce A dish made with the sweetbreads of young animals — veal and lamb. They may be simply fried, or, they may be parboiled, cut into pieces and sautéed in chopped lardo, prosciutto, carrots, onions and celery, and then baked. Just before they've finished cooking, they're covered with a sweet and sour sauce made with vinegar, chopped capers, sugar and olive oil.

Arrostini annegati For this dish, medallions of veal are floured, then fried in butter, pancetta and kidney fat that has been flavored with rosemary and sage. The golden medallions are then covered with white wine and broth and cooked until very tender. They become a *piatto unico* — a one-dish meal — when served with risotto or mashed potatoes.

Bollito lombardo This substantial mixture of boiled meats is very similar to the Piemontese *bollito* (page 13). It consists of rump of veal stuck with garlic and lardo, breast of veal, beef ribs, veal head and tongue, cotechino sausage and stuffed capon. It's typically served with salsa verde, salsa rossa and mostarda di Cremona.

Bottaggio lombardo The Italian name for the French cassoulet (see *casoeûla*, below).

Bruscitt A dish made with very small — bean-sized — pieces of beef that are cooked in butter, lardo, fennel seeds and red wine. Traditionally, bruscitt is served with polenta flavored with garlic, or with mashed potatoes. The dish is typical of the central area of the province of Milan and the area around Varese and Como. It's tasty, but rare.

Busecca The Milanese name for tripe cooked with beans and other ingredients.

Busecca matta See *uova in trippa* (page 55).

Bussechin Large, fat salami made with pig's blood, cream, lardo, butter, Grana cheese, onions and spices stuffed into a cow's-gut casing. It's boiled, and served with fresh bread.

Casoeûla, cassoeûla or **cazzoeûla** Primarily a wintertime dish made with pork ribs, sausages from Monza (see *luganega*, page 59), pork rind, pig's feet, tails and ears, lots of savoy cabbage, celery, carrots and onions. It's often served with polenta.

Costoletta alla valtellinese Veal chops cut from the loin. They should be just a little more than half an inch thick. They're floured, then sautéed in butter, sage and a splash of white wine.

Cotoletta alla milanese These chops, cut from the loin of a milk-fed calf, should be just over half an inch thick. The chops are dipped in egg and freshly ground pepper (no salt), then in breadcrumbs made with only the white part of the bread. The breaded chops are then fried in clarified butter.

Cuz A stew made with a large lamb or sheep cooked in its own fat that has been flavored with various aromatic herbs — in particular, sage — and salt. The stew is stored outdoors in large wooden bowls. The preparation is typical of the Val Camonica.

Faraona alla creta For this preparation, guinea hens are covered with rosemary, sage, oregano and butter, wrapped in parchment paper, completely enclosed with clay, and then baked to serve.

Fegato Liver.

Fegato alla lodigiana Little pieces of pork liver wrapped in prosciutto, flavored with fennel seeds and covered with caul fat. The little "packages" are then fried in butter.

Fegato alla milanese Pieces of calf's liver flavored with parsley, breaded, then fried in butter.

Fritto di lesso alla milanese This recipe is designed to use up leftover pieces of boiled beef. The sliced meat is first dipped in Parmesan cheese, then eggs, and finally breadcrumbs. They are fried like the cotoletta alla milanese. This is an old, almost forgotten Milanese recipe.

Fritto misto alla milanese The true fritto misto is made with a mixture of brains, liver, tendons, lungs and sweetbreads that are cleaned, parboiled, breaded and fried in butter. Sometimes chicken croquettes, sausages from Monza, mushroom caps and sliced zucchini and eggplant are added to the mix.

Frittura piccata See *piccata* page 60.

Lepre crostata A preparation in which hare is spit-roasted while continually being basted with cream. The cooked hare is then covered with a fragrant and tasty crust of amaretti cookies mixed with cream. This specialty of the Valtellina is somewhat rare.

Luganega This sausage — typical of Monza and sometimes simply called "sausage from Monza" — is made by filling lamb casings with a mixture of pork shoulder, various spices and grated cheese. It's good as an accompaniment for risotto or simply fried and finished with white wine.

Lumache Snails.

Lumache alla castellana A dish typical of the province of Pavia in which snails are first boiled then fried with olive oil, garlic and parsley. They are finished with boiled and boned frog's legs, dry white wine and truffles.

Lumache alla comacina For this dish snails are cooked in butter, olive oil and broth, then finished with chopped walnuts and butter.

Messicani Despite the unusual and unexplained name of this dish ("Mexicans"), it is typically Milanese. It consists of thinly sliced pieces of veal or loin of pork stuffed with sausage, Parmesan cheese, eggs and other ingredients that are then rolled into bundles. The bundles are skewered and cooked in a skillet with butter, sage and Marsala wine, or stewed with tomatoes.

Mondeghili See page 48.

Osso buco in gremolada A classic specialty of Milan made with one-inch-thick slices of veal hocks. They're stewed very, very slowly then finished with a gremolada—a mixture of chopped lemon rind, garlic, rosemary, sage, parsley and anchovies. The veal is served as a *piatto unico*, a one-dish meal, on a bed of risotto alla milanese.

Piccata or **piccatina** Thin slices of veal that are floured, then rapidly cooked in butter, then flavored with Marsala wine, lemon and other ingredients and showered with chopped parsley to serve. Today, piccata is often referred to as scallopine and can be garnished with mushrooms, asparagus, or tomatoes, etc.

Pollin cont el pien or **tacchino ripieno** Stuffed turkey par excellence in which the bird is filled with lardo, sausages, liver, chestnuts and prunes, etc. It's a Milanese Christmas dish.

Polpette Meatballs.

Polpette di carne For Lombardians, meatballs are actually little bundles of veal or pork that have been stuffed with chopped meat, pancetta, garlic, Parmesan cheese and breadcrumbs. They're stewed in tomato sauce and served with mashed potatoes, buttered vegetables or polenta.

Polpette di verza These little "suitcases" are made by stuffing cabbage leaves with chopped meat (leftover roast), salami, Parmesan cheese, breadcrumbs, eggs, parsley and garlic. They are sautéed with pancetta, onions and sage.

Polpettine di vitello alla milanese For this dish, thin slices of veal are stuffed with chopped meat, prosciutto, chicken livers, Parmesan cheese, breadcrumbs, eggs, salt, pepper and nutmeg. The bundles are placed on wooden skewers three at a time, with each bundle separated by a piece of prosciutto and a sage leaf. They are placed in a skillet, covered with broth and slowly cooked.

Posciandra Another name for *casoeûla* (page 58).

Rane Frogs.

Rane in guazzetto For this preparation, frogs are cooked in a sauce made with butter, white wine and broth and thickened with flour. The dish is finished with chopped parsley.

Rane in umido alla pavese Frogs sautéed with chopped leeks and finished with tomato sauce.

Rosticciata or **rostisciada** A very rich stew made with a mixture of pork loin, sausages, etc. and onions. Very often white wine and tomatoes are added. The dish wants to be served with polenta.

Rostin negáa See *arrostini annegati* (page 58).

Salsiccia di castrato Made with the meat of a castrated bull, this sausage is usually cooked in a saucepan and served with polenta. It's a dish found in the area around Breno in the Val Camonica.

Tacchina ripiena This very old — antique — recipe for stuffed (female) turkey is a must on the Lombardian Christmas table. The stuffing includes chestnuts, apples, pears, prunes, walnuts, chopped veal, pancetta, rosemary and cognac. The turkey is usually served with boiled potatoes finished in melted butter, butter-sautéed spinach with raisins and accompanied by mostarda di cremona.

Tapulone See *tapulone* (page 20).

Uccellini scappati Small veal roll-ups that are stuffed with slices of pancetta and fresh sage, threaded three at a time onto a skewer, and then sautéed in a skillet with butter and broth and served with slices of toasted polenta.

VEGETABLES

Asparagi alla milanese A dish in which asparagus tips are steamed, covered with grated Parmesan cheese and topped with fried eggs.

Cavolfiore al burro Steamed cauliflower florets that are sautéed with onions and parsley, topped with an abundant amount of grated Parmesan cheese and baked.

Machitt Turnips, cabbage and beans are boiled, then drained and dressed with fried onions to make this dish, a specialty of the Val Travaglia.

Melanzane dorate Vegetable cutlets made by parboiling eggplant slices, squeezing them dry and marinating them in milk. They are then dipped in beaten eggs, a mixture of breadcrumbs and grated Parmesan cheese and fried to serve.

Segrigeula Wild thyme found on the Riviera of Tremezzo.

Soncino This very sought-after salad green is actually the first radicchio cutting. The leaves have a delicate flavor. It's primarily found in the eponymous town of Soncino.

Verdure in intingolo A mixed vegetable stew that includes onions, peppers, zucchini, celery and tomatoes.

Verze imbracate A dish made with thinly sliced cabbage sautéed with onions and pancetta then finished with crumbled bits of salami and a splash of vinegar.

Zucca fritta Slices of winter squash cooked in milk, then breaded and fried in butter.

CHEESE AND DAIRY PRODUCTS

Bagoss A semi-fat cheese made with partially skimmed milk. The paste may be cooked or raw. Of the two, the preferred is the cooked, with its firm and hard rind and its naturally golden color and hard body, which resembles Grana. The cooked version is mildly flavored while the raw has a slightly bitter palate. The flavor is influenced by the kind of grass consumed by the cows while they're grazing. In the village of Bagolino in the province of Brescia where Bagoss is produced, it's often grilled and eaten with polenta.

Bel Casale A very soft cheese typical of the village of Casalpusterlengo in the province of Milan.

Bitto A round, almost flat, semi-cooked, fatty, hard cheese made with four-fifths cow's milk and one-fifth goat's milk. It requires long aging to reach its optimal flavor and its golden straw color. When young, it is mild and lightly aromatic; as it ages, however, it becomes not only more aromatic but quite sharp with an almost dry body that makes it a good grating cheese. Bitto is a cheese typical of the Valtellina, with origins in the town of Morbegno in Val Gerola.

Branzi This mountain cheese is made with whole cow's milk and sometimes a bit of goat's milk. It has a thin, golden rind and a straw yellow body. As it ages, the body gradually turns a deep golden color, more compact and soft. The young Branzi has a mildly aromatic flavor while the aged version is tangier. You'll find this cheese in the Val Brembana in the province of Bergamo.

Cingherlin or **zicarlin** This soft cheese made almost exclusively with goat's milk (it can also be made with a mixture of milks) is aged for three or four weeks to give it just the right tangy palate. It's traditionally dressed with olive oil, vinegar and salt and served with cooked beans and raw onions. The cheese is a product of the pastures between Varese and Como.

Crescenza A fresh whole cow's milk cheese, rindless, with a milky white body, easily spreadable buttery consistency and sweet, if slightly acidic, flavor.

Formai de mut Literally "cheese of the mountain," this cheese originated in the lush pastures of the mountains of the Val Brembana (Bergamo) where cows eat only the summertime grass. It's a fatty cheese with a semi-cooked paste made with whole cow's milk. The golden rind is thin and firm and becomes gray as it ages. The body is elastic and melt-in-your-mouth soft. It smells like alpine grass.

Gorgonzola This raw-paste, fatty, wet cheese is made with whole cow's milk. The body may be yellow or straw colored and veined with blue-green "noble mold." With its creamy texture, agreeable odor and pleasurably tangy palate, it's an ideal cheese for both the table and the kitchen.

Grana padano A semi-fat, cooked cheese with a hard body that is made with partially skimmed milk and must be aged from one to two years before consumption. The golden yellow rind is hard and the granular straw white body breaks away into flakes. Its palate is delicate and fragrant. It's traditionally a table cheese but is mostly used for for grating. In a way, Grana is the Parmesan cheese of Lombardy.

Lodigiano This cheese is in the same family as Grana but is aged for at least six, and up to eight, years. It has tiny little eyes that almost seem to be teardrops. This increasingly rare cheese with its slightly sharp palate is an exceptional table cheese and can also be used for grating.

Mascarpone or **mascherpone** More than a cheese, this is a very delicate snow white to straw-colored cream made with heavy cream that's curdled with organic acids in a double boiler. The whole process takes no more than twenty-four hours. When it's very fresh it is eaten on its own, but mostly mascarpone is used as a main ingredient in desserts and other dishes.

Panerone or **pannerone** A fatty, unsalted, semi-cooked whole cow's milk cheese that needs to be aged for at least two months. Its soft rind is white to golden straw colored, its soft body is filled with small eyes. Once called "white gorgonzola," it's no relation to that cheese but has a similar palate.

Provolone lombardo A cheese, usually found in the southern part of Italy, produced in the provinces of Brescia and Cremona in mild and tangy versions.

Quartirolo This soft, mild whole cow's milk cheese is called the stracchino of Milan. The small, square forms with reddish or grey-green rinds and pale straw-colored, melt-in-your-mouth interiors, have a delicate palate. Quartirolo also may be made with skimmed milk.

Scimud Made with skimmed cow's milk, scimud is aged for a few months in order to achieve a slightly acidic, lightly sharp palate. It's called *casera* or *magro di latteria* — the "in-house" cheese of a dairy. It comes from the Valtellina.

Semuda This rare, tangy cheese, typical of the area around Lake Como, is unusual because it isn't curdled but instead slowly aged, forming a thick, irregular rind.

Stracchino Basically *crescenza* (page 62), although at one time there were differences in the way the two cheeses were processed, their forms and the time they were aged to develop a thin rind. The name of the cheese comes from the word *stracco* (also *stanco* or "tired"). It refers to the length of time the herds of cows were left to graze—all summer, until the end of September. By the time they were milked for the last time, they were *stracche*—tired.

Taleggio A fatty, raw cheese made with cow's milk. Its pinkish rind, thin and soft, darkens with mold as it ages. Its delicately flavored, straw white body is soft and wet. It comes from the eponymous Val Taleggio.

SWEETS AND LIQUEURS

Amaretti Little round cookies made with finely chopped almonds, egg whites and sugar. They may be dry, soft and/ or covered with pearl sugar. Conventional wisdom says the cookie dates from the Venetian Renaissance. Today they're made throughout Italy, however, the best amaretti are said to come from the town of Saronno in the province of Varese and in Sardinia. These long-lasting cookies are often used as an ingredient in both savory and sweet dishes.

Amaretto di Saronno A liqueur made with almonds, cherries, plums, cocoa and other ingredients.

Barbagliata or **barbajada** A hot drink made with cocoa, sugar and coffee that's finished with a dollop of whipped cream. It may be served cold as well. Its creation is attributed to Domenico Barbaja, a music impresario who owned an eponymous café in Milan. It's a typical afternoon drink.

Brodo di giuggiole This very dense syrup, used to enrich tarts, etc., is made with jujubes (*giuggiole*)—quince, lemon peel, raisins and other dried fruits cooked in water and sugar and finished with red wine. It's a specialty of the area around Lake Garda.

Busecchina This antique recipe, a specialty of Milan, is made with peeled, boiled chestnuts that are then re-boiled with white wine then finished with milk and cream.

Chiacchiere These fried, crumbly, ribbon-shaped cookies, covered with powdered sugar, are made during Carnival season. The name of the cookie changes according to region.

Chisola A type of dry cake made with white and yellow flours, salt, yeast, sugar, lardo and lemon zest; a specialty of Mantua.

Chisulin Little cakes made with almost the same ingredients as chisola — with the exception of the yeast and lemon zest. They have a distinctive blackened appearance because they are baked in ashes.

Colomba pasquale A dove-shaped Easter cake, covered with slivered almonds and pearl sugar, made with dough similar to that used for panettone. These days this traditional Milanese cake is made throughout Italy.

Copett A dessert similar to Tuscan *copata* (page 158).

Cotizza or **cutizza** The dough for these fritters is made with flour, milk, sugar, vanilla and eggs. They're sprinkled with granulated sugar to serve.

Fave dei morti Crunchy little sweets made with sugar, almonds, pine nuts, eggs, flour, cinnamon and brandy, traditionally served on November 2, the Day of the Dead.

Farsò or **frittelle alla pavese** Fritters made with flour, eggs, milk, sugar and raisins. At one time they were made on the feast of San Giuseppe, March 19, or for the Day of the Dead.

Fiapon Polenta fritters typical of the bassa Padana, the southern part of Lombardy.

Laciada A simple dish made by layering sweet little omelets (made with eggs, milk and sugar) with marmalade in a baking dish. The baked laciada is flambéed with rum to serve.

Laciaditt Apple fritters typical of Milan.

Mataloc A sweet bread filled with dried fruits and nuts such as raisins, figs, walnuts, hazelnuts, etc., typical of the area around Menaggio in the province of Como.

Meini fini A refined version of *pan de mej* (page 66) covered with sugar syrup, sugar and elderflowers. They are off-white in color.

Meini greggi A glazed version of pan de mej, deep yellow in color.

Miascia A traditional dessert made with stale bread soaked in milk, then mixed with eggs, apples, pears, grapes, raisins, lemon peel and white and yellow flours. Before baking, it's covered with chopped rosemary and sugar.

Monte Bianco The same as the one made in Piedmont (page 26).

Mostaccini Very hard cookies made with flour, sugar, water and spices.

Offelle The common name for small cakes that vary according to region. The best-known version, an oval shortbread, is made in the village of Parona in the province of Pavia. In the province of Mantua they look like ravioli—a shortbread crust filled with a mixture of eggs, sugar and butter.

Oss de mord (ossa da mordere) These very hard (the name means "bones that you can bite into") but crumbly cookies are made with almonds, sugar, flour and various spices. They are usually served with a sweet wine such as Moscato or Vin Santo.

Pallottoline dolci di mascarpone Oval-shaped sweet croquettes—an original nineteenth-century recipe—made with crushed amaretti mixed with mascarpone, eggs, cinnamon, other spices and the surprise addition of grated Parmesan cheese. They are breaded and fried. At one time these croquettes were served with roasted meat.

Pan de mèj or **pàndemèinn (pan di miglio)** Round, flattened cakes made with fine and coarse corn flour, white flour, sugar, bran flour, a bit of milk, elderflowers (*panigada*), yeast and eggs. Native Milanesi make these cakes for April 23, the feast of San Giorgio, the patron saint of milkmen. They are served with cream for dipping.

Pan de mort (pane dei morti) This old-fashioned confection is made like an open-faced sandwich topped with a communion wafer. The dough is made with crushed amaretti or other cookies, flour, sugar, raisins, dried figs, almonds, yeast, egg whites, white wine and cinnamon. Some cooks make the dough even richer by adding hazelnuts, pine nuts and orange peel or candied citron. Traditionally, they're served on the Day of the Dead.

Pane di San Siro A pudding made with layers of cream, hazelnuts and butter, soaked in liqueur, then covered with chocolate; a specialty of the province of Pavia.

Panettone The most famous sweet bread in all of Italy has become a symbol of Italian Christmas. This very yeasty bread/cake is made with flour, natural yeast, butter, sugar, eggs, candied citron and orange peel, and raisins. Because good commercial panettone is so widely available, very few people actually make it at home. According to one of the many stories about panettone's origins, the bread got its name when a young baker, Toni, made it for his sweetheart, who loved it. Subsequently it was made in the bakery where Toni worked and called "*pan de Toni*"—Toni's bread, or panettone.

Persicata Basically, jellied peaches cut into various shapes and covered with sugar. The most typical are the white peach jellies from Brescia cut into little rectangles.

Polenta dolce A preparation in which cornmeal is cooked with milk; egg yolks, crumbled amaretti cookies, butter and cinnamon are then added. The mixture is baked until firm. This sweet polenta "cake" is a specialty of the province of Bergamo.

Polenta e osei dolce A sweet version of the savory dish, "polenta with little birds," made by layering sponge cake with apricot jam, liqueur and other ingredients. It may be glazed, or covered with a mixture of marzipan and cornmeal, then garnished with little chocolate birds that have been brushed with apricot jam; a specialty of the city of Bergamo.

Risulen (ricciolini) Little Carnival-time sweets made with fine cornmeal, white flour, sugar, lardo, Sassolino liqueur, lemon, vanilla, white wine and yeast cut into various shapes such as hearts and flowers, and then glazed with egg whites and sugar; typical of Mantua and the southern area of Lombardy, the bassa Padana.

Rosumàda A dense, restorative drink made with egg yolks whipped with sugar and a little red wine. In the summertime water or milk is used in place of the wine.

Sbrisolona A classic and delicious dry almond crumble made with white and yellow flours, sugar, egg yolks, butter, almonds and spices; a specialty of Mantua.

Sfars See *farsò* (page 65).

Spongarda Made with rustic dough that's filled with honey, hazelnuts, candied citron, raisins, crumbled toast and spices. A specialty of Crema, in Emilia-Romagna it is called *spongata* (page 138).

Suc A simple pudding made with cooked black grapes that are strained, then thickened with flour.

Torta di farina gialla e bianca A crunchy and fragrant tart made with white flour and very fine cornmeal, butter, sugar, white wine and egg yolks; another version is made with only white flour and almonds.

Torta di Menaggio A cake very similar to *torta paradiso* (page 68); a specialty of the village of Menaggio in the province of Como.

Torta di tagliatelline A very special pie made by layering fresh egg tagliolini with dough made with almonds, sugar, vanilla, cocoa and liqueur. It's dotted with butter before baking.

Torta mantovana A very rich cake made with lots of butter, flour, sugar, almonds or pine nuts, eggs and lemon zest. It's garnished with powdered sugar.

Torta paradiso A very soft cake made with white flour, potato flour, butter, eggs and sugar. A specialty of Pavia, it's often served with crema di mascarpone.

Torta sbrisolona A classic and delicious dry almond crumble that is a specialty of Mantua, made with white and yellow flours, sugar, egg yolks, butter, almonds and spices.

Tortelli Sguazzarotti An old-fashioned recipe for tortelli filled with puréed beans, cooked wine (vino cotto), walnuts, pumpkin, orange zest and other spices. They're boiled, drained and then served, at room temperature, with a sauce called saorina, also made with vino cotto.

Tortino di sangue di pollo A small cake made by mixing the blood of a freshly killed chicken with eggs, sugar, milk, crumbled amaretti, lemon zest, raisins, pine nuts and some breadcrumbs. Before baking, the top is covered with sugar and butter.

Tortionata The dough for this dessert is made with flour, butter, sugar, egg yolks, chopped, toasted almonds and lemon zest.

WINES

You could paraphrase Alessandro Manzoni when describing the wines of Lombardy, *"così buoni quando son buoni"* ("when they're good they're so good"), but in fact, in the vast wine-growing area of the region, there are only a few wines of notable quality. For example, the wines of Franciacorta are of very high quality. There are a few other areas where some interesting wines are produced: the Valtellina, the hills surrounding the Riviera of Lake Garda and the Oltrepo pavese.

Botticino The solid presence of the Barbera varietal used to make this wine gives it a robust and decisive flavor. Its flavor is helped along a bit as it ages. It's not a very refined wine, but is good with rustic and hearty dishes.

Colli morenici mantovani There are three wines grouped together in this D.O.C. category: Bianco, a delicate and fragrant white wine that is a good accompaniment to non-demanding first courses; Chiaretto, a very pleasant rosé that's good with cured meat antipasti; and a dry, light, ruby-colored Rosso that goes well with the entire meal.

Franciacorta (province of Brescia) The sparkling version of the Bianco is produced with the Pinot Bianco varietal mixed with both Pinot Nero and Pinot Grigio. This very fragrant, delicate and soft-in-your-mouth deep yellow wine is good with mild first courses and molded vegetable puddings. The best sparkling wines in all of Italy are produced around the town of Erbusco in the province of Brascia using the champagne method. The medium-bodied, lively Rosso becomes more complex as it ages making it the perfect accompaniment for roast meats and game. When it's still young, it easily slips between first courses and non-demanding entrées.

Lugana This not-very-well-known, lightly acidic, highly fragrant Bianco is a good *aperitivo* wine. However, if you happen to find yourself around the town of Sirmione on Lake Garda, be sure to search it out as it goes well with fish from the lake.

Oltrepo pavese In this zone — literally "the other side of the Po (river)" — you'll find wines that are influenced by the varietals of Piedmont like Barbera, Moscato and Cortese. The most interesting red wines of the Oltre Po are the Rosso, perfect with the entire meal; the Barbera, softer than the Piemontese version and perfect with steaks and braised meats; a dry and tannic Bonarda that ages beautifully and works well with rustic foods. There's a very special wine from the area called Barbacarlo, often called Buttafuoco as well; it's nothing more than Barbera mixed with Croatina and Uva Rara varietals. This tannic, winey, currant-fragrant wine sweetens as it ages, making it the perfect dessert drink. The Sangue di Guida is a sweet and sparkling version of Barbacarlo that marries well with plum tarts and fruit salads. Among the white wines of the Ottrepo worth mentioning are the fresh and soft Cortese, perfect with vegetable soups, frogs, snails and fish. The dry, fragrant and deep yellow Reisling is good with any seafood. You can find both still and sparkling versions of the aromatic and lightly sweet Moscato. It's the perfect dessert wine.

Riviera del Garda There are two D.O.C. wines in this category, a Rosso (red) and a Rosato (rosé), both made, for the most part, with the Groppello varietal. The Rosso, which doesn't hold up well to a long aging process, is a good choice with an antipasto of mixed cured meats. The Rosato, also called Chiaretto, is a delicate, soft, fragrant wine that's a perfect accompaniment to sauced first courses and white meats.

Tocai The origins of this fragrant, rather bitter white wine are in the Friuli region, but there's a version made in the town of Battaglia in the province of Brescia. It goes well with fried fish but can work well with the whole meal.

Trebbiano This unpretentious, slightly sour white wine is a good table wine, but works particularly well with fish dishes.

Valcalepio The wines from the Valcalepio area, in the province of Bergamo, range from a full-bodied red wine with an herby aroma made with Cabernet Sauvignon and Merlot varietals — great with roasted or stewed meats — to a dry, delicate white wine good for drinking anytime or, specifically, with fish dishes.

Valtellina Since the sixteenth century these long-lived, robust wines have been famous throughout northern Europe. They are composed of a high percentage of the Nebbiolo varietal (called Chiavennasca locally). These grapes are responsible for the wine's intense fragrance and tannic acid that guarantees long life. The most prized wines of the group are Valtellina Superiore and the Riserva, both of which need at least four years to properly age and release their fragrance of flowers, resin and red fruits; they're good with roasted meats and cheese. The Sassella and Inferno wines are aged for at least eight years; they go well with game. Sfursat or Sforzato is a spicy, very aromatic wine made with partially dried grapes; it goes well with veined cheeses.

Risotto alla Milanese
Serves 6

20 threads of saffron or 3 small packets of
   powdered saffron
6½ cups rich meat broth
3 ounces unsalted butter
1 medium onion, chopped
1 clove garlic, chopped
2 ounces chopped beef marrow
1 cup red or dry white wine
A bit less than 1 pound *superfino* Carnaroli
   rice (It's very important to use the right
   rice when making this risotto — you
   may substitute the Carnaroli rice with
   Vialone Nano rice.)

Place the saffron in a small bowl and cover with a bit of
boiling hot broth.

   Place a saucepan (possibly copper or terra cotta) over
medium heat with 2 ounces of butter, the onions and garlic.
When the onion is translucent, add the marrow and cook
for a few minutes before adding the rice. "Toast" the rice
stirring continuously with a wooden spoon. When the rice
has toasted, pour in the wine and let it evaporate. Add the
broth two cups at a time always stirring with a wooden
spoon until the rice has absorbed it before adding more.
Five minutes before the cooking has been completed, add
the saffron with its broth. Just before serving, add the
remaining butter and grated Parmesan cheese. The risotto
should be soft but not too liquid.

Suggested wine: Tocai San Martino della Battaglia

VENETO

The Veneto is a vast terrain with a constantly changing landscape. There are great stretches of plains, mountains, sloping hills, a coastline and lagoons that meet the Po River delta where the Tagliamento River flows down from the Alps. There are two dominant foods that show up as the base of almost every food preparation in the region: corn polenta and rice, which are either cooked with other ingredients or served as accompaniments to other dishes.

The region has a strong tradition of family vegetable gardens producing delicacies like radicchio di Treviso, castraure (the first artichoke buds that are "castrated" or loped off the plant), Bassano asparagus, Lamon beans and very sweet peas that are the starring ingredient in risi e bisi (rice and peas). The vegetables of the Veneto are as flavor-filled as anything you might find in southern Italy.

The region's seafood is equally dignified. At the seafood market in Chioggia, one of the most famous in Italy, you'll find rare fish from the lagoons, shellfish and crustaceans including incredible moleche (green soft shell crabs) and very tasty granseole (spider crabs).

Preserved fish is part of the region's tradition, too. Nothing says Veneto more than baccalà mantecato, a dish made with softened dry cod whipped into a cloud with olive oil, garlic and parsley. It's served with polenta.

There are meat dishes unique to the region. Pork is made into excellent cured meats and salami. The province of Vicenza is famous for female turkey roasted with pomegranate seeds; Treviso for pigeons made into sopa coada; and the province of Padua for the legendary hen prepared in every possible way.

The gastronomy of the Veneto is essentially Venetian. It was born when basic Romanesque taste met the regional fascination with all things from the Orient. An unforgettable cuisine was created when exotic spices were combined with modest, simple, everyday food.

ANTIPASTI, BREAD, PIZZA, SAVORY TARTS AND FLATBREADS

Baccalà mantecato This very basic typically Venetian recipe is made by whipping steamed salt cod with parsley, garlic and olive oil. The finished dish, with its foam-like texture, is often served with polenta.

Bagigi The Venetian word for peanuts.

Bondola affumicata A type of salami made with a mixture of chopped pork, salt, pepper and red wine stuffed into a turkey bladder or neck. It's smoked for about a month and then aged in a well-ventilated space.

Bondola di Adria Salami similar to the *salama da sugo* or *salamina ferrarese* (page 133), made with ground veal, pork butt, lardo, salt, pepper and red wine. It's aged for at least four months before it's either steamed or slowly poached, then cut into pieces and served on a bed of puréed potatoes.

Bovolo A spiral-shaped roll. In Venetian dialect, a *bovolo* is a snail.

Carciofo A bread shape — "artichoke" — that has its origins in the Veneto but is found all over Italy.

Casatello A plate of assorted fried cheeses. This dish is typical of the area around the province of Belluno, particularly the town of Pieve di Cadore.

Granseola or **grancevola alla veneziana** Boiled crab. The meat is then removed from the shell, mixed with garlic, parsley, lemon juice and olive oil, and then stuffed back into the shell.

Moleche col pien Male soft shell crabs that are eaten in the spring and fall when they're molting. In Venice, they're dipped into a mixture of eggs and Parmesan cheese while still alive and left to eat the mixture until they are full (*col pien*), then they're floured and fried.

Muneghete The Venetian version of popcorn.

Puccia A flatish, round bread made with whole-wheat flour and fennel seeds; typical of the Dolomite Mountains.

Sarde or **sardele in saor** A typically Venetian dish made with fresh sardines that are floured, fried and then marinated in abundant amounts of sliced onions that have been slowly sautéed with vinegar, sugar, pine nuts and raisins. According to record, the habit of marinating food with onions goes back to fourteenth-century Venice.

Schie or **schile** Tiny peeled and boiled shrimp that are either simply dressed with olive oil and lemon, or cooked in a sauce and served with polenta. The typically Venetian shrimp can also be fried.

Scopeton Herring. Usually the fillets are bathed in warm milk, then baked, then finally dressed with olive oil, garlic and parsley.

Sfogi (or sfogie) in saor Just like the sarde in saor preparation except that small sole fillets are marinated with white wine vinegar to achieve a more delicate and refined flavor.

Soppressa Very dense yet tender fresh salami, also known as sopressa del Pasubio, made with 65% lean and 35% fatty pork parts. The meat comes from pigs that are raised more or less in the wild, eating chestnuts and potatoes. Soppressa goes well with roasted polenta.

Soppressa col fil Salami prepared just about the same way as the above, except that this has a piece of pork fillet in the center of the filling blend.

Speck in pasta di pane A dish made by wrapping bread dough around smoked prosciutto (speck), and then baking it. It's a specialty of the province of Belluno, in particular the town of Pieve d'Alpago.

PASTA, GNOCCHI, RICE, POLENTA AND GRAINS

Bigoli Thick, rather coarse, spaghetti-like pasta shape made with a special bronze press, a *bigolaro*. Bigoli are usually made with whole-wheat flour. The following are some of the sauces typically used to dress bigoli:

Bigoli col pocio A sauce made with chopped celery, carrots, onion and veal. Sometimes chopped pork is added to the mixture.

Bigoli con i rovanazzi A sauce made with the "gifts" of the chicken—crests, wattles, etc. (*i rovanazzi* in Venetian dialect).

Bigoli con l'anara A preparation in which the bigoli are cooked in duck broth and then dressed with a sauce made with the duck's innards.

Bigoli in salsa A sauce made by slowly sautéing onions and anchovies, until they melt into the sauté, and parsley.

Castradina See *risotto con la castradina* (page 76).

Casunziei or **casumziei** or **cassunziei ampezzani** Semi-circular ravioli stuffed with beets, smoked ricotta, bread-crumbs, eggs and cheese. They're dressed with melted butter, grated cheese and poppy seeds. This particular dish is a specialty of the area of the mountains called the Ampezzo, where the influence of the food of the neighboring Central European countries is present. There are similar versions in other provinces of the Veneto; in Belluno the pasta is filled with pumpkin and cinnamon, or spinach and prosciutto, then dressed with melted butter and smoked ricotta.

Gnocchi alla cadorina Simple potato gnocchi dressed with melted butter and smoked ricotta.

Lasagne da fornel Simple homemade lasagna noodles dressed with a sauce made with butter, walnuts, raisins, chopped dried figs, grated apples and poppy seeds. Everything is quickly sautéed to serve. The dish is typical of the mountain area around Belluno and is also influenced by the food of Central Europe.

Mosa Polenta cooked with milk instead of water. It's served with butter and cold milk; sometimes sugar and cinnamon are added as well.

Paparele coi bisi These very wide, handmade egg tagliatelle are cooked like a risotto — ladlefuls of broth are added to the pasta as the previously added liquid is absorbed. They are dressed with a sauce made with fresh peas, pancetta, onions and parsley; they're also very good dressed with chicken livers.

Polenta bianca Polenta made with white corn flour. This polenta, used in the Veneto and Friuli regions, has a more delicate flavor than the more common yellow polenta; it marries perfectly with fish dishes.

Risi e bisati A rice and eel dish typically served on Christmas Eve made by cutting eel into pieces and cooking it with olive oil, parsley, bay leaf and a few drops of fresh lemon juice, and then adding the rice at the end.

Risi e bisi A very dense soup made with rice and peas cooked in a broth made with the pea pods. Some of the more ancient recipes call for the addition of fennel seeds. It's a famous Venetian dish.

Risi e bisi con l'oca in onto In this version of risi e bisi, pieces of goose preserved in its own fat are added to the dish.

Risi e bisi e colo de castrà In this version the risi e bisi are cooked in a broth made from the neck of castrated beef.

Risi in cavroman Cavroman are pieces of castrato beef or mutton. The meat, with celery, carrots, onion, cinnamon and cloves, are added to a risotto. The dish has its origins in Dalmatia and Eastern Europe in general.

Riso alla lamonese A dish of boiled rice, puréed beans, butter and cheese. It's a specialty of Lamon, a town known for its extraordinary beans, in the province of Belluno.

Risotto al baccalà Simply a risotto to which *baccalà alla vicentina* (page 78) is added halfway through the cooking process. It's typical of the town of Montegaldella in the province of Vicenza.

Risotto al radicchio trevigiano This relatively new dish provides an opportunity to showcase the extraordinary radicchio di Treviso by including it in a classic risotto.

Risotto al tagio or **tajo** This risotto may be made with shrimp and eel, or peas and artichokes; *tagio* simply means that there are two different ingredients that go into the risotto. It's a specialty of the province of Treviso.

Risotto alla chioggiota or **con i gô** Risotto cooked with a dense broth made with ghiozzi or go, a small fish found in the lagoons of Chioggia. It's finished with chopped parsley and, even though it's a fish dish, garnished with Parmesan cheese.

Risotto alla sbirraglia Risotto made with bits of chicken; a specialty of Treviso.

Risotto alla trevigiana This risotto is started with a base of onions and celery, then finished with crumbled sausage from Treviso.

Risotto con i bruscandoli This risotto gets its slightly bitter and sour flavor from i bruscandoli — hops sprouts (when it's made in Padua) or broom sprouts (when it's made in Verona).

Risotto con i rovinassi Risotto made with pieces of chicken and some of its giblets; a specialty of Padua.

Risotto con la castradina A very-difficult-to-find risotto made with smoked, sun dried, then boiled pieces of castrated beef; an ancient Venetian recipe.

Risotto con le secole Secole are the muscles between beef ribs. This risotto is made with secole mixed with celery, carrots and onions.

Risotto polesano Risotto cooked with a broth made with eel, sea bass and mullet. The risotto is finished with butter, Parmesan cheese and the deboned fish that were used for the broth. Some cooks add a handful of raisins.

Risotto primavera The generic name for all risottos made with fresh, springtime vegetables. Harry's Bar in Venice created the famous dish.

Subioti A Venetian term for tubular pasta shapes that have a small hole running down the middle.

Tirache trevigiane Slightly thick, rustic tagliatelle made with semolina flour and water. They're often used when making pasta e fagioli (pasta with beans). In the Trevigiano dialect, *tirache* means "little suspenders."

SOUPS

Broeto A Venetian fish soup that is made in various ways. It almost always starts with broth made with small fish from the lagoons (*ghiozzi*) and a sauté of onions, carrots and celery. Assorted larger fish are added to the broth.

Minestra di fagioli al magasso Magasso or moriglione is a type of wild duck. For this dish, the duck is deboned, stuffed with a filling made with onions, lardo and assorted herbs and then boiled with beans and other ingredients. The cooked duck is removed from the broth and served as a main course. Pasta or rice is added to the broth to make a tasty soup.

Sopa coàda You'll find this very rich soup, made with beef broth, pigeon, bread and cheese, throughout the Veneto region. *Coàda* means "slowly cooked" in Venetian dialect. In fact, this soup is first cooked on the stovetop and then baked.

Zuppa scaligera The "noble" version of coàda in which, in addition to the pigeon, deboned chicken and turkey are added.

CONDIMENTS, SAUCES, SALSAS AND EGGS

Alla buranella A preparation, usually with pasta, made with a light béchamel and fish sauce. In spite of its name, it has nothing to do with the island of Burano.

Alla carlina A salsa made with tiny capers and raw tomatos, usually served with skillet-fried fish. The name was coined by Giuseppe Cipriani of the renowned Venetian restaurant, Harry's Bar.

Casso pipa A term that indicates that a food is simmered in a heavy-bottomed metal or terra cotta saucepan. *Pipar* means "simmer."

Pearà A medieval sauce with origins in Verona. Made with breadcrumbs, beef marrow, Grana cheese, salt, pepper and diluted with beef broth, it's a good accompaniment for boiled meats.

Peverada This sauce is sometimes mistaken for *pearà* (above). However, peverada is made with toasted bread, saffron, liver and spices that have been pounded together in a mortar and diluted with vinegar, wine or broth. It goes well with boiled meat, poached fish or roasts. There are other peverada recipes: one from Milan, based on the French sauce *poivrade*, and another Venetian version (*soppressa*, page 74), made with anchovies, lemon peel, parsley, olive oil, vinegar and pepper.

Asià The Venetian name for a type of small shark that is skinned then cut into steaks.

Baccalà alla vicentina One of the most famous dishes of the Veneto region, made by cooking pieces of boned salt cod with onions, garlic, parsley and anchovies. Parmesan cheese, olive oil and milk are whipped into the mixture at the end. This dish is traditionally served with polenta.

Bisato Eel, in Venetian dialect.

Bisato in tecia For this simple dish the eel is skinned, cut into pieces, then stewed with onions, herbs, white wine and tomatoes.

Bisato su l'ara Eel simply cooked with bay leaves but no fat. This historic dish has its origins on the island of Murano, where it was traditionally cooked on a shelf in the glassmaking ovens.

Bovoletto or **bovoleto** The Venetian name for sea snails; also bovolone or bogone. In Vicenza they're stewed in a sauce made with olive oil, butter, parsley, garlic and white wine.

Canestrelli A mollusk similar to a small scallop. There are two varieties, the most famous being pettine, which means "comb" and might refer to its ridged surface. You often find canestrelli in the market without their shells. Batter-fried is one of the best ways to enjoy them; Venetians make a good risotto with them as well.

Cannoce The Venetian name for a type of mollusk; also called cannochie because they look like corncobs. They're delicious in a soup but also may be simply steamed open and dressed with olive oil, lemon juice, parsley, salt and pepper.

Caparozzoli The Venetian name for clams. They may be stewed *alla marinara* or tossed with spaghetti.

Cape longhe Razor clams; also called cannolicchi ("telescopes"). In the Veneto they are usually gratinéed to serve. However, there are other ways to cook them — mostly Venetian recipes — in soups, grilled, or in tomato sauce.

Capesante or **cappesante** The Venetian name for conchiglie di San Giacomo or coquilles St. Jacques; scallops. In Italy, scallops are usually served gratinéed. In recent years, because of the influence of French cuisine, many other ways of preparing them are found on menus throughout Italy.

Caragoi Venetian dialect for a conch-like mollusk, garagoli.

Filetti di pesce alla carlina In this dish, sole, turbot or San Pietro fillets are floured and fried until golden then finished in the oven with butter, sliced tomatoes and capers. The name of the dish was invented by Giuseppe Cipriani of Harry's Bar in Venice.

Folpetti The Venetian name for the mollusk called moscardini. Tiny and squid-like (their shells are inside), when fresh, they are sometimes called polpi muschiati or mughetti because of their musk-like fragrance.

Garagoli or **garagoj** or **garusoli** Names used in the Veneto and Marches for a conch-like mollusk, chiocciola. The name is derived from the Spanish, *caracol*. They are delicious when stewed or when cooked in a type of court bouillon and then removed from their shells.

Ghiozzo or **gô** The generic name for the genus of Venetian lagoon fish, gobius. They may be fried, cooked in a sweet and sour broth or in a risotto.

Granseola or **grancevola alla veneziana** See page 73.

Granzoporo or **gransoporo** The Venetian name for a large crab found in the waters near Venice.

Maruzele Tiny sea snails that may be simply steamed or cooked with tomatoes.

Masanete Female crabs.

Moleche col pien See page 73.

Peoci Mussels.

Sardele In Venetian dialect, anchovies or sardines.

Scorpena or **scarpena** Another name for scorpion fish.

Seppie al nero alla veneziana Cuttlefish cooked with onions, garlic, olive oil, white wine, parsley and a bit of tomatoes. The addition of the cuttlefish's black ink defines the dish. In Venice this dish is served with white polenta.

Storione del Po The very refined way in which sturgeon is prepared around Venice and along the Po River. The fish is simply poached and served with olive oil. Just as all the parts of a pig are used in Italian cooking, the same can be said for the sturgeon; the head is used to make a broth for risotto, the eggs are eaten as caviar, the innards are cleaned, then grilled or stewed, and the fish itself can be stewed, smoked, sliced raw for carpaccio, fried or roasted.

MEAT

Anara col pien Duck stuffed with a filling made with crumbled *soppressa* (page 74), a bit of chopped pork and veal, eggs, Parmesan cheese, the white part of bread soaked in milk, mushrooms and pistachios, and then boiled. It's a traditional Venetian custom to serve this dish for the Feast of the Redeemer. For another version of this dish, crumbled amaretti cookies are added to the filling, then the cooked duck is served with *peverada* (page 77) that been diluted with a bit of the duck's cooking liquid. The whole thing is garnished with crumbled amaretti cookies.

Bollito veneto This Venetian version of mixed boiled meats is defined by the use of pieces of pork bladder, and the use of more pork parts in general. Some of the sauces used to accompany the dish are *pearà* (page 77) and chopped mostarda. Sometimes *musetto* (page 81) is used instead of cotechino, and then it's served with mustard.

Cappone alla canevera Capon flavored with mixed herbs and enclosed in beef bladder. To cook, it's placed in a large saucepan, covered with water and then a natural fiber straw (*canevera*) is stuck through the bladder to be used as an air hole. This antique recipe comes from the village of Arzignano in the province of Vicenza.

Capriolo alla caprilese Marinated leg of roebuck cooked with pancetta, veal liver, sage, white wine and other ingredients.

Carpaccio A famous dish made with very thin slices of beef fillet that are dressed in various ways. The most common is a citronette made with extra virgin olive oil, lemon juice, freshly ground white pepper and minced garlic, then garnished with fresh ovoli or porcini mushrooms, shards of Parmesan cheese and shaved white truffles. The dish, which probably has its origins in the Piemontese town of Alba, was baptized for the painter Carpaccio by Giuseppe Cipriani of Harry's Bar in Venice.

Cavreti de Gambellara White baby goats weighing no more than four kilos that are stuffed with aromatic herbs, then spit-roasted; a specialty of the area around the province of Vicenza.

Cavroman A Venetian stew made with the choice parts of castrated beef. The other ingredients are celery, carrots, onions, cinnamon, cloves and sometimes a little tomato sauce. It's served with boiled onions and potatoes.

Faraona in tecia A dish in which an onion and cloves are stuffed into a guinea hen that is then cooked in a terra cotta pot with butter, olive oil, onions and herbs.

Fegato alla sbrodega A preparation of liver that's distinct from the more well-known Venetian version (*alla veneziana*, page 81), in which the liver and onions are stewed instead of sautéed; a specialty of the province of Padua.

Fegato alla tortiera Slices of veal liver that are breaded then fried.

Fegato alla veneziana Thin slices of veal liver cooked very slowly in butter and olive oil with abundant onions. The dish is finished with a shower of freshly chopped parsley.

Figà col rasedelo Pieces of liver wrapped, with sage leaves, in pork caul, then fried in butter.

Figà garbo e dolce Pieces of liver dredged in flour, dipped in egg and breadcrumbs, then fried in butter and finished with sugar and vinegar.

Fongadina A stew made with veal offal (lungs, liver, heart, sweetbreads, spleen, etc.) and fresh and dried mushrooms. This specialty of the province of Belluno is usually served with polenta.

Juganega or **luganega veneta** Typical of Treviso, a type of fresh (raw) salami made with a mixture of chopped pork neck and cheeks. The mixture is stuffed into a relatively short casing then tied with double strings in order to make four sections. Versions that are made with slightly leaner ingredients are good for cooking over wood; a slightly fattier version is good in risotto.

Magasso Venetian dialect for *moriglione* (see below).

Mazaro a la valsana For this dish a mallard is marinated for a day in vinegar, thyme and marjoram, roasted for half its cooking time, then finished in a skillet with butter, anchovies and onions.

Moriglione A wild duck found in the valleys and on the delta of the Po River.

Musetto The best known of all the cooking salamis. It is used throughout the northern Veneto and Friuli. It's made with lean pork parts, pork rind and snout (*muso* is an animal's face), cinnamon, coriander, nutmeg, red pepper flakes, salt and pepper and either Tocai, Picolit or Marsala wine. Musetto is somewhat similar to *cotechino* (page 132), but it's leaner and its ingredients are more finely chopped.

Pastissada or **Pastizzada** A traditional stew of the region generally made with horse or donkey, sometimes beef. The stew is made with meat that has been marinated in red wine then slowly cooked in the marinade, to which assorted herbs and spices are added. In Verona this stew is called pastissada de caval, referring to one of the barbarian battles when the losers had to give their entire cavalry of steeds to the winners. The Veronese invented this dish to use up all the horsemeat.

Pollo alla padovana A fricassee made with pieces of chicken cooked with onions and butter and finished with a mixture of egg yolks and lemon juice.

Secole Muscles between an animal's vertebrae. The usual preparation is to add them to risotto.

Sguazzetto alla bechera Literally, "the butcher's stew." It's made with the parts of an animal that are difficult to sell, the leftovers — tripe, lungs, spleen and tail.

Tacchino alla melagrana Roast turkey served with pan drippings and pomegranate juice and garnished with pomegranate seeds; a specialty of the town of Marostica in the province of Vicenza. In dialect it's called paeta al malgaragno.

Torresani allo spiedo Torraioli — a kind of dove — wrapped in pieces of lardo, skewered and then spit-roasted over a maple- and ash-wood-burning fire. The birds are continually basted with olive oil flavored with juniper berries and coarsely ground pepper. The dish is a specialty of the town of Breganze in the province of Vicenza.

VEGETABLES

Asparagi alla bassanese The famous, thick white asparagus of Bassano that are steamed then served with a sauce made with egg yolks, olive oil, lemon juice and herbs.

Bruscandoli A Venetian term always used in the plural form. It refers to two kinds of wild sprouts: in the province of Padua, hops, in the province of Verona, broom. The first is slightly bitter tasting, the second, acidic. Both are often mistaken for wild asparagus. They're used in risotto.

Carletti The Venetian name for a slightly elongated, wild green leaf (*silene angustifolia*) that is used in salads and risotto. Carletti sprouts are also used in soups, risottos and frittatas.

Castraure These unusually shaped vegetables, found growing in the lagoons of the Veneto, are among the first artichokes to bloom in the spring. They're harvested before maturation from plants that have too many blossoms. They're usually sautéed with olive oil, garlic and parsley to serve. *Castraure* means "to prune."

Cilele The base of the splendid Venetian artichoke. You can find them in markets already prepared, left in lemon water to keep them from turning black. They're traditionally boiled, then served dressed with olive oil, salt, pepper, chopped garlic and parsley.

Radicchio trevigiano Probably the most prestigious variety of red radicchio, it looks like red endive with its long leaves and compact head. There are many ways to prepare it: raw in a salad, roasted, stewed, fried, made into a sauce for pasta, in a stuffing or added to risotto. In the past few years it has become popular to caramelize it.

Sedano rapa Celery root or celeriac; also called sedano di Verona. Often sautéed in butter and served with Parmesan cheese, it may also be cubed, steamed and served with olive oil and vinegar, or eaten raw, cut into matchsticks and dressed with a sauce made with mayonnaise and mustard.

Verze sofegae Shredded cabbage that is cooked in a terra cotta pot with olive oil, garlic, onions, rosemary then *affogata* ("drowned") in broth. Some cooks add chopped lardo or pancetta to the sauté mixture.

CHEESE AND DAIRY PRODUCTS

Asiago This typically Venetian cheese is mostly produced in the summer pastures of the plateaus of the Altopiano d'Asiago. There are two very distinct types of Asiago: *allevato* (raised) and *pressato* (pressed).

Asiago di allevo A semi-fat, partially cooked cow's milk cheese. Its rind is smooth and ranges in color from straw to brown. Depending on its age, the body can range from milky white to straw colored with sparsely spaced, small to medium-sized eyes. It's a fragrant cheese with a flavor that, as it ages, goes from mild to very tasty — it adapts perfectly to prolonged aging.

Asiago pressato Made by large producers in the low-lying areas of the Veneto, this is a fatty cheese with an elastic, thin orange rind and a body that ranges from milky white to straw white with deep, irregularly shaped eyes. It has a very delicate flavor.

Casatella A fatty cheese made with whole cow's milk. It matures in about a week and has no outer rind. Its soft body is milky white. It has a distinctly mild, milky flavor, with a lightly pleasurable, slightly sour streak.

Fioretto or **grasso monte** A very fatty cheese found throughout the Veneto region. It's ready to eat a few days after production.

Morlacco This soft, cooked, low-fat cheese is made with skimmed cow's milk. It's produced in the massive tablelands along the Grappa River. Its rind can sometimes develop a greenish mold that gives the cheese a unique smell referred to as *calcagno* (heel). The body, with its tiny eyes, will harden as it ages. It's a very flavorful, slightly salty cheese that gets stronger as it ages.

Piave This traditional cheese gets its name from the Piave River that stretches its way across the northern part of the region to the lagoons of Venice. It's a cooked, semi-fatty cow's milk cheese. When the cheese is young the rind is pale, tending towards brown as it ages. The compact body ranges from milky white to straw colored. This young, mild cheese melts in your mouth.

Puina In Venetian dialect, smoked ricotta.

Spess A cheese that has just curdled. It's typical of the town of Alleghe in the province of Belluno.

SWEETS AND LIQUEURS

Baìcoli Very thinly sliced biscotti; typical of Venice.

Bigarani These rather provocatively named round cookies have an inward facing point that gives them the appearance of a vulva (*biga*). They are made with flour, eggs, milk, butter, sugar and yeast. At one time these cookies, along with Vin Santo, were brought as gifts to new mothers to help them regain their strength.

Bussolà A type of cake enriched with pine nuts, candied citron, chocolate, almonds, cinnamon, pepper and nutmeg.

Bussoldi See *forti* (below).

Caramei Typically Venetian sweets; skewers on which walnuts, dried figs, dried apricots and prunes are threaded then caramelized.

Favette Sweet fritters typically found in the Veneto during the Carnival period.

Forti or **bussoldi** Crunchy, long-lasting ring-shaped cookies. They're made with flour, sugar, molasses, almonds, butter, eggs, ginger, syrupy red wine, cloves and cinnamon. This specialty of the small city of Bassano del Grappa owes its names to the fact that a paste of white pepper is added to the dough as well making the flavor strong (*forte*).

Fregolotta A cake that's very similar to the sbrisolona from Lombardy. It's a dry, rustic cake filled with crumbled almonds; a specialty of the province of Treviso, especially the town of Castelfranco Veneto.

Fritole The Venetian name for fritters, made during Carnival, with flour, sugar, yeast, liqueur, raisins, pine nuts and candied citron.

Fritole de risi Fritters made with the same ingredients as the above fritters, with the addition of rice that has been cooked in milk.

Fugazza An old-fashioned and odd sweet made with sweet dough, eggs, yeast, iris root, orange peel, cloves, ginger, cinnamon, vanilla and almonds.

Galani The Venetian version of a sweet found in other parts of the country, but with different names, made by knotting ribbons of dough, frying them in lardo, then covering them with powdered sugar.

Gialletti See *zaleti* (page 86).

Golossesi The same as *caramei* (page 84).

Ossi da Morto Cookies called "bones of the dead" because of their cylindrical shape, made with flour, milk, sugar, yeast, butter, olive oil, eggs and orange liqueur. They're baked twice.

Pandoro The Christmas cake of Verona that's found throughout Italy. The industrially produced, tall, star-shaped cake is made with flour, yeast, sugar, eggs and butter, and is as highly yeasted as panettone.

Pavana A small, sweet flat cake enriched with raisins, candied fruits and cinnamon.

Pinza A cake made with white and yellow corn flour; it may be sweet or savory. The corn flour is enriched with fennel seeds, raisins, dried figs, orange peel, pine nuts, candied citron and squash, apples and grappa.

Putana A version of pinza from Vicenza.

Rosada A refined pudding made simply by cooking pastry cream in a water bath.

Smegiazza A very rare, rustic cake from the provinces of Padua and Vicenza made with bits of hardened polenta, smashed cookies, milk, eggs, candied citron, raisins and pine nuts.

Sugoli Jam made with grape juice; a specialty of the province of Padua.

Tiramisù A delicious, simple dessert made by lining a pan with coffee-soaked sponge cake or ladyfingers, filling the pan with mascarpone cream, then covering the whole thing with powdered cocoa.

Torta nicolotta A cake traditionally eaten by fishermen made with milk-soaked breadcrumbs, raisins, sugar, eggs, butter and flour and covered with fennel seeds.

Torta sabbiosa A soft, crumbly cake made with whipped butter, sugar, potato flour, eggs and flour. It's called *sabbiosa* (sandy) because if it's properly made it should melt in your mouth. The cake is native to the Veneto but is found throughout central Italy.

Tortion The Venetian version of apple strudel.

Trandoti The Veronese term for *ossi da morto* (page 85).

Zaleti or **gialetti** Small lozenge-shaped rustic pastries made with flour and corn flour, butter, eggs, sugar, raisins, pine nuts and spices.

WINES

Even though the Veneto is primarily dedicated to white wines, there are some exceptional reds: Cabernet and Merlot, among the great varietals that have their origins in Provence; Bardolino, one of liveliest wines in Italy; and, above all, Amarone, the full-bodied red.

The numerous, very drinkable whites are more than just part of the meal; they are part of a regional philosophy, *minestra e vin* — soup and wine — a natural pairing. Another habit that's entrenched in the ways of the Veneto is the *andar a ombra*, the custom of the evening, before-dinner stroll with friends, from *osteria* to *osteria*, tasting a glass of white wine at each stop.

Bardolino Made with Corvina, Molinara, Rondinella and Negrara grapes, this light-bodied, dry, clear, ruby red wine, with its winey aroma, could be called sprightly, just approaching a sparkle. It can age a bit but is best enjoyed when young and lively. If it's vinified with white wine, a type of Chiaretto or rosé is produced. Bardolino goes well with the entire meal but is particularly good with certain first courses like little gnocchi with spleen and eel soup. It is produced on the banks of Lake Garda.

Bianco di Custoza A mixture of Trebbiano, Garganega and Tocai Friulano grapes, its flat color, decisive aroma, and delicate although slightly bitter flavor makes it the perfect wine to accompany crutaceans and other seafood.

Breganze Wines produced in the area around Breganze in the province of Vicenza. The Bianco is basically a Tocai with small addition of other grapes. It's delicately colored with a winey aroma, and a slightly aggressive but pleasant flavor. Other whites made to accompany fish, especially the signature dish of Vicenza, baccalà, include the mild and fragrant Pinot, and the gritty and persistent Vespaiolo. The full-bodied Rosso is great with roast meats, as are the elegant

Cabernet with its orange reflections and the delicate Pinot Nero, fragrant with wild berries (*frutti di bosco*).

Cabernet The numerous Cabernets of the Veneto each have their own particular characteristics that depend upon the area where they are vinified. One of the most renowned Cabernets is the one from the town of Pramaggiore in the province of Venice. It's a dry wine with a warm, ruby color with garnet reflections, herbaceous with shades of the aroma of sweet peppers, well structured and full of character. Other Cabernets include those produced in the area of the Piave River, in the town of Montello, in Breganze and in the Berici hills.

Gambellara A pleasant white wine made from the Garganega grapes in the hilltop village of Gambellara in the province of Vicenza. It's particularly good with dishes made with the freshwater fish from the lakes, because its slightly acid and bitter flavor is soothed by the fats used in cooking.

Garganega White wine produced in the Berici Hills, very similar to Gambellara that goes well with the same kinds of food.

Merlot This varietal from Bordeaux has found its second home in the Veneto. It's produced in Pramaggiore in the province of Venice, in the area around the Piave in the province of Treviso, in Montello and the Berici Hills. All of the Merlots are dry, tannic, decisively ruby red with a winey aroma. They're not great wines but are very pleasant and good throughout a meal.

Moscato Moscato grapes have made the trip from Piedmont to the Euganei hills where they've caught on perfectly. This sweet, golden wine is very fragrant. Produced both in still and sparkling versions, it's a perfect dessert wine and goes especially well with dry cookies.

Pinot The white, produced in Breganze and the Berici hills, is made from a mixture of grapes that include not only Pinot Bianco but also a small percentage of Pinot Grigio. This easy-to-drink, mild, pale white wine has a slightly fruity aroma. These Pinots can become sparkling wines using *la méthode champenoise*. Pinot Nero is produced only in Breganze. Although it's a full-bodied red, it maintains a delicate flavor and is highly fragrant with fruits of the forest.

Prosecco da Conegliano Produced in an area in the province of Treviso that is referred to by the name of one of its principle towns, Valdobbiadene, the Prosecco-producing vineyards are bordered by the town of Asolo, just beyond the Piave River, making for a contained production area. With its straw yellow color, full but delicate bouquet and flowery fragrance, Prosecco is the most elegant white wine of the Veneto. Prosecco is highly acidic, making it a perfect sparkling wine. It's made into a bubbly wine by using the Charmat method. There are dry and sweet versions. It's often noted that Prosecco is a wine that wants to be drunk when it's young. Cartizze is a superior Prosecco that can handle a year of aging.

Raboso This very acidic and tannic red wine is made with Raboso grapes in the area around Piave. With its high alcohol content it is a good blending wine. However, if it's left to age, it transforms itself into a well-structured wine that goes well with roasted and spit-roasted meats.

Recioto Made with Garganega grapes that are left to wither on trellises after they've been harvested, this golden colored, sweet wine, redolent of spring flowers, is produced in Gambellara and in Soave in the province of Verona. It's a great dessert wine that goes equally well with dry cookies and fruit tarts. There's also a red Recioto that's made with Valpolicella grapes. This sweet, garnet colored wine, fragrant with flowers and vanilla, is perfect with dessert. Another version is called Amarone. This well-structured wine with a high alcohol content is richly dry and decisively flavored; it goes well with complex meat dishes, game and aged cheeses.

Sauvignon A straw colored, fragrant and slightly bitter wine produced in the Berici Hills from grapes of the same name. Because this is a well-structured wine, it accompanies elaborate fish dishes with ease.

Soave A wine, born in the village of Soave in the province of Verona, made with Garganega grapes and a small percentage of Trebbiano grapes. Its flat straw color becomes golden as it ages; however, it should be drunk when young. Its dry, soft flavor is slightly bitter, making it an excellent wine to drink with all fish dishes and especially with the famous baccalà dishes of the region.

Tocai The most famous Tocai of the region is the one produced in the village of Lison in the province of Venice; it is, however, also made in the area around Piave and in the Berici Hills. The vine is Tocai Friulano. This soft, flat, yellow, fresh-tasting, slightly bitter and fruity-fragrant wine goes well with all fish dishes and local first courses, especially seafood and vegetable risotto.

Torcolato Made from a blend of Vespaiolo, Garganega and Tocai grapes that are left to wither all winter before they're vinified. The must is attacked by a noble mold giving the wine an unmistakable soft and persuasive flavor that recalls a Sauterne. This highly fragrant, golden wine is very, but not unpleasantly, sweet due to its high alcohol content. It goes well with foie gras and liver patés.

Valpolicella An intensely red, dry wine fragrant with flowers but with a slightly bitter vein; it goes well with robust meat dishes.

Sarde or sfogi in saor
Serves 6

> 2 pounds of fresh sardines or 1¼ pounds
>   small sole filets
> Flour
> 1 quart peanut oil
> 3 large onions, thinly sliced
> 3 tablespoons olive oil
> 2 cups white wine from the Veneto: Pinot,
>   Soave, etc.
> 2 tablespoons raisins, softened in white wine
> 1 pint white wine vinegar
> 1 teaspoon sugar
> Salt
> Freshly ground white pepper
> 2 tablespoons pine nuts, toasted

Thoroughly clean and skin the sardines or sole. Dredge in flour and fry in abundant peanut oil, then drain on paper towels. Add the onions and olive oil to a skillet over low heat and let them sweat. Stir, and add a tablespoon or two of white wine every now and then. When the onions are very tender, add the raisins, white wine vinegar, a sprinkle of salt and pepper and the sugar. Simmer for a minute or two. Place a layer of fish fillets on a serving platter with sides. Cover them with half of the onions and half of the marinade. Sprinkle half of the pine nuts over the top. Place a second layer of fish fillets on top and cover with the remaining onions, marinade and pine nuts. Let them rest for a few hours—or up to a day or two—before serving.

There is no suggested wine because of the presence of vinegar in the dish.

TRENTINO—ALTO ADIGE

Trentino and Alto Adige stand united because of their combination of diverse traditions, habits and shared landscape. La Chiusa di Salorno in the province of Bolzano—the Salorno lock—on the Adige River is the dividing point between the two cultures and ethnicities who seemed to have found a way to thrive side by side. You will find the "Germans" toward Salorno and the Veneto-influenced Italians in the direction of Avio.

The gastronomy of Trentino-Alto Adige is the result of a strong relationship between historical traditions, but also because for a long period of time the area was a sort of stage for the German, Italian, Austrian, French and sometimes Spanish, Arab and Russian cooks who passed through and left lasting marks of their food on the region.

In Trento, you'll find good examples of a modest cuisine, born out of the necessity to simply survive, as well as the sumptuous dinners prepared for visiting popes, members of the church hierarchy and nobility. The dishes are made with fresh ingredients like mushrooms and wild berries that come out of the mountain valleys and from the banks of lakes, and long-life, cold-weather products such as polenta, cured meats, baccalà and potatoes.

The mountains—which run through the entire region—produce exquisite cheese and butter with an aroma of warm, fresh milk. The floors of the forests are rich with blueberries, raspberries and currants. Trento's market is known throughout Europe for the quality and selection of its wild mushrooms—over 250 varieties.

The rivers and streams are teeming with white and pink trout. The green and highly fragrant meadows offer perfect grazing for cattle. The one animal that's raised everywhere is the pig. Every part of it is used—every part! It's salted, it's smoked, it's cured and it's ground to makes delicious patés. As you descend towards the valleys, you'll find orchards filled with apples, pears and plums.

Alto-Adige is almost not even Italy anymore. The region's cuisine tastes like that of the cozy inns (*stube*) of the border, where the air is fragrant with cumin and anise, and where excellent wine is consumed with slices of speck—salt-cured, smoked ham—and dark, multigrain bread. There are places offering a variety of refined delicacies worthy of the greatest European restaurants.

Carne salata con fagioli or **fasoi e carne salada** Brined leg of beef cut into small pieces, then griddled and served with boiled beans. The dish is dressed in olive oil. It's a specialty of the province of Trento and the Valsugana.

Ciabatta A long, slightly flat white bread, soft on the inside with a crunchy crust. Ciabatta is originally from the area around Trento but is now found throughout Italy.

Ciope The Trentino name for the roll that is called michetta in the Veneto. The ciope is slightly smaller.

Frittata alla trentina A very rich frittata made with sardine fillets, cheese, mushrooms and artichokes.

Gefülltes Gemüse (verdure ripiene) Stuffed vegetables — tomatoes, peppers, zucchini, etc. — filled with a mixture of rice, chopped meat and other ingredients. It's a typical antipasto in the German-speaking area of the region.

Hirn Profesen or **cervella in carrozza** An antipasto from the Sudtirol, the southern Tyrol area. Cooked brains are spread on bread slices, then dipped in batter and fried.

Polpette di fagioli Puréed beans mixed with onions, eggs and breadcrumbs made into small balls and then fried.

Riebl Fritters made with buckwheat flour and milk.

Speck tirolese A type of smoked prosciutto made with pigs butchered in November and December. The shoulder, leg and belly of the pig are rubbed with salt, bay leaf, pepper and grappa, and left to marinate for two weeks. They are then slowly smoked for about three weeks and left to age for at least three months.

Testina di vitello all'agro Boiled veal's head served cold with onions, olive oil, vinegar, salt and pepper.

Türteln Round ravioli filled with sauerkraut, spinach, potatoes and chives, or with spinach and ricotta, then fried. Historically, in the Val Pusteria they were considered *la cena del sabato* — a Saturday meal.

PASTA, GNOCCHI, RICE, POLENTA
AND GRAINS

Canederli or **knödel** Large dumplings (5–10 cm) that are the emblematic food of the Tyrolean kitchen. They are a good way to use leftovers — they're made with stale bread (white or whole wheat) and often include the addition of pieces of speck, cheese, liver or prunes. They may be served in broth or as a side dish with beef stew or game.

Mòncoi Polenta cooked with water and milk, then enriched with pieces of cheese and speck.

Mus Sometimes called mosa or zuf, an "evening dish" found throughout the Tyrolean countryside and especially popular in the area around Trento. It's made with white and yellow cornmeal cooked in two-thirds milk and one-third water and finished with butter. Sometimes poppy seeds and sugar are added as well.

Pasta al sangue Tagliatelle made with flour, eggs and beef blood. It's usually dressed with butter and cheese to serve.

Pasticcio di maccheroni A "pie" made with macaroni dressed with pigeon sauce, then enclosed in sweet dough and baked. It's a specialty of Trento.

Polenta di patate A dish made with sautéed onions, pancetta and boiled potatoes combined with polenta. The ingredients are then passed through a food mill and eaten as a one-course meal with cheese or beef stew. It's made almost exclusively in the village of Conca della Pieve di Bono in the Val Giudicarie in the province of Trento.

Polenta smalzada An historic Trentino dish made with buckwheat flour polenta mixed with white wine and dressed with butter, anchovies and local grated cheese. Very often it's served with baked pork ribs or garzi di ran—sprouts from turnips that have been left in dark cold cellars in winter—that are boiled, then dressed with olive oil and vinegar.

Ravioli della Val Pusteria Ravioli made with whole-wheat pasta, filled with a mixture of spinach, cabbage and sauerkraut, or ricotta and chives, and served with melted butter and breadcrumbs fried in butter.

Roefioej See *strangolapreti* (page 93).

Schlutzkrapen Half-moon-shaped ravioli found throughout Alto-Adige. The dough is usually made with flour, water and a bit of egg; every once in awhile whole-wheat flour is added. The ravioli are generally filled with ricotta cheese and spinach. Sometimes pureed or flaked potatoes, chopped or browned onions and spices are added too. Schlutzkrapen are always dressed with melted butter and grated cheese.

Smacafam Literally a *schiacciafame* ("hunger-smasher"), this old Trentino recipe comes straight from the kitchens of the poor. It's a very dense polenta made with buckwheat flour and milk. The surprise inside the dish is an onion. The outside is covered with lardo or sausages or *luganega* (page 59).

A sweet version of this dish, made with raisins and bread-crumbs in place of onions and sausages, is served during Carnival.

Spätzle Flour dumplings made with their own special gadget, a type of grater with round holes from which the spätzle emerge as squiggly worm-like shapes. There are several versions of spätzle including one made with spinach and served with sauerkraut. Spätzle may be added to soups or served as a side dish to various entrées.

Strangolapreti or **roefioej** In the Trento area these "priest-stranglers" are little dumplings made with chard, stale bread, eggs, flour, milk and Grana cheese, dressed with butter and sage. They're a specialty of the village of Conca della Pieve di Bono in the Val Giudicarie in the province of Trento.

Tagliatelle smalzade e vitello alla trentina Egg tagliatelle served with roast veal and onions.

SOUPS

Frittatensuppe Broth served with strips of crêpes that have been made with eggs, parsley and fresh chives.

Gerstensuppe Barley soup with speck, onions, parsley and other ingredients.

Milzschnittensuppe See *zuppa di milza* (page 94).

Zuppa acida alla bolzanina Broth flavored with chopped onions, parsley, thyme, bay leaf, cumin and nutmeg, then enriched with tripe fillets and sour cream. It's served with pieces of polenta fried in butter or simple flour dumplings. In certain areas, such as the Val Venosta, the soup is finished with sauerkraut.

Zuppa al vino di Terlano A creamy soup made by whipping together — over a low flame, until it's completely smooth — a mixture of condensed beef broth, white wine from Terlano, fresh cream, cinnamon and egg yolks.

Zuppa d'orzo A first-rate soup made with barley, onions or leeks, potatoes, carrots and other ingredients. Very often it's enriched with minced speck and lardo or pork rind, or with the ribs of a castrated animal and smoked meat, or a prosciutto bone.

Zuppa di aglio A soup made with a base of chopped onions sautéed in butter and flour diluted with milk and broth. It's finished with finely chopped garlic and nutmeg along with fresh cream and chopped parsley.

Zuppa di birra A soup made with a base of flour and butter flavored with cloves, cinnamon, lemon peel and sugar. It's diluted and made creamy with a mixture of beer, fresh cream and egg yolks.

Zuppa di crostini di milza See *zuppa di milza* (below).

Zuppa di farina or **brennsuppe** A simple-to-make and very tasty soup that originated in a time of famine. It is made by toasting flour in lardo or butter. The mixture is then diluted with water. A richer version is made with flour, milk, potatoes and lardo.

Zuppa di gulasch A soup made with little pieces of beef, onions, potatoes, paprika, garlic, tomatoes, bay leaf, lemon peel, cumin and marjoram.

Zuppa di milza Meat broth enriched with small butter-toasted "sandwiches" that are filled with a mixture of spleen, eggs and marjoram. The soup, customarily served at wedding dinners, is often garnished with chopped chives.

Zuppa di trippa A light and healthy soup that is emblematic of the cuisine of the Trentino. It's made with tripe and assorted vegetables.

Zuppa Val d'Ultimo Creamed soup made with cabbage, speck and onions. It's an old-fashioned dish from Alto Adige.

CONDIMENTS, SAUCES, SALSAS AND EGGS

Salsa al cren Horseradish sauce, with origins in northern and central Europe, which is a perfect accompaniment to boiled meats. Cren or radice di barbaforte shouldn't be confused with rafano, which is also horseradish, but isn't nearly as sharp as cren.

FISH, CRUSTACEANS AND SHELLFISH

Anguilla alla trentina Cut-up pieces of eel sautéed in butter, onions and other ingredients, flavored with cinnamon and finished with white wine.

Stoccafisso alla trentina or **gröstl di stoccafisso** A very substantial dish made with dried codfish, potatoes and onions cooked in a skillet.

Trota al blu To make this dish, freshly caught trout are left to bathe in warm vinegar for about fifteen minutes, then poached in a white wine court bouillon. The trout turns a bluish shade as a result of the vinegar and the heat from cooking.

Arrosto alla pusterese Roast veal served with cabbage.

Bauernschmaus A mixture of boiled meats—smoked loin of pork, cured tongue, liver sausage, blood sausage and frankfurters—served with cumin-flavored cabbage and canederli.

Beuschel Boiled veal lung cut into pieces and cooked in a saucepan with butter, sugar, onions, anchovies, parsley, vinegar, bay leaf, thyme and lemon peel.

Camoscio alla tirolese A stew made with pieces of mountain goat marinated in red wine, vinegar and assorted herbs. It's cooked in a casserole with the marinade and sour cream.

Grostl Thinly sliced pieces of beef, veal or pork sautéed with potatoes and onions until they become crisp. The dish is served with cabbage and speck salad. Sometimes leftover pieces of meat are used.

Herrngrostl Literally, the "proprietor's dish." It's very much like *grostl* (above).

Lepre alla trentina Hare marinated with pine nuts, raisins, cinnamon, grated lemon zest and sugar before cooking. It's something like a sweet-and-sour salmì.

Lumache alla meranese Boiled cleaned snails, cut into pieces then sautéed with lardo and assorted herbs and finished with white wine, broth and pea purée.

Manzo vecchia Trento Beef stew made with vinegar and milk or cream.

Nidi di rondine Little bundles of veal stuffed with hard-cooked egg yolks wrapped in boiled ham, then cooked in a casserole with butter and broth.

Probusti Invented by Gigi Caresia, a well-known gourmet from the province of Rovereto, these are large, fresh salami made with veal, pork, kidney fat and garlic and smoked over birch and juniper wood. To serve, they are boiled or grilled and accompanied by cabbage.

Schopsernes Lamb, potato and cabbage stew.

Stecchi alla mosiana Kebabs made with pieces of sausage, brined beef, Gruyère cheese, gherkins, green and black olives and red and yellow peppers.

Tafelspitz Boiled beef.

Tonco de Pontesel The Trentino version of goulash albeit a bit less spicy than the classic recipe.

CHEESE AND DAIRY PRODUCTS

Burgeiser A whole cow's milk cheese from Alto Adige with a soft, elastic body and very irregular eyes. Its melt-in-your mouth flavor is sweet and aromatic. The low-fat version is compact with a white body that tends towards straw colored. Its delicate flavor is slightly acidic.

Eisacktaler A fresh or semi-fresh table cheese made in Alto Adige in the valley along the Isarco River. It's recognized by a furrowed rind that develops a subtle, velvety white mold as it ages and by its unmistakable rich and aromatic flavor.

Graukase This readily available Tyrolean cheese is decisively flavored. It's made with low-fat, acidic cow's milk that develops a slight grayish-green mold as it matures. The color gives the cheese its name. It doesn't have a rind. However, as it matures it can develop a yellowish color and become slightly oily. In Alto Adige it's served sliced, dressed (not marinated) with olive oil, vinegar, salt and pepper. It goes exquisitely well with black bread. Graukase is also used to describe a whole family of cheeses that derives from Hand, the German, acid milk cheese molded by hand. Quargel, Hartkase, Kochkase and other cheeses—named according to the regions of their manufacture—are produced with the same method as Graukase.

Ortler Whole cow's milk cheese produced near Dell'Ortles in the province of Bolzano. The paste of this briefly aged fatty cheese is compact and white. Its flavor is refined and delicate with an aromatic streak.

Pestolato Something like *brôs* of Piedmont (page 23) in that it's made with pieces of assorted leftover cheese that are smashed together with a mortar and pestle, then mixed with milk, grappa, white wine and fragrant herbs. The mixture is transferred to glass jars where it's mixed daily for three weeks—the resulting flavor could be defined as explosive!

Spressa A cow's milk cheese typical of the Trentino and in particular the Rendena and Giudicarie valleys. In the past it was produced only during the weeks immediately preceding the herd's departure for the high pastures. Today, it's produced year round. This very digestible, low-fat cheese is made with skimmed milk. Its sweet flavor is pleasingly acidic and lightly aromatic.

Sterzinger Partially skimmed cow's milk cheese typical of the area around Vipiteno in the province of Bolzano. As it ages, its hard, variegated rind turns from off-white to brown.

Its soft body is straw white. This is a full-flavored, lightly sharp and aromatic cheese.

Vezzena A cheese very similar to *asiago* (page 83) but with a grainier body and a sharp streak in its aged form. It was originally produced in the Vezzena plateau in the province of Trento. Today, the production has extended to the areas of Lavarone and Folgaria.

Vollfettkäse Literally, "full-fat cheese." Produced in the Vipiteno area, it's similar to *Sterzinger* (page 96) but slightly sweeter.

SWEETS AND LIQUEURS

Bienenstichtorte A yeast cake filled with pastry cream, covered with almonds and garnished with whipped cream.

Bina badiota A braided, yeasted focaccia enriched with raisins.

Brazadel A yeast donut typical of the area around Trento.

Buchteln A flatbread made up of many little balls filled with jam, then pressed together to make one piece.

Chifelini Rolled pastries very similar to croissants made with potato flour dough and filled with jam.

Christstollen A Christmas yeast cake filled with raisins, candied citron and almonds.

Crostoli Fried pastries, similar to *cenci* (page 158), made in the Trentino-Alto Adige, and in Friuli and the Veneto as well, typically around Carnival time. One version is filled with jam.

Dolce Trento A butter-fragrant cake filled with almonds.

Dorso di capriolo A tender chocolate cake filled with a thin layer of apricot jam, glazed with chocolate, garnished with pine nuts and served with whipped cream.

Ferro di cavallo A large fritter made by threading dried fruits such as apples, pears, prunes, figs and apricots on a horseshoe-shaped wire. The fruit-filled wire is dipped in a special batter and fried. The cooked pastry is cut horizontally to remove the wire, then filled with whipped cream.

Fiadoni Little triangular pastries filled with honey, almonds and rum, flavored with cloves and cinnamon. They are typical of the area around Trento.

Fortaies Italian funnel cake. The batter is fed through a special funnel so that when it drops into oil, it forms concentric shapes. They're served showered with powdered sugar.

Fugazza A simple ring-shaped yeast cake made with flour, butter, sugar, eggs and milk, and flavored with lemon zest or vanilla.

Grostoi dolci Fried rectangular or oval pastries served covered with powdered sugar.

Gugelhupf A ring-shaped yeast cake enriched with raisins and almonds.

Kaiserschmarrn A sweet omelet enriched with raisins and pieces of apple, served with powdered sugar and jam. Variations are made with bread or rice, cherries or ricotta cheese.

Kniekiechl Red currant-filled dumplings served with powdered sugar.

Kugelhupf See *gugelhupf* (above).

Linzer Torte A crostata made with shortbread pastry and filled with red currant jam and almonds found throughout Alto Adige. It's typical of the city of Linz in Austria.

Maniscalchi Pitted prunes that are softened in water, filled with almonds, dipped in batter and fried, then covered with a mixture of grated chocolate and sugar.

Murbe Large, half-moon-shaped ravioli made with wholewheat flour and filled with jam.

Nigelen See *riccetti* (below).

Pinza trentina A cake made with leftover bread soaked in milk, sugar, flour and dried figs.

Rehrucken See *dorso di capriolo* (page 97).

Riccetti Yeasted fritters covered with honey or poppy seeds.

Rosada "Priest's pudding" made with pulverized caramelized almonds, eggs, milk and sugar, also called budino del prete.

Schmarrn See *kaiserschmarrn* (above).

Spitzbuben Tyrolean shortbread cookies with jam.

Straboi or **straboli** The Trentino word for fritters.

Strauben Large grappa-flavored fritters often served with cooked fruit, applesauce or berries.

Strucolo The Italianized word for strudel.

Strudel Literally, "whirlpool." A pastry made by wrapping a very thin sheet of dough around a filling of apples, raisins, pine nuts and butter-toasted breadcrumbs. The fillings may vary — ricotta, walnuts, poppy seeds, cherries and grapes may be used.

Torta di bozzoletti A long-lasting, crunchy cake made with almond crumbs, butter, sugar and flour.

Torta di fregolotti See *torta di bozzoletti* (above).

Torta Simona A tender raisin cake flavored with lemon zest.

Zelten Whole-wheat yeast cake filled with dried fruits,

spices and herbs, then brushed with honey. It's a typical Christmas cake.

WINE

When the Romans arrived in the Trentino Alto-Adige region, they found a population that had already developed an oenology completely different from theirs. For example, unlike the Romans who stored their wine in clay amphorae, the Trentini used wooden barrels for storage as taught to them by the Germans. This German lesson was a way of rewarding the Italians for the rivers of wine that flowed over the Alps to the Danube and Moselle valleys. Then, like now, the wines of this region are prized in all of northern Europe. Trentino is home to some very important reds and Alto-Adige is dominated by its large selection of whites. In the beginning of the nineteenth century, the selection was enriched by the importation of Pinot vines to the region. The altitude, the severe climate and the thermal range all help to make masterful wines. The grapes mature slowly, allowing their pronounced fragrance and acidity to transfer to the must. The resulting wine is filled with the true smell of the grapes of origin. With a strong aroma and loaded with color, the wines of this region are truly elegant— among the best white wines in Italy and the world.

Cabernet This dry, lively red, produced with Cabernet Franc and Cabernet Sauvignon grapes in the province of Trento, has a distinct aroma of peppers and herbs. It's slightly astringent due to the presence of tannins and goes well with hearty meat dishes.

Caldaro Produced with Schiava grapes in the hills around Lake Caldaro in the province of Trento, this wine, with its brick red color, fruity aroma and mild palate, is a bit weak due to low acidity. It's a good table wine. The Caldaro produced in the province of Bolzano has the same characteristics.

Casteller With its winey aroma and dry palate, this red is a good table wine—it goes well with all dishes. It's a rather dull red color.

Eisacktaler—Valle dell'Isarco There are five white wines under this D.O.C.: Traminer Aromatico, Pinot Grigio, Sylvaner, Muller-Thurgau (made with a cross between Sylvaner and Riesling) and Veltliner. They are all dry, pale wines with shades of green. They have a characteristic aroma and are fresh with a slightly bitter streak. They are terrific wines to serve with fish, especially shellfish and crustaceans, and also work well with delicate first courses.

Lagrein This varietal originally came from the area that borders the provinces of Bolzano and Trento. The wine that's produced from it is lightly structured but pleasingly dry with an aroma of roses and violets. It goes well with light antipasti and subtle soups. If it's vinified into a full red, it becomes a more decisive wine perfect to accompany roasted meats.

Marzemino Made from the eponymous grape, this is a dry, slightly tannic, orange-shaded red wine with an aroma of berries. It's a good table wine.

Moscato A golden, pleasingly sweet wine that tastes just like the grapes from which it is made. It's a good dessert wine, perfect with cakes, dry cookies and puddings.

Pinot Trentino Early in the nineteenth century Pinot Bianco, Pinot Nero and Pinot Grigio varietals were imported from Burgundy and planted in the province of Trento. The slightly bitter, ruby-colored Pinot Nero has a mixed berries flavor. It goes well with hearty meat dishes especially those cooked with fruit sauces and preserves, and, even though it is a red wine, it should be tried with fish dishes because it possesses the same kind of bouquet and softness as the best whites. A straw-colored Pinot is produced from the other two varietals. With its delicate aroma and flavor, it goes well with antipasti and light first courses. There's also a sparkling Pinot that makes a good table wine or a perfect aperitif.

Riesling This blending of Riesling Italico and Riesling Renano grapes produces a straw-colored, well-structured, decisively fragrant, slightly acidic, very drinkable wine. It may be served as an aperitif or with an all-fish meal.

S. Maddalena or **S. Magdalener** One of the few reds produced in Alto Adige, this wine, made with Schiava grapes, is ruby colored with brick reflections, and has a winey aroma and fresh flavor. It's well structured enough to hold its own with roasted or braised meats.

Sudtirol—Alto Adige Within this D.O.C. are a group of white and red wines produced in the southern Tyrolean area of Italy. The reds must come from vineyards with elevations not higher than 700 meters and the whites from not higher than 900 meters. Among the whites are Pinot Bianco, Pinot Grigio, Riesling, Muller-Thurgau, Sylvaner, Sauvignon, Goldmuskateller (the local name for yellow Moscato) and Gewürztraminer or aromatic Traminer. They all have intense aromas, and are pale yellow (often with green reflections), fruity and dry with a slightly bitter streak (with the exclusion of the Goldmuskateller, which is decisively sweet). The dry whites, together with some Sardinian whites, are the best Italian wines to accompany crustaceans. The Moscato is a wine to drink at the end of a meal—a dessert wine—or by itself. The few red wines produced are quite elaborate. Blauburgunder or Pinot Nero has a concentrated aroma with forest undergrowth the prevailing perfume. Its mild, sweet palate makes it good with game—try it with venison cooked with blueberries. Lagrein (red and robust), Dunkel (dark) and Kretzer (pink, light and elegant) are wines that go well with meat—red meats with the Lagrein and Dunkel and white, delicate meats with the Kretzer. Last, but not least, the rare and precious Rosenmuskateller or Moscato Rosa is a sweet wine that is surprising with every sip.

Terlaner A town in the province of Bolzano where only white wines are produced: Riesling, Sylvaner, Pinot Bianco, Sauvignon and Muller-Thurgau. Their characteristics and food pairings are the same as other Alto Adige wines.

Teroldego Rotaliano Made with the Teroldego varietal in the area where the valley of the Adige River widens to make the Campo Rotaliano, this is a wine of the plains; however, with its acidity, elegance and fruity aroma, it has all of the characteristics of a mountain wine. The *superiore* is dark pink with overtones of orange and needs to age for at least two years. Its fruity bouquet becomes ethereal with age and its slightly bitter flavor becomes fuller and softer. This is the perfect wine to serve with braised meats and game and it marries well with substantial first courses and aged cheeses.

Traminer aromatico A straw yellow wine with a delicately aromatic palate and bouquet. It works well with crustaceans whose sweet flavor balances the wine's slightly bitter taste.

Valdadige A lightly fragrant and freshly flavored white wine that is straw yellow. It's a good table wine. The red, a dry, ruby-colored wine with a winey bouquet, is made with Schiava, Lambrusco and Pinot Nero grapes. These are not full-bodied wines and they don't age well.

Vin Santo Made with Pinot Bianco and Nosiola grapes that are left to dry on trellises after the harvest, an intensely sweet, amber-colored wine that is aromatically fragrant. If the must is adjusted with alcohol, the wine becomes liqueur-like. It's an end of the meal drink—or one of "meditation."

Canederli allo speck—Specknödel
Serves 6

¾ pound stale bread cut into cubes
½ cup whole milk
¼ pound smoked sausage, diced
⅓ pound speck, diced
½ onion, chopped
1 tablespoon unsalted butter
6 eggs
¼ pound all-purpose flour
½ teaspoon salt
¼ teaspoon freshly ground black pepper
¼ cup chopped chives plus more for garnish
Beef broth
Grated cheese for serving

Soak the bread cubes in the milk. Add the diced sausage and the leanest pieces of the speck. Sauté the onions in the butter, then add the fattiest pieces of speck. Let cool then add to the bread mixture. Add the eggs, flour, salt, pepper and chives. Thoroughly combine until a smooth dough is achieved. Carefully form small or large balls. Cook them in salted, boiling water for 15 minutes. Serve the cooked dumplings in beef broth garnished with chopped chives and grated cheese.

Suggested wine: Lago di Caldaro

FRIULI-VENEZIA GIULIA

While they are two distinct areas — the poorer, but more tenacious part of the region, Friuli, thrives on agriculture, while the more prosperous Venezia-Giulia has a marine-based economy — they are completely entwined with each other.

The agricultural harvest includes excellent produce like the white turnips used in the dish brovada; the small, reddish beans, fagioli della Carnia; Jerusalem artichokes; and the delicate radicchio that is cultivated in the towns of San Giorgio della Richinvelda in the province of Pordenone and Tavagnacco in the province of Udine.

Regional livestock include the prestigious pezzata rossa friulana veal, Martignacco lamb and goats. All sorts of game are popular. While the historical fish tradition of Friuli has been based upon freshwater fish (pike, tench, temoli, eel, freshwater shrimp and trout), the most important saltwater fish market is found in the town of Marano Lagunare in the province of Udine. This market, about twenty-five miles northwest of the seaside city of Trieste, may seem an odd spot for a saltwater fish market; however, at one time the surrounding lagoons and beaches were so marshy that markets were created in cities and large towns inland from the coast. Pork is the most famous meat product of the area and is typified in the great prosciutto, San Daniele.

On the tables of Trieste, with its confluence of cultures and traditions (Levantine, Hapsburg, Venetian and Jewish), you will find the most interesting cuisine of the region.

ANTIPASTI, BREADS, PIZZAS, FLATBREADS AND SAVORY TARTS

Biga A typically Friulana bread shape which is made by putting two rolls together, side by side, while they are rising, in order to make one.

Cevapcici Little sausages of Slavic origin found in the kitchens of Gorizia and Trieste. Made with a mixture of lamb, beef, pork and lots of spice, they're either grilled or pan-fried to serve.

Costa Salami made with pieces of meat that remain when pork ribs are deboned. The meat is rolled into a long, tubular shape.

Frico carnico A peasant dish made with grated Montasio cheese that's cooked in a skillet. It resembles a frittata.

Although this version is from Carnia, there is a frico variation in every Friulian valley. Frico is often served with potatoes, apples and/or onions (see recipe, page 118).

Frize or **frizze** Pork cracklings.

Granseola alla triestina Made with boiled granseola (crabs). The meat is removed from the shells, then sautéed with olive oil, onions, garlic, breadcrumbs, lemon and parsley. The mixture is spread on crostini to serve as appetizers. It's a typical antipasto of the Istrian peninsula.

Liptauer guarnito A creamed cheese made with ricotta or stracchino mixed with onions, cumin, chives, anchovies, butter, mustard, parsley, capers and paprika. It's spread on whole-wheat bread to serve. Liptauer has its origins in Central Europe, specifically, Hungary.

Marcundela Meatloaf made with lungs, liver, sweetbreads, pine nuts and nutmeg, then enclosed in pork caul fat. It's dredged in cornmeal and fried to serve.

Ossocollo Salami made with pork neck meat (not chopped), lardo, salt and spices.

Pan de frizze salato Friulano bread made with flour, yeast, sour cream, butter, pork cracklings and ground lardo.

Prosciutto di sauris Prosciutto smoked with pinewood, myrtle branches and herbs.

Prosciutto in crosta di pane col rafano Ham covered in bread dough, then baked and served sliced, covered with grated horseradish. This is originally a Czech dish.

Rodoleti de persuto Slices of raw or cooked prosciutto wrapped around pickles. In the *osterie* (inns), of the region, they are traditionally served with a glass of wine.

Salame alla friulana Salami of the area cut into slices, sautéed, doused with vinegar and served hot with sliced polenta.

Salviade Sage fritters.

Sardele in sesame Sardines marinated in assorted herbs. The term sesame is Istrian in origin.

Struzza A soft bread found in Friuli. It's long, with three or four slashes at each end.

PASTA, GNOCCHI, RICE, POLENTA AND GRAINS

Bisna An old, traditional rustic dish from the mountains of the region in which beans and cabbage are stirred into polenta, which is then topped with onions fried in lardo.

Cialzons or **cjalzons** Filled pastas based on an antique recipe, which, according to documentation, goes back to at least the fourteenth century. They're typical of the Carnia area. The little semi-circular bundles have sweet and savory fillings that may include spinach, chocolate, raisins, candied citron and whole-wheat bread. They're then dressed with sugar, cinnamon, smoked ricotta and very aged Carnico cheese. Sometimes pears, plums or prunes are used instead of spinach. Another version uses a filling of meat, eggs, cheese and a combination of fresh herbs (basil, mint, sage and marjoram) and yet another might include brains and roast chicken.

Cialzons or **cjalzons della Val Gortana** A simple flour-and-water pasta wrapped around a filling of fresh ricotta, smoked ricotta, buckwheat bread, milk, raisins, grappa, parsley, onions, cinnamon, pepper and sugar.

Cialzons or **cjalzons della Valle del Butsono** A version filled with puréed potatoes, grated smoked ricotta, parsley, basil, mint, melissa, wild fennel, grated pears, jam, bitter chocolate and crumbled ladyfingers.

Cialzons or **cjalzons di Arta** or **ciargnei** Calzones from the province of Udine filled with potatoes, pears, apples, lemon zest, parsley, basil, mint, marjoram, raisins, crumbled cookies, smoked ricotta, chocolate, jam, sugar and cinnamon. They're dressed with melted butter, cinnamon, sugar and grated, smoked ricotta.

Cialzons or **cjalzons di Cercivento** A version filled with potatoes, onions sautéed in butter, chard, melissa, marjoram, mint, basil, parsley, smoked ricotta, cinnamon, bitter chocolate and lemon zest.

Cialzons or **cjalzons di Ovaro** Another variation filled with fresh ricotta, breadcrumbs, grated aged cheese, parsley, lemon zest, wine-soaked raisins and eggs.

Cialzons or **cjalzons di Paularo** A version in which the pasta dough is made with flour and potatoes. The filling is made of pieces of pork crackling.

Cialzons or **cjalzons di Pesaris** Another version with a flour-and-potato dough. They're filled with chopped parsley, basil and leeks and breadcrumbs made from whole wheat, corn and white breads sautéed in butter. Smoked ricotta, grated cheese, eggs, sugar, rum, raisins and lemon zest are added to the mixture.

Cialzons or **cjalzons di Pontebba** A version with a filling made with crumbled smoked ricotta, dried figs, raisins, walnuts, plums, cinnamon and sugar.

Cialzons or **cjalzons di Timau** A pasta made with flour and eggs filled with potatoes, butter, sugar, cinnamon, onions, raisins, parsley, mint, lemon zest and eggs.

Cialzons or **cjalzons di Tolmezzo** A pasta made with flour and potatoes filled with raisins, peanuts, bitter chocolate, walnuts, candied citron, ricotta, ladyfingers, jam, honey, cinnamon and lemon zest.

Cialzons or **cjalzons di Udine** or **di planure** A variation filled with apricot jam, cocoa, sugar, raisins, grated pears, pine nuts, lemon peel and cinnamon.

Ciargnei See *cialzons* (above).

Gnocco di pane A large dumpling made with cubes of stale bread that have been fried in butter, then combined with eggs, milk, flour and chopped prosciutto. The dumpling is steamed and served with melted butter and grated Grana cheese.

Gnocchetti de Gries Small dumplings made with semolina flour that are usually served in broth. They're typical of Friuli.

Gnocchi con il cacao Potato gnocchi dressed with bitter chocolate, candied citron, raisins, cinnamon and sugar.

Gnocchi di prugne or **de susini** Very large potato gnocchi each filled with a prune or dried apricot, then dressed with breadcrumbs browned in butter, cinnamon and sugar. Although this is originally an Austrian dish, over the years, it's become part of the cuisine of Trieste.

Lasagna al papavero Lasagne dressed with melted butter, sugar and poppy seeds. It's a dish from Trieste.

Matufi Polenta cooked in water and milk, then left to solidify on a cutting board. It's cut into slices that are layered with a filling of sautéed sausages, sage, butter and montasio cheese then baked to serve.

Mesta Polenta made with yellow and white cornmeal and served with milk.

Mesta e fasui Similar to the above except that beans and their liquid are cooked with the polenta. It's served with melted butter.

Offelle alla triestina A type of pasta made with potatoes then filled with chopped meat, sausages and spinach. The word *offelle* is used for other food, especially for a type of pastry.

Paparot A soup-like polenta made with white and yellow cornmeal and water in which spinach has cooked. It's finished with spinach, lardo and garlic.

Patugoli Similar to the Venetian *mosa* (page 75), but dressed with grated Grana or ricotta salata as well as butter and milk.

Pistum Gnocchi made with breadcrumbs, sugar, eggs, mixed herbs and soaked raisins, served in a pork broth.

Risot cui cròz A typical risotto made with frogs.

Strucolo de spinaze A roulade (strudel) made with potato pasta that's filled with ricotta, spinach and Parmesan cheese and served with melted butter and browned breadcrumbs.

Zuf Something like *mesta* (page 106) — essentially, yellow cornmeal and white wheat flour cooked together and then served with cold milk. There is also a version in which a purée of winter squash is added about three-quarters of the way through the cooking process.

Zuf di coce Winter squash or pumpkin cooked in water and milk, then puréed and served with cold milk.

SOUP

Acqua bruciata A creamy soup made by toasting flour in butter, then diluting it with milk.

Brodetto alla Triestina Fish soup from Trieste. It's slightly different from the one from Grado (below) because of the addition of tomato conserve, razor clams and large crabs called granciporri.

Brodetto di Grado or **boreto alla graisana** Fish soup made with a base of garlic fried in olive oil and vinegar-flavored herbs, then finished with hot water and pepper. Traditionally, it's cooked with only local fish such as monkfish, scorpion fish, wolf fish, San Pietro fish, etc. Tomatoes are not usually added. The original version of the soup was made only with turbot and served with polenta.

Brodetto di Marano Lagunare Fish soup almost identical to the *brodetto di Grado* (above), except that it's completely strained so there is no sign of bones. There's a great tradition of fish cuisine in Marano Lagunare because it's home to one of the most important fish markets of the region.

Brodetto di seppioline Cuttlefish soup with olive oil, parsley and garlic.

Brodo brustolà A creamy soup made by adding flour to brown butter, then diluting it with broth or water. After removing from the heat, it's finished with beaten eggs, cumin and marjoram. It's served over slices of toasted bread and garnished with grated cheese.

Jota, jote, iota or **ota** Soup made with beans, *brovade* (page 112) or sauerkraut, potatoes, pork and smoked pork rind and a mixture of finely chopped lardo, then thickened with corn or wheat flour. There are variations where the soup is cooked in a mixture of water and milk, and vegetables such as radicchio, chicory, celery, wild herbs and potatoes are added. There are also "lean" versions of the soup made without meat. In Trieste some cooks add barley and some thicken it with winter squash.

Minestra carsolina A soup made from broth to which little crumbs made from an egg and flour dough are added.

Minestra de bobici (granturco) Straight out of the Slavic kitchen, a soup made by boiling beans, potatoes and tomatoes together with a prosciutto bone and a pig's foot. Unripe corn kernels (bobici) are cooked in another pot. Part of the corn and the other vegetables are strained then added back to a single pot in order to thicken the soup. It's flavored with finely chopped lardo and garlic.

Panade A soup made with stale bread flavored with fennel seeds, pepper and Parmesan cheese, then baked. Panade is a specialty of Friuli.

Papazoi A peasant soup made with beans, barley and corn kernels.

Sope de cjaval An interesting soup made by topping sliced bread, covered with brown butter and sugar, with warm red wine.

Suscía Bean soup flavored with onions fried in butter and thickened with a bit of flour. It's garnished with mixed herbs.

Uardi e fasui A classic and tasty soup made with beans and barley.

CONDIMENTS, SAUCES AND EGGS

Salsa di cren A sauce made with freshly grated horseradish and breadcrumbs fried in butter. Grated apples are added to balance the sharpness of the horseradish. It's cooked in wine and broth and is usually served with boiled meats.

Salsa di ribes A dense sweet-and-sour sauce made with red currants, sugar, vinegar, lemon zest and red wine. It's generally served with boiled or roast meats but most often game.

Salsa di rognone A sauce that starts with the painstaking process of purifying veal kidneys by letting them soak in water and vinegar, or covering them with salt. They're then very thinly sliced and sautéed in butter with onions, parsley, sage, basil and rosemary. The cooked sauce is pounded in a mortar and pestle, diluted with orange juice and then cooked again with candied citron, sugar and vinegar.

Tocj di Vòres A creamy sauce made by sautéing grated smoked ricotta in butter, flour and salt, then diluting it with milk. It's used to dress polenta.

Tride A "little" sauce made by sautéing garlic and onions with lardo. It goes very well with *brovade* (page 112), soup and cabbage.

Us in fonghet or **uova al funghetto** A specialty of Venezia Giulia that goes perfectly with polenta. It is made by peeling soft boiled eggs, cutting them in half, then finishing them in a porcini (or other wild mushroom) sauce with a touch of tomato.

FISH, CRUSTACEANS AND SHELLFISH

Baccalà alla cappuccina Dried cod that has been pounded and left to soak in water for hours, then cut into pieces, floured and fried in butter and olive oil with onions. Anchovy fillets, bay leaf, raisins, pine nuts, cinnamon, nutmeg, sugar, salt and pepper are added to the same pot and all the ingredients are cooked together with water and breadcrumbs. This dish loves to be served with polenta.

Bisat nel stec Skewered, grilled pieces of eel flavored with bay leaves.

Bulo The Triestina name for murice, a very large sea snail.

Busara or **buzara di scampi** A dish made with many different kinds of crustaceans, but usually with shrimp, that are quickly sautéed in olive oil and garlic and then finished with white wine, paprika, parsley and breadcrumbs — and sometimes a bit of tomato. It was originally from Istria but is now made throughout the region, as far as Venice.

Caparozzoli The name used in the Veneto and in Friuli for clams.

Capelonghe Razor clams.

Capesante alla triestina Parboiled scallops or oysters that are cut into pieces and sautéed in butter with onions, parsley, watercress and the white part of bread. The mixture is then put into the shells and quickly gratinéed.

Cappe lisce A smooth-shell bivalve.

Datoli Sea urchins.

Dondolo A bivalve, also called tartufo del mare, similar to a clam.

Garuse The Friulan word for the very large sea snails called murici spinosi in Italian.

Giambars Freshwater shrimp. They're usually cooked with fresh herbs and served with polenta.

Granseola or **granzevola** or **grancevola alla triestina** Coarsely chopped meat of a large crab mixed with olive oil, garlic, parsley, lemon and breadcrumbs. The mixture is put into the shells then gratinéed.

Merluzzo all'istriana Cod fillets that have been sautéed in olive oil with onions and a purée of garlic and parsley. The fillets are removed from the skillet and set aside. Capers, chopped sardines, a bit of flour or grated raw potato, hot pepper flakes, broth and lemon juice are added to the skillet and simmered. The cod fillets are placed in the sauce and then served very hot.

Mussoli or **pedoci** Mussels.

Porcheto The same as *bulo* (page 109).

Scazzoni Small river fish usually floured, fried and served covered with chopped parsley and garlic.

Seppie alla gradese Cuttlefish cooked in a saucepan with white wine, garlic and parsley.

Seppioline alla granseola Small cuttlefish stuffed with crab, butter and egg yolks, then baked. This preparation is a specialty of Grado.

Spinarelli Small freshwater fish usually served *in saor* (sweet-and-sour style).

MEAT

Arrosto di manzo alla friulana Beef roast browned in lardo and onions and flavored with cumin seeds, horseradish and cloves.

Bollito friulano A mixture of pork cuts including smoked pieces and *musetto* (page 111) that is boiled, then served with *brovada* (page 112) and horseradish sauce.

Brasadule di Codroipo Roast loin of pork cooked with garlic, sage, rosemary and white wine.

Calandraca A stew made with pieces of veal, mutton or steer (castrated beef), potatoes and other ingredients. The name references the word *calandra,* a medieval boat on which this dish was cooked.

Cotoletta alla viennese or **Weinerschnitzel** Unlike the Milanese veal cutlet, which is made with a loin chop, a cutlet made with sliced leg of veal. The slices are dipped in egg, then in breadcrumbs, and fried in lardo or olive oil. The cutlets are garnished with olives and anchovy fillets. This dish is straight out of the Central European tradition.

Fegato di maiale alla triestina Slices of pork liver wrapped around bay leaves then enclosed in pork caul and baked with white wine.

Gulasch A beef and potato stew spiced with paprika, found in the kitchens of Trieste. Its origins are in Central Europe, specifically Hungary. It may be served, as it is in Hungary, as a soup or, slightly thicker, as an entrée.

Jeurs in salse or **lepre in salsa** Hare that is first marinated for at least twelve hours in a cooked marinade of vinegar, red wine, peppercorns, sage, carrots, celery, parsley, bay leaf, rosemary and oregano. It is then cut into pieces and browned in butter, olive oil, chopped onions, smashed garlic and chopped prosciutto fat and then cooked with white wine and the strained marinade. Toward the end of the cooking process, some butter-toasted flour is added to the pot to thicken the sauce. The hare is served with toasted polenta slices.

Lepre alla boema A sweet-and-sour dish made with pieces of hare that are stewed with various ingredients and herbs, then flavored with sugar and vinegar. It's an example of the strong Hapsburg influence in the kitchens of Trieste.

Mule A blood sausage enriched with whole-wheat flour, sugar, raisins, cinnamon, pepper and breadcrumbs. It's cut into cubes to serve.

Musetto The most famous cooking sausage of its kind in Friuli and in Alto Veneto. It's made with lean pieces of pork, pork rind and head (*muso*), hence the name musetto. It's usually flavored with cinnamon, coriander, nutmeg, hot pepper flakes, salt, pepper and Tocai, Picolit or Marsala wine. It's very much like *cotechino* (page 132) except that it's leaner and the ingredients are more finely chopped. In Friuli it's often served with *brovada* (page 112) or beans.

Pastizzada de anso Boned, larded loin of pork that's slowly stewed with celery, carrots, parsley, rosemary, sage, white wine, salt, pepper and other spices.

Porzina or **porcina** A boiled mixture of both lean and fatty cuts of pork—some smoked, some not. It's eaten hot with cabbage, mustard and horseradish. This dish is popular on the *tavole calde*—hot buffets—in the restaurants around Trieste.

Rambasici Little bundles of cabbage leaves stuffed with ground pork, beef, sausage and garlic, parsley, eggs and paprika. They are cooked in a skillet and finished with a shower of cheese and breadcrumbs. The Slavic dish is sometimes referred to as *uccellini scappati nella verza* ("birds hiding in cabbage").

Selvaggina in paiz Venison — or other "noble" game — that is marinated in white wine, carrots, celery, parsley, aromatic herbs, ginger, cinnamon, cloves and peppercorns for at least three days. The meat is then baked with carrots, parsley, white wine, cream, breadcrumbs and pepper and served with its strained sauce.

Stinco di vitello al forno Veal shank baked with smashed boiled potatoes — the idea is for the potatoes to soak up the cooking juices. This is a classic dish from the kitchens of Trieste.

Testina alla carniola Boiled veal's head cut into strips, then mixed with a sauce made with a purée of boiled brains, olive oil, vinegar, garlic and horseradish.

Toc de purcit A very substantial stew made with beef, liver, white wine, cloves and cinnamon. It goes very well with polenta.

VEGETABLES

Asparagi di Sant'Andrea The unique asparagus grown in the village of Sant'Andrea in the province of Gorizia. They are boiled and served garnished with butter-fried breadcrumbs and a spicy egg sauce.

Brovade or **brovada** or **broade** Sliced white turnips that are left to ferment on grape lees for one to three months. It's served as a side dish with *musetto* (page 111), or sautéed in lardo and garlic, then served with boiled meats, or used as a soup ingredient.

Crauti acidi or **capuzi garbi** A dish — basically, sauerkraut — made with sliced and salted cabbage that's fermented in barrels. It comes to the region from Germany and is a good accompaniment to cooked sausages and smoked pork products.

Fagioli alla smolz Cooked borlotti beans dressed with a sauce made with lardo, butter and onions, then finished with vinegar and a bit of flour to thicken.

Fritole di San Giovanni Long, thin, oblong-shaped fritters made with a mixture of potato purée, flour, salt and seed oil. They are first boiled, then fried in butter and, to serve, topped with butter and cinnamon. In Friuli, they are typically served as an entrée during the festival of San Giovanni.

Matavilz, rucola e fasoi A salad found throughout Trieste made with valerian, arugula and borlotti beans.

Patate in tecia alla friulana or **uso Baviera** Boiled, smashed potatoes that are first sautéed in lardo and onions, then finished by cooking in a bit of broth.

Topinambur Jerusalem artichokes.

Radicchietto nano di Gorizia The first, very tender radicchio leaves, picked when they're about as big as fingernails.

Zartuffi Jerusalem artichokes, or *topinambur* (above).

Zastoch A mixture of cooked green beans, sliced potatoes and pieces of winter squash sautéed in lardo and onions.

CHEESE AND DAIRY PRODUCTS

Asìn A Friuliano cheese made with whole cow's milk and barely aged. It's from the mountain area of Asio—which gives the cheese its name—in the province of Udine.

Carnia Cheese from Friuli made with cow's and sheep's milk. Its thin, smooth rind is yellow tending towards brown. Its body is yellowish-white. It can be a good table cheese, but it's really good grilled or cooked in a skillet and served with polenta.

Montasio A cow's milk cheese from the mountain pastures of the southern part of Friuli. It's a cooked, hard-paste cheese with a smooth, elastic rind that can be golden straw colored to reddish. When fresh, its sweet, compact body is straw white. As it ages its color deepens, the eyes get a bit smaller, the body becomes flaky and it develops a lively, almost sharp flavor.

Pecorino del Selz Sheep's milk cheese made in the Monfalcone area. The light rind is brownish and the compact body is straw colored. It's a very flavorful cheese, almost salty and slightly sharp.

SWEETS

Buchtel Little bundles of dough made with butter, flour, yeast, egg, milk and lemon zest, then filled with jam. This pastry originated in Austria.

Budino di avena A delicious pudding made with toasted oats cooked in milk and thickened with eggs and sugar. The mixture is then poured into a mold that has been bathed with Marsala wine or another liqueur. Once set, it's unmolded to serve.

Budino di patate Pudding made with puréed potatoes, raisins, pine nuts, cream, eggs and a bit of nutmeg, and baked in a water bath.

Buzolai Very simple ring-shaped cookies.

Castagnole di Sacile Chestnut-shaped fried dumplings made with sugar, butter, flour, eggs and lemon zest.

Chifeletti Half-moon-shaped pastries made with potato dough that are fried then covered with powdered sugar and cinnamon.

Crostoli Pastries of fried dough, sometimes filled with jam, served during the Carnival celebrations. They're made not only in Friuli but also in Trentino and the Veneto.

Fiori di sambuco al miele Elderflowers that are dipped in batter, fried and then doused with honey to serve.

Gubana del Friuli A Friulian bread that is part of a great tradition of sweet breads enriched with various ingredients. Gubana is made by layering walnuts, raisins, pine nuts, chocolate, etc., on a sheet of yeast dough then rolling the dough around the filling. The rolled dough is then made into a circle and baked. It's served sprinkled with grappa.

Koch de gries Molded sweet semolina.

Koch de risi Molded sweet rice with raisins, candied citron and orange peel.

Kolazie Ring-shaped cookies made with flour, butter and sugar, then covered with chopped almonds. This recipe has its origins in Slovenia and Austria.

Kugelhupf or **Cuguluf** A quintessentially German recipe for a highly yeasted, ring-shaped cake enriched with raisins and almonds. It's similar to panettone.

Mulis A very tasty, almost impossible-to-find blood sausage from Gorizia.

Mulze Fat, sweet sausages made with cooked pork blood, raisins, pine nuts, sugar and other spices. They're very much like *mulis* (above).

Palatschinken Jam-filled crêpes covered with powdered sugar.

Panafracchi Ring-shaped cookies made with flour, walnuts, almonds, honey, herbs and spices.

Pane indorato A sweet that's as tasty as it is simple, made by dipping bread slices into a sweet batter, then frying them.

Panini di Pasqua Sweet little sandwiches served on Easter in order to insure good times. The yeasted bread is made, according to an antique recipe, with corn flour, sugar, raisins, butter, eggs and milk.

Perseghini Crunchy, ring-shaped cookies made with butter, flour and sugar, typical of the area around the city of Cividale in the Friuli region.

Pistum From an old recipe, dumplings made with sweet bread, breadcrumbs, sugar, eggs, raisins, candied citron, pine nuts, melted butter and cinnamon. They are cooked in a cotechino broth.

Polenta dolce di farina bianca A very simple dessert, much loved by children, made with white polenta cooked with milk and sugar, then enriched with eggs and lemon zest. The polenta is divided in two and cocoa powder is mixed into one half. The mixtures are then layered in a cake dish, with wafers separating the layers, and then baked.

Potizza, putitza or **putizza** A winter holiday cake, typical of the eastern part of Friuli, very similar to the *gubana* (page 114). The major difference is that the gubana is lighter and more yeasty.

Povesen A very rare dessert of Bohemian origins that was, at one time, found all over Trieste. It's very similar to *schnitte* (below) — the only difference is that in povesen, the bread is soaked in white wine instead of milk.

Presnitz An Easter cake in which a simple dough made with flour, butter, sugar and eggs is filled with mixed dried fruits, herbs and spices, then rolled up and twisted into a spiral. For all intents and purposes, this cake is a specialty of Trieste; however, it's originally from the town of Castagnevizza, no longer a part of Italy, and before that, Hungary.

Rosade A type of pudding made with eggs, sugar, milk, lemon peel, cinnamon and sugar.

Schnitte A dish made by soaking slices of bread, sugar and lemon peel in milk. The slices are then dipped in beaten eggs, fried and covered with sugar.

Straube See *crostoli* (page 114).

Strucolo di ricotta Strudel filled with very fresh ricotta. Other versions are filled with walnuts, apples, cherries and other ingredients.

Titole A well-known Easter cake of braided dough with colored, hard-cooked eggs sunk in at each end. It's full of symbolism: the braid references the snake in the Garden of Eden and the eggs, fertility. This cake dates back to the Phoenician era.

There are two areas in Friuli known for their excellent wines: the Collio Goriziano and the Colli Orientali, just beyond Udine and stretching all the way to the Slovenian border. The combination of shale terrain, daily high/low temperatures, winds that travel through the valleys and northern currents blocked by the alpine elevations provide congenial, isolated areas where vines have found an ideal growing spot. Extraordinarily refined wines are the result. For the most part, these are exceptional white wines with the occasional very interesting red. Names of the region's wines that evoke praise and admiration include Sauvignon, Picolit, Ramandolo and Ribolla Gialla. Many of the wines have a thousand-year-old history — Picolit and Ribolla date back to the end of the twelfth century.

Cabernet Cabernet vines are found throughout Friuli and produce important wines, but it's in the area of Collio in the province of Gorizia that Cabernet acquires a certain elegance, producing wines even superior to the Cabernet of the Veneto. This dry wine, with an herbaceous aroma, is a lively ruby red color with a tendency towards garnet as it ages. It's the perfect wine for red meats and game.

Merlot An excellent table wine found throughout Friuli — winey, dry, tannic, and, if it's properly vinified and ages for a few years, quite refined. It goes well with hearty meat dishes.

Picolit An unlucky vine that was abundantly produced, widely distributed and enjoyed fame up until the eighteenth century when disaster struck — the grape blossoms aborted themselves before reaching maturity, so at harvest time the bunches had only a few grapes. However, the obstinate and tenacious Friulani wine growers took the seeds from those few remaining grapes and began the growing process over until they could produce the elegant wine once again. With its rich straw color, its ample floral aroma that evolves into fragrant mature fruit, its alluring, honey-sweet (but not nauseatingly so) flavor, it makes a splendid dessert wine that should be drunk alone.

Pinot Produced throughout Friuli, Pinot Bianco and Pinot Grigio, when young, are clear with greenish reflections. They have a delicate but persistent clean aroma. The dry palate has an aromatic spot that leaves a slightly bitter but pleasing taste in the mouth. Pinot Grigio has a slightly fuller color. Both are great wines to drink with fish dishes.

Ramandolo Made in the eponymous town in the province of Udine, a sweet wine produced with Verduzzo Friulano grapes. The grapes are vinified after drying out from the autumn harvest until March. The result is a Madeira-style wine, amber in color, with an aroma of raisins and mature fruits. The flavor is sweet with a slightly bitter spot that sometimes can be too pronounced. It's delicious with fresh fruit, and incomparable with the classic Friulian cake, gubana.

Refosco Until the nineteenth century, the only red grapes cultivated in Friuli. The wine produced from them is ruby red with shades of violet, with a winey aroma and a fresh, pleasing flavor with a hint of acid that makes it very drinkable. It's a wine to drink when young, with first courses and white meats, but it goes equally well with the entire meal.

Ribolla gialla A straw-colored, well-balanced, full-flavored white wine with an intense aroma. It's a great wine to drink with fish but also with spicy antipasti.

Riesling Made from two different grapes, Riesling Italico and Riesling Renano. The Renano makes a more aromatic, intensely fragrant, dry wine. The Italico has the same structure but makes a less elegant wine. The two grapes can be vinified together or separately. The widely distributed Riesling Renano is produced in the Colli Orientali, Aquileia, Sull'Isonzo and Trieste.

Sauvignon Like Merlot and Cabernet, this varietal comes from Bordeaux. It's straw colored with a delicate, floral bouquet and a full, harmonious flavor making it a splendid wine for fish and shellfish dishes.

Schioppetino An ancient vine that once seemed condemned to extinction. However, in the past few years it's been revived with great success. The wine has a deep red color and intense aroma. Its full flavor is soft, ample and tannic, the perfect accompaniment to meat dishes. There's also a slightly sweet version that makes for a very original dessert wine.

Tocai Very closely related to the Tocai produced in the Veneto in the village of Lison, but unrelated to the wine with the same name produced in Hungary. The Hungarian Tocai is made with the Furmint varietal and is a sweet and syrupy wine. The Italian Tocai is a dry, soft wine with scents of almond. It's straw colored with shades of gold. This wine is meant to be drunk when young. Drink it with fish and vegetable first courses with delicate sauces.

Verduzzo in spite of its name ("greenish"), it's a warm golden color. When young, scents of fruit escape and its dry flavor is sometimes aggressive. It ages well because of its high levels of tannin. It's a table wine but is particularly good with hearty first courses.

Frico

Serves 6

1 thinly sliced onion
Butter or melted lardo
1¼ pounds Montasio cheese, thinly sliced
Optional: 2 eggs

Slowly sauté the onions in the fat—make sure that they do not take on color—for about 20 minutes. Add the sliced cheese, and, if desired, beaten eggs. At this point, raise the heat and let the cheese melt until a little golden crust is formed, making sure not to let it stick to the pan. Turn over the "frittata" by letting it slip onto a dinner plate that's placed over the skillet and quickly turned upside down. It's important to do this as quickly as possible, because the frico needs to stay crunchy on the outside and soft on the inside. Cook it until the other side achieves a golden crust. Add salt and pepper as desired.

There's a version that uses only cheese and another that allows for the addition of grated potatoes and apples.

Suggested wine: Riesling

EMILIA-ROMAGNA

There have been two great schools of gastronomic thought in Italy since the Renaissance and Baroque eras—the papal Romana and Emiliana.

Emilia has produced some of the greatest chefs and authors in Italian history. Just think about the Bolognese, Bartolomeo Stefani, author of *Arte di Ben Cucinare* (*The Art of Good Cooking*); the chefs of the courts of Ferrara, Giovan Battista Rossetti and Cristoforo Messisbugo; Vincenzo Cervio from Parma; and Giulio Cesare Tirelli from Bologna. This culture of great chefs and their recipes have formed the base of the region's food—solid, well dressed, flavorful, generous and substantial.

Emilia-Romagna has two distinct gastronomic temperaments—the Emiliani are tranquil and pleasure-loving while the Romagnoli are sanguine and decisive. The terrain of Emilia is a level landscape, plains that rise gently into hills. Romagna is a bit more severe with the Appenine Mountains on one side and the Adriatic on the other.

Emilia is agricultural, producing the famous Parmesan cheese, sugar beets, Vignola cherries—among the best in Italy—asparagus from Altedo and a thousand other delicacies.

Pork is the meat *per eccellenza* in Emilia—it's added to all the extraordinary salami of the region, used for prosciutto di Parma and Langhirano, for the Bolognese mortadella, salami from Felino, culatello from Zibello and numerous other lesser known delicacies.

Emilia may be the only region in Italy where the tradition of rolling out pasta with a rolling pin is still in widespread use. Maybe it's a myth, but it seems that the Emiliani can't stand the smooth surface of machine-made pasta. They believe that pasta should have a slightly rough surface so it can better absorb sauces and dressings.

The Romagnola cuisine is typified by piadina (griddled flatbread) spit-roasted meats and fragrant, wild vegetables. Pasta is made with water instead of eggs, then is made into uniform shapes like strozzapreti, garganelli and maccheroni. These pasta shapes gave birth to a world of modest but tasty soups.

Romagna, with its coastline, brings a mountain of tasty fish to the table, used in fishermen's soups, grilled or fried. Of note are the sweet eels and freshly caught *pesce azzurro* (bluefish).

Bartolaccio Very large, rectangular ravioli, filled with potato purée, pancetta and Parmesan cheese, a specialty of the town of Tredozio in the province of Forlì. They're cooked on a griddle similar to the one used for making piadina.

Batù d'oca A Romagnola recipe for goose preserved in its own fat, similar to the French confit d'oie.

Belecott A cooked sausage, similar to cotechino, made with both fat and lean pork cuts and flavored with cinnamon, nutmeg and cloves. It's served with piadina in the areas around Russi and Ravenna.

Bevr'in vin A cup of hot beef broth diluted with good red wine. It's a recipe from Mantua.

Bocconcini alla modenese Little delicacies made by first dipping sliced bread in milk, then making them into little sandwiches with prosciutto or mortadella, cheese and white truffles, then dipping them in egg and flour before frying.

Bocconotti alla bolognese Small vol au vent filled with a rich ragù made with chicken giblets, sweetbreads and white truffles.

Bondiola Salami made with the upper muscle of pig's neck and cured in either pork or beef casing. Similar to *coppa d'estate* (page 121), it's mostly made in the province of Piacenza.

Borlenghi or **burlenghi** Very thin disks made with a simple flour, water and salt dough. They are cooked on special irons called *cottole*, greased with pork rind, then cooked over a wood-burning fire. They're filled with pesto made with garlic, lardo and rosemary, folded into four and eaten when hot. There is also a fried version.

Buricche ferraresi Round ravioli made with puff pastry that, because the recipe originates in the Jewish kitchens of Ferrara, is made not with butter but with veal or goose fat. They're filled with chopped chicken and onions browned in olive oil, broth-soaked bread and eggs.

Burt-lèna The Piacentina version of the Bolognese *crescente* (page 121).

Cassoni Piadina filled with chard, spinach or field greens, folded in half and cooked on a scorching hot griddle. Historically, raisins were added to the greens. These days there are many different fillings: tomatoes and mozzarella, sausage, mushrooms, winter squash and potatoes, etc. There is also a fried version.

Chizze reggiane or **chezzi** Dumplings made with dough similar to that of the torta fritta, or of the gnocco or *crescente* (below) except that they're filled with shards of Parmesan cheese before frying. There's also a version filled with greens.

Ciacci A type of *borlenghi* (page 120) made with chestnut flour and eaten with ricotta or another soft cheese. It's a specialty of the foothills of the Alps near Reggio Emilia and Modena.

Ciacci di ricotta Similar to borlenghi except that ricotta and yeast are added to the dough. They are cooked on a waffle iron and usually eaten with prosciutto or coppa.

Ciccioli Little delicacies made with pork or goose cracklings.

Coppa d'estate Salami made with meat from shoulder of pork that is salted, spiced and stuffed into a cylindrically shaped casing. It must be aged for at least six months. The best version comes from Piacenza.

Coppa d'inverno or **coppa di testa** Salami made with meat from the whole head of the pig including the snout, cheeks, tongue and ears. It's completely deboned, broken into pieces then cooked in saltwater and vegetables. After it's cooked, it's rolled into a cloth, weighted and left to cool. It doesn't need to age. It's served sliced.

Coppia, coppieta or **ciùpeta** A typical bread shape from Ferrara.

Cornetto Another bread shape from Ferrara.

Crescente, crescenta, crescentina Crisps made with a dough of flour, water or milk, salt and yeast. It's thinly rolled, cut into squares or rectangles then fried in lardo or oil. They're served with assorted cured meats and cheeses. They're very similar to the *gnocco fritto* (page 122) or the *torta fritta* (page 124). In Bologna crescentine are like the above description, while the gnocco al forno or crescenta is made with yeasted dough mixed with ciccioli, prosciutto or pancetta, then baked and served as bread with cured meats or used to make sandwiches.

Crocetta A cross-shaped bread from Ferrara.

Culatello Extremely prestigious salami produced in the lower area of the region around Parma called the Verdiana, which includes the towns of Zibello, Busseto, Colorno, Soragna and San Secondo. It's made with the rear part of a pork thigh. It's salted and spiced while warm — that is, immediately after the pig has been butchered—then put inside the bladder casing and left to age for at least a year in the humid area of a room usually designated for curing prosciutto.

Erbazzone A thin-crusted tart filled with chard, lardo, herbs and Parmesan cheese. The tart, found in the Reggiano area of the region, can have other names according to the dough or fillings that are used for it: scarpazzone, morazzone, scarpazza and scarpazzit. There's also a sweet version.

Erbazzone fritto A little cake made with chard or spinach, eggs and Parmesan cheese. It's usually made like a frittata and cooked in lardo.

Fiocchetto Raw salami similar to culatello, but of lower quality. The meat comes from the underside of the thigh and the leftovers from making culatello. After salting, fiocchetto is aged for at least three months.

Fiorettino Salami from Reggio Emilia. The way pork fat and lean meat are mixed together gives fiorettino more flavor than the ingredients would be expected to produce.

Galantina A mixture of prosciutto, tongue, black truffles, pistachios, etc., all rolled up in chicken or capon skin, stitched closed, poached and weighted down. It's served sliced, at room temperature, garnished with the gelatin that comes from the poaching liquid.

Gnocco emiliano or **crescente al forno** A type of focaccia, a specialty of Modena, made with a yeasted dough that's mixed with cracklings, prosciutto or pancetta. It's usually served with sliced, cured meats or used to make sandwiches.

Gnocco fritto See *crescente* (page 121).

Guancialino Salami wrapped in a pork jowl. It's a specialty of the town of Spilamberto in the province of Modena.

Gussoni Large, half-moon-shaped vegetable-filled ravioli that are a specialty of the area around the town of Sarsina in the province of Forlì.

Ligaza Dialect for *salame matto* (fake salami) at one time, a peasant preparation.

Manine Ferraresi A bread shape from Ferrara.

Morazzone More or less the same type of savory tart as the *erbazzone* (above). The name refers to the Roman herb, moretum, used in its preparation.

Mortadella Made with 100% pork (60% lean meat from the shoulder or loin and 40% cheek fat) and peppercorns and put into a natural bladder casing. "Real" mortadella—that made with 100% pork—has an S for *suino* (pork) stamped on it.

Piadina romagnola Made with a dough of flour, lardo, water (sometimes milk) and salt, and sometimes yeast. The piadina is made into a disk and cooked on a special griddle. The ingredients and the thickness of the piadina vary from town to town. Near Ravenna it's rather dense, but around Riccione, Rimini and the borders of Marches, it's quite thin. Piadina goes well with salami, field greens and soft cheeses. Its name is derived from the word *piadèna*, a short, wide bowl.

Polpettone Salami, made with goose, that comes out of the Jewish tradition of Reggio Emilia.

Prosciutto di Parma One of the best prosciutto in all of Italy. It's aged for twelve to twenty-four months in rooms with great vertical windows that allow the breeze, called the Rèfolo, to blow in from the Mediterranean Sea. It's this breeze that gives the prosciutto its excellent flavor.

Ragnetti A bread shape from Ferrara.

Riccettina Also a bread shape from Ferrara.

Rifreddo A type of meat terrine that's served with gelatin. In Emilia, it's often made with meat, salami and cheese.

Salame felino A very special, intensely flavorful salami that, despite its name — *felino* means cat — is not made with cat. It is made according to all the proper rules and regulations, in the town of Felino in the province of Parma.

Salame gentile Salami made with lean pork meat, bits of lardo and peppercorns, that is put into a *gentile* or refined bladder casing. It's rather rare salami because you can usually only get two *gentile* salami from a pig. It's found almost exclusively in Ferrara, Ravenna and Forlì.

Scarpazzone A savory tart made with chard that's typical of the Reggiano region (see *erbazzone*, page 122).

Solata or **solada di farina bianca** Fritters made with a batter of flour, water, garlic, rosemary and salt then fried in lardo.

Spalla di San Secondo Pork shoulder that has been salted and spiced, then cooked according to a method used in the area around San Secondo and Busseto in the province of Parma.

Stecchi fritti alla Petroniana Skewers loaded with chunks of veal, pickled tongue, chicken livers, mortadella, sweetbreads, cheese and truffles that are dipped in egg and breadcrumbs and then fried. The skewer ingredients may vary. This is a specialty of Bologna.

Streghe or **streghine** A very tasty kind of diamond-shaped cracker made with rich, fatty ingredients.

Stria Focaccia, a specialty of Modena, made with bread dough, olive oil, salt and chopped lardo.

Tigelle montanare Flatbread—smaller than the similar piadina—made on its own specific griddle. The dough is made with flour, water or milk, lardo and, in some cases, yeast. The tigelle are served hot, filled with a pesto di lardo (chopped lardo, garlic and rosemary) and some grated Parmesan cheese. They're great with salami, or a soft cheese and white truffles. They're a specialty of the Appenine Mountains around Modena.

Tirota Yeasted focaccia enriched with onions that is a specialty of Ferrara.

Torta d'erbe A savory tart filled with chard, cheese, olive oil and salt and covered with very thin pastry. It's a specialty of the Upper Val di Taro.

Torta di patate A savory tart made with bread dough and filled with smashed potatoes mixed with Parmesan cheese, milk, eggs, lardo and other ingredients, it's a specialty of the valleys around Piacenza.

Torta fritta The Parma version of the Bolognese crescentina fritta.

PASTA, GNOCCHI, RICE, POLENTA AND GRAINS

Anolini Ring-shaped ravioli classically filled with a mixture of aged Parmesan cheese, breadcrumbs, eggs, nutmeg and the meat from a beef or donkey pot roast that has cooked from sixteen to thirty-six hours, until the meat is completely falling apart. Usually anolini are served in broth. A leaner version of this dish is from Piacenza.

Bassetti or **bassotti** Very thin egg tagliolini that are layered in a baking dish with butter and Parmesan cheese—and sometimes a giblet ragù—then doused with broth and baked until completely gratinéed. The dish is a specialty of Forlì.

Bomba di riso A molded rice dish that's filled with pigeon, eggs, porcini mushrooms, truffles and giblets or sausage. In Piacenza, the dish is traditionally made for the Festa della Madonna on August 15. In certain areas, especially those that border Tuscany, in particular Lunigiana, the dish includes chard and sausages.

Calzagatti, cazzagai, calzagatt or **paparucci** Yellow polenta dressed with beans. It's probably the oldest and simplest peasant dish of the Reggiano area. In Piacenza fava beans are used. Leftovers are cut into rectangles and fried and served very hot.

Capelli d'angelo Angel hair pasta. It's fresh, long, thin and usually served in broth.

Cappellacci Huge tortelli, a specialty of Ferrara, filled with winter squash and Parmesan cheese (not amaretti and mostarda like they are in Lombardy). Their shape is very much like tortelloni.

Cappelletti Little "hat-shaped" fresh egg pasta that have various fillings depending upon the area where they are made — one way in Reggio Emilia, and another in Romagna, but in both areas they are served in beef broth. Cappelletti are different from tortellini because of their fillings and their size — cappelletti are a bit larger than tortellini.

Cappelletti reggiani Cappelletti with a filling made with four types of meat (veal, pork, beef and prosciutto), Parmesan cheese and breadcrumbs (no eggs). In some areas, after they are cooked in broth, they're finished with a splash of Lambrusco wine.

Cappelletti romagnoli "di grasso" Cappelletti with a filling made with three types of cheese: crescenza or raviggiolo, squacquerone, stracchino or ricotta, and Parmesan — plus chopped capon, veal and pork, eggs and spices.

Cappelletti romagnoli "di magro" Cappelletti made with the same filling as di grasso, but without meat.

Ciribusla In Modena, *calzagatti* (page 124).

Crosetti Little waffle-like pasta disks, very similar to *testaroli* or *testetti* (page 147), made in a special iron, and served boiled, with meat sauce. Crosetti are a specialty of the area around Bedonia, a mountain town in the Appenines near Parma.

Curzoli An almost-forgotten Lenten dish made with flour and water pasta that is dressed with butter, browned prosciutto fat, grated Parmesan cheese and pepper.

Fiuchett See *strichetti* (page 188).

Garganelli A type of penne-shaped pasta made with a flour, egg, Parmesan cheese and nutmeg dough. They're rolled on a stick then marked with a special *pettine per garganelli*, a comb used for this pasta. They're traditionally dressed with meat ragù and peas.

Giuget Little squares made with a dough of white and corn flour and hot water. After they're cooked, they're only slightly drained then dressed with sautéed herbs, sausage and pancetta.

Gramigna con la salsiccia A type of fresh egg pasta, much used in Emilia-Romagna, which looks like short, slightly twisted spaghetti with a hole. They're usually dressed with sausage ragù.

Guscioni alla lastra Large tortelli that look like an open shell. They're made with flour and the water that's used for cooking winter squash, and filled with a mixture of winter squash and potatoes or chard. They're cooked on a sandstone griddle placed over a charcoal grill.

Lasagne Classic lasagne alla Bolognese — made with sheets of spinach pasta layered with meat ragù, béchamel and Parmesan cheese, then gratinéed — is only one of the many creative regional variations of this extraordinary dish.

Maccheroni di Bobbio Maccheroni very similar to those manufactured in the southern part of the country with an instrument similar to a knitting needle, a specialty of the village of Bobbio, in the Appenines near Piacenza. Generally, they're served with a sauce made with pot roast.

Maltagliati Fresh pasta, cut into irregular diamond shapes, mostly used in vegetable soups and found in the Emilia area.

Orecchioni A pasta shape similar to tortelli but filled with vegetables and cheese, then folded into half moons and closed at the edges with a fork. Fillings may include ricotta, Parmesan cheese and parsley, or squacquerone and nettles, or spinach. They may be dressed with tomato and fresh basil or with lean pancetta and fresh tomatoes.

Pappardelle della vigilia Papardelle made from a thin sheet of pasta, served on Christmas Eve with a sauce made with tomatoes and dried mushrooms, or with ricotta, butter and walnuts. The dish is a specialty of the village of Borgotaro in the province of Parma.

Pasticcio alla ferrarese A sumptuous dish originated at the court of the Este family of Ferrara in which a short crust is filled with maccheroni that has been dressed with meat or giblets, mushrooms and béchamel, then gratinéed. White truffle shards are sometimes added as well.

Pattone The Reggiano name for fritters made with leftover tagliatelle, eggs and Parmesan cheese.

Pisarei e fasö The emblematic dish of Piacenza, made with dumplings no larger than beans. The dough is made with the stale white part of bread, milk and flour. These gnocchetti are dressed with beans, tomatoes and pancetta. The sauce must be very tender — sometimes some of the beans are puréed.

Risotto all'imolese Risotto enriched with cabbage, beef, chopped lardo, celery, carrots and onions. Sometimes the mixture is browned with a bit of tomato sauce.

Rotolo ripieno A dish made by filling a sfoglia — a sheet of simple egg pasta — with a mixture of ricotta and spinach, then rolling it up and enclosing it in cloth. It's then boiled, sliced, sauced and gratinéed to serve.

Scifuloti Pasta made with the same dough as garganelli and similar in shape but a bit larger. At one time they were dressed with sugar, cinnamon and Parmesan cheese.

Spoja lorda Small ravioli made by *sporcando* — dirtying or mucking up — a sheet of pasta with soft cheese like squacquerone, Parmesan cheese and nutmeg. Another sheet of pasta is then placed over this "mess" and a special toothed cutter is used to make the small square shapes. After they've dried, they are cooked and served in beef broth.

Stricchetti Emiliano dialect for farfalle (butterfly-shaped pasta). This pasta was originally served in soups. These days they're also dressed with various sauces or ragù to serve.

Stringotti A pasta shape made with flour and water that looks very much like the Venetian *bigoli* (page 74). They are named for their physical resemblance to shoelaces. They are dressed with various sauces or ragù. They are a specialty of the high valley of Savio. In some of the areas of the surrounding hills they are served fried with walnuts and breadcrumbs.

Strozzapreti A pasta found in Romagna. The dough is made with flour, water and milk. It's rolled out and cut into rather thick sticks that are then further pulled out by hand. They're often served with a vegetable sauce. Their name — *strozzapreti* means "priest strangler" — refers to the well-known Romagnoli aversion to the clergy.

Tortelli di erbette or **d'erbe** Square ravioli traditionally filled with freshly made ricotta, very fresh eggs, aged Parmesan — grated at the last minute — and just-picked chard. Cooks who have the good fortune to find a special kind of sweet radicchio, grown in the plains of Parma, will use it in the filling instead of chard. The tortelli are dressed with Parmesan cheese and clarified butter. Although typical of Parma, you'll find this pasta throughout Emilia.

Tortelli di zucca The most typical example of this pasta is the version made in Mantua with a filling of puréed winter squash, crumbled amaretti cookies, mostarda (possibly apple) and Parmesan cheese, served dressed with melted butter and more Parmesan. There are many variations of the recipe in

Emilia. In Reggio Emilia, puréed squash and a sauce made with quince, melon, orange and lemon peel, walnuts and cooked must, called *savor* (page 130), is added. In Modena the filling is made with squash and amaretti cookies and dressed with giblet ragù. In Ferrara, where they're called *cappellacci* (page 125), they may vary in shape from triangular to rectangular. The squash filling varies as well.

Tortellini in brodo Very small egg pasta ravioli filled with loin of pork, mortadella, prosciutto, eggs, Parmesan cheese and nutmeg, and sometimes turkey breast. They must be very small so that each spoonful that's lifted out of a rich beef and capon broth, or beef and chicken broth, contains a few tortellini. This recipe is Bolognese *per excellenza* — so much so, that in the 1960s the recipe was codified and filed with the Chamber of Commerce of Bologna as part of their initiative to preserve and honor the local gastronomy.

Tortelloni burro e oro Tortellini filled with ricotta, Parmesan cheese and parsley. They're dressed with butter and tomato sauce — *burro e oro*.

SOUPS

Arbada A soup, typical of the Reggiano area, made by first sautéing onion, celery and carrots in lardo, then adding black cabbage (cavolo nero), potatoes, green beans and pork cracklings. It's thickened with corn flour.

Brodetto dei pescatori romagnoli A soup made by boiling an abundant amount of chopped onion with vinegar, then adding olive oil. Tomatoes are added when the mixture is soft and slightly browned, followed by white wine, lemon peel, garlic, salt and pepper. Finally, a variety of fish is added — first of all the fish that requires the longest cooking time; then cuttlefish, razor clams, and other kinds of shellfish; and at the end the more delicate dogfish, turbot and sole. This recipe has its origins in the area between the towns of Rimini and Riccione on the Adriatic coast.

Imbalsadura A soup made by first sautéing onions with pancetta, then adding stewed peas, beans, a bit of fresh tomatoes, garlic and parsley. Maltagliati (pasta) are cooked in another pot. The vegetables are added to the cooked pasta and it's served garnished with freshly grated Parmesan cheese.

Malmaritati The Bolognese version of this soup is made with beans and fresh egg maltagliati. It's different from the version from Modena because of the absence of lardo. When ditalini, a short, dry pasta shape, are substituted for the maltagliati, the soup is just called maritati.

Manfrigoli or **manfrigul** or **malfattini** A small pasta—about the size of a large piece of grain—used in broth or with a bean soup.

Minestra matta Little flour and water pasta squares dressed with a tomato sauce made with a sauté of carrots, onions, celery, pancetta and fresh tomatoes.

Minestra nel sacchetto A soup made by wrapping a dough made with flour, eggs, Parmesan cheese and nutmeg in a cloth and boiling it in beef broth. The cooked pasta is cut into small cubes then served in the broth. This is a family recipe found throughout Reggio Emilia and Marches, but its exact origins are difficult to pinpoint.

Minestra paradiso A soup recipe from Pellegrino Artusi's classic cookbook, *The Science of the Kitchen and The Art of Eating Well* (1891). It's made by adding spoonfuls of whipped egg whites mixed with the yolks, breadcrumbs, Parmesan cheese and nutmeg to a rich capon broth.

Minestra reale See *zuppa reale* (below).

Panada In Emiliano dialect, a soup made with stale bread cooked in broth, then finished with butter, olive oil, sage and grated Parmesan cheese.

Passatelli in brodo A soup of pasta served in broth. The pasta dough is made with eggs, Parmesan cheese, breadcrumbs, a bit of beef marrow and nutmeg then cooked on a special large cylindrical iron used for making passatelli. The dish is typically Romagnola but also found, with slight variations, in Emilia and in Marches (page 170).

Sbrofanez A pasta and bean dish.

Tagliatelle della duchessa Tagliatelle dressed with browned chicken livers, then finished with beaten eggs and Parmesan cheese. The preparation is from the village of Bazzano in the province of Bologna.

Zuppa imperiale This is the queen—no, the empress—of the Bolognese broth-based soups. It's made with a semolina, egg, melted butter and Parmesan cheese dough that's either baked or fried, cut into small cubes, then served in a rich beef broth.

Zuppa reale A typical Bolognese soup made by adding tiny beignets made with flour, butter, water, eggs and salt to a rich beef broth.

CONDIMENTS, SAUCES AND EGGS

Aceto balsamico The very esteemed vinegar produced in the area around Modena and Reggio Emilia made with naturally fermented cooked grape must. The vinegar-making process is long. It lasts for at least five years and the better vinegars are left to mature for ten or twelve years. The vinegar is poured into a small wooden barrel and each year is transferred into another barrel made from a different kind of wood. The vinegar starts the aging process in a barrel made of oak, followed, in order, by chestnut, cherry, ash and mulberry. Each variety of wood imparts its own flavor and aroma to the vinegar. The mature vinegar is a deep, shiny brown color; its aroma is complex and penetrating; and its flavor is sweet, sour, balanced and rich with velvety overtones. It's important to look carefully when purchasing balsamic vinegar—if it doesn't cost much that usually indicates an imitation made by adding various ingredients to regular vinegar.

Agresto A very old-fashioned, very acidic juice made from sour-grape seeds. Agresto was very popular in the medieval era. Herbs and spices were added to it, and it was used to add acidity to sauces and condiments and as the base for cooked dishes.

Saba or **sapa** Grape syrup made by boiling the must of white grapes until it's reduced by a third. It's used in many sweet preparations or, when diluted in water, as a drink.

Salsa verde A sauce found throughout Italy, typically used as an accompaniment for mixed boiled meats, made with parsley, hard-cooked egg yolks, the white part of bread or puréed potatoes, a bit of garlic, olive oil, vinegar, capers, anchovies and little pickles, all finely chopped.

Savor or **savore** or **sapore** A preparation made by cooking grape must with various kinds of fruit—quince, apples, pears, pomegranates, figs, almonds, pine nuts, walnuts, hazelnuts, squash, lemon and orange peel and sun-dried melon skin—for a long time. In Emilia it's typically served with boiled meats and soft polenta and used as a filling for squash tortelli.

FISH, CRUSTACEANS AND SHELLFISH

Anguilla alla comacchiese A stew made with chunks of eel first sautéed with garlic and onions, then sharpened with a splash of vinegar and finished with tomato sauce.

Baccalà alla bolognese Softened pieces of salt cod (baccalà), floured, then browned in butter and olive oil and flavored with chopped garlic and parsley and a few drops of lemon juice.

Cannelli The Romagnolo term for cannolicchi, a type of clam. The most popular way to cook them is gratinéed; however, there are cannelli recipes for soups, on the grill or in marinara sauce.

Poveracce or **poverazze** In Romagnolo dialect, clams.

Tonno alla bolognese Tuna belly fillets preserved in oil that have been cooked in a sauce made with celery, carrots, onions, garlic, white wine and fresh parsley.

Uomini nudi Romagnolo dialect for *bianchetti* (page 33).

MEATS

Agnello con piselli alla romagnola Stew made with pieces of lamb that have been sautéed in lardo, pancetta and butter then finished with tomato sauce and fresh peas.

Anatra alla romagnola Duck sautéed with onions, carrots, pancetta, herbs and a splash of white wine, then slowly cooked in broth.

Barzigole A Reggiano specialty made by boning a sheep's spine and then marinating the pieces of meat with garlic, rosemary, salt, pepper and white wine, then grilled to serve.

Bollito misto all'emiliana The region's version of the sumptuous mixture of boiled meats and vegetables served with various sauces. In Emilia the broth is made with the usual carrots, celery, onions and fresh tomatoes; a mixture of beef cuts (more or less like the Lombardian version) with the addition of some hind cuts; pork thigh; veal tongue, head and feet; and large, cooked salami such as zampone or cotechino. Some of the sauces that may accompany the dish are salsa verde, mostarda, la peperonata and il friggione. Side dishes such as puréed potatoes and lentils are often served with it as well. There are two similar specialties, *capello da prete* (below) and *salama da sugo* (page 133) from Ferrara.

Cappello da prete Cooked salami from the area around Parma made with the chopped remains of a pork thigh that has been used to make culatello and fiocchetto. The rest of the mixture is like that for a zampone except the cappello da prete is put into a casing made from the bottom part of a pig's hoof, just above the joint. When the salami is sewn together, its triangular shape resembles the three-cornered hats worn at one time by the clergy, *cappello da prete*.

Castrato A castrated sheep, usually served roasted or grilled.

Coniglio alla cacciatora Rabbit stew made with sautéed onions, celery, carrots and lardo, splashed with white wine and finished with tomatoes and broth.

Coniglio alla reggiana Pieces of rabbit flavored with garlic, rosemary, a bit of olive oil and vinegar then braised with diced pancetta, carrots, celery and onions. The dish is finished with broth and some tomato conserve.

Coppa al forno The end of a pork fillet baked with rosemary, white wine, salt and pepper, a preparation typical of the hills around Piacenza.

Cotechino Cooked salami found throughout Emilia-Romagna made with pork, lardo, spices and pork rind (cotica) that gives the salami its name. It's often cooked with mixed boiled meats, or on its own, and served with puréed potatoes and lentils.

Cotechino in galera A version from Modena in which the cotechino is wrapped in a slice of beef or veal, then covered with prosciutto and cooked in broth and Lambrusco or white wine. In another version, the slices of meat are covered with spinach before they're wrapped around the cotechino.

Cotoletta alla bolognese Sliced veal rump or breast dipped in beaten eggs and a mixture of Parmesan cheese and breadcrumbs, then fried, covered with prosciutto and flaked Parmesan cheese, and baked to serve. In some recipes the veal is bathed with broth or covered with tomato sauce and sage leaves before baking.

Gambon The boned leg of a suckling pig that is covered with salt and spices, then pressed between two wooden planks to age. It's then boiled and served with traditional accompaniments; a specialty of Piacenza.

Lepre sfilata A boiled hare that is boned (*sfilata*), then stewed in a broth made with lardo, onions, basil and parsley. The method is also used to cook rabbit. It is a specialty of the village of Bettola in the province of Piacenza.

Lumache alla bobbiese Snails that have been removed from their shells, browned in butter with leeks, then finished with white wine and fragrant herbs.

Manicotto The name for zampone in the village of Mirandola in the province of Modena.

Picaia Roasted or boiled stuffed veal breast, a specialty of Emilia.

Picula 'd caval Stew made with horsemeat and tomatoes, a specialty of Piacenza.

Pollo alla cacciatora Chicken stew cooked with olive oil, garlic, rosemary and white wine, then finished with tomatoes.

Polpettone di tacchino A "meatloaf" made by pounding a big slice of turkey breast very thinly, then filling it with chopped veal head and other ingredients. The whole thing is wrapped in turkey skin and boiled to serve. It's a specialty of Reggio Emilia.

Salama da sugo or **salamina ferrarese** A sumptuous dish that boasts an historic origin: it's said to have been created by Lucrezia Borgia to serve to men who were returning, tired and hungry, from war. This aged cooked salami is made with liver, tongue, neck meat, red wine, black pepper, nutmeg, cinnamon and cloves. It should be slowly cooked — even better, steamed. It is served with a sauce made with the cooking liquid and puréed potatoes or squash.

Sassolino As well as the name of a liqueur, another name for *zampone* (see below) from the town of Sassuolo in the province of Modena.

Scaloppine alla bolognese Veal medallions covered with sliced, boiled potatoes and prosciutto then dressed with meat sauce, butter and Parmesan cheese.

Stracotto alla piacentina A pot roast known for the richness of its ingredients.

Trippa alla parmigiana Parboiled tripe strips that are stewed with carrots, celery, onions, prosciutto, tomato sauce and broth and covered with grated Parmesan cheese to serve.

Umido incassato A stew made with small veal chops, sweetbreads, chicken giblets, hard-cooked egg yolks, mushrooms and truffles, that is then covered with béchamel and baked.

Valigini "Little suitcases," a specialty of Reggio Emilia made by filling thin meat slices with a mixture of parsley, garlic, Parmesan cheese, eggs and breadcrumbs. They're slowly stewed in a light tomato sauce to serve.

Zampone Large, cooked salami made with a mixture of chopped pork cuts (skin, ears, nerves, snout) and salt, pepper, nutmeg, cinnamon and cloves, wrapped in a casing made with the skin of the rear hocks (*zampe*). It must be very slowly steamed before serving. In this region, it's traditional to serve this salami on New Year's Eve with puréed potatoes and lentils and sometimes with beans and buttered spinach. Zampone is often an essential ingredient of a bollito misto.

Zucco Salami similar to cotechino but with a richer mixture of spices. It's typical of the area of Reggio Emilia.

VEGETABLES

Cardi al forno alla parmigiana Boiled cardoons placed in a baking dish, covered with meat ragù, Parmesan cheese and shaved white truffles, then baked to serve.

Erbette Another word for bietole, chard.

Friggione A slowly cooked tomato-and-onion sauce that's typical of Emilia. The many variations include the addition of sausage or prosciutto or leftover boiled meats, or vegetables such as potatoes, eggplant, zucchini and sweet peppers.

Peperonata A stew typical of Emilia made with sweet peppers, tomatoes and onions.

Striccapugni Bitter field greens, such as chicory.

Strigoli Long, thin green leaves with a slightly bitter flavor found sprouting in the sandy terrain of Romagna.

Trifola Another word for truffle.

CHEESE AND DAIRY PRODUCTS

Castel San Pietro A briefly aged, semi-fat, semi-fresh skimmed cow's milk cheese produced in the eponymous village in the province of Bologna. The thin rind is straw colored and the very subtle paste is white. It's mildly flavored.

Formaggio di fossa A cheese made with sheep's or goat's milk, or a mixture of both. It's covered in leaves, then left to age in very humid caves (*tufacee*) in order to produce the mold that gives it its aroma and unique, piquant flavor. Produced mostly in Romagna, it's also found in Marches. The best-known version is from the village of Sogliano in the province of Forlì. It's a splendid accompaniment for figs — preserved or caramelized — or as an ingredient in cakes or pastries.

Parmigiano reggiano An extraordinary cheese produced throughout the provinces of Parma, Reggio Emilia, Modena, parts of Bologna and Mantua in Lombardy. It's a semi-fat cheese with a hard, cooked paste made with partially skimmed cow's milk. Natural calf's rennet is used to stabilize it. Sometimes anti-fermentation substances are added to the milk as well. The cheese is brined for twenty to thirty days, followed by a slow, natural aging process that lasts until at least the end of the following summer. It may, however, be aged for a longer period of time giving it the very sought-after designation of *stravecchi* or super-aged. The straw-colored rind is stamped with the Parmigiano Reggiano mark. The flaky, fine-grained body is also straw colored with an extraordinary aroma and delicate flavor.

Pecorino del Frignano A typical cheese of the Appenines of Modena made with a mixture of sheep's and cow's milk. Its aromatic, full-flavored, straw white body tends to develop a sharp streak as it ages.

Squacquerone A very fresh cheese made with cow's milk. It has an amorphous consistency without any real shape because of the way the curd coagulates. This typically Romagnolo cheese is usually spread onto fresh, hot *piadine* (page 123).

SWEETS AND LIQUEURS

Africanetti Elongated box-shaped cookies made with whipped zabaione that are a specialty of the village of San Giovanni in Persiceto in the province of Bologna.

Bensone An old-fashioned, rustic, sweet focaccia stuffed with *savor* (page 130) that's typical of Modena but also found in Versilia in Tuscany.

Biscione A pastry, typical of Modena, made with sweet and bitter almonds, sugar and yeast and covered with a mixture of egg whites and sugar then garnished with candied fruits. They are made into large snake shapes (*biscia*).

Boeri Chocolates filled with cherries in liqueur.

Bonissima A shortbread tart, sometimes called sarzenta, filled with walnuts and honey, then covered with chocolate. It's a specialty of Modena.

Bracciatelli Very simple, ring-shaped wedding pastries, sometimes called zuccherini, made with flour, milk, eggs, sugar and yeast. The size can vary according to the location where they're made.

Brazadela A slightly yeasted, ring-shaped cake covered with pearl sugar.

Budino gabinetto A spoon dessert from Pellegrino Artusi's classic cookbook (see page 129) made with ladyfingers, milk, sugar, eggs, black and golden raisins, apricot and quince jam, candied fruits and Kirsch liqueur.

Buricchi Small square pastries, of Jewish origin, that are filled with sugar and almonds.

Burlengo A delicious and unusual dessert made with rice, milk, flour, pig's blood, dried figs, pine nuts, hazelnuts, almonds, raisins, chocolate, chopped candied fruits, quince jam, honey and *saba* (page 130). In some of the villages of Romagna, burlengo is covered with a short crust, making it a type of crostata.

Bustrengo An old-fashioned farmer's tart made with flour, grated Parmesan cheese, breadcrumbs, eggs, milk and grated lemon zest. Very often pine nuts, raisins, walnuts and other pieces of dried fruits are added. The name bustrengo may also be used to define a *sanguinaccio dolce* (sweet blood sausage, *migliaccio*, page 137), a castagnaccio (chestnut tart) or burlengo (a dessert made with rice and milk).

Buzzillan or **Bussolan** A nineteenth-century Reggiano dessert made with flour, sugar, yeast, butter and eggs that's a very close relative to the Tuscan *buccellato* (page 158), which is also produced in the Correggio area. There is a version made with apricot jam.

Cantarelle Crêpes made with a batter of yellow and white flours, warm water and a pinch of salt. They're cooked on a griddle and served covered with sugar and a bit of olive oil. These ancient snacks are typical of the area around Rimini.

Casadello Also called caciatello or latteruolo, an historic Romagnolo sweet made with cream and eggs cooked in a rather tasteless pastry shell whose sole purpose is to be a vessel in which to cook the delicate cream.

Cassatella A type of charlotte, a spoon dessert surrounded by liqueur-soaked (Sassolino or Alchermes) ladyfingers.

Castagnole Sweet fritters whose shape slightly resembles a chestnut (castagna) typical of Emilia-Romagna and served during Carnival.

Certosino A long-lasting Christmastime sweet bread made with flour, honey, orange peel, fruit jam, pine nuts, almonds, chocolate and cinnamon, etc. The loaf-shaped bread is a specialty of Bologna and the surrounding provinces.

Ciabattine di San Antonio Cookies similar to ladyfingers that are a specialty of the village of San Giovanni in Persiceto in the province of Bologna.

Ciacar dal sori The odd Romagnolo name for *sfrappole* (page 138).

Ciambella A soft ring-shaped pastry.

Colomba di Pavullo A substantial cake made by layering cake with apple and pear jam, pine nuts and raisins.

Coppo A stiff pudding baked in a water bath. In the Emiliana countryside, it's sometimes cooked on a grate over a wood-burning fire.

Cucchiarole or **cuciarole** Romagnolo term for dried chestnuts. At one time they were used to make soups that were then flavored with *saba* (page 130).

Erbazzone dolce The sweet version of the savory *erbazzone* (page 122) in which greens, sugar, almonds and other ingredients are baked in a short crust.

Fior di latte A pudding, similar to crème caramel, made with a mixture of milk, eggs and sugar poured into a caramel-lined form and baked in a water bath.

Frappe Crumbly fried pastries covered with powdered sugar and served during Carnival. Their name varies by region.

Gialletti Small rustic pastries that look like a squashed ball, made with whole-wheat and corn flours, butter, eggs, sugar, raisins, pine nuts and spices.

Latte brulè or **alla portoghese** Another pudding similar to crème caramel.

Latteruolo See *casadello* (page 136).

Laurino Bay leaf–flavored liqueur.

Lupini or **Luìn di Ferrara** Flattened sticks of pastry made with flour, sugar, butter, lardo, eggs, rum and lemon that are fried and covered with powdered sugar and served during Carnival. When baked instead of fried, they're called favini.

Mandorlini del ponte Flat, primitive cookies made with flour, almonds, sugar and stiffly beaten egg whites, a specialty of the village of Pontelagoscuro in the province of Ferrara.

Migliaccio Although it means different things in each region, migliaccio basically refers to something made with millet flour (miglio) that nowadays is replaced with corn flour. In Emilia-Romagna the migliaccio is a cake made on the day a pig is slaughtered. In fact, its blood, together with flour, milk, *saba* (page 130*)*, sugar, chocolate and other ingredients, is used to make it.

Mistocchine An old-fashioned specialty made by roadside food vendors. They're small, flat round or oval cakes made with chestnut flour and milk.

Mistrà A type of brandy made by distilling aniseed, very often used to "correct" a coffee.

Mostaccioli In Emilia, ring-shaped cookies made with flour, sugar, cooked must and candied fruit.

Nocino A very old-fashioned liqueur made with not-completely-ripened walnuts (skin on), sugar and alcohol. It's said that the walnuts need to be collected by barefoot females on the night of June 24, San Giovanni's Day, and be cut with a wooden blade—not a metal one.

Panone A sweet from Bologna similar to the *certosino* (page 136).

Pan pepato or **pampepato** An historic cake made with dried fruits, honey, candied fruits, chocolate, pepper and other spices. The ingredients and the shape of the cake, however, may vary by region. In Emilia it's made in a large ring shape with flour, sugar or honey, raisins, almonds, pine nuts, pepper and orange peel.

Pan speziale Another name for *certosino* (page 136).

Pazientini Tiny Lenten pastries made with flour, sugar, stiffly beaten egg whites, pine nuts and zabaione.

Pinza A cake that may be sweet or savory. In Emilia-Romagna it's a sweet preparation made with dough that's similar to shortbread and filled with mostarda. In Bologna it's filled with jam made with various local fruits. It's rolled up and baked.

Raviole Little shortbread cookies typical of Emilia that are filled with jam, marzipan or cream, cut into half-moon shapes and baked. Sometimes after they come out of the oven, they are splashed with a bit of Alchermes liqueur and then covered with sugar.

Sabadoni Sweet ravioli filled with chestnut cream, puréed beans and quince. They're covered with saba to serve.

Salame dolce A traditional Romagnola sweet made with a mixture of butter, cocoa, crumbled amaretti cookies, liqueur and other ingredients made into a long salami-like shape. It's sliced to serve.

Sarzenta See *bonissima* (page 135).

Sassolino Aniseed liqueur originally made in the town of Sassuolo in the province of Modena.

Sfrappole Similar to *frappe* (page 137).

Spongata A long-lasting cake that's made by filling a short crust with honey, mostarda di frutta, breadcrumbs, walnuts, raisins, pine nuts, cinnamon, candied citrus peel, spices, etc. One of the oldest preparations in Italy, it was created in the fifteenth century, at Christmastime, in the village of Brescello in the province of Reggio Emilia. It's made in other provinces of the region and in Liguria where it's called spungata di Sarzana, and in Lombardy where it's called spongarda di Crema.

Sprell Flat strips of dough made with flour, eggs, sugar, butter, yeast, rum and wine, that are fried in lardo, then covered with powdered sugar to serve.

Spumino A small meringue-like sweet.

Stracadent Hard, crunchy, long-lasting pastries made with honey, almonds, flour and stiffly beaten egg whites. *Stracadent* means "tooth-breaker!"

Sughi A grape pudding from Emilia made with must and flour or breadcrumbs.

Torta Barozzi A thin, soft cake made with chocolate, coffee, peanuts and other secret ingredients.

Torta degli addobbi An exquisite rice and almond cake.

Torta di melica A cake made with very fine corn flour, white flour, butter, sugar, almonds and eggs.

Torta di rose A cake made with a type of brioche dough or puff pastry. The sheets of pastry are spread with whipped butter and sugar, then rolled up into a cylinder and sliced. The slices are placed near each other in a baking dish. The baked cake appears to be composed of many roses.

Torta nera A cake that's filled with a mixture of almonds, sugar, cocoa, coffee and egg yolks, then covered with a slightly yeasty short crust. It's typical of the town of San Secondo in the province of Modena.

Torta ricciolina or **di tagliatelline** A tart with a short crust base filled with egg thin tagliatelle (tagliatelline), almonds, candied fruits, etc. After baking, it's covered with powdered sugar. It's found throughout Emilia-Romagna and in Lombardy.

Turchetto A hot drink made with coffee and rum or gin and served with anise, lemon peel and sugar.

Zuccherini Little ring-shaped cookies made with flour, eggs and a pinch of salt, typically served at wedding celebrations.

Zuccheroni montanari Large ring-shaped pastries glazed with sugar and sprinkled with fennel seeds, typical of the mountain villages around Bologna.

Zuppa inglese A spoon dessert made by lining a bowl with slices of sponge cake bathed with Alchermes liqueur, then adding pastry cream and chocolate cream.

WINES

This generous and spirited region has a yearly wine production of nearly 300 million gallons. Rivers of Lambrusco, Sangiovese, Trebbiano and Albana flow together into the *cantine sociali* — the cooperative cellars of the region — for sale and for export. In fact, it's said that there's only one thought in the heads of the vintners of the region: throughout the whole world, to replace Coca-Cola with Lambrusco!

Producing such large quantities of wine hasn't affected its quality. The growers are not afraid to use state-of-the-art equipment without compromising traditional winemaking methods. This is a region with an interesting, continually evolving outlook.

Albana The only wine of the region to have the coveted D.O.C.G., the most stringent of all designations guaranteeing the wine is produced in a certain region by specific methods. Albana is made with eponymous white grapes that are cultivated in the hills around the provinces of Imola, Forlì and Ravenna. It can be dry and very acidic, in which case it marries marvelously with fish. When it's sweet, with aromas of almond and yellow fruit, it becomes a superb dessert wine.

Bianco di Scandiano From a varietal that contains massive quantities of Sauvignon grapes, a faintly aromatic wine produced in the province of Parma. It can be dry or sweet. It's not a very full-bodied wine. However, the dry version is a very pleasing summertime table wine, especially when served chilled, and the sweet version is a good dessert wine.

Gutturnio A dry, easy-to-drink wine made with Barbera and Bonarda grapes in the hills around Piacenza. A pleasing aroma of youth escapes from this ruby-colored wine. It goes well with salami antipasti and may accompany the entire meal. The sweet version is perfect with dry cookies, apple cakes and other simple baked goods.

Lambrusco Mostly produced in the provinces of Modena and Reggio Emilia, types vary according to the grape that's used in its manufacture, but the quintessential one is the Sorbara Lambrusco from Modena. This fresh, slightly fizzy wine has an aroma of violets and a pale, almost dull, ruby red color and pleasingly acidic palate. It goes well with the opulent first courses that come out of the Emiliana kitchen, but its true love is the fat cooked salami called zampone. There are also very good Lambrusco spumati—sparkling wines made with white grapes.

Monterosso val d'Arda A light, intensely yellow wine made with Malvasia di Candia grapes in the province of Piacenza. It goes well with simple fish dishes. The sweet version is a perfect dessert wine.

Sangiovese A 100% Romagnolo wine from the eponymous grape. It seems as if the generosity of the whole region is condensed in it. When young, it's a vivid ruby red color with reflections of violet that, as it ages, tends towards garnet. It has an intense aroma of red fruits and flowers. It's strongly structured but as it ages it weakens a bit, losing its *superiore* qualification — but never losing its elegance. Its dry, bluntly winey and slightly bitter flavor makes it the perfect wine for roast meats. It goes well with farm animals, in particular, lamb. The *superiore* version is just right with red meats.

Trebbiano A typically Romagnolo varietal, intensely straw colored and slightly fragrant with a pleasing flavor. It's an unpretentious, honest wine. Its low alcohol content and acidic streak make it a perfect table wine.

Vini dei Colli Bolognesi A whole group of not-very-high-level, but pleasing and very drinkable wines in this D.O.C. category. For example, among the reds there's a well-structured Barbera that can stand a year or so of aging. It's a good table wine and the Riserva goes particularly well with roast meats. Among the whites there's a Sauvignon that marries well with soups and white meats, a fragrant Riesling Italico perfect with fish and fresh cheeses and a limpid and soft Pinot Bianco that can be served as an aperitif.

Tortellini in brodo alla bolognese

Tortellini in broth, Bologna style
Serves 4 to 6

For the filling:
2 tablespoons unsalted butter
1 tablespoon olive oil
¼ pound loin of pork, cut into 1-inch pieces
¼ pound veal, cut into 1-inch pieces
¼ pound mortadella
¼ pound prosciutto
Optional: 1 tablespoon beef marrow
1 egg
⅓ pound grated Parmesan cheese
A pinch of salt
A bit of freshly grated nutmeg
For the pasta:
1 pound white flour
4 eggs
To serve:
2 quarts good quality beef broth

Melt the butter and olive oil in a skillet over medium-high heat then sear the pork and veal on all sides. Remove the meat from the skillet and finely chop with the mortadella, prosciutto and marrow. Add the egg, Parmesan cheese, nutmeg and salt to the meat mixture and thoroughly combine.

Make dough with the flour and eggs. Roll it out into thin sheets. Cut it into 1½-inch squares. Place a bit of the filling onto each square. Fold it over to make a triangle. Hold two ends of the triangle and fold one over another to make a circle. It's easy to do this if you anchor the triangle on your pinkie finger while you're folding. Place the tortellini on a floured surface and cover with a dishtowel or plastic wrap so they won't dry out as you work. Cook them in a good meat or capon broth. Be careful not to overcook them because they will continue to cook as long as they remain in the broth. Turn off the heat and let them rest for a minute or two before serving.

Suggested wine: Gutturnio

N.B. There are many variations for the tortellini recipe because just about every family in the region has its own version. In some cases all the meat for the filling will start out raw — or some cooks will substitute turkey breast for the veal. Some people cut the pasta into rounds instead of squares. Despite the fact that there is a well-known gastronomic association whose mission it is to guard what they believe to be the only and irreplaceable recipe, there's an ongoing discussion as to which is the original recipe.

TOSCANA (TUSCANY)

The food of Tuscany is sober, elegant and well balanced—it perfectly reflects the landscape of the region. Authentic Tuscan cuisine has roots in peasant food found at inns and wine bars, as well as on noble tables. It's an original and sometimes mysterious mixture of flavors and habits celebrated by Lorenzo the Magnificent in his little poem, "I Beoni," which is actually a list of Florentine *trattorias*. Il Fico, Il Buco and L'Osteria delle Bertucce are just some of the names on the list where people gathered to eat fresh fava beans with pecorino cheese, succulent sausages, crunchy fried frogs, herring, fried crabs and—always—the unfailingly good beans, as well as, of course, lots of good Tuscan wine.

When Caterina de' Medici married the future Henry II, she took Tuscan food to the courts of France and in return brought French cuisine back home to Tuscany, most notably, the recipe for paparo all' arancia (duck with orange) that can be found in a fifteenth-century Tuscan cookbook, *Recettario Toscano*. It was the publication in the late nineteenth century, however, of Pellegrino Artusi's book, *La Scienza in Cucina e l'Arte di Mangiar Bene* (*Science in the Kitchen and the Art of Eating Well*), which brought widespread fame to the Tuscan table. Artusi dedicated a good portion of the book to descriptions of the food of the region.

Good examples of the region's culinary arts are found in its great cured meats (especially salami), excellent cheeses and the incredible extra virgin olive oil that's often eaten in combination with the historic and unique Tuscan bread, which has the ability to highlight any ingredient it accompanies. Soups are extraordinary. Pasta isn't really a traditional Tuscan dish; nevertheless, there are very good and original pasta dishes that reveal the influence of the region's neighbors. There are excellent seafood dishes and the beef found in Tuscany is of the highest quality—the same for game and fowl. It would be foolish not to mention fried food. Everything is fried, with the greatest respect for the starring ingredient, with light, airy and extremely tasty results. The earth is fragrant with wild mushrooms, truffles, aromatic herbs and extraordinary vegetables. Every city, every village, every piece of the countryside and hills has its own personality, which together make up the great Tuscan kitchen.

Antipasto alla toscana Mixed antipasti plate consisting of prosciutto, fett'unta (garlic bread) or panzanella (bread salad), spleen or game crostini, fennel sausage, olives and olive oil–marinated mushrooms. This dish wants to be served with the famous flavorless unsalted Tuscan bread.

Biroldo A blood sausage from the area around the province of Pistoia that's found in Versilia and Garfagnana as well. It's made with veal blood, cheese, innards, a salami mixture and abundant spices. It's often served with turnips.

Bruschetta Slices of rustic bread toasted in an oven or over a grill, then rubbed while still hot with a garlic clove and sprinkled with salt, pepper and top-quality extra virgin olive oil. Some variations are topped with very ripe tomatoes, wild fennel, oregano or a spoonful of *fagioli al fiasco* (see 155). Bruschetta is also called fett'unta or panunto.

Buristo or **burischio** Fresh salami made with meat from a pig's head, fried pork fat, pork blood, innards, spices, lemon and orange peel and garlic. Toasted pine nuts and raisins are sometimes added. The mixture is put into a pig's stomach then very slowly boiled. It's ready to eat the day after cooking — it's not aged. It's truly delicious when served with rustic bread and a good glass of red wine. It seems that the name is derived from the German wurst, or sausage.

Cavolo nero con le fette A modest or "poor" dish made by quickly boiling cavolo nero leaves, toasting slices of rustic bread, rubbing them with garlic then placing alternate slices of the bread and cabbage leaves in a baking dish. The whole thing is covered with top-quality olive oil, salt and freshly ground pepper to serve.

Coppiette Boar or lean beef slices flavored with hot pepper flakes and salt that are dried and then smoked. They are a specialty of the Maremma and are served as an antipasto.

Crostini alla toscana Sliced, toasted bread spread with a mixture of chopped chicken livers and giblets sautéed with anchovies, capers and herbs. In another version, the base of the mixture is veal spleen.

Fett'unta See *bruschetta* (above).

Ficattole di Prato Salted, oval-shaped breads with a slash down the middle that are fried and served with salami and cheese.

Finocchiona Typical Tuscan salami made with finely chopped pork, belly fat, wild fennel seeds, garlic, salt and pepper. Sometimes beef is added to the mixture. It's aged from seven months to a year.

Mallegato Blood sausage found in the area around the provinces of Siena, Lucca and Pistoia, quite similar to the *buristo* (page 144) and the *biroldo* (page 144). It's made with pork blood, candied citron, cracklings, raisins, pine nuts and spices. This blackish colored sausage is usually boiled to serve.

Necci Flatbreads made with chestnut flour, water and milk. They are cooked on special olive oil–greased irons. Necci are served with fresh cheese or ricotta. At one time the chestnut batter was enclosed in chestnut leaves before being cooked on the irons. They are a specialty of the area around Lucca and the Appenines near Pistoia.

Panunto or **Panunta** See *bruschetta* (page 144).

Panzanella A specialty of both Tuscany and Campania that is also made throughout Italy and influenced by the pan bagnat of Nice in France. It's made with hard, stale bread that's softened with water and vinegar, then mixed with sliced tomatoes and onions, cucumbers, anchovies, olives, basil and extra virgin olive oil. There are variations with different ingredients.

Pilze The cured meat typical of the province of Siena.

Prosciutto di lepre Very small prosciutti made from hare's thighs, not easy to find, made exclusively in the village of Sinalunga in the province of Siena.

Prosciutto toscano A very tasty and compact prosciutto to which large amounts of salt are applied during the curing process. To serve, the finished product is cut by hand into slices that, for prosciutto, are rather thick. Because of its intense flavor, it goes perfectly well with bland toasted Tuscan bread.

Rigatino Typical flat Tuscan pancetta.

Roventini or **migliacci** Blood sausages cooked in a skillet and served covered with sugar and grated cheese.

Salame toscano Salami made with ground lean pork meat and fresh clear pieces of pork fat, salt, pepper and a bit of garlic, which is then stuffed into natural casings. The salami is left to dry at room temperature then aged in a cellar. It's a good idea to serve it with a salad of field greens dressed with top-quality olive oil and typical bland Tuscan bread.

Sbriciolona Finocchiona.

Soppressata Usually a type of salami made with both fatty and lean pieces of ground pork that are then "pressed" together. The best-known Tuscan soppressata is from Siena, made with pig's head meat and flavored with the same spices used for *panforte* (page 159): cloves, coriander, black pepper, nutmeg and cinnamon.

Tondone A typically Florentine fried crêpe made with a flour-and-water batter and served with prosciutto or *buristo* (page 144) that dates from the time of the Stenterello, a famous eighteenth-century masked ball.

Torta con le acciughe Flatbread covered with anchovies, thinly sliced onions and fragrant herbs.

PASTA, GNOCCHI, RICE, POLENTA AND GRAINS

Armleti A first course very similar to testaroli from Pontremoli (which, technically, is in Emilia-Romagna).

Bomba di riso alla lunigianese A dish also with origins in Emilia-Romagna made with boned squab that's stuffed into chard leaves then cooked in chicken pan drippings. The packets are then stuffed into rice timbales.

Cuscusso alla livornese Couscous served with stewed cabbage and tomato meatballs, or, a stew made with chicken, beef, tomatoes, winter squash, chard, cardoons, fava beans, chickpeas and assorted spices. It's Arab in origin.

Gnocchi casentinesi Very similar to *strozzapreti* (page 147).

Pappardelle aretine Pappardelle dressed with duck sauce.

Pappardelle sulla lepre The most famous Tuscan pasta dish and perhaps the only authentic one. The word pappardelle comes from *pappare* that, in Tuscan dialect, means to eat with great gusto and appetite. These wide (3 cm) tagliatelle are traditionally dressed with a sauce made with hare stewed in red wine. Pappardelle dressed with rabbit sauce are another Tuscan specialty.

Pasta alla fornaia A pasta dish typical of Livorno. It's any long pasta — linguine, spaghetti or tagliolini — that are dressed with pesto made with walnuts, Parmesan cheese, Pecorino cheese, basil and extra virgin olive oil.

Pasticcio alla fiorentina A short crust pastry filled with maccheroni and meat ragù and, sometimes, shards of black truffles. It is then baked. The dish dates back to the Renaissance.

Pici or **pinci** Large, fat homemade spaghetti that are a specialty of the area around Siena, in particular Chiusi and Chianciano, where they're called pici. In the area around Montalcino they're called pinci. They're made with flour and water dough that is rolled out and cut into rectangles. Each rectangle is then rolled and pulled by hand. They are most notably dressed with crumbled, stale bread — il briciolata (as it is known in this particular province). However, they're often served with a sauce made with onions, a type of pancetta (rigatino) and tomatoes, or a sauce made with sliced mushrooms and tomatoes, or one with lamb ragù.

Polenta di neccio Chestnut-flour polenta that is a specialty of the mountain villages of Amiata in the province of Siena, of the Valle Garfagnana, the Casentino and the Pistoiese. It may be served with fresh cheese, ricotta, herring or pork sauce, or with cooked greens such as turnip greens. In Florence, this polenta is called pattona.

Risotto alla toscana A delicious risotto made with a base of sautéed onions, carrots and celery which is deglazed with red wine, then enriched with ground meat, Parmesan cheese, chicken livers and giblets (or, in some recipes, kidneys).

Risotto nero con le seppie alla toscana A "black" risotto made with cuttlefish and their ink, found in many regional cuisines. The Tuscan version includes beet greens or chard.

Strozzapreti Not only the name of a pasta from Emilia-Romagna but also for Tuscan-style gnocchi made with ricotta and chard or spinach.

Testaroli Crêpes made on special wrought iron or terra cotta griddles, called *testi*, with a batter of flour (sometimes whole-wheat or chestnut), water and salt. The cooked crêpes are cut into diamond shapes, boiled and then dressed with pesto, or meat, game or sausage ragù, or a mushroom sauce. The dish is typical of the area around Pontremoli and throughout the Lunigiana area. Historically, this is considered one of the first ways people cooked pasta. Testetti from the town of Chiavari in Liguria and crosetti from the town of Bedonia in the province of Parma are similar dishes.

Tordelli Typically Tuscan half-moon-shaped egg pasta ravioli filled with a substantial mixture of brains, veal, chard, pecorino cheese, eggs and spices usually dressed with a light, slightly pink veal ragù.

Tortelli di San Lorenzo Egg pasta tortelli filled with potatoes puréed with butter, Parmesan cheese, salt, pepper and nutmeg. They're cooked in broth, then dressed with melted butter, Parmesan and freshly ground black pepper or a meat or tomato sauce. They are specially made for the August 10 feast of the patron of the village of Borgo San Lorenzo near Florence.

SOUPS

Acquacotta A *piatto unico* (one-dish meal) typically prepared at sunrise by the dairy farmers and shepherds of the Maremma area that is meant to be eaten throughout the day without heating. There are a few different versions: one from Grosseto, with onions, peppers, celery, artichokes, tomatoes, olive oil, bread and eggs; another from Grosseto with onions, chard, fava beans, peas, carrots, celery, garlic, herbs, bread and eggs; and one from Siena with porcini mushrooms, tomatoes, garlic, olive oil, eggs and bread.

Bordatino A soup invented to be eaten on board (hence the name) sailing ships that were out at sea for long periods of time. Nowadays you'll find it in almost all seaside towns. The version from Livorno is made with cornmeal, beans and chard.

Briciolata Broth that contains crumbled ricotta and toasted bread typical of the area around Pistoia.

Brodo di fagiano A very refined pheasant broth served as an entrée with toasted bread and butter typical of the Maremma, an area known for its excellent hunting grounds.

Cacciucco The emblematic fish soup of the Tuscan coast, mostly associated with Livorno. The name has its origins either in the Turkish word *kukut*, which means "small pieces," or the Arabic word *shakshukli*, which means "a mixture of various things." In Livorno it's said that in order to make this soup you need to have at least five kinds of fish that have the letter C in the names. In reality many more are used and not necessarily with the letter C—from moray eel to conger eel to scorpion fish to octopus to cuttlefish to mullet and so on. Like most fish soups, cacciucco was originally a food of the poor, a way for fisherman to use the less commercially valuable catch. It's made with onions, garlic, sometimes carrots and celery, hot peppers, vinegar, bay leaf, red wine, tomatoes and parsley and is served with garlic-rubbed pieces of toasted bread. Because of its robust and decisive flavor, red wine is the drink of choice with cacciucco.

Cacciucco di ceci alla toscana A dense chickpea soup with chard, anchovies, tomato sauce, olive oil, garlic and onions served with toasted bread and grated pecorino cheese.

Carabaccia A Florentine-style onion soup with peas and eggs. It's one of those dishes whose origins are in question: was it born in France or in Tuscany? Onions have played an important role in the region's cuisine since the time of the

Etruscans. Testimony to that fact is found in the town of Cerveteri, where the onion bulb repeatedly figures in the *tomba degli stucchi* frescoes. The name of this soup is derived from a recipe called carabazada, made by the sixteenth century cook-servant Cristoforo Messisbugo.

Carcerato A modest soup typical of the area around Pistoia, a broth made with leftover innards or inferior cuts of meat. It's thickened with stale bread, then dressed with extra virgin olive oil, pecorino cheese and fried *rigatino* (page 145), a type of pancetta.

Cinestrata A typical soup of the Chianti area. The recipe dates back to the Renaissance, when it was served to reinvigorate the sick and to newly married couples after their first night together. It's made with chicken broth, egg yolks and Marsala wine or Vin Santo garnished with sugar, cinnamon and nutmeg. Today, this delicious soup has almost disappeared — there are only a few families who make it. It's named for yellow broom flowers (*ginestra*).

Cipollata A traditional Sienese onion soup made with rigatino or pancetta, sausages and pork ribs.

Garmugia A springtime soup from Lucca made with fava beans, peas, artichokes, asparagus, olive oil, pancetta, onions and ground meat. The ingredients vary, like all vegetable dishes, according to what's fresh from the garden.

Ginestrata See *cinestrata* (above).

Infarinata It's said that this dish is where polenta meets soup — it is in fact a very loose polenta to which beans, cavolo nero, lardo, pork skin, garlic and other ingredients are added. It may be eaten immediately before it sets or, after it has chilled and set, cut into pieces and fried. It's typical of the Garfagnana area.

Intruglia Exactly like *infarinata* (above). It's typical of the Versilia area.

Minestra di farro A healthy and nutritious soup made with farro, beans, pork rind, celery, garlic, sage, marjoram, tomatoes and spices. Its origins are remote but it's characteristic of the Tuscan kitchen, specifically, the Garafagnana. It's also made in Lazio, Umbria, Abruzzi and Sardinia.

Minestrone di castagne A simple soup made with dried chestnuts and beans to which a bit of rice and a sauté of lardo and aromatic herbs are added just before serving. This rare and tasty peasant soup is typical of the Lunigiana area.

Pappa col pomodoro This extraordinary but modest soup is made with Tuscan bread, lots of tomatoes, garlic, basil, black pepper and top-quality extra virgin olive oil. This soup reached the pinnacle of fame when it appeared not only in the comic strip *Il Giornalino di Gian Burrasca* but was also immortalized in an eponymous song in the 1960s.

Ribollita A very dense, decidedly wintertime soup made with beans, bread and cavolo nero. It's called ribollita ("reboiled") because after it is made, it's left to rest overnight allowing the flavors to marry each other. It's reboiled the following day to serve. Originally this was such a "poor" dish that it was eaten for many days in a row, becoming more flavorful each time it was reboiled. There are a few variations. In one, the soup is covered with thinly sliced onions, then gratinéed. It should always have a drizzle of good quality extra virgin oil before serving.

Sburrita On the island of Elba, the name for *cacciucco* (page 148).

Zimino di ceci A type of Tuscan and Ligurian preparation that usually involves chard or spinach and cuttlefish, salt cod or other fish. However, fish aren't used for this particular zimino — instead, it has a chickpea sauce enriched with tomatoes, dried mushrooms and, of course, chard or spinach. If the cooking liquid from the chickpeas is added to the other ingredients, it becomes a soup.

Zuppa di agnello A springtime soup made with lamb, dried mushrooms, tomatoes, water and spinach flavored with herbs and cloves. This ancient soup is a specialty of the shepherds from around Grosseto.

Zuppa di lenticchie con fagiano Lentil soup to which pieces of roasted pheasant are added. It's a family recipe, from Siena.

Zuppa frantoiana A dense soup made with beans, cavolo nero (in season), potatoes, winter squash, fennel, borage and other herbs, then flavored with sautéed garlic and lardo. It's served by pouring it over garlic-rubbed pieces of toasted bread that have been covered with the first pressing of olive oil. It's comes from the old peasant custom of offering a meal to the operator of the olive oil press (*frantoio*) that uses the first sharp and pungent oil.

CONDIMENTS, SAUCES AND EGGS

Frittata con gli zoccoli A very simple frittata made with cubes of prosciutto or pancetta. *Zoccoli* are clogs.

Salsa d'agresto A very old recipe for salsa made with

pounded sour grapes (*agresto*), almonds, walnuts, the white part of bread, sugar, onions, garlic, parsley, salt and pepper diluted in broth. It's a good accompaniment to boiled or roasted meats.

Salsa di dragoncello An interesting sauce from Siena made with chopped tarragon, the white part of bread, garlic, olive oil and vinegar. It's delicious with boiled meats.

Sugo di carne alla toscana A sauce made with beef chopped with dried mushrooms, tomatoes, celery, carrots, onions and red wine.

FISH, CRUSTACEANS AND SHELLFISH

Anguilla Eel.

Anguilla all'aretina Chunks of eel skewered with sage leaves and bread cubes.

Anguilla alla fiorentina Chunks of eel quickly sautéed in olive oil with herbs, then breaded and baked in red wine.

Anguilla in umido con piselli Pieces of eel cooked in a sauce made with olive oil, garlic, tomatoes and fresh peas.

Cacciucco See page 148.

Ceche or **cee fritte** The Tuscan name for elvers, baby eels no more than two inches in length. They come out of the sea during the winter months and get caught up in freshwater currents at the mouth of the Arno River, where they are fished at night with tightly woven nets, illuminated by bright lamps shining on the water. They may be fried or prepared in a frittata.

Ceche or **cee fritte alla livornese** Elvers cooked in a skillet with olive oil, garlic, sage, salt and pepper. They become creamy when cooked.

Ceche or **cee fritte alla pisana** Elvers first cooked with olive oil, garlic and sage. Eggs beaten with breadcrumbs, Parmesan cheese, salt and pepper are then added. The dish is baked to serve.

Cicala di mare Clam-like shellfish.

Nicchi The name used in the seaside town of Viareggio for a type of clam usually made into a typical local soup.

Scampi or **gamberi alla viareggina** Boiled, peeled shrimp mixed with boiled cannellini beans, fresh tomatoes, basil and extra virgin olive oil.

Sparnocchi The name used in Viareggio for shrimp.

Stoccafisso or **baccalà alla livornese** Soaked and rehydrated dry or salt cod slowly stewed in olive oil with onions, puréed tomatoes and seasonings, then finished with a splash of Vin Santo.

Triglie alla livornese Mullets cooked in a skillet with olive oil, garlic and tomatoes, then finished with freshly chopped parsley. The recipe was created by Jews who came to Livorno after being expelled from Spain as a way to honor what was, for them, a new vegetable — the tomato.

Zimino di seppie or **totani** See *zimino di ceci* (page 150). This version is made with cuttlefish or squid.

MEAT

Agnello alla cacciatora A stew made with chunks of lamb, olive oil, garlic, onions, tomatoes and white wine.

Arista alla fiorentina A typical Tuscan dish made with saddle or loin of pork covered with fennel seeds, fresh rosemary and garlic, then oven- or spit-roasted. It's served with roasted potatoes and turnip greens or cavolo nero. It may be eaten at room temperature.

Arrosto morto A term used to define the way a roast (beef, veal or chicken, etc.) is finished in a pot with garlic and olive oil after it has been spit-roasted.

Bistecca alla cacciatora A beef chop cooked in a skillet with garlic or onion, salt, pepper, tomatoes and red wine.

Bistecca alla fiorentina A cut of beef that Americans call a porterhouse. A serving may weigh from one pound to two pounds and should be at least three fingers high. A true Fiorentina comes from the Chianina breed of cattle from the Val Chiana. There are very precise cooking directions for this bistecca. It must be left to tenderize for at least five days. It should be cooked over a wood-burning (chestnut, olive or old grape vines) fire. It must be carefully watched as it's cooking — one mistake and it will burn, giving it a disgustingly bitter flavor. In order to avoid any loss of its juices, or getting it too dark, there should be balanced relationship between the dimensions of the steak and its distance from the fire. It should be salted on both sides *after* it's been seared. Last but not least, something that absolutely should not be forgotten: as the steak cooks, little drops of fat want to fall on the embers creating flames that will burn the meat. To avert this, cover the grill with sea salt that will not only keep the fat from dripping but will allow for uniform heat. The steak is served rare with a drizzle of extra virgin olive oil, salt and freshly ground pepper. The simple, well-tended bistecca alla Fiorentina has become the symbol of excellence in the Tuscan kitchen.

Buglione An old-fashioned recipe for stew made with left-over cuts of meat — chicken necks, turkey, pig's feet, lamb shoulder, rabbit liver, etc. — and vegetables and aromatic herbs. By the time it's served over toasted bread, it is practically reduced to a cream. It's a specialty of the area around Siena and Arezzo.

Carne secca or **carnesecca** Tuscan beef pancetta, which is essentially corned beef. It's straight out of the Roman-Jewish kitchen.

Cibreo This emblematic Tuscan dish is a stew made with chicken giblets, cock's combs and testicles, liver and kidneys, then finished with egg yolks and lemon juice, just like a fricassee. The name cibreo comes from the Latin word *zingibereus*, a dish made with ginger (which in Tuscany connotes hot pepper) fit for a king. Pellegrino Artusi calls this dish "a simple, delicate and agreeable stew perfect for those suffering from lack of appetite and for the sickly."

Cinghiale or **cignale in dolce forte** A Renaissance dish made with a combination of complex ingredients that may seem antithetical but actually complement each other: vinegar, raisins, chocolate, candied citron, pine nuts and lots of spices that rise to meet the strongly flavored main ingredient, wild boar. Sometimes a slice of panforte is part of the ingredient list. This dish is found throughout Tuscany but primarily in the Maremma where hunting is prevalent.

Cioncia A stew made with fatty (meaty) parts of the veal: face and ears, etc., and hot peppers, spices and black olives. Cioncia is a specialty of the village of Pescia in the province of Pistoia.

Fegatelli alla toscana A dish made with large pieces of pork liver that are dipped into breadcrumbs flavored with garlic, fennel seeds and spices, then wrapped in pork caul, threaded onto skewers with chunks of bread, pieces of *rigatino* (page 145) and wild fennel branches. The skewers are spit- or oven-roasted. This traditional dish of the Garfagnana area is called fegatelli del mi pa in dialect. At one time, the same ingredients were threaded onto bay leaf branches that had been stripped of bark, allowing their fragrance to flavor the liver, etc.

Fiorentina See *bistecca alla fiorentina* (page 152).

Folaghe alla Puccini Folaghe are little wild birds with a faintly fishy flavor. In this dish the birds are boiled in water and white wine, then served with a very tasty sauce made with anchovies, smoked salmon, caviar, olive oil, fragrant herbs and lemon juice. There are many variations of this dish, which seems to have been invented by the composer Giacomo Puccini, who lived near Lago di Massaciuccoli in Tuscany and hunted for folaghe.

Fritto misto alla toscana An excellent fried mixture that includes chicken and potato croquettes, brains, sweetbreads, artichokes, zucchini, lamb chops, chicken livers, etc. Each ingredient is floured, dipped in beaten eggs then fried in olive oil. It is a light and delicate preparation that respects the freshness of all the ingredients.

Granelli alla Maremmana A very difficult-to-find dish usually made after sheep, calves or horses have been castrated, prepared by dipping the animal testicles in beaten eggs then frying them in olive oil.

Lepre in dolce forte A complex Tuscan dish made by cooking hare in a sauce made with *rigatino* (page 145) or pancetta, prosciutto, pine nuts, candied citron and orange peel, raisins, cocoa, fragrant herbs, spices, dried cookies, red wine, vinegar and sugar.

Lonze A term that has various meanings according to the region: in Tuscany it's used in its plural form to indicate the secondary parts of beef that are usually used for stewing. Generally, the stew is made with the head, cheeks and lips of an ox.

Maiale ubriaco A dish made with pork ribs cooked in a skillet with garlic and parsley and finished by deglazing the skillet with red wine.

Peposo A very spicy stew, typical of the coastal Versilia area, in particular the town of Viareggio, made with beef shank, tomatoes, wine, lots of herbs and — true to its name — lots of pepper.

Pollo Chicken.

Pollo alla diavola A split chicken that is pounded flat then cooked over a wood-burning fire while being continually brushed with a mixture of olive oil, hot pepper flakes or freshly ground black pepper and lemon juice.

Pollo fritto alla toscana Pieces of chicken that are dipped in an egg and flour batter then fried in olive oil.

Pollo ripieno alla lunigianese A boned chicken stuffed with a mixture of chard, ricotta, pecorino cheese, Parmesan cheese and eggs, then sewn closed and poached. It's served with the same kinds of sauces normally served with boiled meats.

Rosticciana Very flavorful grilled pork ribs.

Scottiglia Sometimes called the cacciucco of meat because it's a mixture of different kinds of meat just like the fish stew is a mixture of a variety of fish. The scottiglia can include guinea hen, squab, veal, pork, chicken, other game birds and lamb or goat stewed with tomatoes and a mixture of vegetables and herbs. It's typical of the area around Arezzo but is also found in the Maremma.

Stufatino Veal stew cooked in olive oil, garlic, rosemary, tomatoes and red wine.

Trippa e zampa alla fiorentina Veal tripe and hock that are boiled, then cut into pieces and browned in olive oil with prosciutto fat, celery, carrots and onions and finished in broth with basil or marjoram. Some recipes include tomatoes. It's served covered with grated Parmesan cheese.

VEGETABLES

Asparagi alla fiorentina Boiled, buttered asparagus topped with fried eggs and grated Parmesan cheese to serve.

Braschetta A Tuscan word for *cavolo nero* (below).

Cannellini A white bean of Italian origin found mostly in Tuscany.

Carciofi ritti Cleaned, whole artichokes that are cooked, heads down, in chopped pancetta, parsley and garlic, then slowly stewed in olive oil and water.

Cardi trippati alla toscana Cardoons that are first boiled, then sautéed in butter and onions, flavored with Parmesan cheese and cinnamon, breaded and fried, placed in a baking dish, covered with grated Parmesan cheese and gratinéed.

Cavolo nero The emblematic Tuscan cabbage that doesn't grow as a head but instead as a bunch of very dark green — almost black — crinkly leaves. Its real season is autumn, but it can be found in the wintertime as well. It's the defining ingredient in the famous soup *ribollita* (page 150). It's also called cavolo toscano, cavolo palmizio or cavolo a penna.

Fagioli Beans.

Fagioli al fiasco Celebrated Tuscan bean dish usually made with cannellini beans that are put into a glass flask or narrow-necked jar, a *fiasco,* and dressed with olive oil, garlic, sage, black pepper, rosemary and water. The *fiasco* is placed in a fireplace near a wood-burning fire, so that the beans can cook slowly, absorb all the liquid and become very flavorful.

Fagioli all'uccelletto Another typically Tuscan bean preparation in which the cannellini beans are stewed with tomatoes, olive oil, garlic and sage or rosemary. Sometimes sausages are cooked with the beans. The dish is probably called all'uccelletto because it's cooked the same way as little birds (*uccelletti*) are cooked in Tuscany — with sage.

Fagioli toscanelli See *cannellini* (page 155).

Fagiolini di Sant'Anna Exquisite, tender, unusually long green beans typical of the village of Pescia in the province of Pistoia. These not-very-easy-to-find beans are cooked with olive oil, garlic and fresh tomatoes.

Rape amare or **rapini** Turnip greens.

Sedani alla pratese A dish in which parboiled celery stalks are cut into approximately two-inch pieces, then filled with a mixture of chopped veal and chicken livers bound with eggs. The filled celery pieces are floured and fried, set in a baking dish, covered with meat sauce and gratinéed.

CHEESE AND DAIRY PRODUCTS

Marzolino An historic cheese distributed throughout Europe in the period from the Middle Ages through the Renaissance made from mostly sheep's milk adjusted with a bit of cow's milk. This lightly and pleasingly sharp, semi-fresh cheese is pressed and shaped by hand into small ovals. The thin crust is straw colored while the soft but dry body is white. For the most part the cheese is produced in the Chianti area of the region: Castellina, Radda, Gaiole and Greve. The fresh cheese should be consumed between March (hence the name) and April. The aged version is ready to eat in the autumn of the year of its production.

Pecorino delle crete Delicious but rare sheep's milk cheese from Siena that's used for *formaggio di fossa* (page 134), the cheese that's left to age in a "ditch."

Pecorino toscano A particular cheese that differentiates itself from all other Italian sheep's milk cheeses because of its extremely delicate flavor and, in particular, its mild streak. There's also a difference between the tender and hard versions of the cheese. Both of them are made exclusively with whole sheep's milk and are always produced between the months of September and June. The tender version has a golden yellow crust, a pale straw yellow body and is mild with a sharp streak and the fragrance of the pastures. The crust of the semi-hard version may be brown, chestnut or reddish while the body is intensely colored, almost pale gold.

Raveggiolo White cheese that is tender, mild, creamy—almost buttery—made with goat's or sheep's milk, preferably a combination of both, in Tuscany and Umbria. Its curd is cut into lumps and then simply drained. Because raveggiolo is presented on reed or fern mats, it's sometimes called giuncata or felciata. It needs to be eaten fresh—it shouldn't age.

Toscanello A full-flavored, rich, salty and sharp sheep's milk cheese that needs to be aged for at least six months before serving. In one version whole black peppercorns are mixed into the paste.

SWEETS AND LIQUEURS

Africani or **affricani** Little pastries typical of Greve in Chianti made with egg yolks, butter and sugar and put into paper cups to bake. The name comes from the color of the cooked product (see *poppe di monaca*, page 159).

Alchermes An intensely red liqueur originally made by the Florentine monks at the Santa Maria Novella church by macerating cinnamon, whole cloves, nutmeg, vanilla and fragrant herbs in alcohol, then adding sugar, essences of rose and jasmine and coloring it with cochineal. It's mostly used in pastry making.

Ballotte Chestnuts boiled in their shells.

Befanini Pastries from Viareggio made during the Epiphany celebration with a dough of flour, eggs, sugar, butter, milk, yeast, liqueur and fennel seeds. They are cut into multi-shaped forms: animals, hearts, stars and the old woman who brings gifts to children on Twelfth Night *(befana)* and decorated with colored sprinkles or sugar.

Berlingozzi Ring-shaped sweets typically made during the Carnival celebrations mainly in the area around Pistoia. Both crunchy and crumbly, they are quite an ancient tradition—so much so that none other than Lorenzo de' Medici wrote a little poem about them. The name comes from the word for Fat Thursday, *berlingaccio*.

Biroldo dolce Pork blood sausage flavored with pine nuts, raisins and sugar.

Biscottini di Prato Little dry cookies flavored with whole almonds. They are made like any other biscotto: first the dough is baked in a loaf form, then cut into small slices and baked again. Sometimes pine nuts, hazelnuts or pieces of chocolate are added to the dough. They are often erroneously called *cantucci* (page 158).

Bolli Sweet rolls from the area around Livorno made by adding eggs, olive oil, orange blossom water, anise liqueur, sugar, cinnamon and fennel seeds to bread dough.

Bomboloni Something like jelly doughnuts, sometimes filled with jam and sometimes with pastry cream, the classic bombolone looks more like the classic American doughnut and is simply sprinkled with sugar to serve. They're found throughout Italy but originally are Tuscan.

Brigidini Small, very thin anise-flavored wafers made with special embossed irons. The name comes from the creators of the wafer, the nuns from the convent of Santa Brigida di Pistoia. Today the wafers are considered a specialty of the town of Lamporecchio in the province of Pistoia.

Buccellato A traditional cake from Lucca made for First Communion celebrations. The ring-shaped, yeasted cake is flavored with Marsala wine, fennel seeds, candied citron or raisins and is customarily quite large.

Cantucci Cookies typically made with bread dough, olive oil, sugar and fennel seeds. They're often confused with *biscottini di Prato* (page 157).

Castagnaccio Traditional Tuscan cake made with chestnut flour, water and a bit of olive oil, usually stuffed or garnished with pine nuts, raisins and fresh rosemary. There are fried versions as well.

Cavallucci Diamond-shaped cookies from Siena made with flour, sugar, walnuts, candied orange peel, anise and cinnamon.

Cenci Crumbly fried pastry ribbons covered with powdered sugar typically served during the Carnival celebration. The name varies according to region.

Coccoli Rice fritters very much like *sommommoli* (page 159).

Copata An ancient recipe from Siena made by placing dark or light honey brittle, walnuts and anise seeds between two wafers. Similar preparations include the cubbaita from Sicily, the copete from Basilicata, copeta or cupeta from Puglia and copett from Lombardy.

Corona di San Bartolomeo A very special sweet from Pistoia made for the August 24 feast of San Bartolomeo, composed of baked ball and medallion shapes of assorted candies and chocolates all strung together on a piece of string to make a necklace to honor the patron saint.

Ficattola This very simple cake made with bread dough and figs is a specialty of the area around Chianti.

Frittelle di tondone alla fiorentina Fritters with an unusual name that comes from the way they're made. The first step is to make a large flour and water fritter, taking special care not to let it take on color, called the *tondone*. It's then pounded into pieces in a mortar. The pieces, with the addition of lemon zest, egg yolks, raisins and stiffly beaten egg whites, are made into a new batter. The batter is fried by the spoonful and the cooked fritters covered with powdered sugar to serve.

Fruttini Little fruit-shaped sweets made with marzipan, typical of the pastry makers of Livorno and very similar to those made in Sicily.

Melatelli Humble sweets that are a beekeeper's specialty, made by reducing the water that comes from cleaning the hives into dense, honey-flavored syrup, then mixing it with flour, eggs and grated orange or lemon zest.

Mantovana di Prato A very soft and tender cake with chopped pine nuts and almonds that's a specialty of Prato.

Nociata Tuscan sweet made with chopped walnuts mixed with honey and bay leaves. It's also a specialty of the Lazio region where it's sold as Christmas torrone.

Orecchie di Amman Fried sweets that are similar to the cenci that originated in the Jewish kitchens of Livorno.

Pan di ramerino Little breads made with a sweet yeast dough, olive oil, raisins and rosemary leaves.

Pan pepato or **pampepato** An antique sweet bread usually made with dried fruits, crystallized honey, chocolate, black pepper and other spices. It varies both in ingredients and shape, however, according to province and region.

Panforte di Siena This long-lasting cake is the gastronomic symbol of Siena, made with a recipe with origins in the honey cakes made in the Middle Ages. It's made with flour, almonds, dried and candied fruits and spices.

Pattona See *castagnaccio* (page 158).

Poppe di monaca Little round pastries made with whipped butter, stiffly beaten egg whites and sugar. For practical reasons, they're often served with *africani* (page 157) because one uses egg yolks and the other the whites. They're a specialty of Impruneta.

Ricciarelli Crumbly oval-shaped cookies made with vanilla-flavored almond dough. They are an antique specialty of Siena that seems to have origins in the Muslim world.

Sommommoli or **frittelle bianche di riso** Rice fritters flavored with either lemon or orange zest traditionally made for the March 19 Feast of San Giuseppe.

Stiacciata alla fiorentina Sweet, yeasted loaves based on an ancient Tuscan recipe. They need an inordinate amount of time to rise—two days—and are made with flour, yeast, fennel seeds that have macerated in Vin Santo or Marsala wine, olive oil, eggs, butter and orange blossom water. Another version includes raisins.

Torta coi bischeri A crostata, or tart, filled with a mixture of cooked rice, milk, raisins, candied fruits, pine nuts, chocolate and sugar topped with a cross-hatch made with the same short crust pastry as its shell. You'll find this tart throughout Tuscany but Pistoia is its real home.

Torta Garfagnina An ancient Tuscan cake, prepared for the feast of San Pietro, made with a dough of flour, finely chopped almonds, anise seeds, lemon peel, sugar, eggs, butter, liqueur, milk, bicarbonate of soda and cream of tartar or yeast.

Zuccotto A half sphere–shaped semifreddo dessert made by lining a bowl with pieces of sponge cake, then filling it with pastry cream and whipped cream. The filling may also include bits of chocolate and candied fruits.

WINE

Tuscany can brag about having more D.O.C.G. wines than any other region in Italy: Chianti, Brunello and Vino Nobile di Montepulciano. You would expect nothing less from a region of uninterrupted hills that reach from the Mediterranean Sea to the Appenine foothills—ideal terrain for the cultivation of vineyards. The Etruscans began to cultivate vineyards in the fifth century B.C. and the Romans sent their great sailing cargo ships packed with wine-filled amphorae out of Italy's coastal cities to all of Europe. It was in the eleventh century that vines started to be planted in the Chianti area of the region. The area of the Chiantigiani was almost immediately raided by the Sienesi and the Florentines. In order to protect their zone, the vintners of Chianti banded together in a *lega* or league. The symbol of that league was a black rooster on a gold background, from a painting by Vasari that hangs in the Palazzo Vecchio. Today, the black rooster is the brand image of Chianti classico.

Artimino Less well known than its relative, Carmignano, this red wine has the same characteristics. It does, however, have a shorter life. It's a good table wine.

Bianco valdichiana A bright, straw yellow wine with a fresh, slightly bitter flavor with almond overtones. The overwhelming presence of Trebbiano grapes gives this wine its persistent aroma. It's an excellent table wine that goes particularly well with antipasti, delicate first courses, fish and white meats.

Brunello di Montalcino The great supporting actor to the star, Chianti. It was born in the nineteenth century in the town of Montalcino in the province of Siena when vintners began to make a 100% Sangiovese varietal wine without the addition of Canaiolo and white grapes as they do for Chianti. The result is a beautifully structured wine that is in the same class as the best French wines. In fact, because of its vivid ruby red color, its full, dry flavor and its profound aroma, Brunello may be compared to a Bordeaux or Burgundy. It's terrific with roast meats but at its best with game. Brunello's younger brother is "il Rosso." Even though it's a wine with class and with the structure of a great wine, because of its age and its tannins, it is a good accompaniment to simple dishes.

Candia White wine produced in the hills between Massa and Carrara that definitely feels the influence of the nearby region of Liguria. In fact, it is made with Vermentino and Albarola varietals. The result is a delicate, slightly bitter, faintly floral wine perfect to accompany fish dishes. The sweet and sparkling versions go well with local sweet dishes such as torta di riso (rice tart).

Carmignano Produced in the eponymous area in the province of Florence, a wine made with the same varietal as Chianti—with the addition of Cabernet, which gives it its velvety texture. It emits an intensely violet aroma and marries well with roasts and red meats.

Chianti Starting at the end of the Second World War, when one said "Italian wine," one was talking about Chianti. Very often this wine, in its characteristic straw-covered bottle, wasn't exactly the best quality or the most genuine. Somewhere in the 1970s there was a revolution! New vines like Cabernet were planted next to Sangiovese and Canaiolo and often the white grapes were eliminated; thus, a new, more robust and structured wine, adapted to long aging, was born. You can recognize a good, young Chianti by its brilliant color, winey aroma and dry and justly tannic flavor. It's a perfect companion to roast pork and pappardelle with rabbit or hare sauce. It should also be served with aged pecorino cheese or assorted game dishes from the Maremma.

Elba An excellent table wine that is fresh, dry and slightly bitter. When aged for a little while, it becomes the perfect wine to accompany roasts and more intricate dishes. The Rosso is made mostly from the Sangiovese varietal with a touch of Canaiolo. The Bianco, locally called Procanico, is for all intents and purposes a Trebbiano, a very pleasing straw yellow, slightly floral, fresh and dry wine that's a perfect accompaniment for fish dishes.

Montecarlo Produced in the province of Lucca, the Rosso is ruby red with garnet reflections, a full-bodied, fragrant wine perfect to drink with a roasted guinea hen or little spit-roasted birds. The straw-colored Bianco is slightly fragrant and fresh flavored. It has a rather elevated alcohol content and improves as it ages for a year or two. It goes well with mussel soup, mixed fried fish and other fish entrées.

Montescudaio Another pleasing but simply structured table wine produced in the province of Pisa. The Rosso is tannic and slightly bitter while the Bianco is fresh and delicate.

Morellino A Sangiovese produced in the village of Scansano in the province of Grosseto. The young ruby red wine is pleasingly tasty and tannic. As it ages, it takes on orange overtones, the aroma becomes more refined and it acquires a certain softness. It's good with pasta dishes and risotto with meat sauces. After it ages, however, it can accompany roasts and aged cheeses.

Moscadello A light, fragrant, slightly sparkling white dessert wine produced in the town of Montalcino in the province of Siena.

Parina Produced in the town of Orbetello in the province of Grosseto, the soft, tasty, intensely fragrant Rosso is a high-quality table wine and the Bianco, made with 80% Trebbiano grapes, is fresh and slightly bitter, making it a perfect aperitif wine or an accompaniment to seafood antipasti.

Pomino Produced in the eponymous area in the province of Florence, the soft and fragrant Rosso goes well with roast pork and all barnyard animals and the fragrant, low-acid Bianco goes well with crustaceans.

Rosso lucchese A robust, slightly bitter, vivid ruby red wine produced in the hills around the province of Lucca. It's a good table wine that goes well with hearty meat dishes.

Ugolino Also called Bianco di Donoratico, Ugolino is produced in the eponymous town in the province of Livorno with Trebbiano grapes. It's fresh, fragrant and slightly acidic—perfect to drink with mullet cooked in parchment and fish soups.

Vernaccia di San Gemignano The vines that make this well-structured, compelling dry white wine are native to the area where it's produced. It's soft and with a floral aroma making it a splendid aperitif. Try it with fresh caciotta cheese drizzled with freshly pressed olive oil. It's perfect with fish dishes as well.

Vin Santo The Tuscan kitchen relies on this wine from antipasti to desserts. For the famous appetizer, crostini with chicken livers, this wine is used to macerate the livers. Chicken is covered with beaten eggs and Vin Santo before it's fried, and the wine lends a certain grittiness to roast meat dishes and sauces. Desserts aren't desserts—especially dry cookies such as ricciarelli di Siena or biscottini di Prato—without a glass of Vin Santo. Vin Santo is produced in two versions: dry, which is reminiscent of sherry and makes a perfect aperitif, and the milder version, the great dessert wine with its sweet, slightly bitter flavor. In each case Vin Santo is amber colored, with an ethereal aroma and a strong ambrosial flavor.

Vino Nobile di Montepulciano Made from a varietal very similar to Chianti, full flavored and richly fragrant, with a garnet color that develops shades of orange as it ages. It goes well with roast meats and game.

Ribollita
Serves 6

2 pounds dry cannellini beans soaked
   overnight in cold water with a pinch of
   baking powder
2 onions
2 cloves garlic
Extra virgin olive oil
A prosciutto bone, or a piece of boiled,
   chopped pork rind, or best of all,
      a few tablespoons of chopped *rigatino*
      (page 145)
Water or broth
Salt
2 peeled and seeded tomatoes, chopped
2 carrots, diced
1 rib celery, chopped
1 potato, peeled and diced
1 leek, white part only, chopped
¾ pound purple cabbage or kale, finely
   chopped (tough ribs removed)
Freshly ground black pepper

Chop 1 onion and 1 clove garlic, then sauté them with a bit
of olive oil and the pork ingredient in a large casserole—
terra cotta if possible. Add the soaked beans and cover with
water or broth and simmer for 2 hours. At this point add
salt to taste (adding salt at the beginning would toughen the
skin of the beans). Now, chop the other onion and clove of
garlic and sauté them in a bit of olive oil. Add the tomatoes,
carrots, celery, potato and leek and cover with the cooking
liquid from the beans, some more liquid and 2/3 of the
beans passed through a food mill. When it boils, add the
cabbage. Cook for about another hour. Add more salt as
needed and freshly ground black pepper to taste. Let the
soup cool then reboil it with some very thinly sliced raw
onion. You could also line a deep baking dish with bread,
pour the soup over it, then gratinée it in the oven. Other-
wise serve the soup in individual soup plates over sliced
bread and garnish with freshly pressed olive oil.

Suggested wine: Bianco Valdichiana

MARCHE (MARCHES)

Marches, with its sweet and delicate terrain, is the transition point between northern and southern Italy both physically and culturally. The components of the landscape directly correspond to the production of food in the region: the coastline with its fishermen and sailors, the land with its vintners and farmers and the mountains with their shepherds.

Up until the thirteenth century, the region had a relationship with the East. Ancona was a Doric colony and Numana was founded by the Siculi, an ancient tribe from eastern Sicily. The Greeks, who were frequent visitors to the entire area, introduced a variety of foods to the region. The Romans, who dominated the area, contributed vegetable and grain soups, farro polenta with chickpeas, lentils, fava beans, beans, fresh cheese, honey and eggs to the region's table. During the Barbarian invasion, the varieties of food declined and for nourishment the population began to rely more on fish than on the harvest of the land.

During the Medieval period, vegetables, legumes and small amounts of pork, goose or game were consumed with very spicy sauces. As time passed, the cuisine became richer again. Now, the contemporary Marchigiano cuisine is fundamentally based on the harvest of the land: peas and artichokes from Fossombrone, cauliflower from Jesi and fava beans from Ostra, to name just a few. There's an outstanding selection of salami and cured meats, including the great ciauscolo. There are top-quality fowl, rabbits, pigs, lambs and goats. The excellent beef comes from a breed, razza bianca Marchigiana, which is unique to the region. The forests provide an infinite variety of mushrooms and a splendid truffle, di Aqualagna, that's considered the equivalent—if not better—of those from Alba. Just as the region's geographical position is centered, the true character of the Marchigiano cuisine is balance, as exemplified by its seafood dishes.

ANTIPASTI, CURED MEATS, BREAD, FLATBREADS AND SAVORY TARTS

Barbaja Salted pork cheek.
Caciù Large ravioli filled with puréed fava beans, then fried.
Chichiripieno A type of stuffed focaccia from the area around Offida in the province of Ascoli Piceno. The filling usually includes tuna, anchovies, pickled peppers, capers,

mixed pickled vegetables, little artichokes, parsley and olive oil. As soon as it comes out of the oven, it's brushed with olive oil and a bit of red wine. The name comes from the dialect word for pizza, chichi.

Ciaccia A special pizza made with eggs. It comes from the town of Apecchio in the province of Pesaro-Urbino.

Ciauscolo or **ciabuscolo** or **ciavuscolo** Soft salami made with very finely ground pork, typical of the area around the provinces of Macerata and Ascoli Piceno. Additional ingredients include pork fat, vino cotto, garlic, salt and pepper. After it's put in a soft casing (*budello gentile*), it's slightly smoked over juniper berries. This is one of the few spreadable Italian salami.

Coppa marchigiana A cooked cured meat made with pork rind, parts of the head, black pepper, nutmeg and orange peel. It's a specialty of the province of Ascoli Piceno.

Crescia Pizza made with bread dough. It's dimpled to allow the topping—olive oil, onions, salt and rosemary—to sink in.

Crostoli A flatbread similar to the *piadina romagnola* (page 123) but made with flour, eggs and milk. It's served with prosciutto and cheese in the villages of San Leo, Carpegna and Montefeltro on the border with Emilia-Romagna.

Goletta The salted and aged lower part of a pig's snout.

Lonza Two boned pork loins prepared by salting, then letting them rest for forty-eight hours. They are then washed with warm water and wine, dried and then left in the open air for a day. They are then put into a bull's bladder casing, stuck with smashed garlic cloves, covered with black pepper, then with olive oil, tied up with twine and hung in a well-aired room to age for about two months.

Mazzafegato Salami made with ground pork livers, lungs and assorted spices, slightly smoked in its casing, then aged.

Olive all'ascolana Huge Ascolane olives that are opened with a spiral cut, pitted and then stuffed with a filling made with ground meat and salami, spices, cheese and eggs. They're dipped in beaten eggs, covered with breadcrumbs and fried. It's a mistake to use industrially pitted olives for this dish.

Piconi Ravioli filled with pecorino cheese, eggs and freshly ground black pepper then baked. They're typical of the province of Ascoli Piceno.

Pizza al formaggio A type of savory panettone enriched with ricotta, cubes of fresh pecorino cheese and grated aged pecorino, traditionally served during Easter celebrations in the town of Jesi in the province of Ancona.

Prosciutto di Carpegna A prosciutto unique in all of Italy because of the way it's made. First of all, it comes from a type of lean, black pig. The meat is salted, soaked in vinegar, "massaged" with black pepper and then smoked over acorns and juniper berries.

Prosciutto di Montefeltro A prosciutto first covered with black pepper, then with salt. After it's rinsed with water, it's covered with vino cotto mixed with garlic, bay leaves, sugar and rosemary, then once again covered with black pepper and left to age for at least one year, and up to three years.

Salame di Montefeltro Salami made with pieces of the thigh and loin of the black pigs typically found in Marches.

Soppressata di Fabriano Salami made with assorted finely ground meats, spices and diced pancetta. It's slightly smoked before aging.

Vruscata A flatbread made with cornmeal stuffed into cabbage leaves then cooked over a wood-burning fire.

PASTA, GNOCCHI, RICE, POLENTA AND GRAINS

Bucatini alla marchigiana Bucatini—a kind of thick-ish spaghetti with a hollow center—dressed with a sauce made with celery, carrots, onions, prosciutto, pancetta or lardo, black pepper, tomatoes and a bit of red wine.

Calcioni all'ascolana Very large, square ravioli filled with pecorino cheese, sugar, egg yolks and grated lemon zest, then boiled, placed in a baking dish, covered with grated pecorino and gratinéed.

Canne d'organo Cannelloni made with hand-rolled pasta and dressed with meat sauce. They're a specialty of the town of Tolentino in the province of Macerata.

Capellini di Campofilone See *maccheroncini di Campofilone* (page 168).

Cioncioni or **cencioni** Taglioni—fine, flat pasta in the tagliatelle family—made mostly with fava bean flour. Traditionally, they're eaten in broth or dressed with a sauce made with lardo, sausages and tomatoes. They're a specialty of the province of Pesaro-Urbino.

Cresc'taiat Large pasta squares made with cornmeal flour and dressed like cioncioni to serve.

Frascarelli Liquid polenta cooked in lemon water, which heightens its flavor, then dressed with a sauce made with olive oil, onions, diced prosciutto, crumbled sausage or pancetta, tomato conserve, salt and pepper. The dish is covered with grated Parmesan cheese and eaten with a spoon. During the age of the Ottoman Empire, frascarelli were eaten with cooked wine must (vino cotto).

Jaiett Polenta mixed with egg tagliolini, then dressed with a bean sauce. It's a specialty of the village of Montemaggiore al Metauro in the province of Pesaro-Urbino.

Lasagne incassettate A version of the classic Bolognese lasagne from the province of Ancona made with sheets of pasta layered with a ground meat sauce, chicken, giblets, Parmesan cheese and Gruyère cheese. In the province of Pesaro, the dish is "ennobled" with a garnish of shaved white truffles.

Lumachelle all'urbinate Ring-shaped pasta made by wrapping pieces of tagliatelle around a stick. At one time they were wrapped around textile weaving combs that gave them not only their shape but also a ridged surface. They can be cooked in a chicken giblet broth. Smaller lumachelle used to be called Ave Maria; today they are called ditalini. Similarly, larger lumachelle were called Pater Noster and were dressed with a meat sauce. Nowadays real, homemade lumachelle are almost impossible to find, unless you happen upon that rare convent where the nuns still make them.

Maccheroncini di Campofilone Very thin egg tagliolini, like angel hair pasta, typical of the eponymous town of Campofilone.

Minestra col grasso A dish made with homemade egg tagliolini cooked in broth, then dressed with olive oil, onions, prosciutto, black pepper and tomato conserve.

Pataluc Rather large, whole-wheat flour and cornmeal pasta squares dressed with a hearty bean sauce.

Pezzòle Pasta squares made with flour and water and dressed with a sauce made with lardo or pancetta, onions, celery, carrots and peeled tomatoes. They're typical of the area around the village of Arcevia in the province of Ancona.

Picciasanti A type of soup-polenta made with whole-wheat flour and water that is dressed with either tomato sauce, meat sauce or with onions sautéed in lardo or crumbled sausages. The curious name comes from the habit of gluing a calendar, honoring San Antonio, to a rear stall door of a barn with natural glue made with the same ingredients as this dish—flour and water. *Picciasanti* literally means "glue the saints."

Pingiarelle or **pincinelle** or **pengiarelle** or **pecianelle** Small dumplings made with flour, water, eggs and yeast.

However, in the village of San Ginesio the dough is cut into thin tagliatelle then dressed with any kind of sauce. In the province of Pesaro-Urbino they resemble little balls called pincinelle, and are dressed with meat ragù or pot roast sauce. In the old days, when people made bread at home, it was the custom to break away some of the dough to make pingiarelle.

Ravioli ai filetti di sogliole Ricotta- and parsley-filled ravioli that are dressed with a sauce made with olive oil, garlic, onions, carrots, celery, white wine, tomatoes, fresh parsley and sole fillets. They are a specialty of the coastal area in the province of Pesaro-Urbino.

Ravioli di San Leo Ravioli filled with chard, spinach, borage, marjoram, Parmesan cheese, mild ricotta, lemon zest, cinnamon and nutmeg. They're served dressed with meat ragù.

Spaghetti alle noci A typical Marchigiano Lenten dish of spaghetti dressed with walnut pesto, parsley, garlic and olive oil. In the town of Osimo in the province of Ancona, there's a rather odd custom of eating this dish with forks made with pieces of sugarcane.

Surcitti Dumplings made with cornmeal polenta and served with liver sausage fried in lardo or olive oil and flavored with lemon juice. They're a specialty of the province of Macerata.

Tacconi di biada Large pasta squares made with both white and fava bean flours served with a sauce made with sautéed lardo, onions, olive oil and tomatoes.

Tagliolini di biada Tagliolini made with the same flours as above and served with the same sauce.

Tajulì pilusi Tagliolini made with a flour-and-water dough, then dressed with a sauce made with guanciale (cured pork cheek) and tomatoes and covered with grated pecorino cheese or a crab sauce. They're called pilusi (*pelosi,* or furry) because when they're cooked, they develop a kind of skin that gives them a velvety or furry texture.

Tuffoli (or **maccheroni**) **alla pesarese** Maccheroni filled with a mixture of turkey, cooked ham, truffles and puréed chicken livers. They're layered with meat ragù and grated Gruyère cheese, then gratinéed.

Vincisgrassi A white lasagne typical of Marches, particularly in the province of Macerata where the pasta is layered with a very rich sauce made with béchamel, giblets, gizzards and grated cheese. Sometimes truffles are added as well. Legend has it that this dish was created on a whim by a

Maceratese cook for the Austrian general Windisch-Graez, for whom this dish is named, while he was in Marches during the Napoleonic campaign of 1799.

SOUPS

Ceciarelli A soup made with chickpeas and the little pasta squares called quadrucci.

Ciavarro A very dense soup, a specialty of the village of Ripatransone in the province of Ascoli Piceno, made with chickpeas, farro, beans, cornmeal, lentils, pork rind, tomatoes, salt, pepper and olive oil.

Minestra di cicerchie A very tasty old-fashioned soup made with a somewhat rare legume, cicerchia, which resembles a flattened chickpea. Additional ingredients include olive oil, carrots, celery, marjoram or mint and tomatoes.

Minestra di frascarelli A soup of little dumplings made with cornmeal, eggs and butter served in a rich beef broth (see *frascarelli*, page 167).

Minestrone di Montappone A very odd soup made with fresh beans, immature ears of corn, wheat berries and potatoes.

Passatelli in brodo A typically Romagnolo soup also widely served in Marches, where it's enriched with spinach and beef, chicken or turkey.

Pisellata alla maceratese A soup made with fresh peas, pancetta, onions, garlic, parsley, marjoram and tomatoes found in the area around the towns of Montelupone and Potenza Picena, both in the province of Macerata.

CONDIMENTS, SAUCES, SALSAS AND EGGS

Frittata con le vitalbe A traditional Marchigiano frittata made throughout the region in the springtime with the tender leaves of a white-flowering shrub similar to clematis.

In porchetta A term used to describe any kind of food that uses the same ingredients that are used for preparing roast suckling pig—specifically, tender wild fennel sprigs and garlic. This method is used most often with chicken, rabbit and *crocette* (page 171).

In potacchio A way to stew meat or fish—most of all chicken, rabbit or monkfish —with parsley, rosemary, garlic, olive oil, black pepper, hot pepper flakes and white wine. The name is derived from the French word, potage.

Uova in trippa Frittata strips which are stewed, like tripe, in a casserole, with tomatoes, chopped lardo, onions, marjoram, white wine, lemon peel and nutmeg.

FISH, CRUSTACEANS AND SHELLFISH

Agore Dialect for a very long fish that, in Italian, is called aguglia—but has no other translation.

Aguglia See above.

Arrosto segreto Sardines filled with breadcrumbs, olive oil, salt, pepper and lemon slices, then enclosed in bay leaves and roasted.

Balleri Bivalves that look something like razor clams that are made into a soup. They're also called datteri di mare.

Bombi Large sea snails.

Brodetto all'anconetana A fish soup from the province of Ancona that typically contains thirteen different varieties of fish among which are tiny and large red mullet, mackerel, dogfish, turbot, sea bass, squid, cuttlefish, eel, scrod—all, of course, depending upon market availability. The broth is made in a terra cotta casserole with olive oil, onions, garlic and parsley; the whole thing is then doused with vinegar. As soon as the vinegar evaporates, the tomatoes and fish, according to cooking time, are added to the broth. Some cooks like to flour the fish before adding them to the broth; other cooks like to add wild saffron (zafferanella) to it. If the brodetto is allowed to reduce, it can be used as a pasta sauce or as an accompaniment to polenta.

Cappone di galera A huge salad made with boiled white fish, salmon, anchovies, pickled eel, caviar, green and black olives and truffles. It's typically served on Christmas Eve.

Crocette in porchetta The word used in the province of Ancona for murici (sea snails) prepared in a manner called *in porchetta* (as if it were a roast pig) with wild fennel, rosemary, olive oil, garlic, white wine and a touch of tomato.

Garagoli or **garagoj** The word used, in certain areas of the Veneto and in Marches, to describe sea snails. There's even a festival that celebrates them in the town of Marotta in the province of Pesaro-Urbino. They are prepared *in porchetta*.

Guatti The Marchegiano word for ghiozzi, which are little fish that live both in salt and fresh water.

Muccigna A term used to describe less commercially desirable fish.

Mugelle Dogfish.

Moscioli Anconetano dialect for mussels. They're often stuffed with a mixture of breadcrumbs, garlic, olive oil and prosciutto, then baked or grilled.

Pannocchie Golden brown–colored bivalves. They're also called canocchie.

Papaline Little—about finger-sized—sardines that are usually served fried.

Risetto Newborn anchovies and sardines made into "meat" balls.

Roscoli The Marchigiano name for small red mullets.

Stoccafisso all'anconetana A stew made with pieces of dried codfish, olive oil, a pesto of anchovies and marjoram, onions, carrots, celery, parsley, tomatoes, potato wedges and milk (optional).

Triglie al prosciutto Red mullets flavored with olive oil, garlic and sage, then wrapped in prosciutto and baked.

MEAT

Agnello alla cacciatora Lamb stew cooked in a cast-iron skillet with olive oil, lardo, sage, wild fennel and white wine, but no tomatoes. The recipe is typical of the town of Montefeltro in the province of Pesaro-Urbino.

Bombarelli Little snails.

Braciole all'urbinate Thin slices of beef filled with a cheese frittata and prosciutto slices that are then rolled up and cooked in white wine.

Ciarimboli A dish of modest origins, made with a thoroughly purified pork bladder that's seasoned with salt and spices, then aged. The aged bladder is then cooked with olive oil, garlic, black pepper and rosemary in a skillet over a wood-burning fire. Traditionally ciarimboli are eaten with boiled cabbage.

Coniglio in porchetta A boned rabbit stuffed with wild fennel, garlic, rosemary, pancetta, salami and prosciutto or lardo, then rolled up and cooked in a skillet or baked. The recipe is typical of Marches and Umbria.

Coppiette Pieces of leg and shoulder of mutton that are dried together.

Gummarelli See *bombarelli* (above).

Olivette alla pesarese Veal roll-ups filled with finely chopped prosciutto, anchovy fillets, capers, garlic and parsley mixed with breadcrumbs and a bit of tomato. They're stewed in white wine with the optional addition of fresh tomatoes.

Pasticciata pesarese Stew made with beef top round, lardo, red wine, garlic, cloves, cinnamon and some tomatoes.

Pezzata A shepherd's dish made with pieces of mutton cooked with onions and mint, then served on sliced bread covered with grated pecorino cheese.

Pipicchiotto A specialty of the town of Fabriano in the province of Ancona made by cooking pieces of lamb in a cast-iron skillet with olive oil, whole garlic cloves, rosemary, garlic and wine.

Porchetta alla marchigiana Roast suckling pig stuffed with wild fennel, rosemary, a bit of nutmeg and garlic, lots of freshly ground black pepper and some vino cotto. Cooking the pork over pine, oak and live oak branches gives it its very distinct flavor.

Potacchio See *in potacchio* (page 170).

Tournedos alla Rossini In reality, not an authentic Marchigiano dish, but one found throughout the region, in particular in the province of Pesaro-Urbino, to pay homage to its native son, the composer and gourmand Gioachino Rossini. It's made by sautéing beef fillets in butter then serving them on toasted bread covered with sliced foie gras and a sauce made with beef stock and Madeira or Marsala wine.

Trippa di mongana (vitella da latte) alla canepina A stew made with milk-fed veal tripe, onions, garlic, celery, carrots, parsley, marjoram, lemon peel, tomato sauce, a prosciutto bone and pork rind. It's served covered with grated Parmesan cheese.

VEGETABLES

Budino di gobbi A rather complex molded dish made by layering boiled cardoons that have been dipped in flour and beaten eggs then fried, with giblet ragù, sliced prosciutto, slivered truffles and grated Parmesan cheese.

Fave 'ngrecce Boiled fava beans served as a salad, dressed with olive oil, garlic, salt, pepper and fresh marjoram or mint leaves. This is an antique recipe from the province of Macerata.

Gobbi Cardoons. They're frequently used in Marchigiano cuisine.

Grugni Bitter, wild chicory.

Misticanza A term used throughout central Italy to describe a salad made with mixed wild greens. The mixture depends on what's in season. Generally you'll find dandelion greens, rucola, erba stella, watercress, anise, raperonzolo (which literally means Rapunzel but is campanula), field lettuce and the tops of wild fennel.

Parmigiana di gobbi Pieces of cardoons that are boiled then fried and covered with béchamel and grated Parmesan cheese. The dish is gratinéed to serve.

Peparole The mushroom *lactarius piperatus*.

Pincicarelli A vegetable well known in the province of Ancona but mostly unknown in the rest of Italy. It's a thistle with a flavor very much like its cousin, the artichoke. The meatiest part of the flower is eaten fried, steamed or stewed. Pincicarelli are in season in June and July.

Rosa di verza A sumptuous eighteenth-century dish made by stuffing a whole, intact cabbage, leaf by leaf, with a filling much like the mixture used for meatballs, so that it resembles an overblown rose. It is then cooked in a casserole with tomatoes, mushrooms and Ascolane olives.

Roscani A salad green also known as barba di fratti ("monk's beard").

Spaccasassi A plant very much like purslane. In the town of Monte Conero in the province of Ancona, it's first preserved in vinegar, then in olive oil and served with antipasti. Its name, spaccasassi ("rock-breaker"), refers to the area where the plant grows — in between rocks.

Taccole Also called piselli mangiatutto or fagioloni; taccole are, in fact, snow peas.

CHEESE AND DAIRY PRODUCTS

Bazzotto or **bazzott** A fresh sheep's milk cheese typical of the town of Fano in the province of Pesaro-Urbino.

Cagiòlo An old-fashioned dairy product made with bits of leftovers from other cheese productions with a texture somewhere between a compact cheese and ricotta. It's typical of the area around Osimo.

Casciotta d'Urbino The pearl of Marchigiano dairy production made with 80% sheep's milk and 20% cow's milk. This mildly flavored, slightly fragrant, fatty, semi-cooked, semi-fresh cheese has a soft, straw white paste with tiny eyes and a thin golden rind. Its production is limited to the province of Pesaro-Urbino. There's an often-told story about the first time that Michelangelo tasted the cheese. He was so impressed with the cheese, a gift from his foreman, that he bought property in the region just so he could have the real thing on his table every day.

Formaggio di grotta di Talamello A cheese made with sheep's and goat's milk, covered with walnut leaves and left to age in an earthen grotto until it produces the mold that gives it an intensely aromatic fragrance and unique, tangy flavor. It is produced not only in Marches but also in Emilia-Romagna.

Pecorino di Monterinaldo A particularly refined cheese made with the milk of sheep that have grazed in pastures filled with aromatic herbs and grasses in the area of Monterinaldo in the province of Ascoli Piceno.

Raviggiolo A soft, mild, delicate and buttery cheese made with goat's or sheep's milk. Once the curds are produced, they're drained in wicker baskets. The finished cheese is presented on reed or fern mats. It is sometimes referred to as giuncata or felciata.

Slattato A soft cheese made with whole cow's milk. It's typically prepared in dark, warm environments in order to insure its rind will crack, allowing the fats to leak out and give the cheese its distinct character. In some ways slattato is similar to the squacquerone romagnolo.

SWEETS AND LIQUEURS

Acetello A beverage from the past that's derived from a Roman drink called posca. Quite simply, it's water flavored with a drop of vinegar.

Acquaticcio A liquid made by fermenting grape lees and water in a vat. Every once in a while, when a glass of the liquid is drawn from the vat, it's replaced with an equal amount of water. In the southern part of Marches, the drink is called caccementte ("take out and put in").

Amandovolo See *mandovo* (page 177).

Ammezzato A beverage from an antique recipe made by boiling young wine with water until a low grade of alcohol is achieved.

Beccute Rustic cookies made with cornmeal, pine nuts, walnuts, almonds, dried figs and raisins.

Berlingozzi Crunchy and crumbly ring-shaped cookies typical of the town of Saltara in the province of Pesaro-Urbino. Berlingozzi are also found in Tuscany, especially during the Carnival celebration.

Bostrengo A cake made with rice, chocolate, pine nuts and various herbs. It's readily available in the area around the town of Sant'Angelo in Vado in the province of Pesaro-

Urbino. Its origins, however, seem to be in the town of Piobbico in the same province.

Caciuni or **calcioni** Large ravioli filled with pecorino cheese, egg yolks, sugar and lemon zest. This salty-sweet dish is recognized by a slash in the pasta that allows the filling to leak out as the ravioli bake.

Cavallucci di Apiro Small pastries made from dough of flour, eggs, butter, sugar and yeast. They're then filled with a mixture of walnuts, hazelnuts, almonds, *sapa* (page 177), sugar, breadcrumbs, Alchermes, cognac, amaretto, Marsala, anisette, coffee and grated lemon zest. Once filled, the pastries are rolled into a horseshoe shape and the edges of the pastry are snipped to almost resemble a horse's mane. Originally, each pastry was stamped with an image of a horse. They are typical Christmastime treats in the province of Macerata.

Ciambelle al mosto Ring-shaped cookies made with flour, olive oil, sugar, fennel seeds, yeast and grape must during the grape harvest in the province of Ascoli Piceno.

Ciaramilla urbinate An old-fashioned Easter cake made with flour, eggs, yeast, lardo, lemon peel and Alchermes and garnished with colored sprinkles.

Cicerchiata A Carnival-time confection made with balls of fried sweet dough, almonds and candied fruits held together with honey. The mixture is then formed into a ring or heart shape, or a pile. The name comes from pasta made with *cicerchia* (page 328). Although this dish has its origins in Umbria, it's found throughout Marches and in Abruzzo and Molise.

Cicerù Christmastime pastries made with flour and egg dough that is thinly rolled out, then cut into circles or squares. The pasta shapes are filled with a mixture of puréed chickpeas, sugar and mosto cotto. The raviolotti are then fried and covered with powdered sugar to serve.

Crustingu or **figusu** See *frustingu* (below).

Fiocchi Fried pastries made with a dough of flour, eggs, lemon peel, cinnamon and vanilla. It's rolled out very thinly, cut into strips and tied into bows that are deep-fried in lardo. They're served during Carnival, doused with Alchermes and sprinkled with sugar.

Frustingu An old-fashioned homemade Christmastime cake made with a mixture of white and yellow flours, the white part of bread, chopped dried figs, raisins, walnuts, pine nuts and *sapa* (page 177). They're a specialty of the province of Ancona.

Gnocchi dolci di latte Little dumplings made with wheat starch, sugar, butter, eggs, milk and cinnamon. They're covered with butter, sugar and Parmesan cheese, then gratinéed to serve.

Lattaiolo A confection made with flour, eggs, milk, cinnamon, lemon zest and a pinch of nutmeg. It's baked, covered with powdered sugar then cut into small squares to serve.

Lonza di fico A lonza, or loin, in name only. At one time there were so many figs grown and harvested in the Marchigiano countryside that the residents were constantly looking for ways to store them. This salami or loin-shaped confection was created as a result of that ongoing search. It's made with ground sun-dried figs, saba, anise, almonds and walnuts all wrapped in fig leaves and rolled into a log shape. It's wonderful when sliced and served with pecorino cheese.

Mandovo An almond confection typical of the area around Porto San Giorgio in the province of Ascoli Piceno.

Paccucce Apple and pear wedges that have been dried in the sun then candied with sugar, cloves and must.

Piconi "Ravioli" made by filling short crust pastry with ricotta, eggs, sugar, almonds, chocolate, cinnamon and rum. The pastries are marked with a special tool before they're baked. They're a specialty of the province of Macerata.

Pizzutu A sweet pizza made with cornmeal dough and dried figs, walnuts and raisins.

Sapa White and black grape must that's boiled until it's reduced by one-third.

Scorzette Sun-dried melon rind candied with sugar, cloves and must.

Scroccafusi Baked or fried "pellets" made with a dough of flour, eggs or water, sugar, olive oil or lardo, liqueur and lemon zest. They're covered with sugar to serve and are a Carnival-time specialty of the province of Macerata.

Serpe di Apiro A specialty of the mountainous area around the province of Macerata made with a mixture of almonds, sugar, egg whites, butter, cinnamon and lemon extract. Bits of the mixture are rolled up like snakes, then placed on a wafer, baked, then covered with chocolate or glazed with sugar.

Torta nociata A cake made with bread dough mixed with walnuts, raisins, sugar, dried figs, olive oil, candied fruits, orange marmalade and grated orange and lemon zests. It's typical of the village of San Ginesio in the province of Macerata.

Vino cotto A boiled mixture of grapes that is usually decanted into small bottles, then closed with stoppers made with various kinds of wood that then lend their own perfume to the cooked wine. Vino cotto's alcohol content is around 20%. The flavor of vino cotto improves as it ages. The sale of vino cotto is prohibited by law.

WINE

Marches is one of the most mountainous regions in all of Italy but it has the good fortune to face the Adriatic Sea. In addition to its mountains and coastal area, the region is filled with forests and rivers. The gastronomic offerings of the region clearly reflect the bounty of the diverse terrain: fish, both salt- and freshwater; mushrooms and truffles that are as famous as those of the self-proclaimed truffle capital, Alba; game and a great selection of meat, all of which is cooked over the variety of wood found in the forests.

The wines seem to have been born just to accompany these dishes: Verdicchio, one of the few white wines that's not destroyed when drunk with the vinegar-flavored brodetti (fish soups), and the reds that can just as easily go with stewed conger eel as with polenta with mushrooms, and with kebabs of little birds cooked just like pork — *in porchetta*.

Bianchello del Metauro This vivid straw-colored wine, with hints of green, has a fresh, zesty bouquet. Although it's a dry wine, it has a persistent and lightly spicy base. It makes an ideal aperitif, but can also accompany first courses and fish and white meat dishes with great success.

Falerio This very clear white wine with a delicate bouquet is fresh and dry, making it the perfect companion for shellfish dishes, non-sauced fish and regional first courses. It comes from vines that grow on the hills around the province of Ascoli Piceno.

Rosso Two very important red wines of the region are Rosso Conero, a full-bodied, deep, ruby red wine made with a large percentage of Montepulciano grapes and a small amount of Sangiovese grapes, and Rosso Piceno, just the opposite — made with a large percentage of Sangiovese grapes. It's also a deep ruby red with hints of violet that fade as it ages. They both have a full bouquet that becomes more refined with age until dried fruit and vanilla fragrances are released. Slightly acidic when they're young, they soften and become more convincing as they grow older. The Piceno can almost be called Superiore if it reaches an alcohol content of at least 12 percent. Because of their high level of tannins and slightly bitter flavor, they not only are good companions for hearty, regional first courses, but, when they reach their optimal strength, are the perfect wine to drink with meat and game. Their high level of tannins also allows them to keep for years.

Verdicchio This straw-colored wine with hints of green and a bouquet of fruit and white flowers may be one of the most popular wines of the region. The best-known production is that of Castelli di Jesi but it's the Verdicchio of Matelica that's the most full bodied and refined. Both are produced in the province of Macerata. They're sometimes produced as sparkling wines. Their ideal companions are fish soups but they go equally well with mushrooms and dishes made with cheese and eggs. The recommended combination is a glass of Verdicchio with pizza made with pecorino cheese.

Vernaccia di Serrapetrona A naturally sparkling red wine made with grapes that are harvested before they're ripe so as to avoid the area's typical chilly autumn weather — they're left to wither off the vine. Around Christmastime the wine is produced and then bottled before it has completely fermented. The wine is very slowly fermented in the bottle, sometimes for a year and a half. The result is an exceptional, full-flavored, dry or sweet (depending on sugar content) red wine with a bouquet of violets, faded roses and berries. Because of its very fine foam, it should be served at just the right temperature — a low temperature would "kill" it. It's a splendid dessert wine, perfect with local baked goods, particularly red fruit tarts.

Olive all'ascolana
Serves 6

60 large, brined Ascolane olives
3½ ounces chopped beef
3½ ounces chopped pork
3½ ounces chopped chicken
½ onion stuck with cloves
½ chopped carrot
½ chopped celery stalk
1 tablespoon olive oil
1 teaspoon tomato paste diluted with a bit of water
Salt and freshly ground pepper

1 chicken liver
2½ ounces chopped prosciutto
2½ ounces chopped mortadella
A handful chopped parsley
The white part of a piece of bread soaked in
     broth, then squeezed dry
1 egg, beaten
A pinch grated lemon zest
A pinch nutmeg
A pinch cinnamon
2½ ounces grated Parmesan cheese
1 ounce grated pecorino cheese
Optional: chopped black truffles
Flour
3 eggs, beaten
Breadcrumbs
Vegetable oil for frying

Remove the pits by sticking a sharp knife into the top of the olives and cutting in a spiral down to the other end. The long ribbon will spring back into the olive shape. Place the pitted olives back into their brine while the filling is made. Sauté the beef, pork and chicken in the olive oil with the onion, carrot and celery and add salt and pepper to taste and the tomato paste. When the meat is almost cooked add the chicken liver. When the liver turns pink remove from the heat and add the prosciutto, mortadella and parsley. Add the mixture, including all the juice, to a mixing bowl. Thoroughly combine the soaked bread, 1 beaten egg, lemon zest, nutmeg, cinnamon, Parmesan and pecorino cheeses, more salt and pepper to taste and the truffles to the meat mixture. Stuff the drained olives with the mixture making sure that they reassume their shape. Flour them, dip them in the remaining beaten eggs, cover with the breadcrumbs and then deep fry until golden and drain on paper towels. They should be served hot with lemon wedges.

Suggested wine: Falerio

UMBRIA

You can't really talk about the food of Umbria without first talking about how the borders of the region changed continually during the era when the Sabine tribe inhabited the area. It makes sense that certain Umbrian dishes have hints of the flavors of the neighboring regions of Marches, Lazio, Tuscany and Abruzzo. Umbria is one of the smallest and most secluded — it does not border the sea — of all Italian regions. Its main focus is agricultural. An historic Umbrian meal, dating back to the indigenous Etruscans and still served, would start with farro soup, followed by a piece of spit-roasted wild boar and flatbread made with whole grains and honey. The fireplace, the spit and the *pignatta*, a terra cotta cooking pot with a glazed interior, are the essential Umbrian tools of the trade.

In Norcia, which is considered the gastronomic capital of the region, you'll find amazing cured meats. All over central Italy these products are known as norcino. In addition to cured pork products, the native small, black wild pigs are used to make the glorious porchetta. The lardo and guanciale *must* be dressed with the light, fruity and refined olive oil of the area. This oil elevates every dish that it accompanies.

The Umbrians make sublime roasts and great spits loaded with every kind of fowl: chicken, guinea hens, pheasant, thrush and above all palombacci (wood pigeons). Grilled dishes include the spectacular beef from the area that borders Tuscany.

The hilly terrain, with its clay-rich valleys, provides the perfect ambience for growing the exquisite little Castelluccio lentils. The mushroom and truffle harvest makes autumn the region's outstanding season. The black truffles from the Val Nerina and Spoleto are particularly notable. Other truffles include the bianchetto, and the somewhat less prestigious scorzone and bianco, all of which are used with abandon. They're shaved or julienned, then used as a garnish for everything from eggs to cheese pizza just out of the oven. Famously, they're pounded in a mortar with anchovies, garlic and olive oil, then used to dress homemade pasta or to top crostini, added to ragùs or stuffed into roasts.

Antipasto magro An antipasto that is actually a salad made with a base of cubed potatoes dressed with olive oil, vinegar, salt and pepper that are then covered with tuna preserved in olive oil, and mayonnaise. The salad is garnished with sliced beets, hard-cooked eggs, capers and olives.

Bocconcello Very large ring-shaped bread topped with olive oil and pieces of pecorino cheese and prosciutto.

Capocollo Cured meat found throughout central and southern Italy. It's made with the upper part of the neck and shoulder of a pig, flavored with garlic, fennel seeds, salt and pepper, then covered with butcher's paper and tied like salami. It needs to age for at least three months and up to a year.

Coppa Cured meat made with the meatiest parts of the pig's head. The meat is boiled then flavored with orange peel, black pepper and other spices. The mixture is put into a casing and weighted down to cure.

Crescentini Large ravioli made with a dough of flour, butter, olive oil, milk and water. The ravioli are filled with prosciutto, diced mozzarella or anchovies and then fried.

Crostate alla perugina Little baskets made from loaves of Pullman bread that are then toasted in a skillet with olive oil. To serve, they are filled with roasted, truffled chicken meatballs and browned quail breasts.

Crostini al tartufo all'umbra Toasts made with rustic bread, then covered with a spread made with chopped black truffles from the Norcia area, anchovies and olive oil.

Lonza See *capocollo* (above).

Olive all'arancia Black olives marinated with orange peel, bay leaves, garlic and other herbs.

Pizza al formaggio or **pizza di Pasqua** A savory panettone. Diced fresh pecorino cheese and grated aged pecorino, eggs and olive oil are added to the dough before it's baked. The "pizza" is served with Umbrian cured meats and hard-cooked eggs.

Pizza al testo Flatbread, similar to the *piadina* (page 123), cooked on a terra cotta plate over a wood-burning fire.

Pizza di farina gialla Flatbread made with cornmeal, water and salt. At one time it was cooked in ashes. Nowadays, it's covered with eggs, cheese and olive oil and baked in an oven.

Pizza perugina Covered with grated Grana cheese, diced

prosciutto and fresh pecorino cheese, a pizza that rises in the oven as it bakes.

Scalmarita Dialect for *capocollo* (page 182).

Schiacciata con la cipolla Flatbread covered with sliced onions, sage and olive oil, then baked.

Sfriccioli Pork cracklings.

Torcoletti al formaggio Ring-shaped savory pastries made with yeasted dough and mild pecorino cheese.

Torta di Pasqua con formaggio Yeast bread that's fortified with olive oil, Parmesan cheese, soft pecorino cheese and eggs. During the season, it's garnished with slivers of black truffles. It's usually served with Umbrian cured meats and hard-cooked eggs. It's very similar to *pizza al formaggio* (page 182).

PASTA, GNOCCHI, RICE, POLENTA AND GRAINS

Blò blò Soup made with a very thin flour-and-water fettucine and a sauté of chopped lardo, garlic, marjoram and tomatoes. It's served with grated percorino cheese from Norcia. The name is onomatopoeic for the sound that comes out of the pot as the soup slowly cooks — *blò blò*.

Ciriole or **ceriole** Thick spaghetti made with durum wheat and water. When the spaghetti are wrapped around a special tool to form their shape they're sometimes called *strangozzi* (page 184). The pasta may be simply dressed with garlic and olive oil, or garlicky tomato sauce or meat ragù. They're a specialty of the province of Terni.

Frascarelli Polenta made with whole wheat then simply dressed with raw olive oil. At one time this dish was recommended to new mothers to help with milk production.

"Gnocchi" dolci di Natale Rustic flour-and-water pasta squares that are dressed with walnut pesto, sugar, chocolate, breadcrumbs, Alchermes, lemon peel and cinnamon and served at room temperature.

Impastoiata Polenta to which a bean-and-tomato stew is added near the end of its cooking time. It's a typical peasant dish.

Maccheroni con le noci Pasta, typically served on Christmas Eve, made with homemade flour-and-water tagliatelle or rigatoni or maccheroncini made with semolina flour. They're dressed with cinnamon, sugar, chopped walnuts, breadcrumbs, cocoa, Alchermes, a bit of honey and lemon peel and served at room temperature.

Maccheroni strascinati The Umbrian pasta made with coarse maccheroni or fat, homemade fettucine held together with eggs and Parmesan cheese, then dressed with browned sausages. *Strascinati* means something like "drawn out."

Pasticcio di Jacopone A rich pasta dish, dating back to the Restoration period in the town of Todi in the province of Perugia, made by covering fresh egg pasta sheets with meat, vegetables, ricotta, eggs, cheese and spices. They are rolled into logs, poached, then cut into slices and served with meat ragù and grated cheese.

Risotto alla norcina Plain Parmesan cheese risotto that's finished with an abundant amount of freshly grated black truffles.

Spaghetti alla boscaiola Durum wheat spaghetti dressed with browned pancetta and wild asparagus, then bound together with eggs, grated pecorino and Parmesan cheeses and black pepper.

Spaghetti alla nursina Spaghetti dressed with anchovies dissolved in olive oil and an abundant amount of freshly grated black truffles. This is a specialty of the town of Norcia in the province of Perugia.

Spaghetti col rancetto A specialty of the town of Spoleto in the province of Perugia that is very, very similar to *bucatini all'amatriciana* (page 193). In this version spaghetti are dressed with a sauce made with onion, tomato, pancetta, marjoram (the BIG different ingredient) and lots of freshly ground black pepper, then served with grated pecorino cheese.

Strangozzi or **stringozzi** This pasta, similar to *ciriole* (page 183), is another specialty of Spoleto. They are rough flour-and-water fettuccine that are wrapped around a special tool so they become rustic maccheroncelli bucati — like bucatini, fat spaghetti with a hollow center. They're dressed with meat ragù or tomato sauce.

Strascinati See *maccheroni strascinati* (above).

Umbrici or **umbricelli** Big, fat spaghetti made by rolling each strand of pasta by hand.

SOUPS

Baggiana Fava bean, tomato and basil soup typical of the town of Città di Castello in the province of Perugia.

Minestra alla perugina A condensed broth served with chopped beef, carrots, celery and leeks.

Minestra di pater-noster The Pater Noster is, of course, the Lord's Prayer—and the word for rosary beads. The pasta shape called pater-noster is made by pressing cylindrical pieces of pasta dough, made with flour, eggs, olive oil and nutmeg, through a potato ricer or similar tool. The pasta is served in beef broth with lots of grated Grana cheese.

CONDIMENTS, SAUCES AND EGGS

Salsa ghiotta A sauce used to accompany roast game. It's made by cooking together white and red wine, chopped prosciutto, peeled lemon slices, sage, rosemary, garlic, capers, the white part of bread, juniper berries, olive oil, vinegar and chicken livers or other parts of the game with which it will be served.

FISH, CRUSTACEANS AND SHELLFISH

Anguilla in umido Chunks of eel cooked with olive oil, garlic, onions, white wine, tomato purée and chopped parsley. It's a specialty of the village of Marsciano in Perugia.

Regina in porchetta Boned carp filled with aromatic herbs and other ingredients like the ones used for other dishes cooked *in porchetta* (page 170). The fish is spit-roasted over a wood-burning fire. It's a specialty of the area around Lake Trasimeno in the province of Perugia.

Tegamaccio A soupy stew usually made by fisherman with a combination of fish found in Lake Trasimeno. They're cooked with olive oil, white wine and aromatic herbs.

MEAT

Barbazza or **barbozza** Guanciale or cured pork cheek.

Beccaccia alla norcina The migratory woodcock (*beccaccia*) is a rare and precious ingredient. After it's dressed, it may be prepared in various ways; it's usually roasted, stewed (*in salmì*) or—as it is in this dish—spit-roasted. The birds are filled with a mixture of sausages, giblets, marjoram, thyme and black truffles, then skewered and roasted over a wood-burning fire.

Bistecchine in teglia Thinly sliced beef fillet cooked with dried mushrooms and prosciutto.

Budellacci Pork guts that are salted, flavored with fennel seeds and assorted spices, then smoked. They're grilled to serve.

Lepre alla cacciatora A stew of hare that is marinated with rosemary, sage and red wine then cooked with olive oil, garlic, aromatic herbs and the marinade liquid. Very often the stew is finished with an anchovy-caper sauce.

Mazzafegati Mild, somewhat sweet sausages made with pork liver, lardo, sugar, raisins and pine nuts.

Morsetti in tegame Gizzards browned with onions and a splash of white wine, then finished with tomato sauce and fresh parsley.

Palombacci Wild doves that are continuously glazed with *salsa ghiotta* (page 185) as they're spit-roasted. They're served with black olives.

Palombacci all'uso di Todi In this preparation, doves are spit-roasted until half cooked, then finished in a saucepan with red wine, prosciutto and other ingredients. Chopped gizzards and giblets are added to the pan remains to make a sauce for the birds.

Palombe alla ghiotta Doves cooked just like palombacci.

Pillotto Basically a seasoning ingredient: a piece of lardo that's wrapped in parchment paper, then skewered and placed near spit-roasting meats. The idea is for the lardo to burn, then to melt, allowing it to splash all over the meat, giving it not only extra flavor but extra heat to insure that it's cooked through.

Porchetta A whole, split suckling pig filled with a mixture made of its liver, heart, lungs, freshly ground black pepper, wild fennel, garlic, rosemary and other herbs. It's spit-roasted over a wood-burning fire. Although this style of roasting a pig has its origins in Umbria, you'll find it throughout the neighboring regions.

Quaglie rincartate Quail wrapped in bread dough and baked. They're a specialty of the city of Orvieto in the province of Terni.

Salsicce all'uva Pan-cooked sausages that are finished with grapes. The grapes have two functions: to give the dish its unique and delicate flavor and to help degrease the pan. This is an autumnal peasant dish made around the time of the grape harvest.

Sanguetto A mixture of the guts and coagulated blood of game birds. The hardened mixture is cut into pieces then browned with olive oil, garlic, rosemary, sage, hot peppers and tomatoes.

Scaloppine alla perugina Sliced veal cooked in a sauce made with anchovies, capers, prosciutto, chicken, livers, garlic, lemon zest and juice and sage.

Testicciola d'agnello A boiled, cooled and boned lamb's head, the meat of which—including the brains and all the gelatinous parts—is cut up, floured, dipped in eggs, then fried to serve.

Ventresca Pork belly.

VEGETABLES

Bandiera Something like a peperonata (sweet pepper stew), it's made with onions, peppers from the town of Bettona in the province of Perugia and tomatoes.

Cardi al grifo A "special occasion" dish made by first boiling cardoons, then breading and frying them. The fried cardoons are then layered in a baking dish with tomato sauce and butter-sautéed chopped veal and chicken livers, then gratinéed to serve.

Colcigli A tasty green leaf vegetable similar to spinach found the area of Gualdo Tadino in the province of Perugia.

Gobbi alla perugina Boiled, floured and fried cardoons layered with beef ragù, tomatoes and onions to serve.

Lenticchie di Castelluccio Very small and extraordinary lentils grown exclusively on the Castelluccio di Norcia plain. They're notable because they have a long shelf life, are cultivated without chemicals and because they hold their shape when cooked.

Pomodori ripieni all'umbra Tomatoes stuffed with a filling made with eggs, breadcrumbs, parsley and garlic that are either grilled or cooked in a wood-burning oven.

Scafata A stew made with fresh fava beans, chard, celery, carrots, onions, diced guanciale and puréed tomatoes. The name of the dish comes from the Umbrian dialect—*scafo* is the word for fava bean pod.

Tartufi neri arrostiti Black truffles wrapped in pancetta, then in parchment paper and cooked in ashes or in the oven.

Turini Field mushrooms.

CHEESE AND DAIRY PRODUCTS

Agliato Garlic-flavored cheese.

Cipollato Onion-flavored cheese.

Pecorino di Norcia Sheep's milk cheese with a pleasingly mild streak, just like the milk of the region.

Raveggiolo Just like the Tuscan *raveggiolo* (page 157).

Arvoltoli The Perugino word for *poltricce* (below).

Attorta A specialty of the mountains made with chopped almonds, flour and sugar, that is also called serpe because of its snake-like shape.

Birbanti Walnut-sized pastries made with flour, sugar, pine nuts, cinnamon, lemon or orange peel and whipped egg whites.

Brustengolo A rustic sweet made with cornmeal polenta, apples, pine nuts, walnuts, lemon zest, Mistrà liqueur and sugar.

Ciaramicola A sweet, yeasted focaccia covered with colored sprinkles. It's usually made into a large doughnut shape with two pieces of dough crossed over the center.

Cicerchiata The same as the *cicerchiata* of Marches (page 176).

Frittelle di San Giuseppe Delicious lemon-flavored rice fritters sprinkled with vanilla-flavored sugar.

Pan nociato or **pannociato** A sweet bread made with dough, pecorino cheese, lardo, raisins, walnuts, wine and spices. It's from the area around the town of Todi in the province of Perugia.

Pinoccate Christmastime pastries, a specialty of the province of Perugia, made with pine nuts, flour, sugar and various spices including cocoa, then wrapped in colored paper.

Poltricce Little focaccie served hot with honey or jam.

Rocciata di Assisi A cake filled with walnuts, almonds, raisins, prunes, dried figs, apples and cinnamon, that's put together like a strudel.

Serpentone delle monache cappuccine A cake shaped like a large, fat snake made with flour, almonds, sugar, olive oil, raisins, walnuts, prunes, dried figs, apples and Vin Santo. Two candied cherries or coffee beans are used for the snake's eyes.

Stinchetti Bone (tibia)-shaped cookies made by filling a meringue solidified with potato flour with marzipan and cocoa. This antique confection is also referred to as ossa di morto (bone of the dead). It seems that the authenticity of the recipe was confirmed when an entire skeleton made with a similar recipe was found in an ancient temple in Perugia. These cookies are usually served around Christmastime.

Strichetti Little almond pastries cooked on a wafer base.

Tisichelle A cookie of stiffly beaten egg whites, flour, sugar and anise liqueur traditionally made by the descendants of the ancient Roman tribe, the Sabini.

Torcolo A large, ring-shaped cake from a recipe dating back to the seventeenth century. It's made with flour, eggs, sugar, milk, butter, raisins, pine nuts, aniseeds, orange peel and candied fruits. This specialty of Perugia is served on January 29, the feast of San Costanzo, the patron saint of the city.

Torta di Orvieto A sweet soft bread enriched with candied cherries and citron.

Zuccherini di Bettona Little ring-shaped cookies made with raisins, pine nuts, aniseeds and candied citron.

WINES

When you consider that Umbria is almost a southern region, its wines are uncharacteristically refined and full of aroma. Then you have a look at the region's hilly landscape, cold winters, rainfall throughout the year and good daily temperature ranges, and you soon realize that you have the ideal growing conditions for prestigious wines.

Colli di Trasimeno The varietals Tuscan Trebbiano, Malvasia del Chianti and Verdicchio grow in the hills around Lake Trasimeno. A pleasing Bianco, a light-bodied white wine with a full bouquet, is made from these grapes. It goes well with grilled vegetables and light, lean antipasti. The Rosso is made from Sangiovese grapes with a small percentage of white grapes. The garnet-colored wine gets slightly brown and its light aroma develops into a complex bouquet as it ages — it's dry and full of tannins without being aggressive. It's good with roasted meats, especially pork, and aged cheese. It also wants to be tried with sliced pecorino cheese doused with freshly pressed olive oil and ground black pepper.

Colli perugini This pale yellow Bianco, with its delicate aroma and fruity flavor, goes well with first courses made with river fish and grilled trout. It's great with fatty freshwater fish like carp, tench and pike. Actually, those fish are perfect with the more substantial but always delicate and elegant Rosato as well. The Rosso, a lively ruby red, full-bodied, highly fragrant wine, marries well with roast pork and small game kebabs.

Montefalco A ruby red wine that's slightly sour when young but velvety smooth, exquisitely structured and refined as it ages. It goes well with roast pork and game birds.

Orvieto A clear golden wine with a mild bouquet and a full, pleasing harmonic flavor with a slightly bitter streak. It goes well with lean antipasti and vegetable and fish first courses.

The slightly sweet Orvieto, the *abboccato* version, is the perfect dessert wine. If it's vinified the old-fashioned way—with grapes that have developed *la muffa nobile* (noble rot)—it becomes the perfect "meditation" wine and great with foie gras.

Torgiano The elegant, slightly fruity Torgiano Bianco is a pale but bright yellow wine with a clean, fresh flavor. It goes well with eggs and vegetables, antipasti and first courses, especially those flavored with black truffles from Norcia. The Rosso is made from a mixture of grapes similar to those for Chianti. It's ruby red with a winey nose and a dry full flavor. The Riserva, aged for about eight years, is a great accompaniment to roast meats and aged pecorino cheese.

Pizza di Pasqua al formaggio
Serves 6

¾ pound double zero (00) flour
1¼ ounces yeast (1 package)
2 eggs, beaten
3 teaspoons olive oil
1 teaspoon lardo
Salt and freshly ground pepper
1 teaspoon honey
3½ ounces Parmesan cheese
3½ ounces provolone cheese
3½ ounces pecorino cheese
Egg and milk for glaze

Dissolve the yeast and 3½ ounces of the flour in warm water and let sit, covered, at room temperature for at least two hours. Mix together the remaining flour with the eggs, olive oil, lardo, salt, pepper, honey and a cup of warm water. Grate half of each of the cheeses, dice the other half then combine with the flour mixture. Add the yeast mixture and knead for about 15 minutes. Let the dough rise in a warm, dry spot for at least 2 hours. Knead again, then place in a round, high-sided mold—something like one used for panettone—half-way full, and let rise again. When the dough reaches the top edge of the mold, brush it with a mixture of beaten eggs and milk. Bake it in a thoroughly pre-heated 375° F oven (if possible, wood-burning) for 30–40 minutes.

Suggested wine: Torgiano Bianco

LAZIO

Apicius, a collection of early Roman recipes also known as *De re coquinaria* (*On the Subject of Cooking*), is not recognizable in the recipes of contemporary Rome and the Lazio region in general. *Garum*, the incredible (and stinky) sauce made with macerated fish guts, herbs and salt doesn't exist anymore nor does *moretum*, a type of cheese mixed with garlic and herbs used on bread or with savory tarts or flatbreads.

After the splendid and over-the-top feasts of ancient Rome, modern-day dishes use a much-reduced number of ingredients. Historically, the population of Lazio chose just a few ingredients as the base of their cuisine: lamb, goat, dairy products and wild greens (misticanze). These items gave birth to a tasty, generous, aggressive and abundant cuisine where quantity almost matters more than quality. However, the quality of the products that come from the land, the sea, the lakes, hills, rivers and marshes of the region are truly excellent. Find the best artichokes in Italy (le mammole or cimaroli) — large, round and completely without thorns; sweet peppers; fragrant Roman lettuce with long, crunchy leaves; green beans from Lago Bracciano; white and sweet onions from Marino; delicate peas from Frosinone; scatoloni beans from Accumoli in the province of Rieti and cannellini beans from Atina in the province of Frosinone or the yellow quarantini from Bolsena and Viterbo.

The meat is exquisite: tender little lambs (*gli abbacchi*), tasty castrated sheep and extraordinary pigs. Pork is celebrated in the cuisine of Lazio for cured meats and for the lardo, guanciale or pancetta that's used to dress various dishes. Lazio is home to the world-famous amatriciana and carbonara pasta sauces, both made with guanciale (cured pork jowl). There's a special place in the gastronomy of Lazio for all salt- and freshwater fish. Dairy products are first class: the famous and sought-after ricotta romana, the excellent mozzarella di bufala from Agro Pontino and the fabulous pecorino romano that is generously grated over many pasta dishes.

The food of Rome, the capital city of Lazio, is characterized by the influence of its inhabitants: for example, the ingenious and refined cuisine of the Jews of the ghetto, or the emblematic dish of the city's butchers, quinto quarto, made with leftover beef parts. Roman cuisine has also been influenced by the aristocratic traditions of the city, in particular those of the church and the diplomatic corps; however, above all it is indebted to the trattorias and inns that faithfully serve the local cuisine.

ANTIPASTI, CURED MEATS, BREAD, FLATBREADS AND SAVORY TARTS

Bigne The Roman name for a rose-shaped bread.

Bruschetta Slices of toasted rustic bread that are rubbed with a garlic clove then sprinkled with extra virgin olive oil. This very simple antipasto is typical of the region.

Calascioni Large panzerotti (turnovers) stuffed with ricotta cheese or vegetables then baked.

Cariole The Roman name for long rolls with golden, crunchy crusts and soft interiors.

Crostini alla ponticiana Pieces of bread that are first fried in butter then covered with mozzarella or *provatura* cheese (page 199), prosciutto and sliced mushrooms then baked. The name refers to the historic Roman district where the dish originated.

Crostini col merollo Toasted bread covered with beef marrow and salt.

Crostini di provatura e alici Pieces of bread and fresh anchovies threaded onto a skewer, flavored with butter and cured anchovies then baked.

Fave con pecorino A typical and simple antipasto made with raw, freshly picked fava beans served with slices of pecorino romano or homemade salami.

Filone A long, crusty regional bread similar to the French baguette.

Fiori di zucca farciti e fritti Squash blossoms stuffed with mozzarella, breadcrumbs and anchovies, dipped in batter then fried. The dish is straight out of the Italian-Jewish kitchen.

Pandorato Slices of white bread (from a Pullman loaf) filled with prosciutto and mozzarella, dipped in milk, floured, dipped in eggs then fried.

Pizza con gli sfrizzoli Focaccia, typical of the region, made with pork cracklings.

Provatura fritta The Roman equivalent of *mozzarella in carrozza* (page 222) made with slices of *provatura* cheese (page 199) that are floured, dipped in eggs, then breadcrumbs, and fried.

Scammarita In the province of Viterbo, the word meaning *capocollo* (see 182).

Suppli al telefono Rice croquettes filled with ragù, mushrooms and mozzarella. The term *al telefono* refers to the "wire" or string of cheese that's created when one bites into the croquette.

PASTA, GNOCCHI, RICE, POLENTA AND GRAINS

Bucatini all'amatriciana Fat spaghetti with a hollow center dressed with a sauce made with guanciale (cured pork cheek), onions, tomatoes and freshly ground black pepper served covered with grated pecorino romano cheese. The name of this dish comes from the town of Amatrice in the province of Rieti. Historically the dish was made without tomatoes because they weren't, at that time, grown in Italy. The same goes for the onions.

Carbonara (pasta alla) A relatively recent addition to the Laziale kitchen in which spaghetti are dressed with beaten eggs mixed with grated pecorino or Parmesan cheese; diced, fried guanciale or pancetta; and lots of freshly grated black pepper. There are many stories about the origins of this dish. The most probable one associates it with woodsmen or lumberjacks who searched the forest for wood to make charcoal.

Ciufulitti The term used by the ancient Roman tribe, the Sabini, for homemade fusilli made with a simple flour-and-water dough. Once the dough is cut into strips, they're wrapped around knitting needles to give them their distinct spiral shape. These days, ciufulitti are not easy to find.

Curiole Egg tagliatelle typical of Tivoli on the outskirts of Rome.

Fettuccine alla papalina Cooked egg tagliatelle tossed in beaten eggs, grated Parmesan cheese and black pepper, then dressed with a sauce made with butter, peas and ham.

Fettuccine alla romana Egg tagliatelle dressed with a ragù made with prosciutto fat, onions, dried mushrooms, chicken giblets, tomatoes and the sauce from a pot roast (see *garofolato*, page 197).

Fregnacce Diamond- or triangle-shaped flour-and-water pasta served with tomato sauce and cheese that's a specialty of the province of Viterbo.

Frigulozzi Thin sticks 25 or 30 cm long made with yeasted bread dough that are typical of the town of Montopoli Sabina in the province of Rieti. They're served boiled with a sauce made with tomato sauce or one made with wild mushrooms.

Gnocchi alla romana Gnocchi made with a semolina polenta mixed with butter, cheese and eggs. After the mixture has cooled and set, it's cut into disk shapes. The disks are placed in a baking dish overlapping each other, covered with Parmesan cheese and gratinéed to serve.

Gnocchi di latte Gnocchi made with a mixture of potato flour, egg yolks, a bit of sugar, milk, butter, nutmeg and cinnamon. The mixture is spread out on a cutting board and left to solidify; the set mixture is then cut into diamond shapes. The diamonds are floured, dipped into beaten eggs, then breadcrumbs, and then fried in butter. They're served hot covered with grated cheese.

Gricia Pasta dressed with browned guanciale or sausages — in fact, it's amatriciana in bianco, a white amatriciana sauce (see *bucatini all'amatriciana*, page 193).

Jaccoli or **jacculi** Large, long pieces of homemade spaghetti wound into skeins or hanks served with meat sauce and pecorino cheese. This pasta, typical of the province of Rieti, is also called maccheroni a *fezze*, maccaruni a *matassa*, maccaruni a *cento* or maccaruni a *centinara*.

Pasticcio di maccheroni A sumptuous dish, served during the Carnival celebrations, made by filling a short crust with pastry cream and maccheroni dressed with a rich ragù prepared with sweetbreads, chicken livers and crests, "unborn" eggs, mushrooms, tiny meatballs and sausages.

Penne all'arrabbiata A term ("in an angry style") that usually refers to a spicy preparation. In this case penne is dressed with a sauce made by sautéing diced guanciale or pancetta in olive oil with garlic, onions, tomatoes, an abundant amount of hot pepper flakes and fresh basil or parsley. It's served with grated aged pecorino cheese.

Rigatoni con la pajata Rigatoni served sauced with *pajata* (page 197).

Spaghetti a cacio e pepe One of the oldest and most basic ways to prepare pasta in which cooked spaghetti are tossed with grated pecorino cheese and freshly grated black pepper.

Spaghetti aglio, olio e peperoncino Spaghetti dressed with garlic and hot pepper flakes sautéed in olive oil.

Spaghetti alla Checca Spaghetti cooked *al dente* — with just enough resistance when chewed, not soft — then dressed with raw tomatoes and fennel seeds.

Stracci di Antrodoco Very thin frittati that are filled with browned ground beef and mozzarella, then served covered with tomato sauce and grated cheese. They're a specialty of the province of Rieti.

Timballo alla Bonifacio VIII A sumptuous timballo — a baked pie-like dish — made with maccheroni, meat ragù, chicken giblets, little meatballs, mushrooms and truffles. It's served completely covered in truffles and is a specialty of the town of Anagni in the province of Frosinone.

SOUP

Bazzoffia A soup made with fresh fava beans, fresh peas, artichokes and curly escarole, then enriched with croutons and eggs. It's a specialty of the lower area of the region.

Brodetto pasquale A soup made with a lamb-and-beef broth finished with eggs beaten with lemon juice, fresh marjoram leaves, pieces of toasted bread and grated Parmesan cheese.

Minestra alla viterbese A purée of vegetables thickened with semolina.

Minestra di broccoli alla romana A very tasty soup made with Romanesque broccoli and broken spaghetti.

Pasta e broccoli con brodo di arzilla A soup in which broccoli and pasta are cooked in a skate wing broth.

Semmolella A very simple soup made with broth and semolina.

Stracciatella alla romana A soup made by adding a mixture of beaten eggs, grated Parmesan cheese and nutmeg to boiling hot broth. As the mixture curdles, little flakes or *stracci* (rags) are created and give the soup its name. The soup originated in Rome but is found throughout Italy.

Zuppa di cappone Little dumplings made from stale bread that has been soaked in broth, squeezed dry and then mixed with eggs, flour, prosciutto, beef marrow, nutmeg and salt and cooked in a rich capon broth.

CONDIMENTS, SAUCES, SALSAS AND EGGS

Garofolato See page 197.
Sugo finto A "fake" (*finto*) sauce made with tomatoes, prosciutto fat or lardo, celery, carrots and onions.

Uova in trippa or **trippate** The same as the version made in Marches (page 171).

FISH, CRUSTACEANS AND SHELLFISH

Baccalà in guazzetto A dish made by first flouring, then frying pieces of salt cod. They are finished in a tomato sauce with anchovies, pine nuts and raisins.

Ciriole coi piselli Little eels cooked in a skillet with little fresh peas. If garlic, capers, anchovies and white wine are added to the skillet as well, the dish is called ciriole alla fiumarola.

Mazzancolle The name, in Lazio, for jumbo shrimp.

Mazzancolle al coccio Shrimp cooked with garlic, olive oil, parsley, white wine, white pepper and lemon over a high flame in individual terra cotta pans. In some versions the shrimp are floured, doused with brandy or cognac, then set aflame.

Sbroscia A soup made with freshwater fish that is typical of the area around Lake Bolsena.

MEAT

Abbacchio The regional name for a suckling lamb. The best time to eat these lambs is the springtime, when they are butchered while still being suckled, but they are found all year around, especially in Lazio, where they're a tradition.

Abbacchio alla cacciatora or **alla romana** Lamb cooked in a casserole with garlic, rosemary, white wine, anchovies and hot pepper flakes. This is one of the iconic dishes of the Roman kitchen.

Abbacchio brodettato Pieces of lamb cooked with chopped onions, prosciutto and white wine. The dish is finished with a delicate, creamy sauce of eggs beaten with lemon juice and parsley or marjoram. Artichokes are often added to the stew as well.

Coda alla vaccinara A Roman dish *per eccellenza*. It's the quintessential "butcher's dish" made with the less commercial parts of the beef, the tail and the offal—the parts famously called the *quinto quarto*. The first quarter of the slaughtered beast went to the nobility, the second to the clergy, the third to the borghese or middle-class, the fourth to the military and the remaining fifth quarter to the working class. To make this dish, those inferior parts are slowly stewed with the guancia (called gaffo in dialect), lardo, garlic, parsley, onions, carrots and celery. The stew is finished with more celery and sometimes raisins, pine nuts and cocoa. This is just the kind of dish that you might find in the *trattorie* on the outskirts of Rome.

Coppiette Very flavorful meatballs enriched with the addition of raisins and pine nuts. They're rolled in breadcrumbs, then fried and sometimes stewed as well.

Coratella di abbacchio Coratella is a collective term used to describe the entrails, liver and trachea of the suckling lamb and kid. In the Roman kitchen, the two most popular preparations for these ingredients are coratella with onions and coratella with artichokes.

Fagioli con le cotiche A stew made with beans and pork rind flavored with garlic, prosciutto fat, lardo, parsley and tomato sauce.

Fegatelli di maiale nella rete alla laziale Pieces of pork liver enclosed in pork caul, then placed on skewers between bay leaves and cubes of rustic bread and cooked over a wood-burning fire.

Fritto misto alla romana A great mixture of fried ingredients including brains, sweetbreads, backs, testicles, artichokes, apples, ricotta, broccoli, etc.

Frittura piccata Floured veal scallops fried in butter with strips of prosciutto, cooked with a bit of broth and lemon juice and garnished with chopped parsley.

Garofolato The Roman version of pot roast. A piece of beef is larded, then stuck with cloves (*chiodi di garofano* means "nailed with cloves"), then very slowly stewed with onions, carrots, white wine and tomato sauce. The sauce is used to dress pasta served with the meal.

Lumache alla romana A stew made with snails, garlic, tomatoes, anchovies, fresh mint leaves and hot pepper flakes.

Padellotto A stew made with the entrails of milk-fed veal: spleen, heart, liver, kidneys, pancreas, backs, sweetbreads and *pajata* (see below), cooked in lardo with white wine, broth, salt and pepper. It is usually accompanied by artichokes.

Pajata or **pagliata** A dish from the same ancient Roman tradition as *coda alla vaccinara* (page 196) in which the guts of a milk-fed veal are cut into pieces, then cooked with olive oil, garlic, tomatoes, white wine, parsley and hot pepper flakes. When it's cooked this way, it's used as a sauce for rigatoni. The pajata may also be baked with potatoes, fennel, garlic and rosemary. The name of the dish comes from an old Roman word for the small intestines of veal, beef, lamb or kid that are usually cooked whole.

Pignataccia A very tasty roasted kid or castrato (castrated beef or steer) that's typical of the province of Viterbo.

Pollo alla romana A tasty chicken stew made with lardo, garlic, marjoram and prosciutto, then finished with tomatoes, white wine and grilled peppers.

Porchetta A whole roast pig with origins in Umbria but now, because it's made throughout Lazio, an emblematic dish of the region. It's eaten both hot and at room temperature, usually flavored with pepper, wild fennel and garlic. The ingredients, however, may vary.

Saltimbocca alla romana Veal scallops to which pieces of prosciutto and sage leaves have been attached with a toothpick. They're then quickly sautéed.

Scottadito The Roman name for lamb chops that are cooked in a skillet or grilled. *Scottadito* means something like "burn your fingers"—which is what happens when you pick up the hot chop by its bone.

Stufatino A stew made with lean beef, prosciutto fat, olive oil, garlic, onions, basil, red wine and tomatoes. It's finished similarly to the coda alla vaccinara with pieces of chopped celery.

Torciolo Veal pancreas that is scored, seasoned and then cooked over a wood-burning fire.

Trippa alla trasteverina Tripe slowly stewed in a terra cotta pot with onions, carrots, tomato sauce and white wine. It's finished with fresh mint leaves and served covered with grated pecorino cheese.

VEGETABLES

Agretti The regional word for *barba di frate* (page 327).

Carciofi Artichokes.

Carciofi alla giudia A recipe from the Roman-Jewish kitchen. After the hard leaves from large artichokes are twisted and removed, the artichoke is fried in abundant amounts of olive oil, then drained and fried again. They're served with salt and pepper.

Carciofi alla matticella Artichokes flavored with garlic, mint, olive oil and sea salt, then roasted on a grate over a bundle of wood (*matticella*). This preparation is a specialty of the town of Velletri in the province of Rome.

Carciofi alla romana Artichokes that are slowly cooked in a little water with olive oil, garlic, parsley and mint.

Carciofi con piselli Artichokes that are braised with lardo, onions, prosciutto and tiny, tender peas.

Cazzimperio In central and southern Italy, the term used for pinzimonio.

Erbette Parsley or other aromatic herbs in general.

Lattuga romana A fragrant and tender head of lettuce.

Misticanza See page 173.

Persa The Romanesco word for marjoram.

Porcaccia A green leaf used in salads similar to the small and succulent ones on a portulaca plant.

Puntarelle con salsa di acciughe An emblematic dish of Rome. The ribs of catalogna chicory leaves are patiently removed, then immersed in icy cold water to allow them to curl and twist. They're dried and dressed with olive oil, garlic, lemon juice or vinegar and finely chopped anchovies.

Vignarola A delicate stew made with fava beans, fresh peas, artichokes, lettuce, guanciale and spring onions.

CHEESE AND DAIRY PRODUCTS

Caciottone The paste for this pleasingly mild and rather distinctively flavored goat's milk cheese is cooked twice. It's a product of the province of Rieti.

Pecorino romano A sheep's milk cheese used for grating or at the table. Its slightly crumbly, hard body, with so-called tears (*lacrima*) — which come from the sweating whey — is white with a few small eyes. The rind is straw yellow tinged with greenish black and it's stamped with a D.O.P. mark. The cheese's strong, sharp flavor gives it a starring role in many of the region's dishes.

Provatura An antique stretched curd cheese made, like mozzarella, with buffalo milk. It's a specialty of the Lazio region.

Ricotta romana A top-rated cheese that is coarser, dryer, more compact and lower in fat than most other ricotta.

SWEETS AND LIQUEURS

Bignè di San Giuseppe Fried cream puffs that may or may not be filled with pastry cream. They're covered with sugar to serve.

Budino di ricotta A fresh pudding made with ricotta romana, eggs, sugar, cinnamon, candied orange and lemon peel and rum.

Crostata di ricotta A short crust tart shell filled with a mixture of ricotta romana, egg yolks and pastry cream with sugar, cinnamon and candied fruit.

Crostata di visciole A short crust tart shell filled with visciole (a variety of cherry somewhat like the renowned amarene, but slightly larger, sweeter and a darker color), cinnamon and sugar.

Fave dei morti Small candy-like cookies made with flour, sugar, almonds, pine nuts, cinnamon and brandy.

Gelato di ricotta A semifreddo made with very fresh ricotta romana, sugar, eggs and cognac.

Giglietti Cookies that are a specialty of the town of Palestrina in the province of Rome.

Maritozzi Yeasted sweet buns with raisins. They're served sliced open and filled with whipped cream. The name for these typically Roman treats comes from the popular and disparaging word for husband, *maritozzo*. Because fiancées would give their future husbands these buns during Lent, they are also called quaresimali, which means Lenten.

Nociata Very soft Christmastime nougat (*torrone*) made with egg whites, honey, walnuts and black pepper. The nougat is wrapped in bay leaves and is a specialty of the provinces of Rieti and Viterbo.

Pan giallo A Christmastime cake made with flour, almonds, raisins, walnuts, pine nuts, hazelnuts, dried figs, candied orange and citron peel, honey, bread dough, chocolate, olive oil and spices and covered with a sugar glaze. This cake is typical of the Lazio region. There's a similar version from Umbria.

Pasticcetti di gnocchi Short crust pastries filled with a solid cream made with milk, sugar, cornstarch, flour, eggs, cinnamon, nutmeg and lemon zest.

Pazientini quaresimali Little pastries made with sugar, flour, a few drops of caramel and egg whites. The mixture needs to rest for a day before baking.

Pizza di polenta A cake made with corn flour, ricotta romana, sugar, raisins, pine nuts and cinnamon.

Ponce gelato alla romana A type of sorbet made with sparkling wine, sugar, orange and lemon juices, egg whites and rum. It's garnished with mint leaves to serve.

Sciantigliè con cialdoni Simply, sweetened whipped cream served with rolled wafers. It's the Romanesco version of the word Chantilly.

Tozzetti Stick-shaped pastries with a long shelf life made with almonds, hazelnuts, aniseeds, sugar, eggs, flour, Sambuca liqueur, white wine and vanilla.

Turchetti An antique recipe for oval-shaped buns made with leftover cookies, cakes and pastries, all ground into a sort of flour that's mixed with regular white flour, sugar, chopped almonds, orange zest, eggs and baking powder.

Visner A liqueur made by adding Aleatico red wine to visciole cherries (see *crostata di visciole*, page 200), their smashed pits, sugar, cinnamon, lemon peel and cloves. The mixture needs to steep for forty days. It's then filtered and added to alcohol used for liqueurs.

WINES

It's a known fact that the Latins, an ancient Italian tribe from the area that is now Lazio, learned how to cultivate vines from the Etruscans, an ancient tribe from the area that is now Tuscany. In particular, the wines from the areas around Velletri and Albano (called Albalonga in ancient times) have been famous since the dawn of the Roman civilization—so much so that they were even mentioned in the works of the Roman satirist Juvenal. Nowadays, just about anything, from the election of a new pope to a speech to the population of Rome, is an excuse to let the monuments of the city gush forth with rivers of wine. It's a testament to the fresh, cheerful, new—or at the most two-year-old—wines of the region, that they elicit universal accolades.

Aleatico Made from the eponymous varietal that grows, for the most part, in the town of Gradoli in the province of Viterbo. This sweet, almost syrupy wine is ruby red with violet overtones. Its intense, persistent bouquet has hints of violets and red fruit. It's an after dinner wine, perfect with pastry desserts.

Aprilia Three wines produced in the eponymous town in the province of Latina and in the town of Nettuno in the province of Rome. Merlot is ruby red with a winey nose, dry and light bodied. It's a good table wine when it's young, but it doesn't age well. Sangiovese is pale red and dry with a light bouquet. It also doesn't age well. It's good with local first courses from spaghetti alla carbonara to rigatoni con la pajata, and also goes well with baccalà and eel in tomato sauce. The dry Trebbiano is straw colored with a lightly fruity aroma. It pairs well with fish and vegetables.

Capena A slightly bitter wine that is straw yellow with a lightly fruity aroma. It goes well with the very flavorful first courses of the region and with fried vegetables.

Cerveteri The Bianco, made with a mixture of Trebbiano grapes, is straw-colored with a winey nose, and dry with a faintly bitter streak. It goes well with fish. The Rosso is winey with a mixed berry bouquet and is full of tannins. This garnet-colored wine goes well with white meats — in particular, l'agnello brodettato.

Cesanese Made in the provinces of Frosinone and Rome from the Cesanese varietal, this ruby red wine has a bouquet of red fruit, robust flavor and is slightly tannic with a semi-dry base. The wine's elevated alcohol content makes it a good accompaniment for roasted or stewed meats and pollo alla romana con i peperoni (Roman-style chicken with peppers). There's also a sweet Cesanese that goes well with red fruit tarts.

Colli Albani An aroma of apples just about cancels out the presence of Malvasia grapes used to make this very pale, almost clear, wine. With its lightly acidic, almost bitter, dry flavor, it's a perfect wine to accompany fish. It goes well with the whole meal, in fact, and shouldn't be served too cold.

Cori The Bianco is straw colored with a persistent bouquet and tasty flavor. Its natural companion is fish, but it works well with vegetable soups, too. The Rosso is a pale ruby red with a bouquet of mixed berries and is lightly tannic. It goes with baked or stewed chicken.

Est! Est! Est! There are a few versions of the origins of this enthusiastically named wine. At the beginning of the twelfth century, a German bishop came to Italy to join the army of the Emperor Henry V. In fact, the bishop was more interested in savoring the wines of Italy than following its politics. He sent his servant, Martin, ahead of him to scout out the best inns to sample wines. Martin discovered that excellent wines were to be had in the town of Montefiascone in the province of Viterbo — so good that Martin couldn't refrain from excitedly marking an inn with *est!est!est!* (exclamation points included) to mean *vinum est bonum* — "the wine is good." This pale yellow wine is made with Trebbiano and Malvasia grapes. It's fragrant and tasty with a slightly bitter streak. It goes well with both salt- and freshwater fish. The semi-dry version goes well with ciambelle and desserts made with ricotta.

Frascati Perhaps the best-known wine from the Castelli Romani (the castles of Rome), a group of communities in the province of Rome, Frascati is straw yellow with a persistent bouquet and dry flavor. This lively, light-bodied wine is good with the entire meal. The semi-sweet version, called Cannellino, is more structured and refined. It's a perfect dessert wine as good with sweets as it is with aged cheese.

Marino Another famous wine from the Castelli. It's pale yellow with a bouquet of delicate but persistent fruits. It's full flavored and lively and goes well with fish or the whole meal.

Montecompatri-Colonna A wine with properties similar to Frascati and Marino. It's pale yellow with a winey nose and a dry, slightly bitter flavor. It's a good table wine.

Velletri This light, pleasurable wine is straw colored with a bouquet of fruit, anise and lemon. Its fresh flavor is slightly acidic. It goes well with vegetable antipasti, fish courses and fish. There's also a Velletri Rosso. This ruby-colored wine is dry, tasty and emits a bouquet of mixed berries. This is the wine to drink with porchetta alla romana, l'agnello brodettato and all dishes made with barnyard animals.

Zagarolo Another wine of the Castelli; however, it's more full bodied and refined than the others. It's pale yellow with a bouquet of fruit and anise; its dry flavor has a slightly bitter streak. It marries well with mixed, fried vegetables, with brains and sweetbreads and with a stew made with peas, fava beans and artichokes.

Bucatini all'amatriciana

(the modern version, with tomatoes)
Serves 6

  1 tablespoon extra virgin olive oil
  1 teaspoon lardo
  1 large onion, chopped
  1 bay leaf
  10½ ounces diced *guanciale* (cured pork cheek)
  2 pounds ripe plum tomatoes, parboiled, peeled, seeded and coarsely chopped
  1 teaspoon sugar
  A pinch of hot pepper flakes
  1 teaspoon freshly ground black pepper
  1 pound bucatini
  A handful of grated pecorino romano cheese

Add the olive oil and lardo to a large casserole. When the lardo has melted, brown the onions with the bay leaf. Add all but a handful of the guanciale to the casserole and sauté. Add the tomatoes (taste for acidity and add sugar to correct), lower the heat and cook until the sauce has become dense. Add the hot pepper flakes and black pepper. Taste and add salt as necessary. Add the remaining guanciale to a small skillet and cook until crunchy. Cook the bucatini according to the package directions, then drain and add to a large frying pan. Sprinkle with a handful of pecorino romano, then add the tomato sauce and toss to thoroughly coat the bucatini. Garnish with the crunchy bits of guanciale and serve immediately.

Suggested wine: Orvieto or Aprilia Sangiovese

ABRUZZO AND MOLISE

The cuisine of Abruzzo is characterized, of course, by its geography. The tall mountains that slope down, almost touching the Adriatic Sea, give the region the natural growing area for the ingredients needed for its diverse dishes. The heterogeneous population of the region has influenced the two profoundly distinct parts of the gastronomic traditions, food from the sea and that from the interior.

The one ingredient that's constant throughout the region is the hot pepper. It lends its "diabolical" flavor to everything it touches. The regional olive oil is used to dress just about every dish. Other essential Abruzzese products include grapes, wine and cheese. Abruzzo is where the tradition of using hard wheat begins and it's showcased in the manufacture of pasta — every kind of pasta is made with incredible tools and techniques. Mutton and lamb are the most popular meat choices. You'll find fresh seafood served exclusively along the coast. It's odd that the most precious saffron in all of the country is cultivated in the province of L'Aquila — but the Abruzzese couldn't care less about using it in their kitchens. The Abruzzesi are great eaters — they'll eat until they almost burst; in fact, they define themselves as *bisacce d'Abruzzo*, the "packsaddles of Abruzzo."

The geographical makeup of the region of Molise is less severe — sweeter and more woodsy than its neighbor, Abruzzo — but they share an almost identical cuisine. They use the same methods in agriculture, the same ways of raising animals and producing cheese. In Molise the meat of choice tends to be pork.

ANTIPASTI, CURED MEATS, BREADS, FLATBREADS AND SAVORY TARTS

Calamaretti agli scampi Squid stuffed with a mixture of shrimp, breadcrumbs, garlic, olive oil and parsley and cooked in white wine. The dish is a specialty of the town of Giulianova in the province of Teramo.

Calamaretti all'olio An antipasto, a specialty of the province of Pescara, made with freshly caught tiny squid that are cut in half and served raw with olive oil, vinegar, onions, salt and hot pepper flakes.

Calcioni molisani Round ravioli filled with chopped prosciutto, ricotta and provolone cheese, then fried to serve.

Capelomme Loin of pork that's inserted into a pork casing, then aged, in the beginning near a wood-burning fireplace, then later hung in a cool, dry spot to finish. The capelomme is served in slices that must contain as much fat as they do lean meat.

Coglioni di mulo See *mortadelline di Campotosto* (below).

Croste di pane alla contadina Slices of stale bread covered with a mixture of eggs, milk, cheese and prosciutto and then baked.

Crostini alla chietina Toasts made by cutting rustic bread into triangular-shaped slices, dipping them in eggs and then frying them. They are covered with butter, anchovies and capers to serve.

Insalata all'abruzzese A mixed vegetable salad with zucchini, green beans, tomatoes, onions and peppers, covered with tuna preserved in olive oil and anchovies. It's dressed with olive oil, vinegar, hot pepper flakes, basil and oregano.

Lumellu A loin of pork covered with hot pepper flakes, inserted into a casing and then air-dried.

Mortadelline di Campotosto Small mortadelle, weighing not more than a pound, that are tied, in the way provolone cheese is tied, to make four wedges. They have nothing in common with the more famous mortadella bolognese. These are made with the very lean meat of wild pigs raised along the banks of Lago di Compotosto, in the province of L'Aquila. Cylinders of lardo are added to the center of each mortadellina to soften the mixture. When the mortadellini are sliced they are quite attractive with their white centers and red meat dotted with black pepper. They're also called coglioni di mulo ("mule's balls").

Mulette Salami from Molise that are similar to coppe or capocolli because of the strong presence of hot pepper flakes instead of black pepper like most salami. The mulette from the village of Macchiagodena in the province of Isernia are among the best in the region.

Nirvi e musse A dish from the province of Campobasso in the Molise region very much like the Milanese *nervetti* (chopped tendons in gelatin, page 48) except that the meat is removed from the head of the veal instead of the foot.

Pampanella Pancetta flavored with abundant amounts of hot pepper flakes then oven-dried. An extra special version comes from the village of San Martino in Pènsilis in the province of Campobasso.

Pizza rustica An antique recipe made by filling a sweet

short crust with prosciutto; aged, sliced sausage; scamorza and pecorino cheeses; eggs and cinnamon. The same filling is used for fried panzerotti.

Prosciutto affumicato Cured meat — smoked ham — typical of the mountainous areas of the Abruzzo and Molise regions. The best are found in the town of Spinete in the province of Campobasso and in Rionero Sannitico in the province of Isernia.

Salsicce al finocchio Pork sausages flavored with fennel seeds then preserved in terra cotta pots covered with pork fat. This is the same method used to conserve *salamin d'la duja* (page 5).

Salsicciotto di Torano A fat sausage made with finely ground, lean pork, pieces of fat and abundant amounts of freshly ground black pepper. It's typical of the town of Torano in the province of Teramo.

Scapece alla vastese A way to preserve fish in which fillets of fish and squid are floured and fried, then marinated in a sauté of olive oil, onions, garlic, aromatic herbs and saffron. The liquid is diluted with a bit of vinegar. Sometimes the fish are marinated raw.

Soppressata molisana A big fat sausage made with coarsely chopped pork and preserved in a casing with strips of lardo placed in such a way that when it is cut, there are cross, star or other patterns in each slice.

Ventricina Salami made with both fatty and lean pork parts. It's flavored with salt, hot pepper flakes, fennel seeds and orange peel, then preserved in a casing made from the *ventre*, or stomach of the animal, hence the name. They're a specialty of the province of Chieti.

PASTA, GNOCCHI, RICE, POLENTA AND GRAINS

Ciufulitti The Aquilana word for a type of flour-and-water maccheroni that's pierced, then dressed with mutton ragù and served covered with grated pecorino.

Fracchiata Chickpea-flour polenta that's served with fried anchovies. Sometimes olive oil, hot pepper flakes and fried, dried sweet red peppers are added as well.

Fregnacce Fregnacce, similar to crêpes, are filled with a rich mixture of chicken livers, little meatballs, cheese and chicken breasts, then rolled and baked.

Fusilli alla molisana Fusilli made by twirling pieces of pasta around a spiral tool, then serving them with a tomato and hot pepper sauce.

Gnocchetti a cacio e uova Little flour gnocchi dressed with eggs and grated pecorino cheese, then garnished with chopped, fried pancetta, a recipe similar to pasta alla carbonara from the Lazio region.

Gnocchetti di pasta da pane Dumplings made with bread dough that are boiled and then dressed with beef ragù and grated pecorino cheese.

Gnocchi carrati Flour gnocchi dressed with eggs, pecorino and fried pancetta.

Granitte con le fave Grated pasta cooked like polenta, then dressed with sautéed fava beans and onions.

Laianelle Half-moon-shaped egg-pasta ravioli filled with Molisana ricotta, then dressed with kid ragù and grated cheese. Lainelle are distinguished from other ravioli because the pasta is not rolled out with a rolling pin. Instead, bits of pasta are broken off from the dough and formed into circles by hand.

Macche Sliced cornmeal polenta layered with sausages and baked. It may be served with pork ragù, vino cotto or apples. The dish is typical of the region of Molise.

Maccheroni al rintrocilo Large, square spaghetti, similar to spaghetti alla chitarra, made with a special tool. You'll find this pasta in the town of Lanciano and throughout the province of Chieti.

Maccheroni alla ceppa Pasta made by wrapping pieces of dough around a *ceppa*, a tool that looks like a knitting needle. These maccheroni are served dressed with a simple tomato sauce or giblet ragù.

Maccheroni alla chitarra A typically Abruzzese pasta made with an egg dough kneaded at great length. A *chitarra* is a rectangular wooden loom strung with metal wires placed very near each other. The sheet of pasta, la sfoglia, is placed on top of the frame and pressed through it with a rolling pin to make square-shaped spaghetti. This is a relatively new shape—well, for Italy. It dates back to the middle of the nineteenth century. Before the invention of the *chitarra*, in the province of Chieti, the same shape was made by cutting the pasta with a shoemaker's hammer (*rintrocilo*). Maccheroni alla chitarra is typically dressed with beef or lamb and sweet pepper ragù. Sometimes they're dressed all'Amatriciana or with a tomato and hot pepper sauce.

Maccheroni alla molinara A curious pasta shape made by dividing the dough into little balls, sticking a finger into the balls, then twirling until a wide doughnut-shape is created. These "doughnuts" are lifted from the work surface, then pulled until a long cord that rolls itself until a hank or skein is formed. In the end the idea is to obtain a spaghettone (a huge spaghetto) about fifty meters long!

Maccheroni carrati See *maccheroni alla chitarra* (page 208).

Mappatelle unto e cacio Very thin frittate, similar to crêpes, that are filled with maccheroni alla chitarra dressed with pecorino cheese, parsley and fried pancetta, then folded closed and baked to serve. *Mappa* means napkin. It's a specialty of the Molise region.

Pappicci Flour and water tagliatelle cooked with fresh tomatoes then dressed with onions sautéed in lardo.

Pastuccia A type of polenta baked with sausages, raisins, eggs and guanciale.

Polenta di farro Polenta made with coarsely ground farro and usually served with an abundant amount of ragù all'abruzzese.

Sorcetti verdi Gnocchi made with potatoes and spinach that are dressed with beef ragù.

Stracci di Sella di Corno Crêpes filled with scamorza cheese and veal sauce. The folded crêpes are covered with grated pecorino cheese, baked and served with tomato sauce. This is a traditional dish of the town of Sella di Corno in the province of Aquila.

Strengozze Abruzzese pasta made with flour and water, then cut into irregular shapes.

Surecilli Flour and egg gnocchi dressed with mutton ragù and grated pecorino cheese. They're a specialty of the province of Aquila.

Taccozze See *taccozzelle* (below).

Taccozzelle con ricotta Large pasta squares, similar to maltagliati, that are dressed with fresh ricotta cheese and tomato sauce.

Tajarille Maccheroni alla chitarra cut into pieces.

Tajarille con trote e gamberi Tajarille with tomato sauce with trout and freshwater shrimp.

Tajarille de lu cafone Tajarille with pork liver, olive oil and garlic.

Timballo Crêpes layered with meatballs, scamorza cheese, tomato sauce, grated cheese and chicken giblets, then gratinéed to serve.

Volanelle See *taccozzelle* (above).

SOUPS

Brodetto pescarese A fish soup *in bianco*—without tomato sauce—that contains scorpion fish, catfish, skate, octopus, lobster and other seasonal fish. It's flavored with onions and peppers.

Brodosini Broth with short egg tagliatelle and guanciale sautéed in lardo.

Cardone in brodo con polpettine di carne Cardoon soup enriched with little meatballs, chicken livers and beaten eggs. This specialty of the province of Chieti is usually made during Christmastime.

Cicoria cacio e uova A soup made with wild chicory enriched with chopped lardo and onions, grated pecorino cheese and eggs.

Cipollata dell'ortolano An onion and tomato soup flavored with hot pepper flakes and fresh basil. It's finished with eggs and grated pecorino cheese.

Condita or **connita** A "frugal" or low-cost soup made by boiling a piece of pancetta in water to create a simple broth. It's thickened with eggs and grated pecorino cheese. It's similar to *zuppa alla pavese* from Lombardy (page 55) and straciatella alla romana from Lazio.

Cucine Another name for the soup called *virtù* (page 211).

Fruffella Minestrone enriched with sautéed pancetta, garlic and hot pepper flakes; a specialty of the town of Bojano in the Molise region.

Laganelle e fagioli Soup made with fresh little pieces of lasagna, beans, aromatic herbs and hot pepper flakes.

'mbaniccia Minestrone made with beans, tomatoes, olive oil, garlic, lardo and hot pepper flakes. It's served with pieces of stale bread. There's also a version made with turnips and pork rind, without beans and tomatoes. 'mbaniccia is a specialty of the Molise region.

Minestra marinara A very rich fish soup that includes squid, fillet of sole, hake, red mullet, dogfish, clams and other assorted fish and shellfish. It's cooked with olive oil, garlic, parsley, hot pepper flakes and lemon juice and is a specialty of the town of Giulianova in the province of Teramo.

Scrippelle 'mbusse A specialty of the province of Teramo made with cheese-stuffed crêpes served in broth garnished with more cheese. The name of the dish means "wet crêpes."

Tassa This *tazza*, or cup, of soup is made with bread, wine and hot pepper flakes.

Virtù An Abruzzese soup also called cucina (kitchen) or sette peccati (seven sins). The interesting name refers to the virtues of the housewife and her ability to include all the necessary ingredients to make this soup: seven meats (pork rind, prosciutto, ham bone, ham hocks, pig's ear and snout, and lardo); four different kinds of legumes (chickpeas, lentils, dried peas and dried fava beans); vegetables (escarole, fresh fava beans, fresh peas, endive, chard, spinach and tomatoes); herbs and aromatic vegetables (celery, carrots, onions, garlic, parsley, mint and marjoram); pasta shapes chosen among dry, fresh, egg, long and short; and the time it takes to cook it. The soup is usually served in the countryside during the springtime harvest as a way to empty the pantry and make room for new products. Actually, the *virtù* or virtue is that of the cook who successfully makes good use of the leftover dry goods and the recently harvested crops.

Zocche See *virtù* (above).

CONDIMENTS, SAUCES, SALSAS AND EGGS

Ragù d'agnello e peperoni A typically Abruzzese ragù used to dress, *per eccellenza*, maccheroni alla chitarra.

FISH, CRUSTACEANS AND SHELLFISH

Baccalà mollicato Salt cod that is parboiled then finished in a casserole with the white part of bread, garlic, parsley, olive oil, oregano and hot pepper flakes.

Brodetto alla vastese A fish soup made with tomatoes, garlic, olive oil, sweet peppers and parsley. Some of the seafood that are used in the soup are cod, red mullet, sole, dogfish, skate, squid, lobster, clams and mussels.

Brodetto pescarese See page 210.

Carpeselle Tiny fish that are floured, fried and then put in a sauce made with vino cotto and vinegar.

Coda di rospo alla cacciatora Sliced monkfish sautéed in olive oil with garlic, rosemary and hot pepper flakes that is a specialty of the province of Pescara.

Polpi in purgatorio Octopus slowly stewed with olive oil, garlic, tomatoes, parsley and hot pepper flakes. It's a specialty of the town of Vasto in the province of Chieti.

Roscioli Abruzzese dialect for triglie di scoglie (reef or striped red mullets).

Roscioli freddi allo zafferano all'aquilana Mullets cooked with garlic, coriander, hot peppers, parsley, thyme, bay leaf, saffron, a few pieces of tomato and white wine, then brought to room temperature in the cooking liquid.

Seppioline alla Cetrullo Cuttlefish stuffed with a mixture of bread, parsley, garlic, capers, anchovies and olive oil, then cooked in white wine.

Sogliole alla giuliese Little sole fillets cooked with olive oil, garlic, parsley and lemon juice, garnished with black olives and hot pepper flakes. This is a specialty of the town of Giulianova in the province of Teramo.

Triglie Red mullet.

Triglie alla rosetana Red mullet cooked with prosciutto, bay leaf and white wine.

Triglie ripiene Red mullet stuffed with bread, garlic and rosemary and then pan-fried. It's a specialty of the province of Teramo.

MEAT

Agnello a cacio e uova A stew made with milk-fed lamb that's slowly cooked with olive oil, garlic, rosemary and white wine. It's finished like a fricassee with a mixture of beaten eggs and cheese.

Agnello a cutturo Pieces of lamb cooked in a large copper pot (*cutturo*) with olive oil, lardo, sage, onions, parsley and hot peppers. It's served with big pieces of rustic bread used to sop up the sauce. Years ago, this was considered a typical shepherd's dish.

Agnello alla pecorara Lamb seasoned with a bit of butter and some onions, then hermetically sealed in a special copper pot to cook.

Agnello alla scannese Lamb cooked in a terra cotta pot with olive oil, garlic, rosemary and white wine. The dish is a specialty of the town of Scanno in the province of Aquila.

Alenoto di agnello or **di capretto** A way to prepare the gizzards of lamb or kid. They are flavored with parsley, garlic and hot pepper flakes, then enclosed in pork caul and baked.

Capra alla neretese A leg of mutton boiled with aromatic herbs then simmered in a terra cotta pot with olive oil, onions, tomatoes, sweet peppers, hot peppers, cloves and white wine. This dish is a specialty of the hill town of Nereto in the province of Teramo.

Capretto incaporchiato Extraordinarily tender and tasty meat produced when baby goats are raised in a rather cruel way. The shepherds of the province of Aquila enclose the kids in very tight wicker baskets. They are let out only to milk. Unable to move in their wicker "prisons," they quickly fatten.

Ciavarre or **ciavarra** A word used to describe a sheep who has not yet given birth or one who is sterile but not necessarily a virgin. The sheep is usually stewed with tomatoes, sweet peppers and aromatic herbs and vegetables.

Ciffe ciaffe A pork stew flavored with onions, parsley, marjoram, garlic and hot peppers.

Coatto Leg of mutton stewed with olive oil, onions, garlic, rosemary, sage, marjoram, tomato sauce, white wine, black pepper and hot pepper flakes.

Coniglio alla chietina Baked rabbit stuffed with prosciutto and rosemary.

Cucett alla ragna' Lambs' heads covered with breadcrumbs, parsley, garlic, olive oil, salt and pepper, then baked with sliced onions and potatoes with sausages, garlic and oregano.

Cucette See *cucett alla ragna'* (above).

Cutturiddi A recipe typical not only of the Abruzzo region but also the Campania region, with many variations. The base recipe is a lamb stew with onions, parsley, tomatoes, olive oil, water and cubes of pecorino cheese.

Marritte Chopped kid's gizzards, pancetta, garlic and rosemary enclosed in the kid's caul. It looks something like a sausage and is baked or stewed to serve.

Marro Lamb giblets, pancetta, garlic, rosemary and pepper stuffed into a *rizza*, or lamb's caul. It resembles a large, fat sausage and is spit-roasted or stewed to serve.

Mazzarelle d'agnello A dish, typical of the province of Teramo, made by covering endive and chard leaves with sliced onions and garlic and sliced lamb's lungs. All the ingredients are enclosed in a lamb's gut casing then sautéed in chopped lardo, olive oil and white wine or stewed in tomato sauce.

Mucische A specialty of Molise made with mutton or goat that is salted, nailed to a wooden plank, sun-dried and smoked in a fireplace. It's served sliced, with a drizzle of olive oil, ground hot pepper and oregano.

'ndocca 'ndocca A soupy stew made with various pork parts (hocks, rind, ears and ribs), garlic, bay leaf, rosemary, hot pepper flakes, black pepper and vinegar. The dish may be served cold in its gelatin as well as hot. The name of this specialty from the foothills of the mountains in the province of Teramo means "large pieces."

Nodi di trippa A stew made with the tripe or stomach of a milk-fed lamb cut into rectangles, then filled with pancetta, garlic and parsley. They're rolled and tied into knots (*nodi*), then stewed with tomatoes.

Pezzata Milk-fed lamb stuffed with oil-preserved peppers, olives, capers, anchovies, cubed lamb, breadcrumbs, grated cheese, garlic, parsley and red pepper flakes. It's cooked over a very low flame and basted with white wine.

Pollo alla Franceschiello A chicken stew with green olives, pickled vegetables and herbs. This dish honors Franceso II, the king of the Due Sicilie, the two Sicilys, who hunted around the town of Civitella del Tronto in the province of Tronto.

Rizza Caul that covers lamb and kid intestines. It's used the same way pork caul is—to enclose and tenderize other ingredients.

Rosticini Skewered mutton pieces cooked over a wood-burning flame.

Torcinelli or **turcenelle** A typical shepherd's dish simply made with lamb's or kid's gizzards wound around each other, then stewed in olive oil, lardo, tomato sauce and white wine.

Trippa alla campobassina A dish made with parboiled tripe that's cut into squares, then stewed with celery, carrots, onions, garlic, lardo, marjoram and tomato sauce. It's served covered with grated cheese.

Ventricine di Chieti "Little suitcases" made with chopped lamb's offal, garlic and parsley enclosed in the lamb's caul, then cooked in a skillet.

VEGETABLES

Cazzariello A term used in the provinces of Pescara and Chieti for hot peppers.

Ciabotta A vegetable stew that may include onions, zucchini, potatoes, celery, carrots, tomatoes, sweet peppers and green beans. It's flavored with fresh basil and hot peppers.

Cioffa Local dialect for cauliflower.

Diavolillo Hot pepper.

Fufulloni Large red peppers.

Fuje strascinate Cabbage cooked with olive oil, garlic, bay leaf and white wine.

Ghiotta A "triumph" of baked vegetables: sweet peppers, potatoes, zucchini, tomatoes and other vegetables.

Lazzariello Hot pepper.

Mesticanza A purée of potatoes and cabbage dressed with pancetta sautéed with olive oil and hot pepper flakes that is a specialty of Molise.

Pepentò The word used for hot pepper in the province of Aquila.

Raponzoli Very tasty wild plants that grow in the cracks between rocks. They are not easy to find and are considered a real delicacy.

Saiettino or **saittè** Hot pepper.

CHEESE AND DAIRY PRODUCTS

Caciofiore aquilano A sheep's milk cheese made in January and February. According to tradition, a pinch of saffron is added to the milk before it's curdled with wild cardoons. The cheese, with its soft paste, may be fresh or semi-fresh, and is made into small forms.

Marcetto A very spicy, spreadable cheese similar to the *brôs* of Piedmont (page 23). It's made by chopping pieces of aged pecorino (so old that it has tiny worms) then letting them macerate in fresh sheep's milk, vinegar (to help with fermentation) and hot pepper flakes. It's passed through a sieve, then preserved in glass jars with a layer of olive oil.

Pecorino abruzzese A full-flavored, slightly sharp sheep's milk cheese with a compact, white body with tiny eyes. It's made in a basket that gives it its distinctive furrow-like markings. The young version is usually preserved in olive oil.

SWEETS AND LIQUEURS

Bocconotti dolci Little short crust pastries filled with sugar, almonds, cocoa, crumbled cookies, lemon zest, cinnamon and must or liqueur.

Cacioricotta A sweet dish made with sheep's milk curds, coffee and lemon zest.

Calcionetti Short crust fritters filled with dried and candied fruits and mosto cotto.

Caragnoli Fried fritters made at Christmastime in the province of Campobasso. They're dipped in honey to serve.

Cassata abruzzese A Christmastime cake made by lining a bowl with sponge cake then dousing it with Centerbe ("one hundred herbs") liqueur. It's then filled with layers of various-flavored pastry creams: nougat, crunchy and chocolate. The whole thing is covered with a mixture of the three creams and then chilled to serve. It's a specialty of the town of Sulmona, known for its sugared almonds, in the province of Aquila.

Cervone A cake named for the longest — but completely harmless — snake in Europe. The dough is made with flour, sugar, honey, coffee, nutmeg, liqueur, cloves and orange peel, then filled with sour cherry jam and baked covered with chocolate and a sugar glaze.

Cicerchiata The same as the Umbrian sweet served during Carnival (page 188).

Ferratelle Wafers lightly flavored with anise liqueur. They're made with their own decorated griddles, most of which have been in Abruzzesi and Molisane families for generations.

Fiadoni Half-moon-shaped ravioli made with flour, sugar, lardo and egg dough, then filled with grated, fresh sheep's milk cheese, eggs and cinnamon. The interesting thing about these rather strange pastries is that each one has an olive leaf inside.

Libretto or **libretta** or **librotta di fichi secchi** Layers of dried figs pressed together with a mixture of sugar, cocoa, vanilla, almonds, candied citron and chocolate. At one time these sweets were covered with fig leaves.

Liquore cotognato Quince liqueur flavored with a bit of bitter almond.

Mostaccioli Cookies, usually made with egg whites, honey and dried fruits, found in many regions. In Abruzzo they're made with flour, honey, mosto cotto and almonds, then glazed with chocolate. This is a very old recipe handed down from the time of the Roman Empire by Marco Porcio Catone, a soldier renowned for his rigid, inflexible views about society.

Neole Wafers made with flour, sugar, eggs, olive oil and anisseeds on specially designed griddles.

Nocci attorrati Sugar-coated toasted almonds.

Occhi di Santa Lucia Eye-shaped anise-flavored cookies made for the feast of Santa Lucia in the town of Ortona in the province of Chieti.

Ostia rechiena A mixture of chopped walnuts, honey, vino cotto and chocolate, sandwiched between two very thin wafers.

Parrozzo A rustic, round pastry made with almonds, flour, sugar and eggs, then covered with chocolate. It's a specialty of the province of Pescara.

Pepatelli "Dry" cookies, also called biscotti di cruschello, made with tritello flour (the residue of milled grain), honey, almonds, black pepper, butter and orange peel. Typically, they're made at Christmastime throughout Abruzzo, particularly in the province of Teramo.

Piccellati Rustic pastries, typical of Molise, filled with honey or mosto cotto, grated or fried breadcrumbs or the white part of bread, walnuts, almonds, orange peel, cloves and cinnamon.

Pizza di ricotta A tart filled with ricotta, pastry cream, chocolate, candied fruit and spices.

Pizza dolce A cake made by layering liqueur-soaked sponge cake with chocolate, almond and egg pastry cream. It's glazed to finish.

Sassi d'Abruzzo Toasted, sugar-coated almonds.

Torrone al cioccolato Soft hazelnut nougat, a specialty of the province of Aquila, sometimes covered with chocolate. The defining characteristic is that the nougat maintains its soft texture no matter the temperature.

Torrone chietino ai fichi secchi Sumptuous nougat, a specialty of the province of Chieti, made with walnuts and dried figs.

Uvata A sugarless jam made exclusively with black grapes.

WINES

Because both regions, Abruzzo and Molise, have a similar mountainous and dry landscape with blustery winds whipping through their valleys, it stands to reason they would have the same wines: Trebbiano, Sangiovese and Montepulciano. These wines are distinguished by their strong character and a kind of pleasing roughness. When they're properly vinified they reveal an unexpected elegance.

Biferno Made with the same grapes as Pentro (page 218), and with similar characteristics, but a more structured wine. It's made in three versions: Bianco, Rosato and Rosso. The Bianco goes well with fish and first courses with complex sauces. The Rosato is good with fish broths and seafood soups, while the Rosso is perfect with lamb and pork dishes.

Montepulciano d'Abruzzo A dark red wine with a characteristic violet light while young. As it ages, it develops orange tones. It emits a bouquet of berries during its first two years. With age, it becomes more persuasive as it begins to reveal an inkling of faded flowers and vanilla. It's a bit sour when young but soon softens and becomes velvety. Its slightly tannic quality allows for a long life. It's a perfect accompaniment to meat cooked over a wood-burning flame. The mature version is good with roasts and game. The cherry pink Cerasuolo is obtained when the must is allowed to age in its skin for a very short period of time. Cerasuolo has a winey nose and a clean, slightly bitter palate. It goes magnificently with all local first courses.

Pentro From Molise, a wine made in three different versions: the Bianco is nothing more than a Trebbiano with a small addition of Bombino grapes. It's a pale straw color with a delicate bouquet and fresh palate. It's a great aperitif and goes well with light antipasti or fish dishes. The Rosato, almost without color, has a light bouquet and a palate that reveals a fine structure. It goes well with first courses dressed with spicy sauces. The ruby red Rosso has a light bouquet and a slightly tannic palate. It goes well with grilled meats or any preparations that use barnyard animals and, for that matter, with first course pastas dressed with meat ragù.

Trebbiano d'Abruzzo A clear yellow wine with a light bouquet of unripe fruit and a fresh and slightly bitter palate. It's a superior table wine and goes particularly well with fish dishes and rustic flatbreads made with prosciutto and cheese.

Maccheroni alla chitarra con ragù di agnello e peperoni

Serves 6

For the pasta:
A bit less than 1¼ pounds durum flour
5 eggs
For the sauce:
1 onion, chopped
3 cloves garlic, chopped
3 tablespoons extra virgin olive oil
1 pound lamb cut into little pieces
1 cup dry white wine
1⅓ pound peeled tomatoes
1 bay leaf
½ teaspoon fresh marjoram leaves
A pinch of hot pepper flakes
½ red pepper cut into strips
½ yellow pepper cut into strips
½ green pepper cut into strips
Salt and freshly ground pepper
Grated pecorino cheese for garnish

Make the pasta dough with the flour and eggs and let it rest for at an hour.

Make the ragù. Sauté the onions and garlic in 1½ tablespoons olive oil then add the lamb and brown. Add the wine, tomatoes, bay leaf, marjoram and hot pepper flakes and lower the heat. Add salt and freshly ground pepper to taste.

Meanwhile, make the maccheroni. You'll need the special *chitarra* frame in order to cut the pasta. Roll out the pasta into sheets, place them one at a time on top of the frame and pass a rolling pin over it to form the maccheroni. Reserve the pasta while finishing the sauce.

Sauté the peppers in 1½ tablespoons olive oil. Add salt and pepper to taste.

Cook the pasta in abundant salted water, drain, toss with the peppers, then with the lamb ragù. Serve garnished with grated pecorino cheese.

Suggested wine: Pentro, Rosato or Rosso

CAMPANIA

The cuisine of Campania isn't a regional cuisine but instead one of a kingdom, the ancient realm of Naples. It's a cuisine that has combined Byzantine, Greek, Roman, Arabian, Norman, French, Spanish and even Austrian elements to make one that's decisively Campanian — vital and vivacious.

It's a combination of the food of the general population and that of the aristocracy. The cuisine of the aristocracy includes timbales, elaborate savory pies and stuffed food. It's the cuisine of the *monzù* (dialect for *monsieur*), the great French chefs who were employed by Neapolitan and Sicilian noble families in the eighteenth and nineteenth centuries. Unfortunately, after the unification of Italy, the tradition of using French chefs disappeared. They left, however, a trail of dishes that are still made, most notably sartù del riso.

Maybe the Neapolitans haven't really invented anything in the kitchen, but they have certainly been able to transform everything they've learned from others. They should be applauded for having introduced the tomato into Italian cooking. There have always been flatbreads in every cuisine of the world, but the Neapolitans combined flatbread with tomato and created pizza as we know it today. Nor did the Neapolitans invent pasta, but the people of the entire region are true maccheroni (used interchangeably with pasta) eaters. Pizza, pasta and tomatoes: these are the symbols of the Neapolitan cuisine that has conquered the world.

You'll find extraordinary produce growing in the Campania terrain: the great sauce tomatoes (San Marzano), salad tomatoes (Torre del Greco), potatoes, cauliflower, sweet peppers, onions, artichokes, eggplant, peas, fava beans, broccoli and escarole. You'll also find clever and delicious calzone (stuffed, fried or baked dough); every kind of pizza; mozzarella in carozza (mozzarella sandwiched between sliced bread, then fried); and every sort of fritter, panzerotti and pizzelle. All fried food, according to local custom, must arrive at the table fragrant and boiling hot — just like the well-known dish frijenno magnanno ("eat while frying").

Meat doesn't have a starring role in the region's cuisine. It's used to make salumi or to flavor sauces and soups. Seafood is prepared in the simplest way in order to highlight the freshness of the fish — fish is cooked in soups, pasta sauces, combined with vegetables — all accompanied by tomatoes. The dairy products and cheese of Campania are unmistakable. Outstanding are the cheeses made with stretched paste, like the world famous mozzarella di bufala. Pastry recipes are passed from one family to another and include the extraordinary babà and sfogliatelle.

The originality of the culture, the attention paid to the cultivation of the land and the history and the resources of the sea have combined to make a rich, colorful, ingenious and flavorful cuisine, which is a mirror of the vital population of Campania.

ANTIPASTI, CURED MEATS, BREADS, FLATBREADS AND SAVORY TARTS

Antipasto di Pasqua An Easter plate that contains a green salad, hard-cooked eggs, sliced ricotta salata cheese and salami or capocollo.

Cafone A bread shape typical of the region.

Calzone A folded, stuffed pizza with various fillings, found in many southern regions. The classic calzone, however, is Neapolitan and is usually filled with prosciutto—or salami, mozzarella, ricotta and Parmesan cheese—and sometimes an egg. It may be baked or fried to serve.

Caniscione A very large calzone filled with prosciutto, salami, pecorino and caciocavallo cheeses and an egg. A Lenten version is filled with chard, olives and anchovies.

Caprese The emblematic Italian salad made with tomatoes, buffalo milk mozzarella, extra virgin olive oil and fresh basil or oregano.

Casatiello A braided, ring-shaped savory cake decorated with raw eggs in their shells. Sometimes pork cracklings, salami or cheese is added to the dough. A sweet version is made with brioche dough.

Crostini alla napolitana Buttered bread slices that are covered with mozzarella, fresh tomatoes, anchovies and oregano and then toasted in the oven.

Frittata contadina con insalata di sedani A frittata made with onions, scamorza cheese and fresh basil served at room temperature with celery heart salad.

Gattò di patate or **Santa Chiara** A typically Neapolitan dish made with boiled potatoes smashed and mixed with mozzarella, eggs, prosciutto, salami, provolone and Parmesan cheeses, and then baked. The name, Santa Chiara, comes from the French convent of the Clarisse sisters who made this dish.

Impasticciato A mixture of meat, vegetables, eggs and cheese wrapped in pasta.

Mozzarella in carrozza Mozzarella sandwiched between two slices of bread, dipped in a mixture of eggs and milk then fried.

Pagnottine Santa Chiara Small yeasted focaccine filled with reduced tomatoes and anchovies that have been quickly sautéed in olive oil and vinegar. They're brushed with lardo just before they're baked.

Palata A very large rustic bread (about five pounds) that *must* be baked in a wood-burning oven. The name comes from the fact that this delicacy takes up the entire baking sheet (*palata*).

Palatone A very large loaf-shaped bread.

Panzanella napoletana A specialty of Campania and Tuscany something like the Nicoise pan bagnat. It's made with stale bread or *gallette da marinaio* (sailor's crackers) softened with water and vinegar, then tossed with sliced fresh tomatoes, sliced onions, anchovies, garlic, peppers, green olives, basil and olive oil. The bread is the base, but other ingredients may vary.

Panzerotti or **panzarotti** Something like calzone, they're made with bread dough wrapped around various fillings that can include mozzarella and tomatoes, ricotta and onions fried with tomatoes, or ricotta, anchovies, salami, prosciutto, smoked provolone cheese, etc. They may be fried or baked. There are sweet versions too. In Naples, potato fritters are called panzerotti as well.

Pasta cresciuta Very soft fritters sometimes made with zucchini blossoms or sometimes with tiny fish.

Pepperoni farciti Roasted, peeled peppers stuffed with various fillings: eggplant and tomatoes, sauced pasta, or mixtures that have as their base olives, anchovies, capers, parsley, etc.

Pizza ai cicenielli Pizza topped with tiny fish.

Pizza alla Campofranco Dough made with flour, butter, eggs, milk and yeast with a mozzarella, prosciutto, tomato and Parmesan cheese topping.

Pizza alla marinara One of the most traditional pizzas, topped with tomatoes, olive oil, garlic and oregano or basil.

Pizza di scarola A traditional Christmas Eve pizza, topped with escarole, black olives, raisins, pine nuts, capers and anchovies.

Pizza Margherita A pizza created by the renowned Neapolitan *pizzaiolo* (pizza maker) Peppino Brandi to honor Queen Margherita. It's topped with tomatoes, mozzarella and basil — red, white and green like the Italian flag.

Pizza rustica The Campana version of the very tasty torte found throughout the regions of Abruzzo and Puglia. It's made by filling a sweet short crust with ricotta, prosciutto, mozzarella, eggs, Parmesan cheese, sausages and smoked provolone or scamorza cheese. It may be made with bread dough as well. Some pizze rustiche resemble fried panzerotti.

Pizzelle alla napoletana A Neapolitan preparation that may be plain fried dough, or dough filled with salami, prosciutto, provolone cheese, vegetables or anchovies.

Sangiovannese Typical Neapolitan bread similar to the *palata* (page 222).

Scagliuozzoli Slices of polenta (often leftover) filled with provolone cheese, then fried.

Tarantiello Unique salami made with tuna belly, from the province of Salerno.

Tortano ripieno A ring-shaped savory cake made with yeasted dough enriched with pork cracklings and lardo, often filled with aged cheeses and Neapolitan salami.

Viccillo A ring-shaped savory cake filled with hard-cooked eggs, salami and mozzarella, typical of the province of Salerno.

Zucchine a scapece Thinly sliced fried zucchini that are marinated in water and vinegar with garlic, black pepper and mint.

PASTA, GNOCCHI, RICE, POLENTA AND GRAINS

Cannelloni alla partenopea Cannelloni made with squares of parboiled pasta that are filled with a mixture of ricotta, mozzarella, prosciutto, eggs, Parmesan cheese and parsley, then rolled into cylindrical shapes. They're placed in a baking dish, covered with béchamel or *ragù alla napoletana* (page 227) and gratinéed.

Crespelle ripiene Crêpes made with flour, eggs, milk and Parmesan cheese, then filled with ricotta, Parmesan cheese, mozzarella and parsley. They're rolled into cylinders, placed in a baking dish, covered with tomato sauce and then gratinéed.

Fusilli alla napoletana Twirled pasta shapes dressed with a pot roast sauce (cooked with lardo, celery, carrots, onions, garlic, white wine and tomato sauce), ricotta and little pieces of cubed salami. The pot roast is generally served as the main course.

Fusilli alla vesuviana Twirled pasta shapes dressed with fresh tomato sauce, mozzarella, pecorino and oregano and then baked.

Lagane or **laganelle** An antique recipe typical of the south-central part of Italy. While they are actually lasagne or lasagnette (short lasagne), they have almost nothing to do with the more famous pasta from the Emilia-Romagna region. Although they share more or less the same shape, the Neapolitan version is made with water and semolina flour. They are served in bean soup or with other legumes and sautéed anchovies, cabbage, turnip tops or beef ragù. In Naples they're sometimes called lampe e tuone ("thunder and lightning").

Lasagne di Carnevale A very substantial dish made with parboiled lasagna noodles layered with little meatballs, little sausages or brains, ricotta, mozzarella, other cheeses and hard-cooked eggs, then gratinéed. It's served especially on Fat Thursday during Carnival.

Maccheroni alla napoletana Ziti dressed with veal pot roast sauce and grated caciocavallo cheese. The veal that's used to make the sauce is generally served as the main course.

Maccheroni alla sangiovanniello Pasta dressed with garlicky tomato sauce, prosciutto and fresh basil and served with grated pecorino cheese.

Maccheroni di casa Gnocchi made with flour, semolina, salt and water. They're dressed with tomato sauce or *ragù alla napoletana* (page 227). At one time they were called strangolaprieve ("priest stranglers").

Migliaccio campano Polenta cooked with pork cracklings and sausages, topped with cheese and parsley, then baked.

Munnezzaglia Assorted, leftover pasta shapes usually added to vegetable soups (see *pasta ammiscata*, page 226).

Pasta alla puttanesca A relatively new way of dressing linguine, spaghetti or vermicelli from the island of Ischia. The sauce is made with tomatoes, olive oil, anchovies, capers, black olives, oregano, parsley and hot pepper flakes.

Pasta alla sorrentina A dish made by sautéing pasta with tomato sauce and cubes of scamorza cheese. The heat melts the cheese so it becomes stringy when the pasta is lifted off the plate.

Pasta fritta A typical "recycled" dish made with leftover cooked pasta, typically maccheroni or spaghetti, that's tossed with ragù, meatballs, prosciutto and cheese, held together with eggs and then cooked just like a frittata. It's characteristically crunchy on the outside and soft on the inside.

Perciatelli principi di Napoli Perciatelli are ten-inch long pasta shapes with a hollow center, similar to bucatini, but slightly wider. For this particular "noble" dish (it honors the Neapolitan princes), the pasta is first dressed with Parmesan cheese, chicken fillets, buttered peas and mozzarella cubes. To serve, it's covered with the sauce from a beef pot roast and flakes of butter.

Ravioli alla napoletana Half-moon-shaped ravioli made with egg pasta. They're filled with mozzarella, ricotta, prosciutto, Parmesan cheese and parsley, then dressed with tomato sauce or ragù alla Napoletana.

Sartù di riso The only dish from the aristiocratic Neapolitan kitchen that's still popular. The name comes from the French word, *surtout* ("above all others"). This sumptuous rice timbale is stuffed and garnished with meatballs, chicken giblets, peas and many other things. It is not only an extremely tasty dish, but also a very beautiful one.

Sciaffoni Very rustic, handmade maccheroni usually dressed with a meat ragù or tomato sauce that originated in the province of Avellino.

Strangolapreti Potato gnocchi. Obviously, before the arrival in Europe of the "magic tuber," gnocchi were made with flour, semolina and water. They're usually dressed with tomato sauce and cubes of mozzarella or ragù alla Napoletana.

Strangolaprieve See *maccheroni di casa* (page 224).

Timballo A short crust pastry wrapped around a filling made with meat ragù, chicken giblets, mozzarella, mushrooms and fresh truffles — or with other ingredients.

Timpano A big "mess" made with pasta, vegetables, meats and cheese, then baked with a pasta wrap. Ingredients vary widely.

Zite or **ziti** A fat, long (ten-inch) pasta shape with a hollow center.

SOUPS

Cardone in brodo con polpettine di carne Cardoon soup with chicken livers and tiny meatballs. See *zuppa di cardoni* (page 226).

Farinella con i cicoli A rather liquid polenta enriched with pork cracklings, grated cheese and fresh parsley.

Laganelle e ceci Chickpea soup with olive oil, garlic and pasta in which *lagane* (page 224) are cooked as well.

Minestra maritata A very rich soup that at one time — up until 1800 and the burgeoning popularity of maccheroni — was considered the "queen" of the Neapolitan table. The many, many recipes for this soup, also known as pignato or pignatto grasso, depend on the area where it's made. Most include vegetables (escarole, broccoli, turnip greens, celery, carrots, onions, chard, cabbage, chicory) and meat (mostly pork — like ribs, sausages, ham bone, salami and guanciale) all cooked in broth, then finished with spices and grated, aged caciocavallo cheese.

Minestrone alla napoletana A regional soup distinguished from other minestrones by the large amount of winter squash and the short, dry pasta that's added to it.

Pasta ammiscata Bean soup cooked with assorted pasta shapes. The name of the soup literally means "mixed pasta" and alludes to the days when shopkeepers sold pasta out of barrels and would sell the remains, mixed together, for highly discounted prices.

Pignato or **pignatto grasso** See *minestra maritata* (above).

Soffritto or **saporiglio** or **tosciano** or **zuffritto** A robust Neapolitan soup that is more a loose ragù, made by sautéing pieces of pork lung, heart, windpipe and spleen in olive oil and lardo. It's diluted with tomato sauce and red wine then flavored with bay leaf, rosemary and abundant hot pepper flakes. It's served with toasted bread.

Zuppa di cardoni A very tasty soup, typical of the interior part of the region, made with cardoons, meatballs, chicken pieces, mozzarella, little sausages and broth. See *cardone in brodo* (page 225).

Zuppa di rotelline farcite Rotelline are little round pieces of bread cut from a Pullman loaf. Some are spread with chicken liver paste, some with prosciutto and others with mushrooms. For this soup, they're floured, fried and served in boiling hot broth.

CONDIMENTS, SAUCES, SALSAS AND EGGS

Ragù alla napoletana The emblematic Neapolitan sauce made by sautéing lardo with chopped onions, carrots, celery, garlic and pork or chopped beef in a terra cotta pot. The cooking continues with the addition of red wine (Gragnano or Irpinia), tomato sauce, nutmeg and marjoram. This sauce is cooked very slowly. In another version called guardaporta ("doorman's sauce") little veal roll-ups filled with garlic, parsley, pepper, raisins, pine nuts and grated cheese are substituted for the ground beef.

FISH, CRUSTACEANS AND SHELLFISH

Alici Anchovies.

Alici a scapece Anchovies that are floured and fried then marinated in vinegar, bay leaf, garlic, onions, peppercorns and oregano.

Alici ammollicate Anchovies baked with garlic, olive oil, white wine, parsley and breadcrumbs. Sometimes tomatoes and oregano are added.

Alici areganate Anchovy fillets baked with olive oil, garlic, oregano and freshly ground pepper.

Anguilla Eel.

Anguilla a scapece Chunks of eel that are floured and fried, then marinated in vinegar, garlic, oregano and freshly ground pepper.

Anguilla in umido alla napoletana A stew made by slowly cooking small eels with olive oil, puréed tomatoes, onions, basil, parsley and white wine. It is served on toasted croutons.

Baccalà alla napoletana Carefully soaked and cleaned salt cod that is floured and fried, stewed with tomatoes, garlic, capers, olives, raisins and pine nuts, then baked to serve.

Cecenielli The Neapolitan word for a type of tiny fish. They may be made into pasta cresciuta (fritters) or pizzelle (wafers made with a type of waffle iron) or used in frittatas.

Fragaglie Tiny fish left caught in the nets.

Impepata di cozze An extremely simple dish made with fresh mussels steamed with lemon, parsley, black pepper, olive oil and the liquid that they create as they open.

Musillo The thick, center part of the baccalà (salt cod).

Pesce all'acqua pazza A way of cooking fish with onions sautéed in olive oil, water, white wine and tomatoes.

Pesce alla marinara Fish cooked with olive oil, garlic, oregano, parsley and sometimes tomatoes.

Polpi affogati Octopus slowly cooked with olive oil, garlic, tomatoes, hot pepper flakes and parsley.

Polpi alla luciana A dish named for Santa Lucia, a little fishing village near Naples. The village fishermen boil freshly caught octopus, cut it into pieces, then marinate them with olive oil, garlic, parsley, black pepper and lemon juice.

Sarde alla napoletana Cleaned and boned whole sardines that are baked with tomato fillets, garlic, parsley, oregano and olive oil.

Sauté di vongole A much-used recipe for clams that are simply sautéed in olive oil with garlic, parsley and black pepper.

Spannocchi Canocchie, a type of shellfish.

Stocco a fungitello Pieces of floured stoccafisso (dried cod) stewed with tomatoes, garlic and basil.

Vongole alla napoletana A type of clam stew made with olive oil, garlic, parsley, fresh peeled tomatoes and black pepper.

Zuppa di pesce alla napoletana or **alla marinara** A typically Mediterranean dish made with fish from the Gulf of Naples; dogfish, lucerne, saltwater eel, mullet, squid and shrimp are essential. They are cooked with an abundant amount of tomatoes, olive oil, garlic, parsley, hot peppers and mussels and clams.

MEAT

Bistecca alla re Franceschiello A dish, dedicated to King Francesco II (a glutton!), typical of the province of Caserta. It's a veal steak cooked in parchment paper with mushrooms, pickled vegetables, olive oil–preserved baby artichokes, green olives, prosciutto and Marsala wine.

Braciole di maiale alla napoletana Pork roll-ups filled with chopped capers, prosciutto, breadcrumbs, raisins and pine nuts then cooked in a spicy tomato sauce.

Braciolette A traditional Neapolitan family dish of skewers loaded with chunks of bread, meatballs, lardo and little "sandwiches" of bread stuffed with prosciutto, butter and parsley. As the name of dish tells you, the skewers are cooked *alla brace*, over a wood-burning fire. However, they may be cooked in an oven, too.

Braciolone alla partenopea A wide piece of beef spread with spinach, prosciutto, hard-cooked eggs, parsley, garlic, oregano, raisins and pine nuts then rolled up and cooked in white wine and tomato-vegetable sauce.

Carne or **costata alla pizzaiola** Pieces of beef sautéed with olive oil, garlic, tomato and oregano.

Cervella alla napoletana Brains baked with capers, black olives, breadcrumbs and freshly ground black pepper.

Cervellatine Little Neapolitan-style sausages made with lean pork, lardo, salt, pepper and red wine enclosed in lamb gut casings.

Coniglio all'ischitana Pieces of rabbit browned in olive oil then stewed with tomatoes, rosemary and white wine.

Frijenno e magnanno (friggendo, mangiando) Neapolitan way to describe a way of "frying" then "eating" that alludes to the custom of frying food, then bringing it to table while it's fresh and hot for consumption and before the next item is cooked. Actually, there should be thirty-six different dishes served in this kind of meal including panzerotti, fritters, anchovies, sardines, baccalà, polenta triangles, zucchini blossoms, borage, artichokes, liver, brains, sweetbreads, backs, rice balls, croquettes, etc.

Genovese In spite of its name, this dish is Neapolitan through and through: a pot roast slowly cooked with lardo, olive oil, an abundant amount of onions, carrots and celery and tomato sauce. It may be that the name comes from an historic settlement of Genoese merchants in Naples.

Granatine Meatballs made with chopped beef, lardo, bread, parsley and prosciutto, then flattened into heart shapes and cooked with vegetables and Marsala wine.

Maruzze Snails.

Pariata All of the innards.

Pezzentelle Sausages made with leftover and discarded pork bits.

Saltimbocca alla sorrentina Veal scaloppine cooked in tomato sauce, covered with prosciutto, mozzarella and Parmesan cheese, then baked for a few minutes.

Tracchiolelle Fresh pork ribs.

Trippa alla napoletana Tripe cooked with lardo and onions, removed from the heat and then thickened, like a fricassee, with beaten eggs and cheese.

VEGETABLES

Carciofi ripieni alla napoletana Artichokes that first are cleaned by removing their thick outer leaves, cutting away the sharp points and eliminating the fuzzy choke. They're parboiled, then stuffed with a mixture of tomato sauce, dried mushrooms, onions, chopped leftover boiled meats, parsley and grated cheese, all held together with egg yolks and then baked to finish.

Cianfotta Campania's version of a vegetable stew found throughout southern Italy made with sweet peppers, eggplant, tomatoes, potatoes, onions, celery, garlic, basil and parsley.

Fagioli alla maruzzara Fresh cannellini beans boiled, then enriched with tomatoes, olive oil, oregano and chopped garlic and parsley. The dish is a Neapolitan specialty.

Fiorilli Squash blossoms.

Friarielli Tender and aromatic greens (broccoletti or turnip greens) from the province of Salerno. They're usually sautéed in olive oil with garlic and hot pepper.

Insalata di rinforzo A sumptuous Christmastime salad made with cauliflower, olives, anchovies, capers and assorted pickled vegetables, then dressed with olive oil and vinegar. The name of the salad comes from the tradition of adding new ingredients daily to the leftover salad — reinforcing it (*rinforzato*).

Melanzane Eggplant.

Melanzane a mannella A dish made with eggplant that is first cut into horizontal slices. The slices are marked with slits, then fried and dressed at room temperature with olive oil, oregano and vinegar, then layered and baked. They may be served hot or at room temperature. This is a specialty of Naples.

Melanzane al funghetto or **a fungitielli** A dish found throughout the region made by sautéing pieces of eggplant in olive oil with garlic and parsley — a preparation used for mushrooms. Sometimes tomatoes and capers are added.

Melanzane Capodimonte or **alla partenopea** Fried eggplant slices made into sandwiches with caciocavallo cheese. The sandwiches are lined up in a baking dish, topped with tomato sauce and Parmesan cheese and then baked.

Moglignane Eggplant.

Pappacelle Little round pickled peppers.

Parmigiana di melanzane Sliced, floured and fried eggplant that's then layered in a baking dish with tomato-onion sauce, basil, sliced hard-cooked eggs, mozzarella and grated Parmesan cheese. It's baked and served hot or at room temperature.

Scarola 'mbuttunata Parboiled, tender hearts of escarole that are filled with a mixture of garlic, black olives, anchovies, capers, raisins and pine nuts. After the hearts are closed, they're placed in a baking dish, covered with breadcrumbs and baked.

Spullecarielli Freshly shelled beans cooked with tomato sauce, olive oil, garlic, oregano and hot pepper flakes.

Torzelle Turnip greens.

CHEESE AND DAIRY PRODUCTS

Bocconcini di cardinale Small, almost flavorless balls of mozzarella preserved in milk or cream placed in a special terra cotta, amphora-shaped container called a *langelle*. The little balls are also called uova (eggs) or ovoline di bufala (little buffalo milk eggs).

Burrielli or **Burrini** Small cheeses made with a paste similar to *caciocavallo* (below) or provolone dolce with a lump of delicious butter in the center.

Caciocavallo A pear-shaped cheese whose shape is made when its head is tied with a string and hung to age or to be smoked. Its smooth rind can go from straw yellow to dark brown. Its compact but elastic body may be white or straw colored. This cheese, produced throughout the ancient realm of Naples, is good for slicing.

Cacio forte An extremely sharp cheese made exclusively in the town of Roccaromana in the province of Caserta. It's usually served with an aperitif or with a selection of antipasti.

Caciottella di Sorrento A fresh, mild cheese with a delicate and pleasing flavor usually made with sheep's milk. At one time it was wrapped in grape or fig leaves.

Fiordilatte A cow's milk cheese made in the same way as mozzarella. It may be round or braided.

Formaggetta di Capua A fresh, very pleasing sheep's milk cheese that's flavored with anise.

Mozzarella A cow's milk cheese made throughout the central-southern part of Italy. It's made in various shapes (hazelnut, cherry, small egg, bocconcini, braided, etc.). Traditionally, however, it's globe-shaped. It's a fresh, stretched paste cheese made up of many layers that melt together as they reach the center of the form. Its smooth, shiny surface reveals the "scar" that indicates the area where the cheese was cut away from the mass of curds. In fact, the name mozzarella comes from the antique verb, *mozzare* ("to cut away").

Mozzarella di bufala Made with whole buffalo milk in the same way as the cow's milk version except that its fuller flavor (at least 50 percent fat) is deemed superior. In Campania it's made almost exclusively in the area called dei Mazzoni, between Capua, Nola and Aversa in Capitanata, and in the area around Salerno. These are the areas where buffalo are still raised.

Provola Like mozzarella, a pasta filata, or spun paste cheese. It's made with a mixture of whole buffalo milk and cow's milk. However, unlike mozzarella, provola, with its more stable paste, has a longer shelf life. It's often found in a very tasty smoked version.

Provolone Another stretched paste cheese made with whole cow's milk. Although it originated in southern Italy, it's now made in Lombardy, Emilia-Romagna and other regions. This rich cheese is made into a variety of very distinct shapes. Its thin, smooth, shiny rind can be golden or brownish-yellow. Its compact body makes it a good slicing cheese. Mild provolone is sweet and buttery while the sharper version has a fuller, saltier flavor and is aged for a considerable amount of time.

Ricotta di fuscella A wet, low-fat ricotta cheese usually sold in baskets to allow the excess whey to drain. It's a cheese that wants to be eaten on its own rather than added to cooked foods.

Ricotta salata Sheep's milk ricotta that is preserved in salt.

Saticulano See *cacio forte* (page 231).

SWEETS

Anginetti Small-ring shaped cookies that are completely covered with a sugar glaze.

Auciati Ring-shaped biscuits made with olive oil, white wine and black pepper then marked with a specific tool. They're typical of the town of Sessa Aurunca in the province of Caserta, where they're eaten dipped in sweet wine.

Babà The pride of Neapolitan pastries. This little mushroom-shaped individual cake is baked, then drenched in rum and covered with an apricot glaze. It's said that the pastry originated with the Polish king, Stanislas Leszczynsky, who, when exiled in the Lorraine area of France, decided to renew, or refresh, the local cake, the kugelhupf, by bathing it in rum. The king, a great fan of the *A Thousand and One Nights* stories, named his invention after Ali Baba. The pastry has been made in Naples since the French rule.

Bombonati Little chocolate candies with a cocoa bean inside. They're decorated with white sprinkles.

Cannellini Cinnamon- and vanilla-flavored sugared almonds.

Casatiello dolce A ring-shaped Easter cake made with brioche dough flavored with orange blossom water. It's decorated with raw eggs, in their shells, that are secured to the cake with strips of dough (the eggs cook as the cake does).

Coviglie al caffè Parfaits made with coffee-flavored pastry cream and whipped cream. There's also a cocoa-flavored version.

Graf A large ring-shaped pastry made with dough made of flour, potatoes, eggs and yeast. It's fried and then rolled in sugar.

Mostaccioli Hard cookies found in many regions and made in many different ways. In Campania, where they are typically made at Christmastime, they are triangle shaped with a layer of apricot jam on one side and glazed with cocoa. It's said that they are the last thing that Saint Francis ate before he died.

Pastiera napoletana An extraordinary Easter tart emblematic of Naples made by enclosing in short crust a mixture of wheat berries cooked in milk (at one time rice or barley was used), ricotta, candied fruit, eggs, sugar, orange blossom water and various spices. For a more delicate, softer filling, pastry cream is added.

Pigna di Pasqua See *casatiello dolce* (above).

Pizza dolce A tart made with a pastry dough of flour, lardo, sugar and eggs and filled with a mixture of ricotta, sugar, almonds and cream. The filling may vary as does the custom of adding a layer of pastry cream either under or on top of the filling.

Pizza figliata or **fogliata** A pastry bundle filled with a mixture of honey, walnuts, hazelnuts, almonds, candied citron and spices.

Raffiuoli or **raffioli a cassata** Soft pastries made with a dough of flour, potato flour, egg yolks and stiffly whipped egg whites (pasta margherita). The baked pastry is cut into oval shapes that are sandwiched around a filling made with fresh ricotta, sugar, pieces of candied citron and chocolate. Usually the raffiuoli are garnished with strips of pistachio paste then covered with a simple sugar glaze.

Sfogliatelle Typical Neapolitan pastries. One version is made with layers of crunchy puff pastry. The other is made with a simple short crust. Both are filled with ricotta, semolina, candied fruits, cinnamon and vanilla.

Sproccolati Sun-dried figs filled with fennel seeds, then threaded onto wooden skewers. Sproccolati are found on the Amalfi coast.

Struffoli Like the *cicerchiata* of Marches (page 176), cone- or ring-shaped mounds of fried dough balls held together with honey and candied fruits and decorated with colored sprinkles.

Susamelli S-shaped cookies made with flour, sugar, candied citron or orange, sesame seeds and honey.

Zeppole di San Giuseppe Ring-shaped fritters traditionally made during Carnival. In Campania they're served covered with custard and sour cherry preserves.

WINES

Fiano, Greco, Falerno — the names of the wines reflect the history of the ancient Greek colonization of the region. The Greeks imported vines for cultivation up until the seventh century B.C., and the ruins of cities of Paestum and Capua contain archeological evidence of a flourishing wine industry in the area. The region is home to prestigious white wines, but also one of the best red wines in all of Italy, Taurasi. With its exceptional color, bouquet and structure it can hold its own with the best Piedmontese reds.

Capri Made with the Greco varietal, the Bianco is a fresh and highly fragrant wine that is drunk as an aperitif or goes well with first courses or simple red sauces, and the Rosso is winey and very pleasing in spite of not being highly structured. It goes well with fish stewed with tomatoes and roasted rabbit.

Falerno A dense and bitter wine that the ancient Romans drank diluted with water. Then, it was the only way. Nowadays, this not-very-well-known wine, with its intense red color, persistent bouquet and full flavor is drinkable. It's austere and slightly acidic. Even though it's a southern wine, it ages well. It goes well with roasts, especially chicken and game.

Fiano Made with eponymous grapes that are cultivated in the province of Avellino, this warm, golden full-flavored wine has a characteristic bouquet of toasted hazelnuts. It's an excellent partner to crustaceans, shellfish and white-meat fish.

Greco di tufo or **Greco del Vesuvio** Made with the Greco varietal, which is none other than a twin to the ancient Aminea varietal described in Roman history. This beautifully golden, full-flavored wine has a bouquet of mature fruits and, considering it's a white wine, is highly structured. It marries perfectly with "noble" shellfish — but should be tried with sea bass all'acqua pazza.

Ischia Wine produced on the eponymous island that has been known for its vineyards since the time of Pliny. All the local wines are grouped together into a D.O.C. The pale straw-colored Bianco is dry and lightly aromatic. It goes well with fried fish and spaghetti with rockfish. The Rosso should be drunk when it's young and still slightly tannic and winey. It goes well with white meats but also with salt cod stewed with tomatoes and olives.

Lachryma Christi del Vesuvio liquoroso A very rare, intensely sweet, amber-colored wine. Unfortunately the production, on the slopes of Mount Vesuvius, is limited. Some people think the grapes for this wine are descendents of the grapes used to make Greco del Tufo.

Solopaca Made in the province of Benevento with vines transplanted from Tuscany. The low-acid Bianco is dry with a soft bouquet and goes well with uncomplicated dishes made with eggs or vegetables. Although the Rosso, with its intense color, winey bouquet and full flavor is very good when it's young, it ages well. It's good with baked or stewed barnyard animals and small game.

Taurasi Made with the Aglianico varietal in the province of Avellino and considered one of the best red wines in Italy. Its vivacious color deepens to garnet and amber and its complex aroma of mixed berries becomes spicy as it ages. It's very tannic and slightly sour when young but becomes velvety, harmonious and full-flavored when mature. It's highly tannic quality allows for long aging. It goes very well with roasted red meats and game but is particularly admirable with aged cheese.

Pastiera

For the pastry dough:
14 ounces flour
7 ounces high quality lardo
7 ounces sugar
A pinch of salt
4 egg yolks

For the filling:
5½ ounces wet wheat berries, or 4¼ ounces
    wheat berries that have presoaked for
    15 days in cold water that's been
    changed every 2 days, or packaged
    precooked wheat berries
3¾ quarts whole milk
1 teaspoon high-quality lardo
1 teaspoon sugar
½ vanilla bean
Peel of ½ orange
7 ounces fresh and creamy ricotta
3½ ounces sugar
2 eggs, separated
¾ ounce candied citron, diced
¾ ounce candied orange peel, diced
¾ ounce candied squash (cocozzata), diced
2 teaspoons orange blossom water
A pinch of cinnamon

For the custard:
1 cup whole milk
A piece of lemon peel
2 egg yolks
1¾ ounce sugar
1 ounce flour

For garnish:
2 or 3 tablespoons powdered sugar

One day before assembling the tart, cook the wheat berries in the milk with the teaspoon of lardo, sugar, vanilla bean and orange peel, in a covered casserole, over a very low flame for about four hours or until the mixture is dense, creamy, and the wheat berries are almost falling apart. Be careful, while cooking, that the berries don't stick to the bottom of the casserole. Remove the vanilla bean and orange peel.

To make the dough, add the flour and lardo together, then add the sugar and salt. Make the mixture into a mound and make a well in the middle. Add the yolks and mix together. Cover the dough with plastic wrap and chill in the refrigerator for one half hour. Butter a 10-inch cake pan. Roll out the dough. Cut away three-quarters of it to line the cake pan. Make the custard by boiling the milk with the lemon peel. Meanwhile whip the yolks together with the sugar and flour. Slowly whisk the warm milk into the eggs. Put the mixture back on a very low flame stirring continuously until the custard coats the back of a spoon. Now, strain the ricotta and mix it with the 3½ ounces sugar. Work the mixture for about 10 minutes. Add the yolks, one at a time, then the custard, the wheat berries, orange blossom water, diced candied fruits and cinnamon. Whip the egg whites until stiff and carefully fold into the mixture.

Pour into the cake pan. Cut the remaining dough into 1-inch strips and with them make a lattice pattern over the top of the tart.

Cook in a preheated 350° F oven until the top is golden brown and an inserted tester comes clean, about an hour. Remove from oven and immediately dust with powdered sugar.

The pastiera gets better day by day. It lasts for about ten days.

Suggested wine: Lachryma Christi del Vesuvio liquoroso

PUGLIA AND BASILICATA

Puglia is a generous terrain. It's covered with a vast plain so fertile than it can easily compete with the fecund Po Valley. Grain, olives, grapes and flavorful vegetables grow in abundance in the region. The huge varieties of pasta and bread, which are so central to the region's cuisine, have an almost cult-like reputation.

Even though meat is not always the first choice when putting together a meal, there is a preference for mutton. Fowl, game, beef, horse and pork follow close behind. Even more than meat, regional seafood is a great addition to the gastronomy of the area. The Adriatic and Ionian seas provide the local tables with excellent shellfish like cannolichi, datteri, tartufi — all bivalves — and most of all i ricci (sea urchins). The shellfish are used to make fresh and fragrant pasta sauces. Oysters hold a special place in this cornucopia of shellfish. The Pugliesi say that the best ones grow in their part of the sea.

The vegetables of Puglia are of the highest quality. With their fresh and light flavors they define the Mediterranean diet. Pugliese cheese and dairy products are unforgettable, especially those consumed when very fresh: mozzarella, trecce, burrini, the unrivaled burrata di Andria and the unique manteca.

The cuisine of Basilicata is very often compared to that of Calabria, but that isn't exactly the case. The area around the province of Matera is, in fact, influenced by Puglia whereas the area towards the province of Potenza is influenced by Calabria and, a little bit, by Campania. Basilicata is a hilly and mountainous terrain. The pig is the focal point of the region's cuisine. Its meat is used for individual dishes as well as part of the dressing for others. Of note are the excellent cured meats and lardo, often preserved in olive oil with abundant hot pepper flakes.

ANTIPASTI, CURED MEATS, BREADS, FLATBREADS AND SAVORY TARTS

Abledda A barley flour roll typical of the village of Corigliano d'Otranto in the province of Lecce.

Afseplasti A flatbread made with barley flour typical of the village of Zollino in the province of Lecce. Its name comes from the Greek word *xeplatòs*, a vulgar term that means "shapeless."

Benedetto An Easter antipasto plate, a specialty of the province of Foggia, which consists of hard-cooked poached eggs, salami, oranges or fresh ricotta and wild asparagus.

Calzengiidde See *panzerotti* (page 240).

Calzone di verdura alla lucana Pizza dough folded into a half-moon shape over a filling of chard or chicory that has been sautéed with raisins or black olives and hot pepper flakes. It's baked to serve.

Calzone pugliese Pizza dough folded into a half-moon shape over a filling made with little Pugliese tomatoes and onions, salted ricotta, capers and anchovies. It's baked to serve. Another version uses a filling made with pieces of hard-cooked eggs, salami and fresh caciocavallo, provola or mozzarella.

Calzoni pugliesi See *panzerotti* (page 240).

Capocollo Cured meat prepared in the same way as the Umbrian version (page 182). The loin of pork used in Puglia gives it a slightly more delicate flavor.

Caroselle sott'aceto Fennel flowers preserved in vinegar.

Cervellata A sausage made with mixed pork and veal parts flavored with fennel seeds, a specialty of the town of Martina Franca in the province of Taranto.

Ciardedda or **cialdedda** or **cialda** or **cialledda** A very tasty, very modest dish made with stale bread that's slightly moistened with water, cherry tomatoes, arugula, freshly ground green pepper and black olives, then dressed with olive oil, vinegar and pepper. Another version is made with tomatoes, cooked onions, parsley, oregano and olive oil.

Cozze arracanate A hot antipasto made with mussels baked with olive oil, garlic, tomatoes, white wine, oregano and parsley.

Cruschill The name used in the province of Foggia for bruschetta—toasted whole-wheat bread rubbed with fresh garlic, then brushed with extra virgin olive oil.

Focaccia alla pugliese A tender flatbread made with dough of flour, yeast, butter, milk, sugar, salt and eggs. It's filled with provola or mozzarella and prosciutto.

Focaccia di patate A tender flatbread made with a dough of puréed potatoes, flour, yeast, salt and olive oil. There's also a version that's enriched with pieces of chopped prosciutto, grated cheese, eggs and white wine.

Friselle or **frisedde** or **frise** Ring-shaped biscuits made with wheat, barley or whole-wheat flour. They must be briefly softened in water before they can be eaten. They go well with fresh tomatoes, basil and extra virgin olive oil and other salads and fresh vegetables.

Pane purecasciu Very tender bread with tomatoes, onions and olive oil kneaded into its dough. It is a specialty of the province of Lecce.

Panzerotti or **panzarotti** Fried, half-moon-shaped raviolotti (large ravioli) that have a variety of fillings. They may be filled with chopped pork and herbs; eggs and provola cheese; tomatoes and anchovies; mozzarella, eggs, grated cheese and chopped parsley; fried onions, cherry tomatoes and sharp ricotta, etc.

Pettule Fritters, made with yeasted dough, that are sometimes filled with ricotta or anchovies. See *pitule salate* (below).

Pezzenta A tasty and modest sausage made with pork, veal and beef scraps, spices and hot pepper flakes.

Pittule salate A light, fluffy fritter made with flour, salt, yeast and water. The dough may be enriched with baccalà, brussels sprouts, celery or olives, capers and tomatoes.

Pizza or **pitta di patate** Two layers of a dough made with puréed potatoes, olive oil and salt filled with a mixture of tomatoes, onions, olives, anchovies and capers.

Pizza or **pitta di verdure** Two layers of pizza dough filled with radicchio sautéed with olive oil, garlic, capers and black olives.

Pizza rustica Like the *pizza rustica* of the Abruzzo and Campania regions (pages 206, 223).

Pizzo Somewhat like the *pane purecasciu* (above), with olive oil, cherry tomatoes, black olives and onions kneaded into bread dough.

Pomodori secchi sott'olio Sun-dried San Marzano or other plum tomatoes preserved in olive oil with garlic, capers and herbs.

Popizze See *pettule* (above).

Puccia Bread with black olives from the province of Lecce.

Puddica A pizza, characteristic of the Salento, an area in southeastern Puglia, made by enclosing, in dough, a filling made with cherry tomatoes, onions, black olives and anchovies. There's another version with a topping—of cherry tomatoes, garlic cloves, salt, extra virgin olive oil and oregano—that is not enclosed. The Pugliese love to eat this pizza with raw shellfish.

Ruccul An almost unknown pizza Bianca from Basilicata.

The dough is topped with olive oil, garlic, oregano and hot pepper flakes and then baked.

Rustico Little pizzas made with puff pastry filled with tomatoes, mozzarella and extra virgin olive oil or suet.

Salsiccia leccese A very fragrant and mild sausage made with a mixture of pork and veal flavored with lemon zest, cinnamon and cloves.

Scalcione A mixture of fennel, chicory and onions, boiled or sautéed with olive oil, salt, freshly ground black pepper, anchovies, olives and capers then enclosed in pizza dough. It's served on Good Friday.

Scanata The great Pugliese bread made, in the province of Foggia, with hand-ground durum flour, yeast, salt and boiled potatoes.

Scapece Tiny little fish that are floured and fried, then marinated with vinegar, saffron and large breadcrumbs.

Sfogliata Basically, a rolled-up pizza. The dough is laid out on a work surface then spread with the same type of fillings used for calzones or pizza rustica or with a simple mixture of anchovies and olives. It's rolled up into a snake-like shape, lightly flattened and baked. It may be served hot or at room temperature.

Soppressata Salami very much like the soppressata di Fabriano, Calabrese or Sienese. The Pugliese version is slightly spicier, made with Pugliese wine and hot pepper flakes. The most famous soppressata of the region is made in Martina Franca in the province of Taranto.

Taralli or **tarallucci** Various-sized ring-shaped biscuits. The secret of their success is to boil them for a few seconds before they're baked. They may be flavored with fennel seeds, cumin seeds or hot pepper flakes, etc. There are versions that are made with dough both with and without eggs, with white wine or Marsala wine or with sweet dough. They are a specialty of Puglia.

Tarantello A type of salami made with tuna belly and spices. Its name lets you know that it's a specialty of the province of Taranto, but it's found throughout southern Italy.

Torta di latticini della Basilicata A very unique torte, a specialty of Basilicata, made with a short crust filled with a mixture of ricotta, fresh cheese, chopped prosciutto, grated pecorino, sliced mozzarella, sugar and eggs.

Torta rustica Something like the *pizza rustica* (page 240). The dough for this recipe is made with flour, olive oil, white wine and salt and filled with fresh Pugliese cheese, mozzarella, ricotta, cooked ham, caciocavallo cheese and eggs. The whole thing looks like a crostata with pastry latticework on top.

PASTA, GNOCCHI, RICE, POLENTA AND GRAINS

Bavette ai funghi Long, thin dry pasta shapes typically dressed with mushrooms, tomatoes, onions, basil and parsley from the Daunia area of Puglia, the ancient Greek name for the area that's now the province of Foggia.

Capello da gendarme A timbale — cone-shaped like a sentry's hat — made by filling short crust pastry with a rich filling of maccheroni, fried eggplant and zucchini, pieces of turkey, pork meatballs, hard-cooked eggs and cheese.

Cavatelli or **cavatieddi** or **cecatelli** A shell- or dumpling-shaped maccheroni made with durum wheat and water. Although it's typically Pugliese, you'll find this shape in Abruzzo, Molise and Basilicata. It's dressed with various sauces — among the most typical is arugula, tomato sauce and olive oil. Sometime the arugula is cooked with the cavatelli, drained and then dressed with garlic and anchovies sautéed in olive oil. Other vegetables such as turnip greens may be used as well.

Cazini or **calzoncini lucani** Small half-moon-shaped ravioli with a slightly sweet filling made with ricotta, sugar, cinnamon and nutmeg. They are served dressed with lamb or beef ragù and are typical of the province of Matera.

Chiancarelle Small orecchiette usually dressed with turnip greens.

Ciceri e tria Chickpeas boiled together with durum wheat tagliatelle then dressed with onions sautéed in olive oil.

Coculedde di patate Orb-shaped dumplings made with puréed potatoes, pecorino cheese, flour, parsley, salt and pepper. They're dressed with fresh tomato sauce and cheese.

Grano al ragù Wheat berries that have been soaked overnight, boiled and then dressed with meat ragù and pecorino cheese. In this area, Basilicata, the meat is typically ground *after* it's cooked.

Lagane al sugo di anguilla Homemade ribbon-shaped flour-and-water pasta dressed with eel that has been fried, then stewed with tomatoes, olive oil, garlic, parsley and basil.

Lagane e fagioli Typical tagliatelle from Basilicata made with durum wheat and water and dressed with beans sautéed in lardo or olive oil, garlic and hot pepper flakes. Sometimes chickpeas or lentils are used in place of the beans.

Lanache di casa Homemade tagliatelle made with durum wheat and dressed with mussels that have been filled with a mixture of breadcrumbs, eggs and pecorino cheese then stewed in tomato sauce. After the pasta is dressed, it's covered with grated pecorino cheese to serve.

Lasagne di San Giuseppe Typical of Mola in Basilicata province, homemade fettuccine dressed with tomatoes cooked with olive oil, garlic and basil. The dressed pasta is garnished with toasted chopped almonds, anchovies and breadcrumbs.

Maccheroni con pomodori al forno Boiled maccheroni dressed with tomatoes that have been baked with olive oil, garlic and parsley. It's garnished with grated pecorino to serve.

Maccheroni di fuoco A fat pasta shape such as bucatini dressed with pesto made with hot red peppers and garlic sautéed in olive oil. It's a very, very spicy dish.

Minestra strascinata Pasta made with a dough of flour, lardo and water and cut into squares, with a tool very much like the chitarra of Abruzzo, then cooked and dressed with tomato sauce and grated pecorino cheese. The dish is a specialty of the province of Potenza.

Minuich or **minnicchi** or **mascined** or **macarun chi fir** Tube-shaped maccheroni, typical of Basilicata, made with a durum-wheat-and-water dough. The pasta is rolled around a knitting needle or chopstick to make the shape. It's usually dressed with cauliflower and tomato sauce, or simply with garlic and hot peppers sautéed in olive oil. They're great as a side dish with hare stew.

Muerzi fritti A pasta-less first course made with turnip greens, chunks of bread and beans sautéed in olive oil.

Orecchiette The emblematic Pugliese pasta shape. The dough is made with durum wheat, sometimes mixed with plain flour, and water. The dough is rolled into ropes then cut into small pieces that are formed into shell or ear shapes by pressing the round end of a dinner knife or a thumb into each piece. The shape makes it all the easier to contain various sauces. The orecchiette are known by many other names: stacchiotte in the province of Brindisi; chiancanelle or cicatelli in the province of Foggia; ricchielle, recchiatelle, coppetielle, strascinati, recchitelle, recchie, stacchiodde, or pestazzuole in other Pugliese towns; ricchie e' prievidi in

Calabria and Basilicata and so on. When they're served with turnip greens, the pasta and the greens are cooked together, then dressed with garlic, hot pepper flakes and anchovies sautéed in olive oil. Other typical dressings are tomato sauce with grated hard ricotta; a sauce made with beef roll-ups; cauliflower and lardo; sausage sauce; and one made with potatoes, arugula and fresh tomatoes.

Pasta al forno alla pugliese A baked pasta dish made with penne or ziti pasta shapes. The pasta is cooked *al dente*, then layered with a sauce made with sausage, little meatballs, sliced mozzarella and grated pecorino cheese and then gratinéed.

Pasta alla catalogna A dish in which the pasta — half or broken ziti — is cooked with catalogna (a variety of chicory), drained and then dressed with fresh tomato and garlic sauce. It's garnished with grated pecorino cheese.

Penne con gli asparagi A dish in which cooked penne are dressed, as soon as they're drained, with beaten eggs, cooked asparagus points, tomato sauce, freshly ground black pepper and grated pecorino cheese.

Pestazzule Pasta disks like *pociacche* (below) but without the indentation.

Pociacche Large orecchiette.

Ravioli di Potenza Square ravioli filled with a mixture of ricotta, chopped prosciutto, eggs, parsley and freshly ground black pepper. They're usually served with meat ragù and grated ricotta salata or sharp pecorino cheese.

Regine alle arche di Noè Pasta dressed with *arche di Noè* (page 247) sauce prepared with olive oil, garlic, parsley and fresh tomatoes.

Rigatoni imbottiti A dish made with half-cooked rigatoni that are filled with a mixture of chopped meat sautéed in olive oil with onions, mozzarella, provolone cheese and mortadella. The stuffed rigatoni are placed in a baking dish with a sauce made with tomatoes, onions, garlic, arugula and thyme, then covered with grated pecorino cheese and baked.

Risotto mar Piccolo Risotto with mussels.

Sagne 'ncannulate A ribbon-shaped pasta, such as fettuccine or tagliatelle, that's rolled on a knitting needle or chopstick to form a spiral. They may be dressed with a meat or chickpea sauce.

Simmuledda alla foggiana Cornmeal polenta cooked with wild fennel and sliced potatoes. To serve, it's covered with grated cheese.

Spaghetti alla zappatora A modest dish typical of the

countryside around the province of Foggia. The spaghetti is dressed with garlic and abundant hot pepper flakes sautéed in olive oil.

Spaghetti con le seppie ripiene Spaghetti dressed with cuttlefish filled with a mixture of the white part of bread, parsley, garlic and chopped tentacles stewed in tomatoes and onions.

Spaghetti con sugo della pizzaiola Spaghetti dressed with a sauce made with sliced beef, olive oil, tomatoes, parsley, garlic and capers. The beef is removed from the sauce and served separately with seasonal vegetables.

Spaghetti di Maratea Spaghetti dressed with raw plum tomatoes, garlic and extra virgin olive oil.

Strascinati or **strascenate** Another name for *orecchiette* (page 243). It's also the name of another pasta shape that's made with flour, lardo and water. The shapes are made by rolling rectangular pieces of dough using a ridged rectangular wooden utensil that leaves a pattern on the pasta.

Tiella di riso e cozze Rice baked with potatoes and mussels.

Timballo di riso di magro all'antica A dish in which a mixture of boiled *al dente* rice, eggs and butter is used to line a baking dish and its sides. The dish is then filled with a mixture of floured fried fish, shellfish, shrimp and a sauce made with tomatoes, onions, anchovy pesto and nutmeg. The whole thing is covered with another layer of the rice mixture and baked to serve.

Tria or **ytria** or **ytrya** Derived from the Arabic meaning "little worms," a long, flat vermicelli made with durum wheat and bran flours found not only in Puglia but in Sicily usually served dressed with lentils or chickpeas.

Troccoli Very similar to the Pugliese *maccheroni alla chitarra* (page 208). The name of the pasta comes from the instrument—a grooved wood or brass rolling pin—used to make the shape.

Vermicelli alla sangiovannello Spaghetti or vermicelli dressed with olive oil, garlic, anchovies, capers, parsley, hot pepper flakes and fresh tomatoes. It's a specialty of the province of Bari.

SOUP

Bombolini in brodo Semolina polenta prepared with milk and butter then mixed with eggs, grated cheese and nutmeg.

The mixture is baked in a water bath then cut into cubes that are added, along with tiny little meatballs, to a broth. At one time this soup was called cunsulu because it was served the night following a funeral to console families in mourning.

Cialdedda or **cialda** or **cialledda** A very modest but tasty soup made with bread, tomatoes, boiled onions, parsley, oregano and good olive oil.

Incapriata See *minestrone 'ncapriata* (below).

Minestra in brodo di pesce A dish made with tomatoes, a bit of olive oil, garlic, parsley and hake. The hake is then served as the main course and pasta is added to the broth to serve.

Minestra maritata One of many soups in southern Italy with this name. The Pugliese version, which has Greek origins, from the Daunia (the Greek name for what is now the province of Foggia) area, is made with escarole, mild and bitter chicory, celery and fennel layered with lardo or pancetta and pecorino cheese. It's covered with broth then baked for a few minutes to serve.

Minestrone di castrato Made with steer (*castrato*) cooked in water with zucchini, potatoes, tomatoes, celery, onions and other seasonal vegetables. This recipe comes from the area around Santa Maria di Leuca, in particular, the village of Alessano in the province of Lecce.

Minestrone 'ncapriata The pride of central Puglia and the Basilicata region, a purée of dried fava beans served on the same plate as boiled wild chicory or turnip greens dressed with olive oil. It's not a real soup but is served in place of one. In the town of Martina Franca, in the province of Taranto, this dish is made with boiled *lampascioni* (page 251). This is one of the oldest dishes in the Mediterranean area, dating back to pre-dynastic Egypt where a similar dish was made.

Pancotto con rucola e patate A soup made with stale bread soaked in the cooking liquid from the arugula and potatoes that go into it as well. It's finished with garlic and hot peppers sautéed in olive oil and is a specialty of the province of Foggia.

Pasta e lenticchie A delicious soup made with lentils and broken spaghetti.

Zuppa di Maratea A tasty soup made with beans, potatoes, onions and other vegetables.

CONDIMENTS, SAUCES AND EGGS

Salsa alla sangiovannello A pasta sauce made with olive oil, garlic, anchovies, capers, parsley, hot peppers and tomatoes.

Marmellata di lampascioni Jam made with *lampascioni* (page 251), vinegar, black pepper and cinnamon. It's eaten as an accompaniment to meat and bread and as a filling for certain kinds of pizza.

FISH, CRUSTACEANS AND SHELLFISH

Agostinelle Tiny mullets, floured, fried and served with a few drops of lemon juice. They're not easy to find.

Alici Anchovies.

Alici arracanate Boned, fresh anchovies that are layered in a baking dish, covered with a mixture of breadcrumbs, garlic, mint, capers, oregano and olive oil, then baked to serve. This is a dish found throughout the province of Bari.

Alici in tortiera Boned, fresh anchovies layered in a baking dish, covered with a mixture of breadcrumbs, parsley, garlic and olive oil, then baked to serve.

Anguille all'acqua di mare A very rare preparation from the province of Foggia made with newly born eels that are immersed in seawater then left to dry in the sun. They are dressed with olive oil and vinegar to serve. They're naturally salted with the sea salt that remains after they've dried.

Arche di Noè Cone-shaped mollusks with undulating and furrowed shells. The name means Noah's Ark. They're also called javetune.

Cotolette di sarde Cleaned fresh sardines that are butterflied, pairs placed together skin sides out, breaded and fried.

Cozze alla leccese or **cozze a 'lampa** Mussels that are dressed, when just opened and still hot, with extra virgin olive oil, lemon juice, chopped parsley and freshly ground black pepper.

Cozze ripiene al sugo Mussels that are opened uncooked, carefully washed, then filled with a mixture of breadcrumbs, garlic, parsley and eggs. They're then closed with a piece of thin string and stewed in tomato sauce. They're served with boiled rice.

Fracaja A mixture of tiny little fish that are floured and fried.

Frittura di cozze Mussels that are opened uncooked, taken out of their shells, breaded and fried.

Javetune See *arche di Noè* (page 247).

Orata alla pugliese Sea bass baked with sliced potatoes, garlic, chopped parsley, olive oil and grated pecorino cheese.

Ostriche alla tarantina Oysters that are opened, covered with a mixture of breadcrumbs, chopped parsley and olive oil, then gratinéed.

Pinne Large mollusks also called astare or pinne nobili, recognized by their triangular shape. They're very popular on the Ionian Sea coast where they're eaten raw with a drizzle of olive oil, lemon juice, parsley and freshly ground pepper.

Polpi sott'aceto Cooked octopus preserved in glass jars with garlic, mint leaves and vinegar.

Pupiddi Assorted tiny fish. They're often fried then preserved in a saffron marinade.

Schiuma di mare Very small anchovies, washed with seawater then covered with fresh lemon juice, olive oil and freshly ground black pepper. After marinating for ten minutes, they're ready to eat.

Sgombri all'aceto Filleted mackerel, wrapped together in cheesecloth, poached then marinated for a few hours in vinegar. After they're unwrapped, they're dressed with olive oil, salt, chopped garlic and mint.

Tortiera di cozze A dish made by layering sliced potatoes, sliced onions, mussels (taken out of their shells), zucchini, tomatoes and grated pecorino cheese. It's baked to serve.

Triglie alla pugliese A dish made with a layer of mullet fillets and pesto made with parsley, basil, garlic, olive oil and breadcrumbs. Just before it's baked, it's sprinkled with a mixture of chopped rosemary, sage, marjoram, breadcrumbs and olive oil.

Zuppa alla greca A delicious soup from the province of Brindisi made with scorpion fish, potatoes, onions and celery.

MEAT

Agnello ai funghi cardoncelli A baked lamb stew made with *cardoncelli* mushrooms (page 250), which are typical of the region, olive oil, garlic and hot pepper flakes.

Agnello al calderotto A specialty of the province of Taranto, a stew made by browning pieces of lamb with onions, parsley, tomatoes and olive oil. The dish gets its unique flavor from the addition of wild chicory. It's garnished with grated pecorino cheese to serve.

Agnello alla carbonara Pieces of lamb that are wrapped in butcher's paper then covered with salt and baked. The fat is absorbed by the paper, leaving the lamb lean and crisp. This recipe is named for the village of Carbonara, a suburb of Bari.

Agnello allo squero Lamb spit-roasted over brushwood with sprigs of thyme and other fragrant herbs.

Agnello con spaghetti al cuturiello alla foggiana Lamb cooked in a casserole with olive oil, garlic, parsley and water, then served with spaghetti dressed with a sauce made with the reduced cooking liquid.

Braciole di melanzane Sliced, fried eggplant roll-ups filled with a mixture of chopped salami, diced mozzarella, garlic, hard-boiled eggs, salt, pepper, mint and parsley. They're covered with tomato and oregano sauce and baked.

Braciolette di peperoni Sections of roasted peppers filled with a mixture of breadcrumbs, parsley, capers, anchovies, pine nuts and raisins, rolled up and baked with tomato sauce and grated cheese.

Brasciole alla barese In Puglia, brasciole or braciole are usually veal roll-ups filled with a mixture of prosciutto, parsley and pecorino cheese, then slowly cooked in tomatoes, olive oil, garlic and other herbs.

Caldariello A mixture of pieces of lamb or mutton, olive oil, garlic, onions, sheep's milk and wild fennel cooked in a copper pot. This somewhat rare preparation is a typical shepherd's dish served with pieces of stale bread for dipping in the sauce.

Capuzzelle Lamb or kid's head, split in two then baked in a casserole with olive oil, garlic, oregano and potatoes.

Cazzmar A mixture of lamb's guts, liver, sweetbreads and giblets enclosed in pork caul and then baked. It's sliced to serve. Sometimes it is simply roll-ups made with liver-stuffed sweetbreads enclosed in pork caul.

Cotechinata Pork rind roll-ups filled with a mixture of lardo, garlic and parsley cooked in tomato sauce that can be used to dress pasta. Cotechinata is a specialty of Basilicata.

Cutturidde Lamb stew made with olive oil, water, small onions, parsley, tomatoes and cubes of pecorino cheese.

Gnummerieddi or **gnomirelli** or **gnemmarieddi** Lamb's innards and giblets wound together, then enclosed in pork caul. They are baked, grilled or cooked with potatoes to serve.

Marro Larger version of *gnummerieddi* (above).

Migliulatiello See *cazzmar* (above).

Monachelle alla pugliese or **moniceddi** Small snails found in vineyards. After they're cleaned, they are cooked with olive oil, rosemary, hot pepper flakes and wild fennel.

P' deja Either mutton or beef belly filled with a mixture of pecorino cheese, salami, hard-cooked eggs and parsley. They're rolled up then stewed with fresh tomatoes, olive oil and garlic. The dish is a specialty of the province of Foggia.

Quagghiariedde A mixture of mutton innards, scamorza cheese, salami, eggs, arugula and other ingredients, enclosed in pork caul or in a boned mutton breast and then baked. This is a rare dish typical of the village of Andria in the province of Bari.

Rot Lamb's head and innards baked in a copper pan with potatoes and *lampascioni* (page 251).

Spiedo martinese A skewer loaded with pieces of lamb, kid, veal rump and sausage. It's baked in a wood-burning oven or spit-roasted over oak or live oak and is a specialty of the town of Martina Franca in the province of Taranto.

Tiella di San Nicandro A *tiella* is a type of low, wide baking dish. In this recipe a lamb's head, split open, is baked in a *tiella* with little balls of lamb innards, potatoes and *lampascioni* (page 251).

Torcinelli or **turcineddi** See *cazzmar* (page 249).

Turde 'n zulze or **tordi in solso** Thrushes boiled with fennel seeds and bay leaves after marinating in a terra cotta pot with robust white wine and bay leaves. They're ready to cook and eat in about a week.

Zampitti Finger-sized sausages made with leftover pieces of veal, lamb and pork flavored with hot pepper flakes. They're sold already grilled.

VEGETABLES

Burracci Borage leaves (*borragine*, page 328). They're usually blanched then sautéed with olive oil, garlic, anchovy fillets and a bit of wild fennel.

Cardi alla pugliese A recipe based on cardoons, which are very popular in Puglia. They're found everywhere, prepared in various ways, but always must be parboiled before further preparation. For this dish the cardoons are cooked with black olives, fillets of anchovies and olive oil, then made into a "fake" fricassee with the addition of eggs and cheese.

Cardoncelli Mushrooms that grow on the barren—almost uncultivable—plateau in southern Puglia.

Carnucieddi A baked dish, typical of Basilicata, made with cardoons, black olives, anchovies, pecorino cheese, capers and breadcrumbs.

Ciambotta or **ciammotta** A dish made with assorted vegetables (eggplant, sweet peppers, potatoes, onions, celery and tomatoes) that are sautéed separately, then tossed together with black olives to serve. Sometimes, just before serving, scrambled eggs are added to the dish. It's a specialty of Basilicata.

Ciaudedda Typical of Basilicata, a vegetable stew made with fava beans, artichokes, potatoes and onions cooked with lardo and good-quality olive oil.

Cicoria in brodo Chicory that is parboiled, sautéed with cubes of prosciutto, then stewed in broth and finished with grated pecorino cheese.

Lampascioni Actually, wild hyacinth bulbs. They have a pleasing but slightly bitter flavor. They're also called lampagioni, lampasciuoli, pampasciuni, cipollacci or muscari. They're used when fresh, or preserved in vinegar or in olive oil. They may be grilled, boiled, stewed or cooked with other vegetables. Because of their slightly bitter flavor, it's wise to leave them in running water for a day or to parboil them before proceeding with other preparations.

Lampascioni alla vetrettese Lampascioni that have been reduced to a jam-like texture to which some vino cotto is added.

Mandorlata di peperoni A stew made with sweet peppers, tomatoes and chopped almonds flavored with vinegar, sugar and raisins. It's a specialty of Basilicata.

Melanzanata (di Sant'Oronzo) Sliced eggplant that is floured, dipped in eggs, fried and then baked in layers with tomatoes, onions, basil and pecorino cheese. It's a specialty of the province of Lecce.

Melanzane ripiene Stuffed eggplant. After scooping the pulp out of the small, oblong eggplants, the shell is filled with a mixture of the chopped pulp, olives, anchovies, capers, tomatoes and other ingredients. They're gratinéed to serve.

Muscari, lampasciuni See *lampascioni* (above).

Paparine Wild, almost sweet greens that look something like poppy plants. They're cooked in very little water with black olives and hot pepper flakes.

Paparuli Mushrooms found in the forests of the Gargano area of Puglia.

Peperoni alla pizzaiola Sweet peppers sautéed with tomatoes, hot peppers, capers, parsley, oregano and garlic. They're a specialty of the Salentina peninsula.

Pomodori arracanati Halved, seeded tomatoes filled with a mixture of parsley, mint, breadcrumbs, pecorino cheese, olive oil, salt and pepper. They're gratinéed to serve.

Scattiata A version of the stew, made with sweet peppers, called peperonata. This one is made with green peppers, onions, tomatoes, parsley, olive oil and garlic. It's often used as a pasta sauce.

Sinepi Mustard greens. In Puglia, the spicy greens are boiled and served with olive oil or with fried anchovies.

Sprusciani Wild winter greens. They are often cooked with leeks and served with freshly pressed olive oil.

Spunzali Leeks.

Tiella di verdure A layered mixture of mushrooms (especially *cardoncelli*, page 250), onions, potatoes, olive oil and garlic. The dish is named for the *tiella*, the low, wide dish in which it's baked.

Verrùch A type of turnip similar to a radish. It's covered with salt in order to drain away some liquid then dressed just like any other salad.

Zanguni A bitter field green.

CHEESE AND DAIRY PRODUCTS

Burrata A cow's milk cheese, stretched, like mozzarella, to make its body. It then is filled with other pieces of the stretched paste and fresh cream. The whole thing is covered with the leaves of the asphodel plant or soaked in salty brine. It's consumed while very fresh. This cheese originated in the town of Andria in the province of Bari at the beginning of the eighteenth century.

Cacioricotta Salted ricotta used for grating.

Manteca Another cow's milk cheese stretched to the same pear shape as caciocavallo. Its core is filled with butter. In fact, its name is of Spanish origin and means butter.

Mercia A rare mozzarella made with sheep's milk.

Palloni di Gravina A stretched cow's milk cheese formed by hand into *palloni* or balloon shapes made in the eponymous town, Gravina, in the province of Bari.

Ricotta schianta or **'scante** A cheese, made weekly from February to July, also called cacioricotta or formaggio di Lecce. After the mass has fermented, it's placed in terra cotta containers covered with grape or fig leaves, then turned upside-down on a layer of lime to allow the excess liquid to filter through. The anti-bacterial lime also maintains the ricotta in pristine conditions. This robustly flavored, unique ricotta is perfect for spreading on toasted bread.

SWEETS AND LIQUEURS

Amarella Basically a Rosolio (a liqueur made with rose petals that's often used as the base for other liqueurs) made with white wine and the leaves of the sour cherry (amarena) tree. It's a specialty of the village of Torremaggiore in the province of Foggia.

Amaro San Marzano A liqueur and a digestif flavored with bitter almonds, chocolate and vanilla. It's a specialty of the province of Taranto.

Anseri Chestnuts that have been left to soak, or are boiled, then smoked.

Bocche di dama Little glazed pastries filled with pastry cream and garnished with candied cherries.

Carteddate or **cartellate** Long, thin ribbons of dough twisted into a spiral, then pinched to make little basins. They're fried and then covered in honey or vino cotto and powdered sugar and cinnamon. These pastries started out as a Christmastime treat but are now made throughout the year in Puglia. There are numerous variations.

Castagnedde Little ball-shaped pastries made with chopped, toasted almonds, sugar, flour, baking soda and lemon zest. To serve, they're covered with cocoa, which gives them the appearance of chestnuts (castagne).

Cauciuni Very unique Pugliese pastries made by filling dough with a mixture of chocolate, cooked chickpeas, vino cotto, cinnamon and sugar. They're fried and then served hot or at room temperature.

Cicirata The same as the Umbrian *cicerchiata* (page 188) and Marches (page 176) — fried balls of dough covered with honey.

Corrucolo A sweet, braided, ring-shaped Easter cake garnished with raw eggs that cook as the cake bakes.

Cotto di fichi Figs, harvested during the last two weeks of August when they're very ripe, that are put into a large vat over a wood-burning fire and cooked for hours. The fig concentrate is then put into cloth sacks and hung to allow liquid to filter out. The obtained liquid is then slowly cooked for four hours and preserved in sterile glass bottles.

Cupeta A brittle made with chopped almonds and lightly caramelized sugar. It's often decorated with colored sprinkles.

Dita di apostoli Little egg-white omelets rolled around in a mixture of ricotta, sugar, cocoa and liqueur. They are traditional Pugliese pastries.

Fruttone A short crust pastry filled with jam and almond paste. The top is covered with chocolate.

Giulebbe Sugar syrup clarified with egg whites.

Palomba In the province of Bari, *corrucolo* (page 253).

Panvinesco A pastry made with semolina flour and vino cotto garnished with colored sprinkles.

Panzerotti dolci alla lucana Half-moon-shaped pastries filled with puréed chickpeas, chocolate, sugar and cinnamon. They may be fried or baked and are covered with sugar or honey to serve.

Pasta di mandorle An almond paste very similar to the Sicilian version made into fish shapes for Christmas and lambs for Easter. Roasted coffee beans are used for the eyes.

Pasticciotto A baked oval pastry made with short crust filled with pastry cream.

Peperato A ring-shaped pastry served during Carnival. The dough is made with durum wheat, eggs, cotto di fichi (also called miele di fichi or fig honey), sugar, olive oil, orange peel, cinnamon, cloves and black pepper. They're not always easy to find, but several little villages (Sannicandro Garganico and Monte Sant'Angelo) in the province of Foggia still make them.

Pittedre Little jam-filled half-moon-shaped pastries typical of the province of Lecce.

Pittule or **pettole dolci** Soft, puffy fritters made with flour, yeast and puréed potatoes. Some cooks add pine nuts and raisins to the dough. They're served with honey or vino cotto; a specialty of the Salento area of Puglia at the heel of Italy.

Pupurat See *peperato* (above).

Purcedduzzi Similar to cicirata or cicerchiata, a pile of little balls of fried dough covered with honey, then garnished with pine nuts, colored sprinkles and cinnamon.

Scarcedda A typical Easter sweet bread decorated with eggs in their shells.

Scarciofa The word used for *corrucolo* (page 253) in the village of Bitonto in the province of Bari.

Strangolapreti lucani Little shell-shaped pastries made with flour, eggs and lemon zest. They're fried, then served with sweet wine.

Susamelli S-shaped cookies made with flour, sugar, candied citron and orange, sesame seeds and honey. The name comes from the fusion of the words for two of the main ingredients, sesame seeds and honey.

Vino cotto The result of a long, slow cooking of grape must. This preparation may be made with fresh grapes or figs. The finished product is used as an ingredient for many sweets.

WINES

Nowadays, Puglia is called "Italy's wine cellar" because of the large quantity of wine produced in the region. Unfortunately, the quality of the wine doesn't always correspond to the quantity for a variety of reasons — not the least of which is the arid climate. The majority of the region's wines are coarse, low in acid with a short shelf life. Even so, they're exported all over the world, and even to northern Italy where they're added to other wines to give them more body and elevate their alcohol content. The predominant varietal of the area, Aglianico, flourishes in a terrain that is mostly volcanic. However, the presence of massive hills provides the kind of continental climate that allows the Aglianico grape to thrive, producing wines that stand on their own beside those of northern Italy. The classic southern Italian wines, Moscato, Aleatico and Malvasia, are becoming rarer in this region, have limited production and need to be searched out in small villages where they're often made by individual families. The hunt for these wines can become a full-time occupation but for those with a good nose — and patience — it's a worthwhile venture.

Aglianico del Vulture Vulture, a dead volcano that faces east towards the Appenines, at an elevation of 1,300 meters, is the perfect host to Aglianico vines. This ruby red wine tends toward garnet as it ages. When it's young, it has an intense winey nose that develops into a more complex bouquet as it ages. Its full, round flavor holds up to more than five years of aging when it becomes *riserva*. The young wine is a good accompaniment for grilled meats. Aged, it's a splendid drink with hearty roasts and aged cheese.

Aleatico A wine made in two versions: Dolce naturale and Liquoroso naturale (for this version the alcohol content is adjusted to bring it up to eighteen and a half percent). Both have a deep, rich garnet color, with a refined bouquet and a full, velvety flavor. They go well with the local pastries, fruit salad, semifreddi and dried fruits. The Dolce naturale goes well with aged and sharp cheese.

Cacce e mitte A ruby red, full-flavored wine with a penetrating aroma produced in the towns of Lucera, Troia and Biccari in the province of Foggia. It goes well with fish soups, white meats and local cured meats. It should be served slightly chilled at about 55° F.

Castel del Monte This wine, produced in the province of Bari, is found in various types. The Bianco is fresh and pleasing with a winey nose that goes well with antipasti, seafood first courses and fried fish. The Rosato has a fruity bouquet and is so pleasingly tannic when it's young, it goes well with both octopus salad and with mixed grilled meats. The Rosso is winey with just enough tannin to allow it to age for a few years, making it the perfect accompaniment to roast meats. When it's young, it goes well with soups with tomatoes.

Copertino A typical wine of the province of Lecce. The Rosato is a deep pink color with a persistent bouquet and a palate of bitter herbs. It goes well with mussel soup and vegetable first courses (try it with *orecchiette con cime di rapa*—see recipe page 258). The Rosso, after it's aged for at least two years, takes on hints of orange and a full, velvety flavor. It goes well with roast white meat and is perfect with lamb.

Five Roses There's a charming story attached to this wine that, for Italy, is curiously named. It seems that during the Second World War, it was so loved by the American soldiers who drank it that they named it after their favorite whiskey, Four Roses. True or invented, the name honors this very good, antique rose-colored wine with a pleasing bouquet and dry, full-bodied flavor. Its alcoholic content, fourteen percent, makes it a fine wine to accompany roast meats and aged cheese.

Locorotondo A deep straw-colored wine with hints of green. It should be drunk when young—aged for about a year in order to preserve its pleasing, winey nose and its fresh, delicate palate. It's the perfect partner for seafood first courses and fresh cheese.

Martina Franca Named for the historic hill town of Martina Franca, it's made from the same grapes as the Locorotondo and is very similar to it. A bit more structured than Locorotondo, this one can age for up to two years. It goes with the same kinds of food as the Locorotondo.

Martino After a year the Martino Rosato turns from a pale pink wine to one with hints of gold without ever losing its winey nose and dry palate. It's a good table wine. The Rosso ages well too. When it's young, it's ruby red with a winey nose and dry palate. It goes well with just about everything but is particularly good with grilled meats.

Moscato di Trani Produced in Dolce Naturale and Liquoroso versions, both of which are golden with a richly aromatic bouquet and a full and velvety palate. They go well with all the traditional Pugliese cakes and pastries.

Ostuni A summertime wine *per eccellenza* that wants to be drunk chilled, with simple fish dishes. Named for an historic town in the province of Brindisi, this wine is deep yellow with a fruity aroma and a dry palate. It may be used as a table wine, because it works so well with first courses, vegetables and rustic tortes made with cheese and prosciutto.

Ottavianello Produced in the town of Ostuni, a cherry-colored wine with a delicate aroma and dry palate. It goes well with grilled meats, especially veal, and lamb roll-ups.

Primitivo di Manduria A red wine with an outstanding and fiery personality. It's deep violet with an aggressive palate. It goes well with cured meats and bread. As it ages, it softens and becomes more persuasive, making it the perfect wine for roasted red meats. There are sparkling and semi-sweet versions also.

Rosato del Salento An intensely red wine that, as it ages, develops hints of brick red. It emits a rather weak, fruity aroma and may have a dry or slightly sweet palate. It's an excellent table wine but is particularly good with roasted white meats.

Rosso pugliese Made throughout the provinces of Foggia and Bari mostly from the Troia varietal. There are actually three different red wines with this name that have similar characteristics — ruby red color with hints of garnet, a winey aroma and a dry, lightly tannic flavor. Rosso Canosa and Rosso Cerignola include not only the Troia varietal but also Sangiovese and Montepulciano. The Rosso Barletta is made exclusively with Troia. All three are good table wines but, after they've aged for a few years, they can accompany roasts and small game.

Salice Salentino Of all those produced on the Salento peninsula, the wine with the most personality. Its two versions, Rosso and Rosato, are made with the Negroamaro varietal. Both have a pleasing, winey aroma and a full, velvety and harmonious palate. Their colors go from cherry red for the Rosato to ruby red for the Rosso. They're typically served with regional lamb dishes. Thanks to their elevated alcohol content and light tannic quality, they are structured well enough to accompany fatty meats.

San Severo A wine produced in the province of Foggia. The Bianco is fresh and winey, making it an ideal accompaniment for local flatbread filled with vegetables and cheese. The Rosato has a refined, fruity aroma and a dry, tasty palate that goes well with all sauced pasta dishes and cured meats. The Rosso has the same characteristics as the Rosato, although with a more pronounced color and flavor. It goes well with roast meats.

Squinzano A Rosato, made with the Negroamaro varietal, with notable alcoholic content and characteristics similar to the Salice Salentino. It may be cherry- or ruby red in color, with a winey aroma and a full and velvety palate. It goes well with white meats and pasta dishes with "important" sauces. There's also a Squinzano Rosso that takes on hints of orange as it ages. It goes well with substantial roasts.

Orecchiette con cime di rapa'

Oricchiettte with turnip greens
Serves 6

1¼ pounds orecchiette
2 pounds turnip greens or broccoli rabe
Extra virgin olive oil
3 cloves garlic, smashed
5 anchovy fillets
A pinch of ground hot pepper
A few grindings of black pepper
Salt

Clean the greens and peel the tough stems. Boil them in abundant salted water until tender. Remove with a wire mesh strainer and reserve. Save the water for cooking the pasta. Add the olive oil to a large skillet over a low flame and brown the garlic. Add the anchovies. When they've melted, add the hot pepper and black pepper. Bring the greens' water back to a boil and cook the orecchiette according to the package directions. Add the cooked greens to the skillet. Add the cooked pasta and ¼ cup of the pasta water directly into the skillet and cook for another minute or two until all the ingredients soften. Remove the garlic and serve with grated pecorino or aged ricotta cheese.

Suggested wine: Copertino Rosato

CALABRIA

Calabria's terrain is full of sharp contrasts—it's mountainous, yet almost completely surrounded by the sea. Its almost-secretive cuisine is inspired by the customs of the people who passed through the region or landed on its shores: the Greeks, Albanians, Latini, Arabs, Normans, Spanish and French.

Antipasti aren't really served in the southern provinces, but in Calabria, a *piattino* of food is served before the main meal. This "little plate" may be filled with salami and cured meats, smashed spicy olives, eggplant and tomatoes covered with olive oil, and fried or pickled sweet peppers. The well-aged, always-spicy salami goes well with the original *pitte* (flatbreads) fresh out of the oven. The basic, always-homemade pastas have odd names. Soups are made with legumes, grains, eggs and onions.

Pork is the first meat choice. Very often it's preserved in one way or another. Pork's popularity is followed by mutton and every kind of offal. Meats may be spit-roasted, grilled or baked. Game contributes to the daily menu as well: wild boar, quail, partridge, woodcock, hare and duck. Interestingly, the Calabrese don't hang game to age or tenderize it before cooking. The Ionian and Mediterranean seas, which give the region their splendid coastlines, provide bluefish, tuna and swordfish. Cooking methods for these fish are strongly influenced by those of western Sicily. Cheese is top quality and flavorful.

Calabria is full of citrus fruit orchards. Citron and bergamots are grown not only for their fragrant essences but also to make exquisite jams. The hot pepper is omnipresent, yet sweet peppers also have a place of honor on the regional table, as do the famous Tropea red onions. The Calabresi are great eaters of eggplant, especially the extremely tasty and prestigious violette lunghe. A wide variety of mushrooms are found in the wooded mountains in the area around Saracena and Santo Stefano in Aspromonte. In this area is found the fabulous *pietra da fungo*, or mushroom rock, porous stone capable of capturing spores from up to eight inches below the earth's surface, and then producing every kind of edible—and precious—mushroom.

Capocollo Cured meat found throughout central and southern Italy similar to coppa piacentina. In Calabria, it's made with the upper part of the neck and shoulder of a pig. It's covered with salt, then left to rest for two days, during which it is occasionally turned. It is then washed with hearty red wine and covered with freshly ground black pepper and hot pepper flakes, enclosed in a natural casing, tied and hung to age for three months to a year. Often, capocollo is slightly smoked.

Cervellata A type of sausage made with mixed pork parts that are finely ground, then flavored with hot pepper flakes and white wine.

Cucùli Small yeasted flatbreads stuffed with hard-cooked eggs in their shells.

Cullurielli Large, ring-shaped pastries made with potato dough, that are fried to serve.

Frisuli Pieces of pancetta, pork rind, tough pork parts and "hints" of fat that are slowly stewed in a large copper pot with salt and hot peppers. Frisuli is eaten at room temperature with pitta or cornmeal rolls, or added to a springtime vegetable soup.

Frisulimiti See *frisuli*, above.

Granzaredda or **fresa cunzata** Toasted, ring-shaped flatbread made with whole-wheat flour. It's topped with olive oil, vinegar and oregano, and sometimes rubbed with fresh tomatoes as well.

Morzeddu A Calabrese sandwich filled with meat ragù.

Mustica Newborn anchovies or sardines (bianchetti or gianchetti) covered with hot pepper flakes, then sun dried and preserved in olive oil.

'ndugghia or **'nnuglia** or **'nduglia** A sausage made with pork meat, lardo, liver and lungs and flavored with freshly ground black pepper, ground hot pepper and fennel seeds. Sometimes the tongue and tripe are added to the mixture. It's dried, but not aged or smoked. It's scalded in hot water, then stewed in tomato sauce — which makes a good pasta sauce — or cooked with chicory and wild fennel. It's also one of the ingredients that goes into *minestra maritata* (page 226). The name of this sausage is derived from the French andouille.

Ovotarica Salted, sun-dried tuna bottarga (roe) served in thin slices dressed with olive oil and fresh tomatoes.

Panzarotti alla calabrese Dough wrapped around a filling made with chicken sautéed in olive oil, pecorino cheese, parsley, eggs and freshly ground black pepper. The half-moon-shaped pastries are fried or baked to serve.

Pitta The Calabrese term for pizza. Generally, they are large ring shapes or circles ready to accept a variety of tasty toppings.

Pitta chicculiata Folded pizza filled with chopped tomatoes, olive oil, garlic, parsley and hot pepper flakes. Sometimes capers, olives and tuna preserved in olive oil are added.

Pitta maniata Pizza covered with another pizza, filled with hard-cooked eggs, ricotta and provolone cheese, Calabrese soppressata or salami and hot pepper flakes.

Pizza di Maiyu Bread dough stuffed with pork cracklings, salami, ricotta cheese, eggs, mozzarella or provoletta cheese. This specialty of the town of Ardore in the province of Reggio Calabria is baked to serve.

Risimogli See *frisuli* (page 260).

Rosamarina See *mustica* (page 260).

Salsiccia calabrese or **sazizza** Sausage made with chopped pork meat and fat and flavored with salt, hot pepper flakes and fennel seeds. To age, they're hung on special poles.

Sarde alla cetrarese Sardines baked with olive oil and oregano. This specialty of the town of Cetraro in the province of Cesenza can be served hot or at room temperature.

Scarafuogli See *frisuli* (page 260).

Soppressata calabrese Rustic, raw-pressed salami. It's made with "knife-chopped" pork, red wine, salt and hot pepper flakes. Before it's smoke-aged in the fresh air, it's covered with a cutting board and weighed down with large stones.

PASTA, GNOCCHI, RICE, POLENTA AND GRAINS

Cannaruozzoli or **canneroni** Homemade egg pasta cut into squares that are then rolled around a stick to achieve their tubular shape. They're covered with grated pecorino cheese then dressed with lamb ragù, meat ragù alla Calabrese or pork, chicken, mushroom, tomato and basil, or anchovy and tuna sauces.

Cappieddi 'i prievidi Egg pasta squares folded into a three-cornered-hat shape. They're dressed with grated pecorino cheese or a Calabrese sauce as above.

Ciufftì Spaghetti dressed with olive oil, garlic and hot pepper flakes. The name of the dish refers to the sound made when the hot, cooked spaghetti are placed in the pan containing the sauce.

Ferrazzuoli alla ricca Homemade pasta dressed with ragù made with pork, lamb, veal, turkey, onions and tomatoes.

Filatelli or **filatieddi** Fat, homemade spaghetti-like pasta (about 3 mm thick). It's dressed with grated pecorino cheese and a salsa Calabrese like those used for *cannaruozzoli* (page 261).

Fischietti or **fusilli** See *maccarruni 'i casa* (below).

Lagane or **laganelle** Just like the version made in Campania (page 224) and not at all like the ones made in Emilia-Romagna (page 126); in Calabria, the long, rectangular-shaped pasta is dressed with ricotta cheese and freshly ground black pepper, or used in chickpea soup garnished with garlic and hot pepper flakes sautéed in olive oil. Another popular way to dress the lagane is to first cook them in milk, then cover them with grated pecorino cheese and butter.

Maccheroni alla toranese Maccheroni dressed with onions and diced guanciale or pancetta sautéed in olive oil, then garnished with grated pecorino cheese and ground hot pepper; typical of the town of Torano Castello in the province of Cosenza.

Maccarruni 'i casa or **a firriettu** Fresh, homemade pasta squares that are wrapped around a special iron tool or knitting needle to achieve its tubular shape. They're dressed with pecorino cheese and a salsa Calabrese (see *cannaruozzoli*, page 261*)*.

Nocchetedde Pasta squares pinched in the middle to make the farfalle or "butterfly" shape. They're dressed with grated pecorino cheese and a salsa Calabrese.

Paternostri Short, tubular-shaped pasta shapes dressed with grated pecorino cheese and a salsa Calabrese.

Rascatieddi or **rascatelli** Similar to the Pugliese *cavatelli* (page 242). The dough contains one-third boiled potatoes.

Ravioli alla calabrese Pasta squares or circles filled with chopped soppressata, provola cheese, hard-cooked eggs and freshly ground black pepper.

Ricchielle, ricchie 'i previti See *rascatieddi* (above).

Ricci di donna Cord-like lengths of pasta that are wrapped around a knitting needle to achieve their spiral shape.

Rigatoni or **maccheroni alla pastora** Ridged pasta dressed with sausage ragù (sometimes), smoked ricotta cheese and freshly ground black pepper.

Risotto alla calabrese or **riso in tortiera** Molded rice filled with ragù alla Calabrese, hard-cooked eggs, little meatballs, mozzarella and pecorino cheese. It's gratinéed to serve.

Sagne chine A term that means "lasagne, stuffed or filled." This special-occasion dish is made by layering sheets of pasta with little meatballs, hard-cooked eggs, scamorza cheese, mozzarella and pecorino—and, in season, artichokes and fresh peas—and sometimes, mushrooms. It's similar to the Neapolitan *lasagne di Carnevale* (page 224).

Schiaffettoni Rectangular stuffed pasta shapes filled with chopped beef, salami, sausage, hard-cooked eggs, black pepper and chopped celery, onions and carrots sautéed in lardo. They're served dressed with tomato sauce and pecorino cheese.

Scivateddi or **scilatelli** Handmade spaghetti dressed with pork ragù and smoked ricotta salata cheese; a specialty of the area around the province of Catanzaro.

Strangolapreti or **strangugliaprièviti** The name of this dish usually indicates homemade pasta made with flour, puréed potatoes and water. They're similar to *cavatelli* (page 242) or *rascatieddi* (page 262). They're dressed with spicy tomato sauce, lamb ragù or beef and tomato sauce.

SOUPS

Accia Celery soup served with sliced hard-cooked eggs, caciocavallo cheese, soppressata, sausage, grated pecorino cheese and black pepper.

Brodo chjnu A typical Easter soup; a type of stracciatella made by adding eggs beaten with grated pecorino cheese, breadcrumbs and parsley to beef broth.

Licurdia Vegetable soup made with potatoes, carrots, chard, escarole or lettuce, then fortified with cipolle di Tropea, a type of red onion, and hot pepper flakes sautéed in lardo. It's served on top of toasted bread. The name comes from Cosenza and refers to the two distinct preparations that go into the dish: a soup and a sauce.

Macco di fave A type of soft polenta made with dried fava beans, onions and tomatoes. It's served with separately cooked broken spaghetti, olive oil, grated pecorino cheese and black pepper or hot pepper flakes.

Mariola Beef broth with strips or small triangles of frittata made with eggs, a bit of flour, breadcrumbs, grated pecorino cheese, parsley and basil or marjoram.

Millecosedde Mixed vegetable soup that includes savoy cabbage, mushrooms and short pasta shapes.

Zuppa d'accio See *accia* (page 263).

CONDIMENTS, SAUCES, SALSAS AND EGGS

Licurdia This name refers to a soup as well as a salsa made by slowly sautéing onions, garlic and hot peppers in lardo until a dense and creamy sauce is achieved. The salsa goes well with toasted, rustic bread.

Salsa calabra Salsa made with tomatoes, lardo, onions, garlic, prosciutto, basil and hot peppers. It's very dense and goes well with boiled meats or pasta.

FISH, CRUSTACEANS AND SHELLFISH

Alalunga all'agrodolce For this dish, alalunga, a type of tuna, is sliced, floured, fried, drained and then dressed with an onion, sugar and vinegar sauce and served at room temperature; a specialty of the town of Bagnara Calabra in the province of Reggio Calabria.

Alici Anchovies.

Alici alla fuscaldese Anchovies that are baked after covering with breadcrumbs, black pepper, hot pepper flakes, oregano, olive oil and lemon juice; a specialty of the town of Fuscaldo in the province of Cosenza.

Alici alla reggina Anchovies covered with breadcrumbs, green olives, capers, garlic, parsley, black pepper and olive oil, then baked.

Baccalà alla verbicarese Softened pieces of salt cod baked with potatoes and sweet peppers; a specialty of the village of Verbicaro in province of Cosenza.

Braciolette di alici Fresh anchovies that are split open like a book, then filled with breadcrumbs, grated pecorino cheese, oregano, parsley and garlic. They are rolled up (*a braciola*), floured and fried, and sometimes served with a tomato salsa.

Costardelle ripiene Similar to *aguglia* (page 317). For this dish, the heads and tails of the fish are removed; the fish are then boned and filled with chopped parsley, garlic, breadcrumbs, oregano, black pepper and olive oil, then sautéed in olive oil with tomatoes to serve.

Pesce spada alla bagnarese Swordfish slices that are poached in olive oil, lemon juice, parsley, oregano and capers; a specialty of the town of Bagnara Calabra in the province of Reggio Calabria.

Quadaro Soup made with a variety of fish: dogfish, lucerna, octopus, mussels, shrimp, etc., and tomatoes, garlic, olive oil, seaweed, parsley and sweet pepper conserve. This specialty of the province of Crotone is served on toasted, rustic bread.

Saraca ara cinnara Herring cooked over hot coals.

Spiedini di anguilla con crostini A dish made with chunks of eel marinated in lemon juice, salt and black pepper. The chunks are threaded onto skewers with fresh bay leaves and pieces of bread then cooked over a wood-burning grill.

MEATS

Agnello alla coriglianese Lamb larded with pancetta and chopped garlic, oregano and vinegar, then roasted; a specialty of the town of Corigliano Calabro in the province of Cosenza.

Braciole alla brugia A dish made by wrapping thin slices of pork around a filling made with lardo, cubes of pecorino cheese, sliced garlic, chopped parsley and freshly ground black pepper. The roll-ups are enclosed in pork caul then cooked in a skillet with lardo and tomato sauce.

Braciole di maiale In spite of its name—pork roll-ups—this is actually a preserved dish. It's made by wrapping thin slices of pork around a filling made with pecorino cheese, parsley, garlic and freshly ground pepper. The rolls are cooked in lardo and may be served immediately or covered with their cooking fat and preserved in terra cotta jars. To serve after they've been conserved, they're browned with sliced potatoes and tomato sauce.

Capretto alla silana Kid stewed in a terra cotta pot with onions, potato wedges and peeled tomatoes. It's cooked very slowly on top of the stove or in the oven and flavored with grated pecorino cheese, freshly ground black pepper, oregano and olive oil.

Capretto ripieno di vermicelli Kid stuffed with cooked vermicelli dressed with a sauce made with lamb's guts and assorted herbs. It's baked to serve. Rabbit may be prepared in the same way.

Carne alla pecorara Pork marinated in olive oil, garlic and black pepper then browned in the marinade, covered with onions, cooked in a bit of lardo, sprinkled with grated cheese then baked. In another version the meat — veal, lamb or chicken — is cooked with olive oil, garlic, tomatoes and oregano.

Carne 'ncantarata Pork preserved in terra cotta jars (in Greek, *kantaros*) with salt, hot pepper flakes and fennel seeds. After the meat has aged for a few months, it's soaked, overnight, in cold water then stewed with tomatoes, chicory and wild fennel, or it's used for sauces or soups.

Cinghiale all'Aspromonte Saddle of wild boar covered with chopped bay leaves, then spit-roasted.

Costolette d'agnello alla calabrese Lamb cutlets browned in olive oil, then finished with tomato sauce made with onions, sweet peppers, green olives and parsley. The dish is a specialty of Cosenza.

Cuccia calabrese A very special, traditional Calabrese dish made in various villages in the foothills of the Silana mountains — in particular, in Pedace in the province of Cosenza — for the Festa della pecorella, the Madonna Addolorata, on the last Sunday of September. The cuccìa (wheat berries) are soaked overnight, then slowly cooked in abundant water for five or six hours. Meanwhile, pieces of kid and pork are cooked. The dish is assembled by covering the bottom of a terra cotta pot with a layer of cooked wheat berries, then the meat. The whole thing is then covered with the remaining wheat berries, baked in a wood-burning oven, then served piping hot.

Frittuli A mixture of pieces of pork rind, snout and ears that are blanched, covered with salt and hot pepper flakes, then cooked, in a copper pot, in lardo; the mixture is covered in salt to preserve.

Marro Little bundles of kid's innards wrapped up in caul with diced pecorino and provoletta cheese, pancetta, chopped garlic and parsley and freshly ground black pepper. They're cooked in olive oil and served with fried potatoes and other side dishes.

Morseddu Pork innards stewed with tomatoes, red wine, oregano and hot pepper flakes; served with rolls or *pitta* (page 261).

Scarafuoghi Fatty and tough pork parts stewed with lardo and water. The stew is finished with hot pepper flakes then served with soft foccacie.

Stigghioli Kid's innards cooked with lardo, tomatoes and strips of hot red peppers.

Trippa alla carbonara Tripe served in tomato and onion sauce with eggplant and fried potatoes.

VEGETABLES

Ciambotta or **ciambrotta** Mixed vegetable stew made with eggplant, zucchini, tomatoes, sweet peppers, potatoes, onions, garlic, celery and olives. Eggs, scrambled with oregano, a pinch of saffron, parsley and marjoram, are added to the stew just before it's served. This is a typical Calabrese dish.

Curriuoli Zucchini cut into strips and dried in the sun. In the wintertime, they're reconstituted in warm water, dipped in batter and fried. They also may be fried without the batter, in olive oil with garlic and oregano.

Gianfottere See *ciambotta* (above).

Insalata calabrese A salad made with potatoes (baked in their skins and then sliced), green peppers and sliced red Tropea onions, dressed with olive oil and salt.

Mappina Christmastime salad made with white frisée lettuce, sweet red peppers, garlic, olive oil and salt; a specialty of the province of Cosenza.

Melanzane alla cariatese Sliced eggplant filled with a mixture of the white part of bread, anchovies, olives, garlic and olive oil.

Melanzane alla finitese A dish in which eggplant slices are blanched, then sandwiched with a filling made with caciocavallo cheese and basil. The "sandwiches" are floured, dipped in eggs, then breadcrumbs, and fried to serve. This dish is a specialty of the town of San Martino di Finita in the province of Cosenza.

Scuma di patati A potato soufflé made with potatoes, butter, eggs, grated cheese and parsley; it's filled with fresh provola cheese and soppressata.

Strascinati Vegetable stew made with onions, zucchini, potatoes, sweet peppers and eggplant cooked in olive oil and garlic.

Zinurra Boiled and drained wild artichokes dressed with olive oil, parsley and black pepper to serve.

Zinurra cà trimma Wild artichokes that are blanched then fried in olive oil with eggs scrambled with pecorino cheese and black pepper.

Zucca ripiena Stuffed winter squash. They're typical of the province of Cosenza.

Zuppa di ripieni Stuffed vegetables — potato, winter squash, zucchini, eggplant, sweet peppers and tomatoes — that are filled with a mixture of chopped meat, breadcrumbs, cheese, garlic, parsley and egg whites, and then slowly stewed in tomato sauce to serve.

CHEESE AND DAIRY PRODUCTS

Abbespata A special salted and smoked ricotta from the area around the Silana mountains and the province of Crotone.

Furmagghiu du quagghiu or **formaggio del caglio** Very strong, aged pecorino cheese filled with tiny worms. It seems that the worms are a result of an imperfection that occurs when the cheese is curdled; it's illegal to sell this cheese.

Pecorino crotonese The best pecorino cheese of the entire region. This faintly pink cheese is consistently tender, with intense flavor and aroma; there's also a version made with black peppercorns.

Ricotta calabrese A unique goat's or sheep's milk ricotta made with whey or water, lightly salted, then curdled over a fig-wood fire.

Sciungata Cheese with a high whey content that should be consumed when very fresh, soft and delicate.

Silano Fresh scamorza cheese.

SWEETS AND LIQUEURS

Anime beate See *vecchiarelle* (page 271).

Bocconotti Short crust pastries filled with jam or pastry cream.

Bratte Figs threaded onto a wooden skewer and then baked.

Cannariculi Stick-shaped pastries made with flour and vino cotto or mosto cotto (cooked grape must), fried and then soaked in honey.

Chinulille or **cassatedde** or **chinuchille** or **chiinule** Round or square ravioli filled with a mixture of ricotta, eggs, sugar, orange and lemon zest, and then fried; a Christmastime specialty of the town of Diamante Calabro in the province of Cosenza. Another filling is made with chestnut purée, cocoa, chocolate fondant, candied fruit, nougat, ground vanilla-covered almonds, sugar, cinnamon and cloves. This version is soaked in honey to serve. There's still another filling made with a base of puréed chickpeas.

Cicirata A Calabrese Christmastime sweet that's very similar to the *struffoli* of Campania (page 234) and *cicerchiata* of Umbria (page 188). The name may also refer to special, half-moon-shaped sweets filled with a mixture made with puréed chickpeas, honey or cooked grape must, liqueur, cloves, cinnamon and grated orange zest, which are then fried in lardo.

Coddura See *piccillato* (page 270).

Collaccio Flower- and animal-shaped cookies made with flour, eggs, honey, suet and yeast. They are covered with a white sugar glaze and decorated with colored sprinkles.

Crucette or **crocette** Figs that are filled with walnuts, almonds and citron zest, then baked.

Cumpittu Soft nougat, obviously of Arab origin, made with honey, sesame seeds and almonds.

Cuzzupa See *piccillato* (page 270).

Fichi ripieni alla sibarita Dried figs filled with a mixture of chopped walnuts, almonds or peanuts and powdered cocoa and candied fruits. They're immersed in cooked grape must then baked.

Ficu du casciuni Figs that are boiled then preserved in large wooden barrels where they develop a white, sugary surface.

Ginetti Ring-shaped cookies that are first boiled, then baked and covered in a lemon glaze.

Giurgiulena See *cumpittu* (above).

Grispelle See *vecchiarelle* (page 271).

Jette See *bratte* (page 268).

Majatiche Little rolled and fried pastries served with fig honey.

Nepitelle Square or round ravioli filled with a mixture of grape purée, grated chocolate, chopped almonds, cinnamon, cooked grape must, sugar, orange and lemon zest, then baked to serve.

Palloni or **padruni** Large, boiled, dried fig balls (*pallini*) that are filled with a mixture of walnuts and chopped citron zest, then soaked in cooked fig must, wrapped in orange leaves, fastened with broom stems and left to dry in the oven.

Pane schiavone Special mostarda made with grape juice, flour, toasted almonds and candied orange zest.

Panicielli d'uva passula Little bunches of grapes wrapped in citron leaves and put in the oven to dry; the pits soften, and the fruit keeps its primitive and aromatic, sweet flavor.

Passulate A type of brittle made with almonds, walnuts, raisins, honey, spices and lemon zest; a Christmastime specialty of the town of Ardore in the province of Reggio Calabria.

Pastiddri or **pastilli** or **pistilli** Skinless dried chestnuts. Those from the village of Montalto Uffugo in the province of Cosenza are particularly renowned.

Piccillato Yeasted cake decorated with eggs in their shells that is an Easter specialty from the province of Catanzaro.

Pitta 'nchiusa Sweet pizza topped with a mixture of walnuts, raisins and vino cotto, covered with another disk of dough, then baked to serve.

Pittapie, pittapia or **nepitte** See *nepitelle* (page 269).

Sammartina Short crust pastry filled with a mixture of almonds, walnuts, raisins, cooked grape must, then decorated with colored sprinkles.

Scalille or **scaledde** or **scaliddre** The dough for these spiral-shaped pastries is made with flour, eggs, lardo and anise liqueur. It is then cut into strips, wound around a chopstick (7 cm long) and fried. They're dipped in giulebbe (a syrup made with sugar and other ingredients) or honey. These pastries are typically served around Christmas and New Year's celebrations.

Scirubetta Fresh snow drenched with fig honey or cooked grape must. In order to make this dish in the summertime, great quantities of snow were covered with straw then buried in a deep trench in the deepest cellar. Near the cathedral, in the city of Cosenza there's a little street called *a vineddra da nivi* ("Snow Alley") because there's a whole series of cellars dedicated to its storage.

Squadatieddri Ring-shaped pastries made with chestnut flour that are first boiled and then fried.

Torrone gelato Made with ghiaccia (powdered sugar whipped into a cream with egg whites) then layered into a cylinder or stick form using various colors and adding pieces of candied citron, tangerines and oranges, and almonds. The forms are then presented, covered with chocolate. In fact, it's not a gelato at all—the name probably refers to the powdered or "icing" sugar used in its preparation.

Tòrtano see *piccillato* (above).

Turtiddi or **turdilli** or **turdiddri** Large, fried, sweet dumplings dipped in honey and orange when they're still hot; Christmastime specialties.

Uova alla monacella This rather elaborate preparation is made with hard-cooked eggs that are cut in half; the yolks are put through a sieve then mixed with cocoa, sugar and cinnamon. The egg yolk mixture is then added back into the whites, rolled in cocoa and cinnamon, dipped in whipped egg whites, then fried to serve. They're a specialty of the town of Castrovillari in the province of Cosenza.

Vecchiarelle Ring-shaped fritters, similar to donuts, made with flour, yeast and water. They are served after dipping in warm honey, or with pastry cream and jam or grape mostarda.

WINES

The wines of this region were celebrated in the past almost like the wines of the area around Mount Vesuvius because of their similar strong, robust and aromatic qualities. Cirò, Greco Bianco, Cosentino, Regium and Sibaris, names that recall the region's original Greek colonizers, were exported all over the Mediterranean basin. Nowadays, Calabria produces just a few, but very interesting wines — even if they're not always made with technically proper methods.

Cirò The Rosso is made with the Gaglioppo varietal. It's a wine that develops a lively ruby red color with hints of garnet and an intense winey nose as it successfully ages. It's dry, full-flavored and strongly tannic when it's young and softens, gaining structure and austerity with age. It's a great wine for roast meats. The Rosato is endowed with the same full body and aroma — in fact, its structure is just like red wine. It's a good companion to lamb and robust first courses dressed with hearty ragùs. The pale, straw-colored Bianco has a decisive, harmonious flavor. It goes well with grilled fish and sauces made with tuna or swordfish and tomatoes and hot peppers.

Donnici Made with the Gaglioppo varietal in the province of Cosenza, this red wine is prized for light aroma, dry and harmonious flavor, and its color, which is sometimes a clear cherry red. It's the ideal partner for stuffed eggplant and all the other vegetable specialties for which Calabria is justly proud. The wine's good vintages go well with stewed meats and first courses with tomato sauce.

Greco di Gerace Made from the Greco Bianco varietal, and its name tells you everything about its origins. The wine, produced in very limited quantities, is a warm yellow gold. If you are able to find a bottle of it, you will be seduced by its delicate aroma of orange blossoms and its sweet but not cloying flavor. When it's still young, it goes well with dry pastries and cookies—when it gets older it should be appreciated for its beautiful golden color and its persuasive, velvety texture. It's a good aperitif and goes well with crustaceans.

Lamezia An honest, pale red dry wine with a winey aroma. In its best years, if well produced, it can accompany grilled meats.

Moscato di Saracena This first-rate dessert wine is made from the Moscatello grapes grown in the town of Saracena in the province of Cosenza. Its pale gold color, all-encompassing aroma and honey-like flavor make it a rare and elegant wine. It goes perfectly with all local pastries, especially those made with almonds, honey and dried figs that evoke an exotic atmosphere.

Pollino This wine gets its name from the massive mountain that straddles the provinces of Cosenza and Potenza. The chalky, clay-like terrain there provides the perfect growing conditions for this rich, structured wine. It's a shame that the methods used for vinification in this area don't always do justice to the wine. This soft, dry, pale ruby red wine with its intense but delicate aroma becomes a good companion for roast meats and game when well vinified.

Savuto Produced in the villages that sit at the foothills of the Sila mountains, this pale red wine tends towards garnet as it ages is. It's dry with a winey nose and goes well with all the local cured meats, spicy sausages, soppressata preserved in olive oil—as well as with the entire meal, from a spicy tomato-sauced first course to stuffed eggplant, and skillet-sautéed potatoes and green peppers.

Ciambotta

Serves 6

1 large onion, sliced
Extra virgin olive oil
Salt
3 eggplants, sliced
2 large tomatoes
2 large sweet peppers
3 potatoes, sliced
2 celery ribs, cut into pieces
A handful of spicy green olives, pitted and
    coarsely chopped
Salt and freshly ground pepper to taste
A pinch of hot pepper flakes

In a large casserole over medium heat, sauté the onions in some olive oil and a few drops of water. Put the eggplant slices in a colander, sprinkle with salt and let them drain for about a half an hour. Blanch the tomatoes in boiling water, peel, seed and quarter.

Fry the peppers in olive oil, turning occasionally, until you're able to peel them but they retain their "raw" quality. Peel, rinse, remove seeds and cut them into strips.

Add all of the vegetables to the casserole, lower the heat and cook until tender. Taste for salt and pepper and add as desired. Add the olives and hot pepper flakes.

Suggested wine: Savuto

SICILIA (SICILY)

Sicilian cuisine is filled with generous flavors and strong contrasts characterized by the populations who have dominated the island over its history. Sicily can thank the ancient Greeks for introducing the simple and austere preparations tied to the natural products of the land. This is especially true on the eastern part of the island, closest to Greece. The Normans imported both dried cod (stoccafisso) and salt cod (baccalà). Arabs introduced fragrant and spicy food. Their way of cooking is especially evident in the sweet and sour preparations that use raisins and pine nuts to balance spicy dishes. The regular use of almonds, couscous, cinnamon, marzipan, sesame nougat and the emblematic cake, cassata, can be attributed to the Arabs as well. In Trapani, on the island's west coast, there's an Arab neighborhood.

During the Baroque period when Sicily was ruled—in name only—by Spain, the tradition of highly decorated and sumptuous desserts came into being. Pan de Spagna (sponge cake) and chocolate were a few of the more important Spanish additions to the Sicilian table.

The French introduced the custom of slowly browning onions instead of garlic to flavor dishes, as well as the traditions of timbales and savory pies encased in short crust pastry. It was a French dish that inspired the quintessentially Sicilian dish farsumagru or falso magro—stuffed, rolled beef.

With its *friggitorie* (fried food shops), *focaccerie* (shops that sell flatbreads and pizza) and great open markets, Palermo is the undisputed capital of the island's gastronomy. There, as in Naples, there's the Monzù ("Monsieur") tradition, which refers to the French chefs who were employed by aristocratic families in the eighteenth and nineteenth centuries.

The region has obvious ties to seafood and fish with tuna holding a place of honor on island menus. The recipes from the town of Favignana, where the historic tuna slaughter, the *tonnara dei Florio*, is held, are incomparable. The cities on the east coast of the island, Syracuse and Ragusa, are known for their refined cuisine, genuine and authentic, and more influenced by the Greeks than the Arabs and the French. Catania, considered the literary capital of the island, has a culinary tradition tied to both the land and the sea.

Bread is still freshly baked at home (it's a ritual); fresh and fragrant vegetables are consumed; meat is roasted over wood-burning fires; and spaghetti al nero di seppia (black cuttlefish spaghetti) is a favorite.

Messina, the city closest to the "continent," is the epicenter of all the island's commercial trade. With products arriving from all over Italy (and the world), an interesting cuisine evolved. For example, it was through Messina that rice found its way into Sicily. While some of the dishes are the same as in the rest of the region, they are all cooked in a slightly different way. Pasta is made into timbales, arancini or sweets. The Sicilian tradition of pastries, cakes and all confectioneries is legendary; this is where the Arab influence in combination with secrets from convent kitchens explode with variety and opulent colors: cassate, cannoli, exquisite gelati, granite, sorbets and marzipan.

ANTIPASTI, BREAD, PIZZA, FLATBREADS AND SAVORY TARTS

Arancini or **arancine di riso** Rice balls usually filled with beef ragù, peas and cubes of cheese that are then breaded and fried. Pine nuts and raisins are added to the filling of those made in the city of Palermo, undoubtedly a nod to Arab influence on the island's food. In restaurants, they're served as antipasti and are a constant presence, as a take-out item, in *rosticcerie* (a kind of deli) and pizzerias.

Bottarga Roe of cefalo grey mullet or muggine tuna that are salted, pressed and aged for four or five months. It's usually made into round or rectangular salami; it's served thinly sliced dressed with olive oil and lemon juice, and added to salads or spaghetti. In Sicily, in particular in the city of Marsala, bottarga is used with olives and shrimp as a filling for fresh tomatoes. Bottarga is also a specialty of Sardinia, Liguria and Calabria.

Cabucio A specialty of the province of Trapani made by shaping bread dough into slightly squashed rolls, then baking them in an extremely hot oven. To serve, they're split open and filled with sliced tomatoes, anchovies, salt, pepper, oregano and extra virgin olive oil.

Caciu all'argintera Made with slices of Sicilian cheese (caciocavallo or canestrato) that are browned in olive oil and garlic then dressed, while still on the flame, with salt, pepper and vinegar. This dish is very much like the Greek fried cheese saganaki; the only difference is that in the Greek version lemon juice is used instead of vinegar.

Cannoli di tuma Blanched slices of fresh tuma cheese that are filled with veal ragù, floured and then fried; a specialty of the province of Trapani.

Caponata A mixture of vegetables that may include eggplant, onions, tomatoes, sweet peppers, spinach, cauliflower, endive and celery that are fried, then marinated in a sweet and sour dressing with anchovies, capers, basil, pine nuts, raisins, cinnamon, cloves, almonds, sliced pears, sugar and vinegar; some recipes include powdered cocoa as well.

Carrubelle Blanched slices of fresh tuma cheese that are filled with anchovies, floured and then fried; a specialty of the province of Catania.

Cassateddi di caciu or **cassatelle di formaggio** Little panzerotti made with a dough made with semolina, eggs, lardo and water. The half-moon-shaped, fried pastries are filled with caciocavallo cheese or anchovies.

Cazzilli A type of simplified potato croquette made by adding garlic, parsley, salt and pepper to puréed potatoes formed into ovals, then fried to serve.

Chichiru See *ferro di cavallo* (below).

Crispeddi Fritters typically found in the *friggitorie* — shops specializing in fried foods — in the city of Catania. Round crespeddi are filled with ricotta, while the long ones are filled with anchovies and fennel seeds. In some areas they are made for Christmastime and in others they're made on November 11, the feast of San Martino.

Cudduruni Focaccia covered with olive oil and sliced garlic, then baked in a wood-burning oven.

Ferro di cavallo Horseshoe-shaped bread.

Ficazza A very spicy soppressata made with tuna guts; a specialty of the provinces of Palermo and Trapani.

Fillata Sicilian term used to describe soppressata made with diced pork thigh and shoulder mixed with cubed lardo.

Fritteddi See *crispeddi* (above).

Fuate A sort of pizza made with rustic bread dough covered with peeled tomatoes, garlic, salted sardines, pecorino cheese, olive oil, salt and pepper; a specialty of the village of Pietraperzia in the province of Caltanisetta.

Guastedde ennesi Pizza covered with fresh tomatoes and pancetta or artichokes, anchovies, ricotta salata, olive oil, salt and pepper.

Guastedde palermitane Soft, sesame seed-covered rolls filled with spleen that has been fried in lardo, sheep's milk ricotta and caciocavallo cheese. In Palermo, they're sold in special shops or from street carts. Guastedde that are referred to as schette or "nubile," don't have much filling, while the ones called maritate or "married," are full of ingredients.

Impanate siracusane Focaccie made with rustic bread dough then filled with broccoletti, pork sausage, primosale cheese, olive oil and red pepper flakes; sometimes potatoes, tomatoes and onions are included. They're very similar to the *pastizzu* (below) from the province of Ragusa and the *scacciata* (page 278) from the province of Catania.

Millassata Large garlic- and parsley-flavored frittata filled with artichoke hearts and wild asparagus buds.

Muffulettu See *cabucio* (page 275).

Musseddu In Trapani, a word used to describe sun-dried dolphin; it's just like *mosciame* from Liguria (page 35). It's served thinly sliced with green salad.

Nunnata The Sicilian word for the tiny fish elsewhere called bianchetti. For the most popular preparation, see *sfigghiata* (page 278).

Olive farcite Green olives stuffed with capers and anchovies, brined and preserved in olive oil.

Olive schiacciate Brined olives, smashed, pits removed, then dressed with olive oil, garlic, red pepper flakes, oregano and vinegar.

Olive verdi alla siciliana Pitted green olives that are filled with tomato and sweet pepper purées and capers.

Pane a caponata Chunks of toasted rustic bread that are dipped in cold water for an instant, then added to a large bowl and tossed with tomato wedges, olive oil, garlic, salt, pepper and abundant amounts of fresh basil; a specialty of the island of Lipari.

Panelle A chickpea and parsley dough that's put in specially stamped wooden molds. The dough is left to solidify, then removed and fried to serve. When the molds aren't available, the dough is rolled out, cut into rectangles and fried. In Palermo the custom is to eat panelle boiled, flavored with a few drops of lemon juice, sandwiched between two slices of bread.

Pastizzu Focaccia typical of the province of Ragusa but very similar to the *scacciata* (page 278) from Catania. In Ragusa the pastizzu are cooked already filled. The fillings can include chopped pork dressed with salt and abundant amounts of freshly ground pepper; cubed, fried eggplant, freshly peeled tomatoes, lots of fresh basil, sliced primosale cheese, grated pecorino or caciocavallo cheeses, olive oil, salt and pepper; ricotta, stewed peas and onions and primosale cheese; or, quartered artichokes cooked with olive oil, garlic, parsley, eggs, anchovies and tuma cheese.

Pisci A typical Sicilian bread shape.

Primosale fritto con l'acciuga A little snack made with triangular pieces of primosale cheese filled with anchovies, floured, then fried to serve.

Rianata Pizza made with bread dough that's topped with peeled, fresh tomatoes, garlic, anchovies, grated pecorino cheese, olive oil, salt, pepper and lots of oregano. It's served very hot. The pizza, from the area around Trapani, gets its name from the amount of oregano (origano) used to garnish it.

Rotolo rustico See *sfigghiulata* (below).

Sarde a beccafico Sardines that have been cleaned, deboned, had the heads removed, opened and laid flat in an olive oil–greased pan, then covered with breadcrumbs, anchovies, pine nuts, cinnamon, raisins and other ingredients. They're baked then splashed with fresh lemon or orange juice. In Catania the sardines are soaked in vinegar, then covered with grated cheese, parsley and garlic and fried to serve. In Messina they're also sautéed with tomatoes, capers and olives.

Scacciata A specialty of Catania made with rustic bread dough that is baked and then stuffed with various fillings. Some of the fillings include tuma cheese, anchovies, olive oil and pepper; boiled, sautéed cauliflower, peppered cheese, anchovies, garlic and olive oil; anchovies, tuma cheese, scallions, olive oil and pepper; and lastly one with boiled, sautéed broccoletti (sparacelli), black olives, primosale cheese, garlic, anchovies, olive oil and pepper.

Scaccie The same dough as the *scacciata* (above) made into flat rounds, stuffed with various fillings then rolled up like a strudel. They're brushed with olive oil and baked. Some of the fillings include ripe tomatoes fried with onions, grated caciocavallo cheese and hot red peppers; fried eggplant, fresh peeled tomatoes, grated caciocavallo cheese, fresh basil, salt and pepper; or ricotta cheese, spring onions, grated caciocavallo cheese, eggs, salt and pepper.

Sciaguazza or **sciavazza** See *sfincione* (page 279).

Sfigghiata Sicilian word for the tiny fish elsewhere called bianchetti. They may be served barely boiled dressed with olive oil and fresh lemon juice, or fried, in a frittata or in fritters.

Sfigghiulata or **rotolo rustico** An old Sicilian dish made by filling a rectangle of bread dough with fresh pecorino or cubes of caciotta cheese, anchovies and oregano. It's rolled up and baked. Another filling includes cheese and dry sausage or rustic salami.

Sfincione or **sfinciuni di agrigento** Similar to the *scacciata* (page 278), the sfincione is bread dough filled with potatoes, tomatoes, onions, black olives and grated Parmesan cheese.

Spincione or **sfinciunipalermitano** Prepared with a lighter dough made with oo flour, a bit of olive oil and yeast, this version is a kind savory tart filled with primosale, pecorino or caciocavallo cheese, anchovies, onions, breadcrumbs, oregano, parsley, olive oil, salt, pepper and tomato sauce.

Susu Gelatin-covered terrine made with pork belly, snout, rind, ears, jowl and feet, flavored with bay leaf, black pepper, vinegar and lemon juice.

Vastedda Large round bread made with elderberry flowers mixed into the dough, traditionally made in Ragusa for the feast of the Pentecost.

PASTA, GNOCCHI, RICE, POLENTA AND GRAINS

Anelletti Sicilian ring-shaped dry pasta.

Attuppateddi Sicilian word for ditalini.

Cannelloni alla siciliana Cannelloni filled with beef pot roast and grated caciocavallo cheese, then covered with beaten eggs, pot roast sauce and grated caciocavallo cheese and baked to serve.

Cavatiddi Little shell-like pasta shapes similar to cavatelli that may be dressed with a sauce made with Belice eels, with pork rind ragù, "alla Norma," with the sauce made from cooking the beef roll-ups and so on. In Caltanissetta they're called cavati, in Palermo gnucchitteddi or gnocculi, and in Ragusa cavasuneddi.

Ciceri ca pasta or **pasta con ceci** Pasta (ditalini or sedani) dressed with a sauce made with chickpeas, pancetta or lardo, onions, olive oil, tomato sauce, red pepper flakes, sage and rosemary.

Cruselli alla siciliana See *rosette alla siciliana* (page 281).

Cuscusu or **uscuso** or **muscuso** Couscous. The dish came from Tunisia to Sicily through the Sicilian Canal and landed in Marsala and Trapani. This is a rather complicated dish. First comes the *incocciata*, which is the transformation of flour into small grains, achieved by placing flour in an appropriate terra cotta pot called a *mafaradda*, then dribbling it with just enough water to start to work the dough into small grains. The couscous is then sieved several times in order to eliminate any residual flour and form a uniform size. The grains are sun-dried. The dish is cooked by putting the couscous back into the *mafaradda* and dressing it with olive oil, salt, pepper and grated onions. The dressed couscous is placed in an onion-lined *pignata*, another terra cotta pot with holes in the bottom, like a colander, and set over a water- and vegetable-filled saucepan. The *pignata* is sealed with a flour and water paste so that steam won't escape while it cooks on very low heat for about two hours. The couscous is then bathed in the cooking broth, covered and left to rest before it's served. Sicilian couscous is served with a loose fish soup, or fish broth, or little fish and fried eggplant, or chicken and fried broccoli, or lamb stew.

Frasquatulidda Semolina polenta.

Gnocculi See *cavatiddi* (page 279).

Lasagne cacate Large, rippled lasagne (dry, not fresh) dressed with a type of pork and veal or beef ragù made with red wine, tomatoes and onions and garnished with fresh sheep's milk ricotta and ricotta salata; a New Year's Day specialty of Palermo and the town of Modica in the province of Ragusa.

Maccaruna di casa See *pasta busiata* (below).

Pasta a "picchi pacchiu" Dry pasta, usually spaghetti, dressed with chopped raw tomatoes marinated in olive oil with garlic, basil and red pepper flakes, then served garnished with grated caciocavallo cheese.

Pasta alla carrettiera Spaghetti or bucatini dressed with raw tomato sauce made with olive oil, garlic and fresh basil.

Pasta alla Norma Dry pasta, usually spaghetti or penne, dressed with tomato sauce (optional), fresh basil and ricotta salata, then covered with sliced, fried eggplant. This emblematic Sicilian dish originated in Catania to honor Bellini's opera "Norma."

Pasta busiata con il pesto trapanese Fresh pasta (also called maccaruna di casa) shaped by wrapping rectangles of the dough around a knitting needle. It's dressed with an interesting sauce made by pounding together basil, garlic, olive oil, salt, tomatoes and almonds in a mortar.

Pasta 'cca muddica Literally, "pasta with bread crumbs." It's usually made with spaghetti dressed with a sauce made with olive oil, garlic and anchovies enriched and bound together with the grated white part of bread. Another version is simply dressed with sugar and the white part of bread. At one time this dish was served on the feast of San Giuseppe, March 19.

Pasta 'cchi masculini Usually spaghetti dressed with tiny and very tasty anchovies (masculini) sautéed in olive oil, garlic and parsley and garnished with grated, sharp pecorino cheese or grated ricotta salata.

Pasta con il 'richiagghiu Spaghetti or short pasta dressed with beaten eggs, chopped parsley and grated Sicilian cheese.

Pasta con le sarde The crowning pasta achievement of Sicilian fishermen, a dish made by cooking spaghetti or bucatini in wild fennel-flavored water, then dressing it with sardine fillets, capers, anchovies, chopped onions, pine nuts, raisins, pepper and more wild fennel; sometimes saffron is added as well. It's garnished with chopped, toasted almonds. The dish was born in the area between the towns of Cefalù, Bagheria and Palermo but is made all over the island.

Pasta 'ncasciata A timbale made with cooked, short pasta, meat ragù, little meatballs, hard-cooked egg slices, fried egg-plant, peas, salami and caciocavallo cheese. It is baked then served with meat ragù.

Pasta palina Ziti cooked in the same water where cauliflower has been cooked then dressed with cauliflower florets sautéed in olive oil with garlic, onions, sardines, anchovies, cloves and a little tomato sauce.

Ripiddu nivicatu A relatively new dish, a black (cuttlefish) risotto, created by Giuseppe La Rosa, owner of the restaurant La Siciliana in Catania. It's presented in a cone shape to resemble the volcano of Mt. Etna and garnished with grated ricotta salata and tomato sauce to represent flowing lava. *Ripiddu* is the word for the tiny, black beach gravel that comes from lava debris.

Rosette alla siciliana Boiled egg pasta squares filled with meat ragù, fried zucchini and grated caciocavallo cheese, rolled up, then baked to serve.

Spaghetti alla siracusana Spaghetti dressed with bottarga (dried tuna roe), smoked herring, olive oil and various herbs.

Tiano d'Aragona Rigatoni dressed with meat ragù then layered with tuma cheese, peas and an incredible amount of eggs beaten with grated pecorino cheese. It's made around Easter in the interior part of the island.

Tria The word used in Sicily and Puglia for a type of spaghetti or tagliatelle made with durum wheat; *tria bastarda* signifies the addition of bran flour to the dough. It's often dressed with lentil or chickpea sauce. The word is derived from the Arabic word for vermicelli, and may be the base of the word trenette, also a long pasta, from Liguria.

Zite or **ziti** A pasta shape that originated in Campania but is popular all over Sicily as well. This large, wide pasta is made industrially, or at home, with durum wheat; it's often used to makes timbales.

SOUPS

Frascatela A soup of boiled cauliflower and its flour-thickened cooking liquid garnished with fried pancetta and freshly ground black pepper; a specialty of the town of Sperlinga in the province of Enna.

Ghiotta di patate Dense potato soup flavored with olive oil, onions, garlic, tomatoes and basil, then garnished with grated pecorino cheese. Pieces of eggplant and zucchini are sometimes added in season.

Maccu One of the most ancient dishes in the Mediterranean area dating back to pre-dynasty Egypt. Maccu refers to the way fava beans are smashed (*ammaccate*) to make a purée. It showed up again in the fourteenth century on the Italian tables of Puglia and Basilicata with the name 'ncapriata. The Sicilian version is made with puréed fava beans and wild fennel and garnished with top quality extra virgin olive oil. It's not a real soup but is served in place of one. Sometimes it's dressed with sautéed onions and tomatoes and served with a dish of pasta. In Palermo it's garnished with sautéed squash.

Maccu di San Giuseppe Soup made with fava beans, peas, lentils, chickpeas, beans and dried chestnuts dressed with sun-dried tomatoes, celery, olive oil, salt and pepper. Fresh vegetables such as borage, escarole, fennel, other greens and pasta are sometimes added.

Minestra di tenerumi (tinnirumi) Soup made with the leaves and sprouts of a very tender and thin zucchini that grows around Palermo. The soup is flavored with peeled tomatoes, garlic, anchovies, salt and pepper; a short pasta shape is added.

Sciuscieddu An Easter soup, probably of French origin, made thick by adding a mixture of eggs, grated cheese, breadcrumbs, parsley and garlic to broth. A richer version is made by adding badduzzi (meatballs) and fresh ricotta whipped with eggs whites to the broth then baking it; it becomes a type of zuppa soffiata or souffléd soup.

CONDIMENTS, SALSAS, SAUCES AND EGGS

Arriminata Any stirred dish.

Cipollata Slowly browned onions to which a bit of vinegar and fresh mint are added; used with tuna, mullet or fried fish; without vinegar, it goes well with liver or other meat.

Ghiotta or **agghiotta** Tomato stew with capers and olives.

Pesto siciliano A sauce made by pounding peeled tomatoes, pine nuts, garlic, basil, parsley, celery, olive oil, salt and pepper in a mortar; in Trapani almonds are used instead of pine nuts.

Picchi pacchiu See *pasta a "picchi pacchiu"* (page 280).

Ragù alla siciliana Lardo, pork rind, sausages, chicken or rabbit thighs and meatballs browned with onions, then slowly cooked with tomato purée.

Salamureci A special pesto from Trapani made with fresh tomatoes, basil and garlic. It's used to dress pasta that's garnished with grated almonds, or as a soup base.

Salmoriglio A simple Sicilian sauce made by cooking very distinctly flavored olive oil with garlic, lemon juice, parsley and oregano in a water bath. Purists maintain that the sauce *must* have a few drops of seawater. Mostly it accompanies grilled swordfish, but other fish as well. Another version is made with grilled tomatoes. It's called sarmorigghiu russu and is used with all kinds of bluefish.

Salsa San Bernardo An unusual and original sweet-and-sour sauce made with toasted almonds and toasted bread pounded in a mortar with anchovies and orange juice, finished with a mixture of sugar, vinegar, cocoa and water; used to dress steamed artichoke hearts, shrimp caponata and shellfish.

Stemperata Condiment made with capers, boiled carrots, green olives, celery and garlic, vinegar and fresh mint.

FISH, CRUSTACEANS AND SHELLFISH

Acciughe all'arancia Fresh anchovies layered with olives, capers, lemon slices and other ingredients, then covered with orange juice and baked.

Alalunga A type of high-quality tuna.

Alalunga a ragù Tuna topped with chopped garlic, mint and salt, browned in olive oil, bathed with white wine, then cooked with onions, garlic, tomatoes and hot peppers.

Alaustra The Sicilian word for lobster.

Alose in camicia A dish in which alose or saracche, a type of sardine, are cleaned, dressed in olive oil, salt and red pepper flakes, then wrapped in sheets of pasta dough and baked; a specialty of the town of Cattolica Eraclea in the province of Agrigento.

Babbaluci Snails.

Braciole di pesce spada Thin slices of swordfish filled with provolone cheese, breadcrumbs, garlic, basil, parsley, eggs and swordfish innards sautéed with chopped onions. They're rolled up, grilled and served with salsa *salmoriglio* (page 283).

Braciole di tonno fresco Thin slices of tuna filled with breadcrumbs, parsley, garlic, chopped hard-cooked eggs, grated pecorino cheese and chopped tuna. Once they're rolled up, they're cooked in a tomato-and-onion sauce.

Caponata di scampi e molluschi A labor-intensive dish made with lobster and shrimp, celery and floured and fried eggplant that are cooked in a sauce made with onions, vinegar, sugar, fresh tomatoes, garlic, parsley, capers and olives. The cooked mixture is chilled, then served with *salsa San Bernardo* (page 283) and garnished with sliced hard-cooked eggs and shrimp. These days it's not as easy to find this caponata as the one that's made exclusively with vegetables.

Cincina Tiny, little fish.

Cipollata di cincina Tiny, little fish that are floured, fried and served with *cipollata* (page 283).

Cocciule ricce Sea urchins.

Crispeddi di nunnata See *purpetti* (page 285).

Cuccu or **facianu** Capone, a fish similar to mullet; also called coccio.

Faggiani impiriali Capone; also known as gallinella.

Furcatu Capone; also known as lira.

Impanata A type of fish tart.

Impanata di palombo Puff pastry filled with ghiotta, a sauce made with onions, tomatoes, celery, olives, capers, small pieces of dogfish and batter-fried zucchini.

Impanata di pesce spada A well-known and very refined recipe from Messina, probably of French origin, made by layering puff pastry with pieces of swordfish cooked in a sauce made with olive oil, tomatoes, onions, celery, olives and capers, and with fried zucchini and another layer of swordfish that is then covered with another layer of puff pastry and baked. The dish sometimes includes artichokes and peas.

Lattume Part of the reproductive apparatus of a tuna that is cut into pieces and fried; a preparation found in areas around tuna fishing.

Maiaticu The word used in Messina for newborn sardines.

Martiduzzu impiriali Capone, a type of mullet also called ubriaco.

Mascolini Tiny little fish in the anchovy family. They're cooked in various ways in the area around Catania and also eaten raw, marinated in fresh lemon juice, olive oil, garlic, parsley, salt and pepper.

Mazzunara The word used in Messina for tiny, little fish.

'mpanata di palombo See *impanata di palombo* (page 284).

Muccu The word in Catania for tiny little fish.

Mulinaro The fish also known as capone or coccio.

Nasello alla palermitana Hake covered with olive oil, various herbs and anchovies and then baked.

Pesce spada a ghiotta Slices of swordfish cooked in a skillet with tomato sauce, potatoes, olives, capers and celery; a specialty of Messina.

Pesce stocco a ghiotta Pieces of rehydrated dry cod that are floured, fried and then cooked with a substantial sauce made with tomatoes, herbs, pine nuts, raisins, anchovies, olives and potatoes; a specialty of Messina.

Pisci papa Capone or ubriaco.

Purpetti (or **crispeddi**) **di nunnata** Delicious fritters made with nunnata (tiny, little fish) mixed with beaten eggs, chopped parsley and garlic, then fried by the teaspoonful.

Russuliddu Small mullets.

Sarde a beccafico See page 278.

Sasizza di tonno Sausage made with coarsely chopped tuna mixed with breadcrumbs, grated caciocavallo cheese, salt, black pepper, red pepper flakes, cloves and chopped parsley. The mixture is put into a pork casing, then formed into little sausages and cooked in a sauce made with tomatoes, onions and white wine.

Sciabbacchieddu fritti alla messinese A typical and popular fishermen's dish made with tiny little fish from the Straits of Messina that are fried, then flavored with garlic.

Sfigghiata See page 278.

Sparacanaci The term used in Messina to describe minute, newly born fish.

Tiega Capone or gurno, a type of mullet.

Tonno a sfincione The most popular way to cook tuna in Palermo in which slices of tuna are layered with olive oil, salt and oregano, then covered with sliced onions and peeled and seeded tomatoes and baked.

Tonno 'muttunato The part of tuna called tarantello is used to make this dish. The tuna is stuck with fresh mint leaves, garlic, rosemary and basil then stewed with tomatoes, onions and white wine.

Tunnina fritta Tunnina is a female tuna. It's cut into one-inch thick pieces called tarantello or curidda, browned on both sides, then flavored with lemon and oregano.

MEATS

Carne aglassata or **aggrassata** or **aggrasatu** A "noble" Sicilian dish that most likely comes from the French kitchen. It's roast beef very slowly cooked with lardo, onions, white wine, rosemary, salt and pepper.

Badduzze Sicilian word for meatballs. They're often cooked in tomato sauce.

Beccafico 'nna a cipudda Onions stuffed with little birds that have been stuffed with figs. They're cooked in a terra cotta pot or grilled and dressed with oil and vinegar to serve.

Capretto a sciusciareddu Kid, first browned in olive oil and onions, then stewed in tomato sauce. It's enriched with asparagus tips and fried artichokes. The stew is covered with eggs beaten with grated cheese and chopped parsley, then gratinéed to serve; a specialty of Palermo.

Capuliatu Chopped meat.

Coniglio a' purtuisa An elaborate dish made with cut-up rabbit sautéed in olive oil with olives, onions, celery and capers. The dish is enriched with eggplant, potatoes, fried sweet peppers, sugar and vinegar and finished with chopped garlic, mint and basil.

Coniglio a' stimpirata Rabbit that is first marinated in red wine, onions, bay leaves and peppercorns, then floured and fried. The fried rabbit is then stewed with chopped lardo and onions, celery, olives, capers, pine nuts, raisins, vinegar and sugar to make this sweet-and-sour dish.

Costoletta or **cotoletta alla siciliana** Boneless steak marinated in vinegar, then covered with grated cheese mixed with garlic and parsley. The steak is dipped in eggs, then breadcrumbs, and fried to serve.

Farsu magru Dialect for one of the most famous Sicilian dishes, stuffed meat. It's made with a large piece of beef or veal that's filled with hard-cooked eggs, cheese, prosciutto, lardo, peas or raisins, pine nuts, sausage and herbs.

Grassatu Stew made with lamb or kid cooked in red wine with potatoes, lardo and fried onions, garlic and parsley. It's finished with grated caciocavallo and pecorino cheeses and is used to dress pasta.

Sancele or **sanceli** or **sancucauru** or **sancunazzu** Sausage made with pork blood, chopped walnuts (sometimes almonds or pine nuts), milk or ricotta, grated pecorino cheese, breadcrumbs, raisins, honey, cinnamon and cloves, and then boiled. The boiled sausage is sliced, then fried in olive oil with onions to serve. There are a few variations; for example, it can be made with two parts pork blood and one part water, garlic, parsley, salt and abundant freshly grated black pepper. There are also sweet versions.

Sasizzeddi Veal roll-ups filled with eggs, onions, salami and cheese.

Stigghiole Kid or castrated beef guts wrapped around lardo flavored with parsley or scallions, then cooked over a wood-burning fire.

Trippa all'olivitana Pan-cooked tripe layered with fried eggplant, cheese, hard-cooked eggs, etc. then baked; a specialty of Enna.

Truscello A rare and old dish made by layering a mixture of ricotta cheese, other cheese, eggs, salt, pepper and cloves with tiny meatballs that have been cooked in broth; a specialty of Messina.

Truscia di cutina Similar to farsu magru; made by filling pork skin with a mixture of beef and pork.

Turcinuna A dish made by wrapping kid or castrated beef guts around pieces of lardo, then cooking them with olive oil, lardo, chopped chives, basil and fresh lemon juice; a specialty of the area around Ragusa.

Turtidduzza A stew made with lamb or kid lungs, liver, heart and guts cooked with olive oil, garlic, parsley and tomato sauce. The oldest version of this dish uses red wine instead of tomato sauce.

VEGETABLES

Bbruocculi incuddati Broccoli incollati; very similar to *cavolfiore a vastedda* (below).

Caponata See page 276.

Cavolfiore a vastedda Cauliflower florets dipped in an

anchovy-flavored batter, then fried. They may be served at room temperature as well as hot.

Cazzilli Potato, cheese and prosciutto croquettes.

Ciciri Chickpeas.

Ficato d'i setti cannòla Sliced, fried winter squash that is made sweet and sour with vinegar, sugar, garlic and mint. The rather strange name comes from an ancient piazza in Palermo known for its vegetable vendors — there are seven *cannòla* (fountains) in the piazza.

Frascatela Cauliflower florets bound together with flour, then flavored with pancetta.

Frittedda A classic Sicilian preparation made with sautéed artichokes, scallions, peas and fava beans. In the area around Palermo, it's made sweet and sour with vinegar or lemon and sugar and is served at room temperature. In the province of Enna and the villages near the Madonie mountains, bunches of wild fennel are added to the vegetables. The dish is typically made for the feast of San Giuseppe, March 19, to symbolize the beginning of spring and the new harvest.

Giri A Sicilian vegetable similar to beets.

Insalata turca Grilled vegetables dressed with good olive oil, garlic, salt and pepper and served at room temperature.

Matarocco An odd dish, a hybrid of salad and soup. It's probably derived from the Spanish gazpacho. It's made by pounding peeled and seeded tomatoes in a mortar with olive oil, garlic, basil, salt and pepper, then adding pieces of slightly green tomatoes. It's served as a mid-morning snack with durum wheat bread.

Melanzane a quaglie Small eggplants cut into four slices down to their base, then cut to make sixteen sticks (always attached to the base) and fried; a preparation typical of Palermo.

Milinciani 'ncudduriati Eggplant roll-ups filled with a mixture of breadcrumbs, pecorino cheese, tomatoes, basil and parsley, then grilled.

Olive alla stemperata Pitted olives sautéed with capers, carrots and artichoke hearts, then flavored with celery, vinegar and mint. In Sicily, olives are often used as a vegetable side dish.

Pipi 'ncudduriati Roast sweet pepper roll-ups filled with breadcrumbs, pecorino cheese, basil and parsley.

Pitaggio Stewed peas, fava beans and artichoke hearts; a specialty of Agrigento often served with roasted sausages.

Salàmoreci A salad made with fresh tomatoes, pieces of dry bread soaked in water, basil, olive oil, salt and pepper.

Sparacelli Broccoletti.

Tenerumi Zucchini leaves.

Trunza di fera Thinly sliced red cabbage sautéed with olive oil, then flavored with vinegar, pitted olives and capers.

CHEESE AND DAIRY PRODUCTS

Caciocavallo A cheese produced throughout the Ancient Realm of Naples. It starts out round then is tied at one end giving it its classic pear shape. The string that ties it is also used to hang it to age and smoke. It has a smooth, pale-to-dark-brown rind and an elastic, white-to-straw-colored body.

Pecorino siciliano Raw, whole sheep's milk cheese with a compact, hard body, formed in a basket. Its rind is yellow-ish-white and body yellow to straw colored. The sharply flavored cheese contains more than 40% fat.

Pepato The same as above, with the addition of black peppercorns in its paste.

Piacintinu A saffron-flavored basket cheese from the province of Messina.

Primosale Fresh, just-salted pecorino, not aged.

Ragusano In the same family of "stretched" cheeses as caciocavallo, with a large, rectangular form. Made with whole cow's milk, it must contain at least 44% fat. It has characteristic markings along its body where it's been tied to hang. The smooth rind is straw to light golden colored when it's young and becomes dark brown as it ages; the body goes from white to straw-color as it ages. The young cheese is compact and delicately flavored; the aged cheese is flaky and pleasingly sharp—a good grating cheese.

Ricotta canestrata Made with sheep's buttermilk; it's salted and aged in a basket.

Ricotta infornata Baked ricotta; typically Sicilian.

Ricotta secca Sun-dried ricotta; a specialty of the area around Paterno and Pollina.

Tuma A freshly curdled, unsalted basket cheese. It needs to be consumed almost as soon as it's made.

SWEETS AND LIQUEURS

Affuca parrinu Dry cookies made with flour, eggs, suet and sugar that are boiled then baked. The name means "priest chokers."

Agnello pasquale A classic Easter sweet—a citron marmalade-filled, lamb-shaped cake either sugar-glazed or covered with marzipan and garnished with marzipan fruits. The best-known agnello pasquale comes from the town of Erice in the province of Trapani.

Baduzzi di cacao Cocoa-covered almonds.

Biancomangiare A classic Sicilian pudding made with skinned powdered almonds, starch and milk. According to tradition, any food — sweet or savory — made with powdered almonds and milk is called *biancomangiare*.

Buccellato siciliano or **purciddata** A ring-shaped, short crust Christmas cake filled with dried fruits.

Cannistreddu A type of *buccellato siciliano* (above).

Cannoli alla siciliana Pastries made by rolling a piece of dough to make tube shapes that are then fried or baked. They're filled with pastry cream or sweet ricotta with candied fruits and bits of chocolate.

Cardinali Little pastries made with almonds, candied fruits, lemon peel, egg whites and pistachios. The baked pastries are covered with a chocolate glaze then decorated with "arabesques" made of sugar.

Carrobisi Sweet ravioli made with dough that has been enriched with almond and lemon and tangerine zest then filled with dried figs cooked in wine and cinnamon.

Cassarulata di gelato A dome-shaped semifreddo made with pistachio, cream and candied fruit gelato.

Cassata alla siciliana An emblematic Sicilian sweet made by filling sponge cake with sweet ricotta, pieces of chocolate, vanilla, candied fruit and liqueur — usually Maraschino. It's covered with a green glaze very often made with pistachios, then garnished with whole, candied fruits. The cassata, which is Arab in origin, is made to perfection in various convents around the island. Towards the end of the sixteenth century, the religious authorities in the town of Marzara del Vallo in the province of Trapani prohibited the preparation of this sweet in all convents because they thought that the nuns paid more attention to its manufacture than to their religious duties.

Cassata gelato Ice cream made with all the same ingredients as the *cassata alla siciliana* (above); these days it's industrially produced throughout Italy.

Cassateddi dolci Panzerotti filled with ricotta, cinnamon and sugar, then fried; the sweet version of *cassateddi di caciu* (page 276).

Ciaurrina A very unusual sweet made by reducing honey until just before it begins to separate, then whipping it, hanging it on a hook and pulling it until it turns white and re-forms itself into circles or twisted shapes. It was born in the town of Barcellona in the province of Messina. Called sanfirrìccia, sanfurrìccia or bombolone in the south-eastern area of the island, it's made for the Day of the Dead on November 2 and for Christmas and New Year's celebrations.

Ciciliu A ring-shaped Easter cake garnished with eggs in their shells and colored sprinkles.

Cileppu or **giulebbe** or **giulebbo** A liqueur made by boiling sugar with various herbs or fruits; then clarifying it with egg whites.

Collure messinesi Ring-shaped pastries made with sugar coated bread dough enriched with pieces of chocolate and garnished, before baking, with a hard-cooked egg.

Conchiglie Shell-shaped almond pastries filled with citron marmalade, typical of Palermo and Noto.

Crispeddi di riso alla benedettina Round or oblong rice fritters served very hot, covered with powdered sugar, cinnamon or honey.

Crispeddi di San Giuseppe Yeasted dough fritters served covered with granulated sugar or honey; made for the feasts of San Martino, San Giuseppe and Christmas.

Cubbàita Soft nougat made with honey, almonds and sesame seeds; Arab in origin.

Cucchiteddi di sciacca Little pastries made with almond dough, filled with candied squash, baked and then glazed.

Cuccìa Dialect for chicco, which is a typical Sicilian pastry of Arab origin. It's made with wheat berries cooked with sugar or honey, then mixed with ricotta cream or milk, candied fruits and chocolate; the ingredients may vary. It's also called grano dolce or grano di Santa Lucia. It's made in memory of a ship that miraculously appeared in the port of Palermo on December 13, 1600 (the feast day of Santa Lucia) filled with wheat that saved the famished population. The starving citizens couldn't wait for the wheat to be made into flour for bread so they ate it simply boiled, dressed with a bit of olive oil. As time passed, more ingredients were added until the present day recipe was achieved. There are similar preparations in Calabria and Basilicata.

Cucciddatu Ring-shaped pastries filled with dried fruits. Their size changes according to the area where they're produced.

Cuddura di Pasqua A sweet bread made in the shape of a

heart, chicken, lamb or ring. Hard-cooked eggs are placed in the shapes then covered with a crosshatch of dough.

Cuscusu dolce Couscous sweetened with a mixture of sugar, pistachios, cocoa, candied fruits, cinnamon and other ingredients. The dish originated in the Santo Spirito Monastery of Agrigento.

Diavolina Tiny colored squares usually used as garnishes.

Dolci di riposto The name used to indicate little pastries made with marzipan filled with various jams and covered with sugar glaze.

Frutta alla Martorana Marzipan made into fruit shapes.

Gelo di anguria or **di melone** Gelatin made with strained watermelon flavored with chocolate, cinnamon, candied squash and vanilla, then stabilized with starch; variations are made with lemon and jasmine. It's made in Palermo for Ferragosto, August 15.

Giggì eoliani Fried dough sticks immersed in vino cotto.

Giuggiulena or **giurgiulena** Very much like *cubbàita* (page 291), a soft nougat made with honey, almonds and sesame seeds sometimes covered with *diavolina* (above).

Grano dolce or **di Santa Lucia** See *cuccìa* (page 291).

Impanatiglie modicane Ravioli made with dough that has been sweetened with Marsala wine and filled with chopped meat, almonds, chocolate, walnuts, sugar, cinnamon and cloves.

Iris con ricotta Small, dry rolls, the interiors of which have been pulled out before soaking in milk. They're then filled with ricotta cream, dipped in eggs, covered with flour and breadcrumbs and fried; typical of Palermo.

Latte di mandorle A beverage made with ground almonds. It's diluted with chilled water to drink.

Luna di Maometto Half-moon-shaped pastry filled with honey, sugar, Marsala wine, dried figs, walnuts and chopped almonds.

Mandolini A mixture of honey, flour, water and cinnamon that is cooked, then formed into a cylinder shape, cut into slices, garnished with almonds and baked.

Marzapane Marzipan. Made with egg whites, sweet almonds and sugar; also called pasta reale or pasta di mandorle. The name comes from the Arabic, *mauthaban*, which means a coin; it came to mean a measure and finally the container in which the marzipan was preserved. In Sicily, marzipan is traditionally made into beautiful fruit, vegetable and other edible product shapes and polished with colored Arabic gum resin to finish; also known as *frutta alla Martorana* (page 292).

Mazaresi al pistacchio Oval, "meditation" pastries (so-called because they go well with a glass of Malvasia or vino passito, wines meant to be sipped slowly in a mood of contemplation) made with pistachios and orange peel.

Minni 'i virgini (mammelle di vergine) The name refers to the sweet's similarity to a young breast. The short crust pastries, from Catania, are filled with ricotta, chocolate and candied squash then topped with lemon glaze. They are made for the feast of Sant'Agata.

Mostaccioli or **mustazzoli di Messina** Antique recipe for dry cookies that keep for a long time made with almonds, cinnamon and cloves.

Mostaccioli or **mustazzolidi Modica** Cookies made with flour, water, vino cotto or reduced honey, rolled out on a marble board, cut into diamond shapes, covered with almonds and honey and then baked; also called rami i meli.

Mostarda A conserve made by cooking together grape must or prickly pear juice. They're put into specific terra cotta molds and sun-dried.

Nacatuli liparesi Small pasta bundles filled with pounded almonds, rose water and sugar.

Occhietti di Santa Lucia Pastries made with a thin sheet of dough made with flour, egg, milk and sugar. The pastry sheet is covered with sugar, then rolled and sliced; the slices are fried then covered with sugar.

Orzata A refreshing beverage made with barley sprouts, almonds and sugar diluted in water. Orzata is also a syrup made with sweet almonds and melon seeds.

Pasta reale See *marzapane* (page 292).

Petramennula or **petrafennula** A candy made by boiling honey with orange peel, then adding chopped almonds. The mixture is spread out and left to solidify before it's cut into pieces.

Pignoccata Small pasta balls fried in lardo, held together with honey diluted with orange-blossom water, then made into a cone shape and garnished with cinnamon; at one time the traditional sweet served on Sunday during the Carnival period in the southeastern part of Sicily.

Pignolata Fried or baked pastry balls. One half is dipped in sugar glaze, the other half in chocolate glaze then the two balls are pressed together to form a bi-color cone shape.

Piparelli Toasted cookies made with almond flour, honey, sugar, lardo, cloves, orange peel and black pepper.

Pizzicata di Palermo Small fried balls of pastry held together with honey and candied fruit.

Purciddata See *buccellato siciliano* (page 290).

Sanfirrìccia or **sanfurrìccia** See *ciaurrina* (page 290).

Sciuretti di Siracusa A type of sweet quenelle made with stiffly beaten egg whites and sugar poached in milk, then served covered in pistachio cream.

Scumuni Chocolate or pistachio ice cream filled with zabaione.

Sfinci or **sfince di San Giuseppe** Small, fried doughnuts filled with ricotta cream and sprinkled with vanilla-flavored sugar.

Sfoglia madonita A short crust tart filled with sweet cheese.

Spongata Assorted gelati held together with a liqueur.

Spongato di caffè Coffee-flavored crushed ice served with whipped cream.

Trionfo di gola A very elaborate Sicilian cake made by spreading apricot and pistachio jam on sponge cake. It's topped with a layer of short crust pastry spread with either pastry cream or ricotta cream mixed with citron and candied squash. The cake is finished with a layer of marzipan.

WINES

Sicilian wines may be compared to the intoxicating nectars described in mythological tales. Alongside the island's stunning dessert wines, Marsala, Moscato and Malvasia, you'll find persuasive dry whites and hearty reds reminiscent of wines found in continental Italy. The wines are symbols of the dual soul of the region that lies between the Orient and Occident.

Alcamo With its slightly green color and light, fruity perfume, similar to the white wines found in central Italy, this dry wine should be consumed when still young, chilled. It's good with local fish and vegetable dishes.

Cerasuolo di Vittoria The beautiful, pale, cherry red color of this wine, made with Frappato di Vittoria and Calabrese varietals, comes from briefly macerating the grape skins. It's dry, with a winey aroma, a wine that goes with high-quality food but also with lamb and beef roll-ups filled with salami and caciocavallo cheese.

Corvo From one of the oldest and most famous wineries in Sicily, Duca di Salaparuta in the province of Palermo. The straw-colored Bianco is fruity, dry and lightly acidic, not only a splendid accompaniment to fish but also to more complex and refined dishes. The Rosso is a brilliant ruby red and emits penetrating aromas. It's full and harmoniously flavored and goes well with local meat dishes like farsu magru or l'agglassato alla palermitana — but not too well with international cuisine. It's also produced in a sparkling version.

Etna A wine from vines planted on the slopes of the volcanic Mt. Etna. The Bianco is pale straw colored with golden reflections and a fruity, fresh flavor. It goes well with all fish dishes — even the most complex ones like *sarde a beccafico* (page 285), or stuffed calamari, or mixed, fried seafood. The Rosato has a winey aroma and dry flavor. It goes well with fish soups and dishes made with tuna. The Rosso is a beautiful ruby red when it's young and tends towards garnet as it ages. It's full flavored with an intense aroma and stands up well to aged cured meats and robust meat dishes.

Faro A ruby red wine with brick reflections produced in the hills around Messina. It has an ethereal aroma and dry flavor. It's a medium-structured wine but if well vinified, it gains strength and becomes a good wine to serve with roast meat and game.

Malvasia delle Lipari The Malvasia varietal born in the archipelago of the Aeolian and Lipari islands. A golden nectar with amber reflections and the aroma of yellow fruits, it has a sweet, ample and persuasive flavor that lingers in the mouth. It's produced in two versions — a natural, passito (wine made from raisins and semi-dried grapes) and a fortified passito. The fortified version has almost 20% alcohol content, making it more a liqueur than a wine. It goes well with cannoli or with cassata; it's also a great "meditation" and in-between-meals wine, especially the fortified version.

Marsala In 1773 the English merchant, John Woodhouse, came to Sicily looking for new experiences and business. As soon as he tasted Marsala wine, he realized its potential and began to produce it, using the same technique used for two other wines that are much loved by the English — Madeira and Sherry. The must is left to oxidize in barrels with *sifone* — cooked must — then fortified with alcohol and transferred to smaller barrels to age. The best wines — the *selezionati* — are aged with a Solera system which consists of decanting and blending younger wines with older ones, a way to keep the wine of a consistent quality. It's a complete success. The five-year-old Marsala Vergine is a product of this method. It's a warm amber-colored wine that emits lingering aromas of broom, almond and wood with a round, soft fundamentally dry flavor. Marsala is not, despite what many people believe, only a dessert wine. Its real strength is as an aperitif or as a between-meal beverage. However, the best marriage is with veined cheeses because of the decisive contrasting flavors.

Moscato A descendant of the antique Bibliano produced in the hills around Siracusa. Grapes are collected during a late harvest, then left to dry in lofts. The amber-colored, full, sweetly flavored wine is vinified with sugar or added alcohol. It's a classic dessert wine that goes well with regional sweets made with marzipan. Moscato di Noto is less sweet but more fragrant. It's pale yellow and can also be sparkling. It goes well with fruit salads and all desserts made with fruit. Last, but not least, is Moscato di Pantelleria, produced on the eponymous island. It's made with the Zibibbo varietal that grows in holes dug into the terrain to protect the vines from the sun and wind. The dry island climate allows the grape sugar to concentrate, making a very sweet, amber-colored wine with a persistent aroma. If the must from the drying and fermenting grapes is corrected with Moscato brandy, it becomes a traditional passito—a fortified wine with 24% alcohol content. The highly structured wine holds its own with gelato desserts without competing with them. The natural Moscato goes well with dry pastries and sharp and veined cheeses.

Regaleali The name of the former fiefdom where the varietals that make these wines originate. The freshly flavored and delicately fragrant Bianco is straw colored with golden reflections, good with fish and vegetable antipasti and perfect with pasta con le sarde. The dry, pale ruby red Rosso and Rosato have winey aromas and marry well with meat dishes.

Pasta con le sarde

Serves 6

6–8 sprigs wild fennel
1 large onion, finely chopped
Olive oil
4 salted anchovies
1½ ounces raisins
1 ounce pine nuts
2½ ounces slivered almonds
2 envelopes powdered saffron
1¾ pounds cleaned, fresh sardines
3½ ounces toasted breadcrumbs made
    from the white part only
1⅓ pounds pasta (bucatini or perciatelli)
Salt and pepper

Bring a large pot of salted water to a boil. Add the fennel and cook for a few minutes. Remove the fennel and reserve the flavored water. Chop the fennel.

Sauté the chopped onion in olive oil in a large skillet. Add the anchovies; after they melt add the raisins, pine nuts and almonds. Dissolve the saffron in a bit of warm water and add to the skillet. Remove from the heat. In another pan, quickly sauté the sardines in a bit of olive oil, then carefully remove them from the pan. Fry the cooked fennel, then add back the sardines and mash them with the back of a wooden spoon. Cook the pasta in the fennel-flavored water. Dress them with the onion sauce and some of the fennel. Layer the dressed pasta in a serving dish with fennel and breadcrumbs, finishing with the sardines. Add freshly ground pepper to taste. Let it rest for ten minutes before serving. If you want to serve it hot — even though it's good at room temperature or cold — let it rest in a warm oven.

Suggested wine: Etna Superiore bianco

SARDEGNA (SARDINIA)

Sardinian cuisine can't be clearly defined. It's a combination of the culinary traditions left on the island by the people who have lived there—Phoenicians, Spanish, Genovese and, most recently, Piemontese.

The most important element in the Sardinian diet is bread. Imbued with symbolism, it is held in such high esteem that it's never cut with a knife but is instead—so as not to dishonor its value—broken by hand. It's almost impossible to list all the breads of the region because every province, city and town has its own version. There are specific shapes that are eaten at weddings, births, funerals or on feast days. Bread is made with de sceddi (sifted flour), crivaxiu (bran), orzatu (barley) or de simbula (semolina). The island's grain production has given birth to not only bread but also to unique pasta shapes: angiolottus, cullurzones, filindeu and malloreddus.

It's hard to believe that the Sardinians, surrounded by the sea, have an instinctive aversion to the water; the region's fishing industry has more or less been put in the hands of Sicilians, Neapolitans, Ponzesi (from the island of Ponza) and the Catalani (from the city of Alghero on the island's northwest coast). Sardinians know how to cook the daily catch, however—wonderful seafood and fish dishes are found all over the island. Whole, ungutted and unscaled fish are roasted to tasty perfection, filled with the flavor of the sea.

Mutton and pork are spit-roasted on aromatic wood such as juniper or myrtle, which imparts its flavor to the meat. This technique is called *furria furria* ("quickly") because the meat is constantly turning on the spit. Although many Sardinians aren't familiar with it, one preparation for roast meats, the malloru de su sabatteri ("bull of the shoemaker"), may be the most memorable: a small bull or calf is stuffed with a wild goat or a suckling pig, which has been stuffed with a hare, which has been stuffed with partridges stuffed with two little birds. The thread that's used to sew up this "pregnant" animal is the same type that's used by shoemakers—hence the name.

Sardinia produces thousands of cheeses. The many varieties are served every day at every meal, from antipasti and first courses through the end of the meal (often with the exquisite, slightly bitter Sardinian honey, miele di corbezzolo). Dairy products include yogurt, which is not, as might be expected, a recent addition to the island's culinary tradition; instead, it dates back a thousand years to the time when there were Roman colonies in Bulgaria.

The flavorful vegetables and fragrant herbs grown on the island include cardoons, artichokes, potatoes, thyme, mint and basil. Regional sweets are excellent and include the unique-in-all-of-Italy sebadas, a cheese-filled pastry served hot, covered with very sweet honey.

ANTIPASTI, CURED MEAT, BREADS, FLATBREADS AND SAVORY TARTS

Bottarga or **buttariga** Salted, cured fish eggs made into a flattened salami shape; the most popular and delicately flavored version is made with the eggs of the female mullet. It's covered in wax to age. Bottarga made with tuna eggs tastes like the sea. Both types are eaten thinly sliced, dressed and added to salads, especially ones made with tomatoes and celery. It's also grated and used as a topping on spaghetti. The most prestigious version comes from the island of Carloforte, just off the west coast of Sardinia, in the province of Cagliari; it's also produced in Liguria, Calabria and Sicily.

Capponata An antipasto with Ligurian origins made with sailor's biscuits (gallete da marinaio) soaked in vinegar and water, then covered with sliced tomatoes, tuna and olive oil. It's very popular on the island of Carloforte in the province of Cagliari where many immigrants from Genoa live.

Carta da musica Very thin and crunchy long-lasting Sardinian bread made with semolina and white flours, water and yeast.

Casadinas salate Little bowl-shaped pasta shapes filled with fresh cheese and mint.

Cocciula a schiscionera Small clams (*arselle*, page 317), cooked with olive oil, garlic and parsley, then finished with a sprinkling of breadcrumbs.

Coccois de Gerda A particularly tasty flatbread enriched with pork cracklings or pieces of lardo, salty cheese and fresh mint.

Cocoi Durum wheat bread best known for its jagged surface.

Gioga minuda Land snails cooked in garlic-flavored water, then again in tomato sauce.

Impanadas Calzones filled with chopped meat, peas, artichokes, olives and other vegetables.

Merca A special salami made with mullet, then tied with eel grass (*salicornia*). The time it needs to age depends upon the saltiness of the fish. Merca is mostly found in the area around the saltwater ponds of the town of Cabras in the province of Oristano.

Mugheddu Salted, dried and smoked mullet that's dressed with olive oil, vinegar, garlic and parsley to serve.

Pane carasau Very thin, circular-shaped bread made with durum wheat flour. It's left to rise, baked, then cut into two and baked again — *carasare* means twice baked. It's very similar to *carta da musica* (page 299) and is found throughout the province of Nuoro.

Pane d'orzo Flat rolls made with barley flour, water and salt.

Pane di Ozieri Disks of flatbread preserved in stacks.

Pane guttiau *Carta da musica* (page 299) dressed with olive oil and salt; sometimes garlic is added as well. At one time the bread was put under roasting meat so it could be flavored with the dripping fat.

Pesci scabecciau Fried mullet marinated in olive oil, garlic, vinegar and tomatoes.

Pingiadeddas Little semolina pasta and potato timbales filled with fried pork and olives.

Pizza alla cagliaritana Pizza made with a dough of flour, milk, yeast and mashed potatoes. It's topped with fresh cow's milk cheese, tomatoes, anchovies, grated pecorino cheese and oregano.

Spianata The bread from which *carta da musica* (page 299) is made; it's double the size, however, and is not twice baked.

Stripiddi Flatbreads made with barley flour, yeast, water and salt.

Tacculas See page 306.

Torta di fave A type of frittata made with eggs, breadcrumbs, sugar and fresh fava beans.

PASTA, GNOCCHI, RICE, POLENTA AND GRAINS

Angiolottus or **anzolottos** Sardinian ravioli made with durum wheat dough filled with very fresh sheep's milk cheese, spinach or chard, eggs and saffron — usually not meat, but it can vary. They're dressed with tomato sauce and cheese — but sometimes meat sauce.

Cascà or **cascasa** Couscous served with a vegetable sauce made with peas, cauliflower, etc. and spiced chopped meat. This dish is found on the island of Carloforte in the province of Cagliari where most of the residents are descendents of the Genoese who, before coming to Sardinia, lived for almost two hundred years on an island along the Tunisian coast called Tabarca.

Ciciones Small dumplings made with semolina, water and a pinch of saffron; typical of the province of Sassari and similar to *malloreddus* (below).

Culingiones, culurjones, cullurzones, gurigliones Ravioli similar to *angiolottus* (page 300), half-moon shapes filled with potatoes, pecorino cheese, garlic and mint; found in the province of Ogliastra.

Filindeu A type of angel hair pasta from the province of Nuoro. In this case the name means "God's hair." Its manufacture is a rather complicated process. The dough is made with finely ground durum wheat, water and salt. After it's made, very tender pieces of the dough are pulled away and stretched, by hand, until they reach almost one meter in length. This process is repeated until all the dough is used then each length is made into thin sheets, pidzos. The sheets of pasta are left to dry, then cut into pieces and used to make a soup with mutton broth and very fresh, slightly acidic cheese. These days, it's difficult to find this dish; you may run across it at festivals in and around the mountainous interior of Barbagia.

Maccarones a ferritus Pasta made by wrapping dough, made with durum flour and water, around a knitting needle (*ferritus*) or a reed to form its shape. Among its most popular dressings are ricotta cheese, fresh pecorino cheese, tomato sauce, meat sauce or a walnut sauce similar to one used in Liguria.

Malloreddus Dialect for a popular pasta (it means "calves") also called gnocchetti sardi, ciciones, aidos and cravaos. The dough is made with semolina, water, salt and saffron that is first made into little stick shapes, then pressed against the *ciurliri*, a sieve made with reeds, to form their final shape. Traditionally, they're made in three different colors: yellow, red and green. They're dressed with tomato sauce, lamb or sausage ragù and pecorino sardo cheese.

Ministru A dish made with angel hair pasta or semolina dressed with casu ispiattadu (fresh cooked cheese), sausage and ciccioli (dried pork fat).

Pillas or **pillus** Sheets of pasta made with semolina, milk, butter, eggs and nutmeg that are then layered with a rich meat ragù and pecorino cheese and gratinéed to serve.

Polenta alla sarda A type of polenta pie made with Sardinian sausage and cheese.

Spaghetti alla carlofortina Spaghetti dressed with pieces of tuna browned in olive oil, anchovies and chopped olives. It's a specialty of the island of Carloforte in the province of Cagliari, known for its tuna fishing industry.

Spighitta Ravioli similar to *angiolottus* (page 300). The dough is made with semolina and water and the filling with boiled potatoes, brined pecorino cheese, garlic and fresh mint. They're shaped like little squashed figs and sealed at the edges in a herringbone pattern.

SOUPS

Ambulau Soup made with barley flour and flavored with onions and vinegar.

Cassòla A term that refers not only to various tomato-based stews, but also to a fish soup (and the name of the pot in which it's cooked) found all over Sardinia's west coast. The very rich soup is made with olive oil, garlic, onions, hot pepper flakes, tomatoes and basil; at least twelve different types of fin fish, crustaceans and shellfish are then added including conger eel, scorpion fish, clams, octopus, calamari, crabs, etc.

Cavolata or **caulada** A rustic soup made with cabbage, sausages, dried fava beans, lardo, veal and pork flavored with mint, wild fennel and garlic.

Curritholata Bean soup flavored with wild fennel, lardo, potatoes and sausages, found throughout the province of Nuoro.

Farru or **su farru** An antique peasant recipe made with cooked farro to which milk and broth is then added. It's flavored with fresh mint leaves.

Fasoli ghisau Bean soup made with tomatoes and onions.

Favata Dried fava beans cooked with lardo, sausages, pork rind, pork ribs, wild fennel, scallions, tomatoes, garlic, mint or basil, parsley and sage.

Fregula Little pasta balls made with flour, water and saffron, then cooked in broth and covered with brined, fresh pecorino cheese. In another version, without cheese, fregula is cooked in a fish and vegetable broth flavored with fresh mint.

Lepudrida A substantial meat and vegetable soup made throughout the province of Cagliari based on the Spanish pork, bean and vegetable stew called olla podrida.

Mazzamurru Slices of soaked, stale semolina bread layered with tomato sauce and grated pecorino cheese.

Minestra di frue Vegetable soup enriched with *frue* cheese (page 308).

Pane frattau *Carta da musica* or *pane carasau* (pages 299 and 300) that has been soaked in boiling water or broth, then placed directly into individual soup plates and covered with squashed tomatoes, tomato sauce or lamb ragù and grated pecorino cheese. It's topped with a poached egg.

Patedda Broth made with wild boar, veal, mutton, goat, squab and vegetables and served with egg pasta and grated pecorino cheese.

Pisci a collettu A dense soup made with dried fava beans and garlic, found throughout the province of Cagliari.

Succu tundu Similar to *fregula* (page 302).

Suppa quatta Slices of bread and slices of cheese that are layered, then covered with a lamb and vegetable broth; a specialty of the Gallura area in the province of Olbia-Tempio.

Zuppa alla gallurese Sliced bread layered with sliced, fresh, slightly acidic cheese, chopped lardo, garlic, parsley and pepper, then covered with mutton broth. It's gratinéed to serve.

Zuppa di finocchietti selvatici Soup made with bread, cheese and cooked wild fennel. It's diluted with the fennel's cooking water. Sometimes chickpeas and potatoes are added.

CONDIMENTS, SAUCES, SALSAS AND EGGS

Mazzafrissa Cream cooked in a casserole with flour and water. It's watched very carefully while it cooks so no lumps form. The substantial amount of fat that rises to the top is used as a condiment with hot flatbreads; it may also be used to dress pastas, to flavor boiled fava beans or as an accompaniment for a salad.

FISH, CRUSTACEANS AND SHELLFISH

Bucconis A type of large sea snail (murici) blanched and dressed with olive oil, lemon juice, salt and pepper to serve.

Burrida The Sardinian way of serving dogfish (gattuccio) and other fish in the shark family, or skate. The fish is poached in an aromatic vegetable broth then dressed with a sauce made with olive oil, garlic, vinegar, pine nuts and walnuts. It's usually eaten the day after it's marinated in the sauce. Even though some people say the liver of the dogfish is toxic, a true Sardinian won't sit down to eat this dish if the fresh, raw liver of the fish isn't included in its preparation.

Cassola Soup made with a mixture of fish including scorpion fish, white bream, mullet, sea bass, kingfish, eel, cuttlefish, clams, sea snails, etc. cooked with onions, garlic, fresh or sun-dried tomatoes, parsley, basil and hot pepper flakes; a specialty of Cagliari.

Filatrota or **filatrotta** A type of large eel similar to a conger eel that is fished just as it's ready to enter the sea to reproduce; often cooked with seaweed — either salicornia or zibba.

Lattume Part of the reproductive organs of a tuna. In Sassari it's cut into pieces and fried; in Cagliari it's roasted.

Orata alla vernaccia Sea bass stewed with fresh tomatoes and Vernaccia wine.

Panada di anguille A timbale made by filling pasta dough, made with white or semolina flour, lardo and salt, with layers of sun-dried tomatoes preserved in olive oil, pieces of eel and parsley.

Pesce arrosto alla sarda Fish that is brined in hot salt water for a few minutes before it's grilled over a wood-burning fire. It's scaled and gutted to serve. This is how Sardinians prefer to cook fish — whole, complete with scales, gills and guts. They feel this method protects the fish's flavor.

Surra Tuna belly.

Triglie alla vernaccia Mullet fillets placed on a sauce made with fresh tomatoes, olive oil, garlic and parsley, then covered with very thin lemon slices and Vernaccia wine.

Trote nelle felci A captivating, almost primordial recipe made with whole trout (not gutted, not scaled) placed on smoldering firewood, then covered with ferns and buried with a thin layer of earth. When they've cooked for about half an hour, they're removed, cleaned and served. They have a unique flavor and aroma.

MEATS

Agnello con finocchietti Pieces of lamb cooked in a casserole with olive oil, tomatoes and onions. The dish is flavored with boiled wild fennel and its cooking water. This is a typical springtime dish in the province of Nuoro.

Bombas Meatballs stewed in tomatoes and onions.

Brent'e sanguni The word used in the provinces of Ogliastra and Nuoro to describe *zurrette* (page 307).

Carrargiu or **carraxiu** A unique preparation made by stuffing a suckling pig or kid with game birds — thrushes, blackbirds, partridges, etc. — and garlic, bay leaf, juniper berries, rosemary, thyme, oregano and wild mint. The animal is bound with aromatic branches then buried in a hole lined with stones placed on embers. The whole thing is covered with earth and then another fire is lit over the top. The extraordinary roast is ready to eat after it cooks for four or five hours. *Carraxiu* means buried.

Cinghiale alla montagnina Wild boar stew made with pieces of meat that have been marinated in red wine, celery, carrots, garlic, rosemary and marjoram then cooked in a casserole with olive oil, onions, the wine from the marinade and black olives. The dish is a specialty of the mountains in the province of Nuoro.

Coccoiddus A stew, a specialty of the province of Sassari, made with large land snails cooked with olive oil, garlic, parsley, tomatoes and basil.

Coiettas Cabbage leaf roll-ups filled with meat ragù, or beef roll-ups filled with finely chopped garlic, lardo and parsley simply cooked in a skillet.

Cordula, corda or **cordedda** Braids or skeins of lamb or kid's guts that are grilled, stewed with peas or baked with potatoes. In the town of Oliena in the province of Nuoro the cordula is made by loading a skewer with pieces of lamb's or kid's liver, lungs, spleen, etc. and pieces of lardo, then covering it, for protection, with braided guts. The skewers are spit-roasted to serve.

Gallina al mirto A boiled hen covered with myrtle branches then chilled for two days before serving.

Ghisau Beef pot roast cooked with tomatoes, onions and potatoes. It's typical of the province of Alghero and reminiscent of the Spanish guisado.

Giogga Small land snails.

Gran premio Interesting name for a boned horsemeat steak that's grilled to serve.

Grive Spit-roasted, myrtle-flavored thrushes. The cooked birds may be preserved in olive oil.

Impanadas Small timbales filled with chopped lamb and pork, sun-dried tomatoes, parsley and saffron.

Is longus Grilled or spit-roasted cow or ox guts.

Longus and **manareddas** Two different types of veal guts that are cleaned, defatted, turned inside out, cut into pieces, then fried or roasted to serve.

Malloro Veal.

Monzette The name, in the province of Sassari, for land snails that are gathered in the wintertime during their hibernation.

Padedda A very brothy stew made with beef, chicken and squab cooked with celery, onions, tomatoes and parsley. The broth is used as soup and the meat as an entrée.

Pastu mistu A large turkey stuffed with a chicken or hare then bound with fragrant branches and cooked in the earth on top of aromatic wood.

Pernice alla sarda Partridge that is boiled, then cut into pieces and marinated in olive oil, vinegar, parsley and capers. It's served at room temperature with potatoes and its broth on the side. In Sardinia, partridges are also preserved in olive oil.

Pilafi or **pilau** Pot-roasted kid cooked with olive oil, lardo, thyme, bay leaf, rosemary, garlic and white wine. The cooked kid is removed from the cooking liquid and set aside. The liquid is then thickened with egg yolks beaten with fresh lemon juice and used to dress boiled rice that is served with the kid.

Pingiada or **pignatta** Stew made with a mixture of mutton, beef, kid, squab and wild boar cooked with onions, celery and parsley.

Piocu a carraxiu See *pastu mistu* (above).

Porceddu The Sardinian name for roast or baked suckling pig. It's not exactly easy to prepare. You need a top-quality pig, the spit needs to be made with *corbezzolo* (strawberry tree) and the fire on which it's roasted must be made with an aromatic wood such as juniper, myrtle, olive, laurel, etc. The pig itself may be flavored with myrtle, thyme, bay leaf and wild fennel. As it spit-roasts, it's basted with lardo. It must be served hot with very crispy skin. It's covered in myrtle branches — adding yet another flavor — and served at room temperature or cold.

Puddighinos Dialect for roast chickens stuffed with their own chopped gizzards mixed with hard-cooked egg yolks, breadcrumbs, cream and chopped sun-dried tomatoes.

Schidoni Spit-roasted skewers of assorted meats. Sometimes chunks of cheese are added as well.

Sizzigorrus Land snails stewed with olive oil, onions and tomatoes. The sauce is flavored with oregano and bound together with breadcrumbs.

Spinu Cut-up pieces of pork ribs cooked with olive oil, garlic, parsley, bay leaf, white wine and black olives.

Succhittu de conillu A stew made by browning pieces of rabbit in olive oil, garlic and parsley that is then enriched with capers and olives.

Tacculas Boiled then drained thrushes enclosed with tender myrtle branches in cloth bags. They're eaten at room temperature—even as an antipasto—after two days. This is a rarely made rustic dish. Its name refers to a brace of eight or twelve thrushes or blackbirds.

Tappadas The word used in Cagliari for *monzette* (page 305).

Trattalìa or **tattaliu** Sheep or lamb innards (liver, lungs, heart, sweetbreads) that are loaded onto skewers with pieces of lardo, bay leaves and chunks of bread. The skewers are covered with pork caul and braided guts, then spit-roasted over a wood-burning fire.

Uscellè Lamb innards (liver, lungs, heart, sweetbreads) cut into pieces and cooked in a casserole with olive oil, onions and vinegar.

Ziminada A stew made with veal innards and meat, onions, tomatoes and other herbs and flavorings sautéed in olive oil, then finished with chopped garlic and parsley.

Zurrette Lamb's stomach filled with the animal's blood, sautéed lardo, bread and fresh, acidic cheese. It's tied up, boiled and served hot.

VEGETABLES

Asparagi selvatici alla sarda Thin and extremely tasty asparagus found in the woods. They are boiled, then sautéed in olive oil, lemon juice, anchovies and parsley to serve.

Carciofi al verde Artichoke wedges cooked with water, olive oil, garlic and parsley, then finished with beaten eggs.

Cardi alla sarda Parboiled cardoons placed in a baking dish, covered with chopped hard-cooked eggs, parsley and sautéed breadcrumbs and briefly baked to serve.

Fagioli alla gallurese Beans stewed with wild fennel, savoy cabbage, onions and tomatoes and finished with chopped lardo and parsley.

Frittelle di finocchio Fritters of boiled, chopped wild fennel tops that are added to an egg batter then fried by the spoonful.

Pomodori ripieni alla sarda Tomatoes, cut in half, seeded and baked, then filled with a mixture of sardines, eggplant cooked in olive oil, tuna and butter. They're covered with breadcrumbs, then gratinéed to serve.

Tuvuras di is arenas or **tartufi di sabbia** A very rare sand truffle. Its scientific name is *terfetia*. It's possible to find them, with lots of good luck and ability, along the sandy coastline near the city of Oristano. They have rough skins and soft, pink flesh. They may be marinated in white wine (Vernaccia) then cooked with butter, garlic, onions and parsley.

Zucchine a cassola Zucchini cooked with olive oil, onions, parsley, basil and sometimes tomatoes. Just before the dish is taken off the heat, it's covered with fresh, acidic cheese.

CHEESE AND DAIRY PRODUCTS

Bonassai A fresh, fatty soft-bodied cheese curdled with cow's milk. It's square with a fine-lined white, slightly straw-colored rind. Its buttery body is white and compact with a slightly acidic flavor similar to yogurt.

Caciotta pecorina An aromatic, sweetly flavored, cylinder-shaped fresh sheep's milk cheese.

Calcagno A raw, hard-bodied cheese curdled with goat's milk, sometimes mixed with sheep's milk. This sharp, pungent cheese is eaten fresh or aged.

Casu marzu or **muchidu** A type of Sardinian pecorino cheese that has been aged in a way to allow the flavor to become very strong. It has a creamy body. Often maggots are present.

Cazu Dried, suckling lamb's stomach. It's heated up a bit to make it creamy before it's consumed. This strongly flavored product is eaten by the spoonful.

Dolce di macomer Soft, low-fat cow's milk cheese.

Dolce sardo Cow's milk cheese produced in the area around the town of Arborea in the province of Oristano.

Dolce Tirso Cow's milk cheese produced in the province of Oristano.

Fiore Sardo A typical, raw, hard-bodied Sardinian cheese made with whole cow's milk. It's unusual shape is that of two truncated cones joined at their wider base. It's a more or less sharply flavored cheese, depending on how long it has aged.

Fresa Fresh, buttery cow's milk cheese, very similar to stracchino, made into flat, round forms. The best versions are produced in the fall in the town of Macomer in the province of Nuoro.

Frue See *viscidu* (page 309).

Gioddu or **juncata** A fresh, curdled sheep, goat or cow's milk cheese with a flavor similar to yogurt.

Gioghittus de casu Literally "toys made from cheese" — soft cheese made into little horse, goat or statue shapes.

Merca The word used in the province of Nuoro for *viscidu* (page 309).

Pecorino semicotto Cylinder-shaped, semi-cooked sheep's milk cheese ripened in a basket. It has a smooth rind and a compact, white to straw-colored body. Its aroma and sweet flavor become more intense as it ages.

Taedda Cow's milk caciocavallo.

Viscidu Sliced, curdled goat's milk cheese preserved in brine. Its acidic flavor makes it a perfect accompaniment to tomatoes.

SWEETS AND LIQUEURS

Amaretti sardi Cookies made with chopped sweet and bitter almonds, egg whites and sugar. They're distinguished from other amaretti by their large size. The most notable Sardinian amaretti come from the island of Carloforte in the province of Cagliari and from Oristano.

Angulis Ring-shaped Easter cakes from Carloforte decorated with painted eggs in their shells.

Anicini Dry, anise-flavored cookies usually served with a glass of Vernaccia di Oristano wine.

Aranzada A mixture of candied orange peel, almonds and honey usually made into triangular or nest shapes and served on orange leaves. It's a specialty of Nuoro.

Arrubiòlus Fried doughnuts made with a mixture of fresh, slightly acidic cheese, fine semolina, eggs, sugar, orange zest and saffron.

Bianchittus Meringues with almonds or hazelnuts and grated lemon zest.

Biscotti di Sorgono Stick-shaped cookies made with flour, sugar, egg yolks and stiffly beaten egg whites. They're covered with powdered sugar just before baking.

Bugnoletti di patate Fritters made with puréed potatoes, sugar, flour, eggs and grated lemon zest.

Caefus Little balls made with finely chopped chocolate and almonds that are rolled in sugar and colored sprinkles.

Candelaus Little bowls made with dense sugar syrup and chopped almonds that are baked and then glazed. They're filled with a mixture of sugar, almonds, egg whites, lemon zest and orange blossom water. In some areas of Sardinia the candelaus are made into amphora, animal and flower shapes.

Casadinas The southern version of *pardulas* (page 311). They may be made into little pasta bowls that are filled with fresh cheese and mint. There are savory versions as well.

Caschéttas Rectangular pastries made with flour, water

and lardo, then filled with honey, oranges and hazelnuts or almonds.

Casgjatìni Little pasta bowls filled with a mixture of caciocavallo or sardo cheese, ricotta cheese, eggs, sugar, orange and lemon zest. They're a specialty of the village of Luogosanto in the province of Sassari.

Cattas The Sardinian word for zeppole (see *zippulas*, page 312).

Cocciuleddas de meli Little snail-shaped pastries, a specialty of Gallura in the northeast area of Sardinia, made with a simple dough filled with a mixture of walnuts, candied orange zest, almonds, cinnamon, cocoa and honey.

Copuleddas Little pastries filled with a mixture of stiffly beaten egg whites, sugar and chopped almonds.

Culingionis dolci Large rectangular ravioli filled with a mixture of sugar, almonds, lemon zest, vanilla and orange blossom water, then fried.

Filu 'e ferru Brandy or "*acqua di Sardegna.*"

Gattò Almond and chopped-lemon brittle.

Gesminus Cookies made with sugar, stiffly beaten egg whites, almonds, lemon juice and orange blossom water. They're a specialty of the city of Quartu Sant'Elena in the province of Cagliari and the Campidano plain in southwestern Sardinia.

Gueffus Round candies, a specialty of Quartu Sant'Elena, made with almond flour, sugar syrup, lemon zest, orange blossom water and a special liqueur called Villacidro.

Marigosos Special little meringues flavored with almonds and grated orange zest.

Meravìglias Fried pastries made in the shape of a hand with fingers spread apart, often covered with orange- or lemon-peel-infused bitter honey.

Mirto Sardinian liqueur *per eccellenza* made with an infusion of myrtle berries and leaves. It's delicious served with sliced peaches.

Niuleddas de meli Small, soft nougats made with candied orange zest, walnuts, almonds, pieces of *carta da musica* (page 299), cinnamon, honey, cocoa and other ingredients.

Opinus Cone-shaped pastries composed of balls of fried pastry held together with honey, orange and lemon zest and orange blossom water.

Orullettas Fried nests, bows or other shapes made with tagliatelle, then covered with loose honey.

Pabassinas di Cagliari A mixture of raisins, chopped walnuts, slivered almonds, pieces of orange peel, aniseeds and nutmeg bound together with sapa (cooked grape must), then baked. The baked sweets are dipped in sapa then covered with colored sprinkles. Besides Cagliari, they're also made, with some variations, in Sassari and the town of Ghilarza in the province of Oristano.

Pane di sapa Little rolls with sapa, cinnamon, cloves, walnuts and pine nuts mixed into its dough. The baked rolls are covered with sapa and sprinkles.

Papassinas di Nuoro Diamond-shaped pastries made with flour, raisins, almonds, lardo, sugar, eggs, grated orange and lemon zests, baked and then glazed with egg whites and sugar.

Pappai biancu The same as the Sicilian *biancomangiare* (page 290). It's made with wheat or rice starch, milk, lemon peel and orange blossom water.

Pardulas Small pastry baskets, made at Easter, filled with fresh cheese and saffron. They may be served with honey.

Pastissus Pastries filled with a mixture of sugar, almonds and eggs and finished with a simple glaze.

Pirichittus Little pastry logs covered with a sugar and lemon glaze.

Pistiddu di Doraglia Disks of yeast pastry filled with a mixture of sapa (wine syrup) orange zest and semolina then baked.

Pistoccos finis Classic baptism and first communion cookies made with flour, sugar, eggs, yeast and lardo.

Pompie Candied bitter orange, citron or grapefruit peel.

Quaglio dolce Sweetened milk curdled with lemon.

Sebadas or **seadas** or **sevadas** Large round sweet ravioli filled with fresh, slightly acidic pecorino cheese, fried, then covered with hot honey. This typically Sardinian specialty originated in the town of Oliena in the province of Nuoro.

Suspirus Cookies made with a mixture of chopped almonds cooked with sugar and stiffly beaten egg whites. When the mixture thickens, it's divided into little balls, then baked and covered in a lemon glaze. They are a specialty of the town of Ozieri in the province of Sassari.

Tericas Little rectangular pastries filled with a mixture of almonds, flour, sapa (cooked grape must) and orange peel. The top is slashed open to allow a bit of the filling to escape.

Tiliccas Small round pastries filled with *aranzada* (page 309).

Torta al formaggio A tart filled with lots of grated, fresh, slightly acidic pecorino sardo cheese, flour, sugar, saffron and eggs. It's served hot.

Torta di latte A spoon dessert made with milk, eggs, sugar, vanilla, lemon and amaretti cookies.

Traggera Colored sprinkles.

Tumbada A pudding made with milk, eggs, ground amaretti cookies and lemon juice.

Uvusones Fritters, made at Carnival time, filled with acacia blossom honey mixed with brandy.

Ziddìnis Diamond-shaped pastries filled with a mixture of honey, flour, almonds, orange and lemon peel and cinnamon.

Zippulas Fritters made with flour, yeast, boiled potatoes, eggs, orange juice, milk, brandy, sugar and saffron that are dipped in sugar to serve. They're made at Carnival time.

Zirìccas Little ring-shaped pastries filled with a mixture of prickly pears and flour, then garnished with colored sprinkles. They're a specialty of the town of Sedilo in the province of Oristano.

WINES

Sardinian oenology is filled with contradictions. On one hand, there are the high-quality wines — Sardinian dessert wines are among the most respected in all of Italy. On the other hand, there are too many vintners who have relied on fancy techniques of modern technology while ignoring the wisdom and experience of their predecessors. There's hope, because modern Sardinian winemaking is still very young.

Cannonau Pale red when young, it assumes orange overtones as it ages. It may be dry (a perfect table wine) or slightly sweet (great with local pastries). There are also fortified versions. The dry is perfect with roast game and aged cheese, and the very good sweet — hot and spicy — is an ideal dessert wine.

Carignano di Sulcis Resistant to sea breezes, the Carignano varietal is cultivated along Sardinia's coastline. The Rosso is a strong ruby color. There's a Rosato as well. Both have a winey aroma and a dry, slightly salty flavor. The Rosato is best with cured meat antipasti and first courses and the Rosso goes well with simple meat dishes.

Girò di Cagliari A pale red wine of Spanish origins with a winey aroma, full flavor and velvety texture. The dry version is ideal with cheese and cured meats and the sweet version is very good with local pastries. There are also dry and sweet versions fortified with must alcohol.

Malvasia In antique documents, the Malvasia varietal is called Uva Greca. At one time all the wines of the region with high alcohol content were called Malvasia. Actually, there are two rather famous Malvasie: one is Bosa (barrel-aged), allowing it to ferment and oxidize so that it develops a *flor*, or veil of yeast that gives it its characteristic, sherry-like aroma. It's pale yellow with amber reflections. Its intense aroma has almond overtones and it's decisively sweet, or dry. Malvasia di Cagliari has characteristics similar to the preceding one, but with slightly more acid which makes it less adaptable to oxidation. It's usually removed from barrels just before the warm season. Both wines are incomparable with crustaceans and fish in general. The sweet version goes well with desserts.

Monica Pale red, developing orange overtones as it ages, Monica di Cagliari, with its aroma of withered grapes and velvety flavor, may be dry, sweet or fortified with must alcohol. The dry version goes well with roast meats and the sweet with desserts. Monica di Sardinia is made exclusively in a dry version and goes well with an entire meal.

Moscato Produced, for the most part, in and around Gallura on Sardinia's northeast coast, the grapes of this varietal develop a nice acidic quality from the area's sandy soil. The wine may be sparkling while maintaining a nice, fruity aroma. It's straw colored without golden reflections—unusual for a Sardinian wine. Its lightly sweet flavor makes it a good dessert wine that goes especially well with dry pastries. The most prestigious type is made in the town of Tempio Pausania in the province of Sassari. There's also a golden yellow Moscato di Cagliari with an intense sweetness. The non-sparkling fortified version is perfect with spoon desserts. Moscato di Sorso has a stronger color and flavor than the previous two.

Nasco A yellow gold wine with the characteristic musky aroma and pleasing, slightly bitter vein of the Nuscu varietal. There's also a sweet version. The dry version is perfect with grilled fish, the sweet with desserts and the dry, fortified version is a splendid aperitif.

Nuragus Mature Nuragu grapes are deep red but the wine that's made with them is straw colored with a sour apple aroma and slightly acidic flavor. When at its best, it's sensational with burrida, the local fish soup, or spaghetti with bottarga.

Vermentino Made in the Gallura area with the eponymous

varietal from Liguria, this refined and elegant wine, with its pale color and persistent aroma of the grapes of its varietals, stands out among Sardinian wines. Its slightly bitter taste gives it a fresh flavor despite the high alcohol level. It goes well with all fish dishes.

Vernaccia di Oristano Barrel-aged and oxidized, this wine is amber-colored with an ethereal aroma and a refined, velvety flavor with hints of bitter almonds. The dry version is a great aperitif and a splendid wine with fish dishes. The sweet version is good with desserts and a *vino da meditazione*—a thought-provoking wine—when it's aged.

Pane frattau

Serves 6

1 finely chopped onion
Olive oil
3 tablespoons water
Pinch of saffron
A few parsley or basil leaves and stems
2 pounds peeled and seeded tomatoes
    passed through a food mill
1 teaspoon sugar
Salt and freshly ground black pepper
1 teaspoon vinegar
12 rounds of pane frattau or carta da musica
    or another thin, crunchy bread, broken
    into pieces
1⅓ pounds grated pecorino sardo
6 eggs

Make the tomato sauce: sauté the onion in olive oil over low heat. After about three minutes add the 3 tablespoons water and lightly salt. Continue to cook until the onion is transparent and soft. Soak the saffron in warm water and add to the onions. Add the parsley stems, tomatoes and sugar. Bring to a soft boil and cook until dense—about forty-five minutes. Toward the end, remove the parsley stems and add the leaves, salt and pepper to taste. Bring a large pot of salted water and the vinegar to a boil. In the meantime, add a layer of tomato sauce to the bottom of the soup plates. Sprinkle grated cheese over the sauce. Quickly—so they don't fall apart—soak pieces of the bread in warm water; pull them out and layer on top of the grated cheese. Continue layering each plate with sauce, cheese and bread until all the ingredients are used. Poach the eggs in the vinegar water for three to four minutes. Top each plate with a poached egg and serve immediately.

Suggested wine: Carignano di Sulcis rosato

GLOSSARY

FISH, SHELLFISH AND CRUSTACEANS

Acciughe Anchovies. There are many names for this small bluish-silver fish with a smooth, scaleless belly. They're called amplove in Liguria, sardele or sardon in the Veneto, lilla or magnana in Marches and speronare in Puglia.

Agoni A freshwater fish mostly found in the pre-alpine lakes, Garda and Maggiore.

Aguglia A long, needle-nosed saltwater fish.

Alborelle Very small fish that live close to the surface of bodies of fresh water.

Alici See *acciughe* (above).

Alosa A long saltwater fish also called saracca.

Aragosta Lobster. A crustacean with a reddish, moiré-patterned shell, it's also called agosta or lagusta in Veneto, aligusta in Central Italy and alaustra in Sicily. It's different from the *astice* (below) because it has two antennae while the astice has two claws and is usually a darker color, and its flesh is more refined with a very delicate flavor. Today, many lobsters are farmed.

Arselle Ligurian or Tuscan dialect for clams in general. In some places it can also mean tartufi di mare, Venus clams.

Astice or **astaco** The largest crustacean in the Mediterranean Sea, it has large claws and a spotted deep blue — almost black — shell. When it's cooked the shell becomes scarlet colored. It differs from the aragosta because of its more distinctive flavor and its claws (instead of antennae).

Baccalà In most of Italy, Atlantic Ocean codfish that has been preserved in salt — except in the Veneto, where the word baccalà refers to dried Atlantic Ocean codfish (stoccafisso). The word baccalà is Spanish in origin.

Bianchetti Newborn anchovies or sardines. They can only be fished from December 1 through April 30. During the in-between months rossetti — which stay small even as adults — may be substituted. Rossetti are distinguished from bianchetti by a tiny red spot on the abdomen. The tiny anchovies are called gianchetti in Liguria, nudini or paronzoli in Marches, janculilli in Campania and sfigghiata in Sicily. The tiny sardines are called pontine in Liguria, palassiole in the Veneto, falloppe in Puglia and nunnata in Sicily.

Branzino Sea bass. This saltwater fish is also called spigola, ragno or pesce lupo and is usually found in slightly choppy waters near the coastline; there's also a freshwater type.

Calamari and **calamaretti** Squid. Cephalopods (their shells are inside their bodies) that are often confused with another cephalopod, *totani* (page 325), which has tougher flesh. The ink from both types is inferior to that of the cuttlefish, *seppie* (page 324).

Canestrelli Shellfish very similar to *capesante* (below) or conchiglie di San Giacomo, but a bit smaller. There are two varieties; one of the two is called pettine. They're often sold without their shells.

Cannolicchi Razor clams. In the Veneto they're called cape lunghe, in Liguria maneghi de cutelo, in Sardinia arrasojas, in Romagna cannelli. They live buried in the sand and are quite easy to gather.

Canochie Mantis shrimp, also called pannocchie. They're called canoce in the Veneto, cicale in Tuscany and Liguria, caraviedde in Puglia and astre in Sicily. They're best eaten in the wintertime—the months with "r" in their names—when the presence of eggs in their bodies doubles the edible portion.

Capesante or **cappesante** Scallops. This is the original Venetian name of conchiglie di San Giacomo or Jacopo (coquilles St. Jacques). The shellfish are also called pettini, ventagli, pellegrine or conchiglie del pellegrino. They were found in abundance on the beaches of Galicia in Spain by pilgrims making their way to the sanctuary of Santiago de Compostela. When the pilgrims arrived at the sanctuary, they attached a scallop shell to their walking sticks as a symbol of the journey. The scallop design is often depicted in religious art, especially that which features the Madonna and other saints.

Capitone A large, mature female eel usually eaten on Christmas Eve.

Capone or **cappone** The generic name for a whole group of red, pinkish, orange-and-yellowish or chestnut-colored, bottom-dwelling saltwater fish sometimes called tub gurnard, Tom Grimard or sea robins. The most common varieties are capone coccio, capone lira, capone ubriaco, capone gallinella and capone gurno. There are so many local names for the fish that it can sometimes be confusing—in some regions capone or cappone can be the names for a completely different variety of fish, like in Tuscany, where they may be used interchangeably with scorfano (scorpion fish), or in Puglia where they can be used for lampuga (red snapper). Capone is a firm-fleshed fish with a delicate flavor, similar to the scorfano.

Carpione An antipasto typical of the lake districts in which fish are floured, fried and then marinated with vinegar, onions or garlic and other ingredients. The name comes from an esteemed freshwater fish, the carpione, a trout-like fish related to salmon.

Cavedano Chub, the most common freshwater fish in Italy. It's full of little bones.

Cernia Grouper, a stout saltwater fish with a large mouth. Its high-quality flesh lends itself to many kinds of preparations.

Coda di rospo Monkfish. Coda di rospo is the commercial Italian name for *rana pescatrice* (page 323).

Corvina Croaker, a high-quality saltwater fish similar to the *ombrina* (page 321). Because of its delicate flesh it's sometimes used for the same kinds of preparations as *branzino* (page 317).

Cuore di mare Shellfish named for its beauty (*cuore* means heart, or love). It's yellowish with very thin ribs, but not particularly tasty.

Datteri di mare The common name for a chestnut-colored, small, oval bivalve that looks something like a date. In Italy they're mostly found in the Gulf of La Spezia and in Puglia. They're also found in Istria. Datteri are among the most valuable and sought-after shellfish in the country.

Dentice Red snapper. From the same family as the pagello, the pagro and the sarago, dentice is distinguished by its large, canine teeth — *dente*.

Fasolari Large brick- or chestnut-colored, smooth-shelled clams sometimes called rubber slippers in English. They're known as cappa chione or Venere chione in Italian. They may be eaten raw or in soup.

Fritto di paranza A fried mixture of tiny fish and tiny shellfish found along the coasts of the Adriatic and Tyrrhenian seas. The name comes from fishing boats with sails that worked side by side (*in paranza*), each one pulling a "wing" of the net. The boats were in operation up until the 1950s.

Gallinella The Ligurian name for *capone* (page 318).

Gamberetti Small saltwater shrimp.

Gamberi Shrimp. Gamberi are different from *scampi* (page 324) because of their softer shells and because they have antennae instead of claws. They're delicious when fresh but less refined and delicate than scampi.

Gamberi di fiume Shrimp found in brooks and along riverbanks hiding under rocks and in between the roots of water plants. They're easy to fish at nighttime when they're out looking for food. Unfortunately, they're becoming more difficult to find in Italy because of polluted water. Most of the freshwater shrimp in Italian markets comes from south Asia. Some are farmed. These reddish-black shrimp have claws and harder shells than saltwater shrimp. Their flesh is delicate and refined.

Gamberoni Large shrimp from 20 to 30 centimeters in length. Their decisive taste allows them to be cooked with strongly flavored ingredients.

Gattuccio Dogfish, a spotted pinkish-gray fish.

Gianchetti See *bianchetti* (page 317).

Granciporro or **granchio poro** Similar to the American blue crab, in Venice it's called granzoporo or gransoporo. It's not blue but instead a pale brownish-yellow color with a smooth shell and two large claws. It's occasionally fished in the autumn and wintertime in the Venetian lagoon, but for the most part is imported. Like most crab varieties, granci-porro is good boiled—the simpler the preparation the better it tastes.

Granseola or **grancevola** Spider crab. A round, red, hairy crab with two very small claws, found in abundance from the middle of December through the middle of February It's also called maia. In Liguria, it's known as faolo or gritton; in Venezia Giulia, musciarola or granzo; in Tuscany, margherita; in Campania, rance 'e tartanella; in Sicily, tarantula; and in Sardinia, marotta or pilargiu.

Grongo Conger eel; also known as brongo, tiagallo, peregallo or felat in Liguria and ruongo in southern Italy. Its firm flesh is distinctively flavored.

Lampreda Lamprey eel; called succhiapesce in dialect. Although it lives in salt water, it reproduces in freshwater rivers. This fish, which is now quite rare in Italy, is more delicately flavored than eel.

Latterino Smelt. Even although they look like anchovies, they shouldn't be confused with them.

Lavarello Freshwater lake fish also called coregone. It's often cooked like trout or perch.

Leccia Pompano, a large saltwater fish.

Lucerna Tub gurnard, the largest of the gurnard group of fish. It's also called pesce prete, uranoscopo, cozzolo or mesoro. It's known for its squat, hard, bulldog-like mouth and upward-tilted eyes. Its delicious flesh has a delicate flavor.

Lucioperca Pike-perch, a freshwater fish found in the southern part of central Italy.

Mazzancolle In Lazio, the name for jumbo shrimp. They're something like tiger shrimp, but distinguished from other shrimp by the color—gray with darker, almost violet, spots and stripes—and a dark band around the stomach.

Mazzola or **mazzolina** The Marchigiano name for a type of *capone* (page 318).

Merlano Saltwater fish something like cod; also called molo.

Merluzzo Cod; the Italian name for nasello or merluzzo argentato. In the international marketplace it refers to the common cod. In Italy only the smallest cod are used for fresh preparations while the larger fish are used to make baccalà or *stoccafisso* (page 324).

Mitili Mussels. In central Italy, called cozze; in Liguria and Tuscany, muscoli; and in the area around the Veneto, peoci.

Moleche See *moleche col pien* (page 73).

Moletti Small *merlano* (above). They're used primarily in fried dishes.

Mormora Striped sea bream, called pagello mormora or marmora or casciola in Puglia and ajola in Sicily. It's one of the best fishes of the Italian coasts and is very often found fresh. Its best seasons are summer and fall.

Moscardini Small cephalopods also called polpi muschiati or mughetti; they're called folpetti in Venice. They look like very small octopuses and if very fresh, smell like musk.

Muggine Mullet. Muggine is a Tuscan name for the fish; it's also used in Sardinia to describe an entire variety of mullets.

Murena Moray eel. It's said that this small-headed eel, with a yellow and black spotted body, has a *cattiva* or nasty expression on its face. However, its flesh is exquisite.

Murice Murex, large, hard-shelled, cone-shaped sea snails found in great quantities in the Veneto and Marches. In Liguria they're called cornetti de ma; in the Veneto and Marches, garusoli or garagoli; in Campania, sconcigli; in Puglia, quecciuoli; and in Sicily and Sardinia, buccuni.

Muscoli Another name for *mitili* (above) or cozze, mussels.

Nasello Hake, or *merluzzo* (above).

Occhiata Saddled bream, an ocean fish with thin blackish-blue stripes and a very showy black spot near its tail. It must be consumed when very fresh because it begins to smell very quickly.

Ombrina Shi drum, a saltwater fish that lives in rocky coastal areas. It's not easy to find; its delicate flavor is similar to sea bass.

Orata Sea bream, a highly esteemed saltwater fish sometimes confused with *sarago* (page 323), which is identified by the golden color between its eyes. With its firm but elastic flesh and strong, recognizable flavor of the sea, it works well with almost any recipe.

Pagello Sea bream. There are three types of this saltwater fish: pagello fragolino, which has a red back, pinkish-silver sides and a pointed face; pagello bastardo, a more slender pinkish fish with a round face and a black spot near its pectoral fin; and pagello occhialone, which has a prominent front end and protruding eyes.

Pagro Red porgy. This saltwater fish is sometimes confused with *dentice* (page 319), which is pinker with larger eyes. There are a few varieties of pagro that are fished in the warm weather months.

Palombo Dogfish. The most common palombo is smooth-skinned and a pale hazelnut color. It's difficult to distinguish it from the other shark-like fish sold as palombo. You need to look for a Maltese Cross shape in its vertebra to know it's the real thing. It's especially popular in non-coastal Italian cities such as Rome and Milan where its flesh lends itself well to the local cuisine.

Pannocchie See *canochie* (page 318).

Paranza See *fritto di paranza* (page 319).

Passera A type of flounder; a flat saltwater fish but with more of a triangle shape than the oval-shaped flounder.

Peoci The Venetian name for mussels; see *mitili* (page 321) or cozze.

Persico trota, boccalone, or **branzino d'acqua dolce** Large-mouth black bass. This freshwater fish is found in Italy but is usually imported from America. Its firm flesh is very flavorful and slightly musky. Even though it's common, it's still difficult to find in markets.

Pescatrice See *rana pescatrice* (page 323).

Pesce angelo Another name for monkfish; also called *squadro*.

Pesce capone See *capone* (page 318).

Pesce gatto Catfish, a completely smooth-skinned freshwater fish known for its "whiskers." Its flavor depends upon its habitat. If it lives in clean, running water it's excellent.

Pesce lucerna See *lucerna* (page 320).

Pesce persico Perch. A freshwater fish also called perca or persico reale.

Pesce prete Another name for *lucerna* (page 320).

Pesce San Pietro See *San Pietro* (below).

Pettine Another name for conchiglia di San Giacomo or *canestrelli* (page 318).

Piè di Pellicano Shellfish similar to the *murice* (page 321); also called crocette, garusoli or garagoli.

Piovra The word used for all large octopus.

Platessa Plaice — an Atlantic Ocean fish — usually sold as frozen fillets in Italy.

Polipo or **polpo** Octopus; a large cephalopod. It's often called piovre. It must be tenderized to cook.

Rana pescatrice Monkfish. Also known as coda di rospo, it's called budego or budegasso in Liguria; boldrò in Tuscany and Liguria; rospo in Central Italy; and diavolo di mare in the Veneto and Sicily. It has a huge, monstrous head, which is why it's usually sold without its head. Its firm but elastic flesh is pale pink and tastes vaguely like lobster.

Razza Skate. The word is used for various similar fish with wide pectoral fins from the same species, *Raja*. The best parts of the fish are the wings (fins) and the cheeks.

Ricci di mare Sea urchins. It's important to know how to gather these spiny shellfish — not all of them are edible. Their season is from the end of winter to the beginning of springtime. They are most delicious when eaten raw with a few drops of lemon juice.

Ricciola Amberjack. A large (up to two meters) deep-sea fish found in markets throughout spring until the beginning of summer.

Rombo Turbot. Two types of turbot are found in Italy: the tastiest of the two, rombo chiodato ("nailed turbot"), characterized by numerous boney, triangle-shaped protrusions over its body, and rombo liscio ("smooth turbot"), which is lighter in color and has a round silhouette. It's also very good.

San Pietro John Dory. A saltwater fish with very tasty flesh, unique for its oval, almost rotund shape and round black spots on its sides. It lives in sandy and muddy ocean bottoms. Its name is based on the legend of Saint Peter catching this fish in Lake Tiberius with his hands (the spots on either side of the fish are his "fingerprints") and finding a coin in its mouth — enough money to "render unto Caesar" his taxes.

Sarago White sea bream. Sarago actually is a name that refers to various members of the *Diplodus* species of fish. They are silver or golden, flat, oval-shaped fish that live in rocky and seaweed-filled areas of the sea. Their good quality flesh must be eaten when very fresh.

Sarde Sardines, commonly used for fresh sardine preparations.

Sardelle Another name for sardines.

Sardine Tiny saltwater fish that are fished from March through September. They're eaten fresh or preserved in oil or salt. This fatty fish belongs to the bluefish group and for that reason must be eaten when fresh. It's easy to confuse sardines with anchovies; the difference is in the shape of their heads — the anchovy's upper jaw is longer than the bottom — and the anchovy's flesh is less perishable than the sardine's.

Sardoni Venetian dialect for anchovy and, sometimes, for sarda or sardina.

Scampi The same variety of lobster denoted by the English word scampi; sometimes called prawns or langoustines, distinguished from saltwater shrimp by having claws instead of antennae. They vaguely resemble the *astice* (page 317).

Seppie Cuttlefish. Cephalopods with ten tentacles — eight short ones and two longer ones. It's easy to confuse them with totani or *calamari* (page 318) not only because their bodies are similarly shaped but also because of the bone, *osso di seppia*, inside.

Sgombro Mackerel. A fatty saltwater fish that belongs to the bluefish group. It's good only when very fresh. It's suitable for sauces, for preserving in oil or brine, or it can be smoked.

Spannocchi The name used in Campania for *canochie* (page 318), mantis shrimp.

Spigola Another name for sea bass, *branzino* (page 317).

Stoccafisso Either dehydrated or air-dried Atlantic Ocean codfish. Its name comes from the German *stock fisch* ("stick fish") or pesce bastone. The highest quality version is called *ragno*, from the most famous Norwegian exporter of the fish, Ragnar. It needs to be tenderized before cooking by soaking in water for five or six days.

Storione Sturgeon, a saltwater fish that deposits its eggs in freshwater rivers in order to reproduce. The sturgeons that have hatched in the river are caught when they return to the ocean as newly developed adults and are vulnerable. They have exquisite, delicate, fatty flesh but are also known for their eggs, caviar. The sturgeon found in Italian markets is usually farm-raised. It's excellent when smoked.

Tartufi di mare Clams; also called cappe verrucose or Venere tartufi. In Liguria they're called *arselle* (page 317); in the Veneto, liberòn; in Campania, taratùfoli; in Puglia, nuci riali; and in Sicily, *cocciule ricce.* They're one of the best shellfish to eat raw.

Telline Wedge shells. These small, smooth-shell, triangle-shaped clams live in the sandy bottom of the sea. These delicious shellfish have only one drawback—the size of their shells makes them difficult to open.

Temolo A freshwater fish with a thin, tapered body. Its brown back is shaded to silver-gray on its yellow-striped, black-dotted sides. Its name comes from the vague odor of thyme that emanates from its flesh.

Tinca Tench. This freshwater fish with a long, rather thick body has a brownish-green back, golden-brown sides and a white belly. Theoretically, its flesh is delicious, but it's full of bones and sometimes tastes like mud. There are several ways to remove the muddy flavor: buy them still alive, then put them in fresh water for a few days so that they can purge themselves or, traditionally, while they're still alive, give them a teaspoon of strong vinegar to drink.

Totani A cephalopod very similar to *calamari* (page 318), but with tougher flesh and a bit less flavor.

Triglia Mullet. Triglia is the name for two different types of mullet: triglia di scoglio ("rock mullet") and triglia di fango ("mud mullet"). The rock mullet has three or four yellow vertical stripes that pale with time until they disappear, and an angled face that the mud mullet doesn't have, giving it a snub-nosed appearance.

Trota Trout. A freshwater fish found in rivers where, like salmon, it swims to deposit its eggs. The kind of trout called salmonata, with its pinkish flesh, is different from other types because of what it eats: crustaceans and crustacean meal. Trout in general is a versatile fish; it lends itself to many cooking methods and is excellent smoked.

Uovo di mare Conifer-shaped shellfish found in salt water; called limone di mare in Liguria, carnumme in Campania and spuenzete in Puglia. It attaches itself to rocks or the sandy floor of the sea. Its dark, warty shell contains yellow-orange flesh that looks like an egg yolk. It's best eaten raw with a drop of fresh lemon juice. It has a slightly iodine flavor.

Ventresca di tonno The most valuable part of the tuna belly. It's preserved in olive oil.

Beccaccia Woodcock. A rare and prized migratory bird, in Northern Italy it's also called gallinazza, arria, ravagnan, pizzacra or pola. In Southern Italy it's called pizzarda or arcera. After it's hung and cleaned, it may be prepared in various ways but is usually roasted or marinated.

Beccaccino Snipe. A smaller version of the *beccaccia* (above), in Northern Italy it's also called pizzarda, sgnepa or becanoto. In the central part of the country it's called senèppia, and, in the south, arcigghiola. It may be prepared using the same recipes as for beccaccia.

Beccafico Warbler, a small wild bird that loves to eat figs, hence its name. In Northern Italy it's also called cannavrola, pittafigh, sardagna or fabbro. In central Italy it's called gricciarola or stropparella, and, in the south, fravetta.

Boccone del prete A term used to define the best part of any preparation, but above all, that which involves meat (it literally means "the priest's mouthful"). It's often used to describe the thighs or rear parts of a chicken.

Cappone Capon, a male hen that's castrated when it's sixty or seventy days old. The castration helps fatten up the bird, resulting in soft, delicately flavored meat. Capon is usually butchered at six or seven months.

Castrato Castrated male sheep. Castration results in more tender and flavorful meat.

Foiolo A regional name for a part of the tripe also called l'omaso, millefogli, centopelli, or libro because the structure of the mucus membranes (the stomach lining) is vaguely similar to pages (*foglie*) of a book (*libro*).

Folaghe Coot. Because these waterfowl live in swamps or marshes their flesh has a slightly fishy flavor.

Fricandò A regional name for a cut of beef. The word, derived from the French *fricandeau*, can also mean veal stew.

Fricassea Fricassee; veal, chicken or lamb stewed with eggs and lemon juice. In regional tradition it's synonymous with preparations called *alla borghese*, *alla provinciale* or *brodettate*.

Lonza A word that can mean various things depending upon the region where it's used. In Northern Italy it means loin or fillet of pork; in Tuscany it's used in the plural, lonze, to indicate secondary cuts of beef usually used to make stews; in central Italy it refers to the neck and the lean back sections of a pig; in Lazio, it's cured meat similar to coppa piacentina and in the south it refers to capocollo, or the smallest, least fatty part of the pig.

Pollo Chicken. It's called pollastro until it's three or four months old and weighs 600 grams (about a pound and a third). A young male chicken is a galletto and a fattened female is a pollanca.

Spuntature di maiale The ends of pork ribs, usually cooked over a wood-burning fire or stewed.

Stracotto Slowly stewed, aged meat. In many places horse or donkey can be used. Stracotto can be used as the base for fillings or as a pasta sauce. It goes very well with polenta. It's different from stufato because wine and other ingredients are added while it's cooking and the meat is not marinated first.

Stufato Meat that's marinated in wine, aromatic herbs and vegetables before it's stewed. The name comes from the word *stufa*—a stove used to heat the home. Most *stufe* have a plate that can accommodate a stewpot.

Trippa Tripe.

VEGETABLES

Barbabietola Beet. The word can mean a sugar, distillery, foraged or vegetable garden beet; all the varieties contain sucrose. The vegetable garden beet is divided into two categories: barbabietola rossa (red beet), including rapa rossa (red turnip), carota rossa (red carrot) and bietola rossa (a round or long, slightly squashed, sweet, wine-red root); and bieta and bietola (beet greens), including erbette, bietola da coste, coste d'argento, bietola da erbucce and cardonetto—all chard-like greens.

Barba di frate or **barba del Negus** A small herbaceous plant found in Northern Italy. It's also known as barba di cappuccino or roscano. The string-like, slightly acidic leaves are gathered in the spring when they're still very tender. Even though they may be eaten raw in salad, it's a good idea to boil them for five to ten minutes before consuming. Barba di frate literally means "monk's beard."

Bietola or **bieta** Chard; called erbetta in Emilia. There are quite a few varieties. Among the most common are bietola verde a costa larga argentata (green chard with wide silver ribs), erbetta verde da taglio riccia (green chard with curly leaves) and erbetta verde da taglio liscia (green chard with smooth leaves).

Borragine Borage. It may be cultivated or found growing wild in warm environments, fields or in rubble. It's harvested in the summertime. Only the leaves are used in cooking.

Cannellini A small white bean grown in central Italy, most commonly in Tuscany.

Catalogna A type of chicory distinguished by its long, narrow leaves and carefully delineated borders, particularly at the lower part of the leaf. Noted for a slightly bitter flavor, the lower part of the leaf and its rib are the edible parts of the plant. The variety of catalogna harvested in the fall and winter is divided into two groups: that which is cultivated in heads and that which is called *puntarelle* (page 199), the young, tender leaves that form the inside of a head. Among the most common head catalogna are jagged-leaf Brindisina or Pugliese; large-leafed Veneta; and Gigante di Chioggia and Catalogna a foglia frastagliata—jagged, with thin green ribs. Jagged-leafed Catalogna abruzzese, long and thin-leafed Catalogna asparago and the swollen-stemmed Catalogna di Galantina (called *a pigna*, "like a fir cone") are the varieties cultivated for puntarelle. All catalogna may be used in recipes that call for chicory.

Cavolo nero Black cabbage or Tuscan kale; also called cavolo toscano, cavolo palmizio or cavolo a penna. It does not grow in heads, but is cultivated for its crimped, deep green—almost black—leaves. Its seasons are fall and winter. It's the starring ingredient in the famous Tuscan soup *ribollita* (page 150).

Cazzimperio The Southern Italian term for *pinzimonio* (page 329).

Cicerchia A rather uncommon, prehistoric legume that looks something like a squashed chickpea. The very small (not wider than a centimeter) off-white or greenish legume is packed with protein. It should be consumed with caution because it is difficult to digest. Its skin is tough and its flavor—something between a pea and a fava bean—quite strong. It may be used in all recipes that call for chickpeas. It can be stored, dried, for up to two years.

Cime di rapa Turnip greens that are harvested just before the plant begins to flower.

Coste d'argento A type of chard with very wide ribs.

Crauti Sauerkraut; sliced cabbage that is fermented in brine. Although the preparation originated in Germany it's common in Italy in the Friuli Venezia Giulia and the Trentino

Alto Adige regions. It's great with cooked sausages and any pork product.

Cren Horseradish. Grated or in sauces usually accompanying boiled meats, it's very common in the Alto Adige region.

Crescione Cress. It's eaten raw in salads or in complex cooked dishes. There are three basic varieties: crescione d'acqua (watercress), crescione inglese (English cress) and crescione dei prati (field cress).

Critmo Samphire or glasswort, also known as finocchio marino. It grows between rocks and along rocky beaches; its jagged, succulent leaves have an intense iodine and slightly bitter flavor. It's used in salads or preserved in vinegar.

Erba cipollina Chives, a common field herb.

Erba San Pietro or **Santa Maria** A fragrant herb with long, thin leaves. It's always used cooked, to flavor soups or stuffing.

Erbette Chard. In Emilia, chard is called *bietola* (page 327). In Lazio, erbette is parsley.

Fagopiro Another word for buckwheat.

Finocchio or **finocchietto selvatico** Fennel. This fragrant plant is also affectionately called finocchiella. It is characteristic of the Mediterranean kitchen and is widely used in Sicily, Calabria, Puglia and Sardinia.

Gobbi Cardoons, in Lazio.

Grano saraceno Buckwheat. This ancient cereal is characterized by its triangle-shaped grain and deep brown color. In Italy it's often used to make a particular kind of polenta, especially in the northern part of the country in the Valtellina.

Grassa gallina The regional name for a type of salad leaf (lamb's lettuce) also called valerianella or soncino.

Pinzimonio Assorted raw vegetables that are served with bowls of olive oil, salt and pepper for dipping.

Piselli mangiatutto Snow peas; another name for *taccole* (page 330).

Rafano Horseradish. This type of cruciferous plant includes *ramolaccio* (below) and ravanello (radish). It's often confused with *cren* (above), a slightly different type of root.

Ramolaccio A type of horseradish. It may be sharp or slightly sweet depending on the plant. It's usually grated, or diced and added to salads that are dressed with vinaigrette. It is also called *rafano*.

Raperonzolo A small wild root similar to a turnip.

Rocàmbola A type of garlic, also called aglio romano, aglio d'India or aglio di Spagna. This small plant may also be found in the wild. It's prized for its small bulbs that are well-suited for preserving in vinegar.

Roscani Another name for *barba di frate* (page 327).

Santoreggia Summer savory, an aromatic herb with straight stems and little bunches of needle-shaped leaves. It smells like a combination of mint and thyme. It's good with vegetables.

Scalogno Shallot. It's used as a substitute for garlic or onions in the Italian kitchen. In Romagna it's preserved in vinegar. Scalogno can also mean a green onion or scallion.

Scorzobianca Salsify, a root with yellowish skin and white flesh. It's also called salsefica or daikon. It may be eaten raw or cooked.

Scorzone A type of black truffle found in all seasons except spring. It has a pleasing flavor which is much less intense than the real black truffle.

Scorzonera Black salsify, a slightly bitter, but delicately fla-vored root with black skin and white flesh. Interestingly, its name doesn't come from the color of its skin but rather from the Catalan word for viper, *escorso*. In medieval times it was thought that the root was an antidote to snake bites. It's usually boiled to serve but may be used in all recipes that call for carrots.

Sedano rapa or **sedano di Verona** Celery root or celeriac.

Soncino The northern Italian name for valerianella.

Taccole Snow peas; also called piselli mangiatutto. Taccole are usually a bit wider and longer than snow peas.

Topinambur Jerusalem artichokes. They are the root of a common, daisy-like yellow flower and taste something like artichokes. They are in season in autumn. They need to be bathed in acidulated water before cooking.

Valerianella Lamb's lettuce, a buttery, spoon-shaped salad leaf also called lattughino, lattughella, dolcetta, gallinella or *soncino* (above). It grows in small heads.

BIBLIOGRAPHY

AA VV, *Enciclopedia della cucina*, Novara, De Agostini, 1990.

AA VV, *Grande enciclopedia illustrata della gastronomia*, Milano, Selezione dal Reader's Digest, 1990

Accolti P.- Cibotto G.A. (a cura di), *Lo stivale allo spiedo. Viaggio attraverso la cucina italiana*, Roma, Canesi, s.d.

Alberini Massimo, Mistretta Giorgio, *Guida all'Italia gastronomica*, Milano, Touring Club Italiano, 1984.

Alberini Massimo, *Piemontesi a tavola*, Milano, Longanesi, 1967.

Alberini Massimo, *Antica cucina veneziana*, Casale Monferrato, Piemme, 1990.

Alberini Massimo, *Storia della cucina italiana*, Casale Monferrato, Piemme, 1992.

Artusi Pellegrino, *La scienza in cucina e l'arte di mangiar bene*, Firenze, Giunti Marzocco, 1960.

Baldassarri Montevecchi Bitta, *La buona cucina dell'Emilia-Romagna. Le autentiche, antiche ricette di casa*, Milano, Franco Angeli, 1980.

Bevilacqua Osvaldo-Mantovano Giuseppe, *Laboratori del gusto*, Milano, SugarCo, 1982.

Boni Ada, *Il talismano della felicità*, Roma, Colombo, 1979.

Bonia Ada, *La cucina romana*, Roma, Newton Compton, 1983.

Braccili Luigi, *Abruzzo in cucina*, Pescara, Didattica Constantini, 1978.

Carnacina Luigi-Veronelli Luigi, *La cucina rustica regionale*, Milano, Rizzoli, 1966.

Chiodi Elio, *Quando lo chef è donna. Ritratti e ricette di 21 ristoratrici italiane,* Milano, Acanthus, 1989.

Codacci Leo, *Civiltà della tavola contadina in Toscana* Milano, Idealibri, 1990.

Corsi Guglielma, *Un secolo di cucina umbra*, Assisi, Edizioni Porziuncola, 1980.

Cunsolo Felice, *Guida gastronomica d'Italia*, Novara, De Agostini, 1975.

Di Leo Maria Adele, *La cucina siciliana*, Roma, Newton Compton, 1993.

Faccioli Emilio (a cura di), *L'arte della cucina in Italia. Libri di ricette e trattati sulla civiltà della tavola dal XVI al XIX secolo*, Torino, Einaudi, 1987.

Faggioni Silvano, *L'alto Adige in cucina*, Trento, Reverdito, 1984.

Francesconi Jeanne Caròla, *La cucina napoletana*, Roma, Newton Compton, 1992.

Goria Giovanni, *La cucina del Piemonte. Il mangiare di ieri e di oggi del Piemonte collinare e vignaiolo*, Padova, Muzzio, 1990.

Gosetti della Salda Anna, *Le ricette regionali*, Milano, Solares, 1967.

Gozzini Giacosa Iliari, *A cena du Lucullo*, Casale Monferrato, Piemme 1986.

Guarnaschelli Gotti Marco, *La cucina milanese. Canali, riso e ingegno*, Padova, Muzzio, 1991.

Hellrigl Andreas, *La cucina dell'Alto Adige*, Milano, Franco Angeli, 1983.

Lingua Paolo, *La cucina dei genovesi*, Padova, Muzzio, 1989.

Maffioli Giuseppe, *Storia piacevole della gastronomia*, Milano, Bietti, 1976.

Mallo Beppe, *Calabria e Lucania in bocca*, Palermo, Il Vespro, 1979.

Marchese Salvatore, *La cucina ligure di levante. Le fonti, le storie, le ricette*, Padova, Muzzio, 1990.

Marchesi Gualtiero, *La cucina regionale italiana*, Milano, Arnoldo Mondadori, 1989.

Mazzara Morresi Nicola, *La cucina marchigiana tra storia e folclore*, Ancona, Aniballi, 1978.

Migliari Maria Luisa, Azzola Alida, *Storia della gastronomia*, Novara, Edipem, 1978.

Monelli Paolo, *Il ghiottone errante*, Milano Treves, 1935.

Montanari Massimo, *Convivio. Storia e cultura dei piaceri della tavola*, Bari, Laterza, 1989.

Montanari Massimo, *Nuovo convivio. Storia e cultura dei piaceri della tavola nell'età moderna*, Bari, Laterza, 1991.

Montanari Massimo, *Convivio oggi. Storia e cultura dei piaceri tavola nell'età contemporanea*, Bari, Laterza, 1992.

Paglia Gianni, *Breviario della buona cucina bolognese*, Bologna, Calderini, 1959.

Perisi Giuseppina, *Cucine di Sardegna*, Padova, Muzzio, 1989.

Piccinardi Antonio, *L'olio a tavola*, Milano, Giorgio Mondadori, 1988.

Pomar Anna, *La cucina siciliana,* Roma, Colonna, 1988.

Prato Katharina, *Manuale di cucina*, Gorizia, Editrice Goriziana, 1991.

Righi Parenti Giovanni, *La grande cucina Toscana (I & II),* Milano SugarCo, 1976.

Salvatori de Zuliani Mariú, *A tola co i nostri veci. La cucina veneziana*, Milano, Franco Angeli, 1992.

Sassu Antonio, *La vera cucina in Sardegna*, Roma, Colonna, 1988.

Tannahill Reay, *Storia del cibo*, Milano, Rizzoli, 1987.

Valli Emilia, *La cucina friulana*, Padova, Muzzio, 1992.

RINGRAZIAMENTI

Vorrei ringraziare i seguenti "consiglieri":

Martino Ragusa, per la sua grande competenza in tema di cucina siciliana;

Franceso Di Natale, aspirante "Monzú" di origine siciliana;

Isabella e Rita Armati (Marche);

Rina Pulixi e Giancarlo Mannoni (Sardegna);

Sergio Rotino (Puglia):

Lia Ambrosini Li Marzi (Piemonte):

Mario Ventimiglia (Liguria)

Gualtiero Marchesi (Lombardia);

sig. Presenza (ristoratore abruzzese);

Michela Scibilia e Rebecca Bragadin (Veneto);

Eugenia Vanelli Cosmi (Friuli-Venezia Giulia);

Rosina Cesari, Nara Bertocchi e Giulian Tassinari (Emilia-Romagna);

Adis Baroni Bertocchi (straordinari cuoca e sfoglina bolognese);

Anna Tognini (Reggio Emilia);

Guido Paulato, Stefano Artuoso e Veronia Franchini (Trentino-Alto Adige);

Frederico e Silvano Bardazzi (Toscana);

dott. Profazio (Calabria);

Franco Mioni (operatore turistico e gastronomo);

Enrico Guagnini (gastronomo);

Giuseppe Pittano (filologo).

INDEX

Monica Sartoni Cesari has had a long career in the world of Italian gastronomy. She was the educational director of the prestigious school of La Cucina Italiana and was awarded the distinguished Commandeur de la Commanderie des Cordons Bleus de France. She is the author of several books, including *La Cucina Bolognese*. Along with organizing numerous food exhibitions and shows, she has contributed to many well-known Italian food magazines, including *Sale e Pepe*, *Cucina Moderna* and *A Tavola*. She is currently the senior editor of *Cucina No Problem*.

Susan Simon, a writer and event planner in New York City, is the author of several cookbooks including *Visual Vegetables*, *The Nantucket Table*, *The Nantucket Holiday Table*, *Contorni*, *Insalate*, and, most recently, writer of the James Beard Award-winning *Pasta Sfoglia*. She is also the author of the guidebook *Shopping in Marrakech*. She writes a bi-monthly food column for *The Nantucket Inquirer & Mirror* and contributes to *Nantucket Today*.